SKOOKUM

An
Oregon Pioneer
Family's
History and Lore

SHANNON APPLEGATE

Quill
William Morrow
New York

Library of Congress Cataloging-in-Publication Data

Applegate, Shannon.
  Skookum: an Oregon pioneer family's history and lore/Shannon
Applegate.—1st Quill ed.
     p.   cm.
  Includes bibliographical references.
  ISBN 0-688-09512-7
  1. Applegate family. 2. Oregon—Biography. 3. Pioneers—Oregon—
Biography. 4. Oregon—Genealogy. 5. Frontier and pioneer life—
Oregon. I. Title.
[CT274.A77A77   1990]
929'.2'0973—dc20   89-39551
                                                                      CIP

Printed in the United States of America

  2   3   4   5   6   7   8   9   10

BOOK DESIGN BY PATRICE FODERO

"Carpent poma netotes"

"Let the grandchildren gather the apples"

This book is dedicated to all young Applegates everywhere, to my little cousins Daniel, Levi, Seth, Garth, Jennifer, Lindsay Jo, and Meghan, to my nephew Carlos-Mariano and, most especially, to Jessica, Colin, Ione, Max, Edane, and Kate—the children with whom I have gratefully shared my love and life and who have encouraged me even when times were hard indeed.

Contents

CONTENTS

INTRODUCTION

Sometimes we are disappointed when we submit any good family story to too much historical scrutiny. Yet rarely have I felt disappointed these last seventeen years and more as I have researched and written about the Applegates.

Their story, which I have chosen to relate through a series of interlocking narratives, encompasses many of the predominant historical themes of the early American West: Among these is the overland crossing via the old Oregon Trail in 1843, which profoundly affected the family's sense of identity as well as its destiny for generations to come. Other themes, such as the quirky restlessness of Applegate men, closely link them to the experience of countless other Oregon-bound emigrants who, even after reaching the "promised land," permitted their travel-worn families to rest only for a while. The effects of the intermittent gold rushes that continued to upset family life on the Pacific Slope long after 1849, the troubled relations between the settler and the Indian, and the use of land and other natural resources are topics that will also be found shaping or underlying many of the narratives in this book. So, too, will some unexpected and curious connections between various Applegates and nationally prominent political figures during the difficult Civil War period.

While history, and one family's history in particular, form the ostensible subject matter of this book, I have been equally interested not only in what has happened but in what it meant, and might mean yet: How did it feel to be a mother witnessing the death of her child on the way to Oregon, or to be a settler's son watching his Indian friends and old playmates rounded up in the dead of winter and marched off to the reserves? What did it do to the course of a young woman's life when she learned that her father had scratched her name from the family Bible? What sort of world was it where an old blue sugarbowl filled with gold dust might be unconcernedly set out in "plain sight"?

To answer these and other questions I have found it necessary to delve beyond the more well-known and occasionally illustrious lives of male Applegates, in whose honor were named a trail, a town, a river, and even a mountain peak. After "making" history, many of these men wrote about their experiences. While extremely valuable, these published accounts represent only a portion of a truly voluminous Applegate archives.

Here I should like to emphasize the many important contributions Applegate women have made to their family's history and its preservation. As surely as certain stitches, they have held the generations together. Their experiences as westering women and early settlers thread through all of *Skookum*'s narratives.

The family women kept the time: The literally thousands of family documents, which include letters, journals, recollections, manuscripts (both published and unpublished), as well as sketchbooks, and a truly vast array of camera works, have survived largely because they were cherished and protected by the generations of female relatives before me. In the days before public and private institutions made room for such collections, Applegate women affixed labels and tags and tied their family's treasures into neat bundles, which for long years were stored in chests of aromatic cedar and Douglas fir.

Many of these women might have written history as well as lived it if the attitudes prevalent in their respective eras and their truly overwhelming responsibilities as wives, mothers, and caretakers had not made such an endeavor unlikely and, perhaps, impossible. Even so, several Applegate women have made little-known contributions to the world of arts and letters. I am particularly indebted to the historical writings by Anne Applegate Kruse (1875–1960). The inspiration and assistance I have gratefully received from others is acknowledged elsewhere, but it is "Annie's" work, and the example provided by "Annie" herself, that have sustained me in times of doubt.

We have both turned respectfully toward the kinswomen of previous generations. These women stand behind me. I have felt what might be called a genetic obligation to tell not only something about their lives, but of the family as a whole whom they loved so dearly and served so well.

A NOTE ABOUT THE CHINOOK JARGON

Words and phrases from the Chinook jargon, an early trade language of the Pacific Northwest, appear throughout this book. First used by natives of the region, these expressions have found their way into the lexicon of present-day northwesterners. Chinook rendered service to traders, Indians, and settlers. Its roots may be found in several cultures. From the Nootkan came *tyee* (chief, headman), and *illahee* (country, earth, field, ranch, home); from the English came *oleman* (old man); and from the French came *siwash* (a native rendition of the French *sauvage*, meaning native or aboriginal).

The word *skookum* is still in frequent use in the present era. Its special meaning to the Applegate family may be found within the pages of this book.

The Applegates of Oregon—
Sons of
Daniel Applegate and Rachel Lindsay

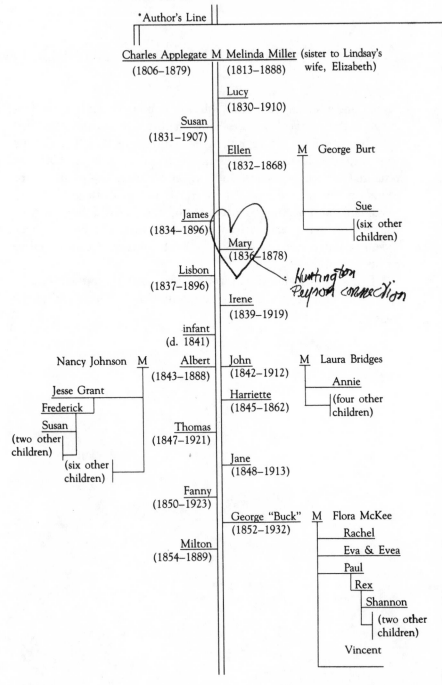

•Author's Line

Charles Applegate M Melinda Miller (sister to Lindsay's
(1806–1879)   (1813–1888)   wife, Elizabeth)

Lucy
(1830–1910)

Susan
(1831–1907)

Ellen   M   George Burt
(1832–1868)

Sue

(six other children)

James
(1834–1896)

Mary
(1836–1878)

Lisbon
(1837–1896)

≃ Huntington
Payson connection

Irene
(1839–1919)

infant
(d. 1841)

Nancy Johnson M   Albert   John   M   Laura Bridges
(1843–1888)   (1842–1912)

Annie

Jesse Grant   Harriette   (four other
Frederick   (1845–1862)   children)
Susan
(two other   Thomas
children)   (1847–1921)
          (six other
          children)   Jane
                                (1848–1913)

Fanny
(1850–1923)

George "Buck" M Flora McKee
(1852–1932)   Rachel

Milton   Eva & Evea
(1854–1889)   Paul
                                Rex
                                Shannon
                                   (two other
                                   children)
                                Vincent

Lindsay M Elizabeth Miller	Jesse M Cynthia Parker
(1808–1892) (1816–1882)	(1811–1888) (1813–1881)

Elisha
(1832–1896)

Rozelle
(1832–1861)

Warren
(1834–1843)
Drowned in the
Columbia River

Edward Bates
(1833–1843)
Drowned in the
Columbia River

Jesse A.
(1835–1918)

Theresa
(1838–1875)

Ivan
(1840–1918)

Milburn
(1836–1839)

Lucien
(1842–1926)

Alexander McClellan
(1838–1902)

Oliver Cromwell
(1845–1938)

Robert Shortess
(1839–1893)

Annie
(1847–1870)

William Henry H.
(1841–1912)

Frank
(1850–1872)

Gertrude
(1841–1867)

Alice
(1852–1934)

Daniel Webster
(1845–1896)

Jerome
(1855–1856)

Sallie
(1848–1912)

Rachel Lindsay
(1857–1940)

Peter Skeen Ogden
(1851–1916)

Alena/Ellen
(?–?)

Flora
(b. ca. 1859–?)

May we not call them Men of Destiny?

Jesse Applegate,
"The Day with the Cow Column: An Essay,"
Overland Monthly Magazine,
San Francisco, California, August, 1868

PART ONE

THE NARRATIVES
1843–1867

WHAT BELONGS
TO THE RIVER

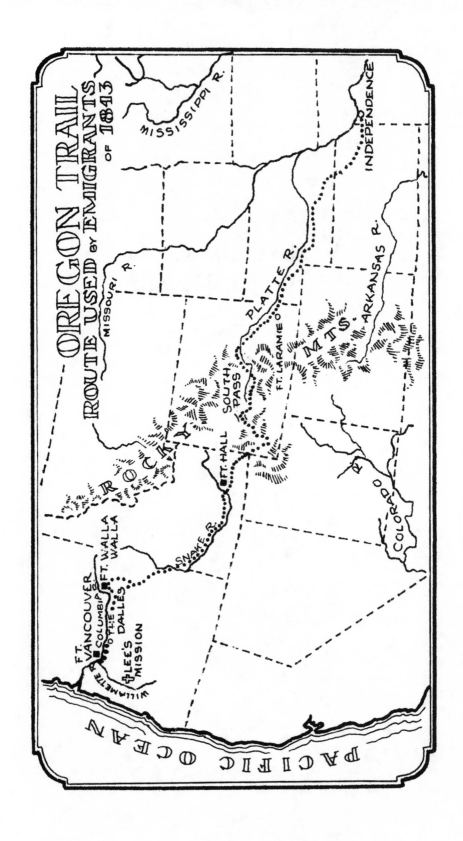

OREGON TRAIL
ROUTE USED by EMIGRANTS
of 1843

MISSISSIPPI R.

INDEPENDENCE

MISSOURI R.

PLATTE R.

FT. LARAMIE

ARKANSAS R.

SOUTH PASS

MTS.

ROCKY

FT. HALL

COLORADO R.

SNAKE R.

FT. WALLA WALLA

FT. VANCOUVER

COLUMBIA R.

THE DALLES

LEE'S MISSION

WILLAMETTE R.

PACIFIC OCEAN

St. Clair Co., Missouri
April 11, 1843

Dear Lisbon,

I will start with our brothers to the Oregon ty. this spring—Lindsay and perhaps Charles go with me. This resolution has been conceived in a very short time, but it is probably Destiny, to which account I place it having neither time nor good reasons to offer in defence of so wild an undertaking and I only snatch this opportunity to write to you for the purpose of ascertaining if the same species of madness exists on your side of the Missouri.

If you are going to Oregon by all means go this Spring for if Linn's bill passes every man's neighbor and friends will move in that direction.

Write *immediately* and meet us armed and equipped as the journey requires.

In Haste, I am,
Your Brother
Jesse Applegate

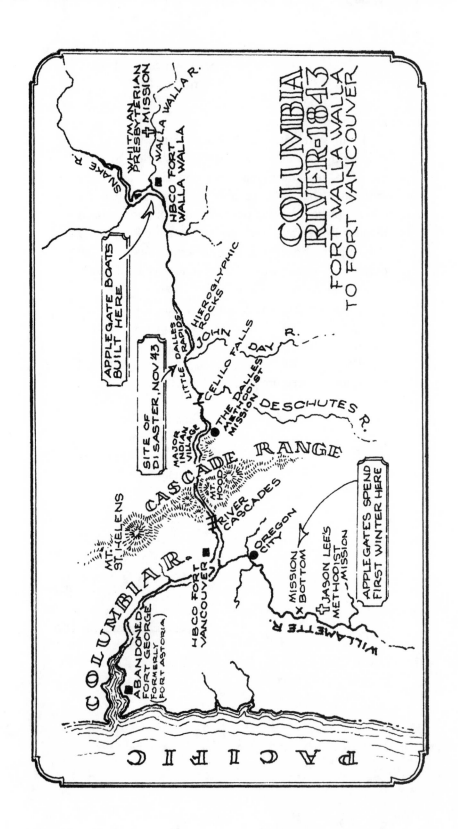

COLUMBIA RIVER-1843

FORT WALLA WALLA TO FORT VANCOUVER

SNAKE R.

WALLA WALLA R.

WHITMAN PRESBYTERIAN MISSION

HBCO FORT WALLA WALLA

APPLEGATE BOATS BUILT HERE

HIEROGLYPHIC ROCKS

JOHN DAY R.

DALLES LITTLE RAPIDS

CELILO FALLS

THE DALLES METHODIST MISSION

DESCHUTES R.

SITE OF DISASTER, NOV. '43

MAJOR INDIAN VILLAGE

CASCADE RANGE

MT. HOOD

MT. ST. HELENS

RIVER CASCADES

APPLEGATES SPEND FIRST WINTER HERE

OREGON CITY

MISSION BOTTOM

JASON LEE'S METHODIST MISSION

COLUMBIA R.

HBCO FORT VANCOUVER

ABANDONED FORT GEORGE (FORMERLY FORT ASTORIA)

WILLAMETTE R.

PACIFIC

Destiny's Man

October 29, 1843
Fort Walla Walla

Destiny's man stands alone, relighting his pipe, watching its pale smoke lift and meet the tendriling mists that move over waters both wide and deep. Beneath the vapors rolls the bold Columbia, pulling its newest captive—the river called Walla Walla—toward the western sea, for this is the confluence. Above him, streaked with fast-changing light, so that the walls of the adobe fort on the hill behind are stained faintly pink, is a sky that is almost Oregon's. Jesse Applegate is but two hundred and ninety-three miles from his destination, Fort Vancouver. Once there, where he and his family will go and where they will winter during the rain-soaked months ahead remains to be seen. But on this day, as the winds of morning so peculiar to the region whip about his trousers and put out his pipe, his concerns are more immediate. He has just finished examining the work of a fortnight: six mackinaws and one little skiff. While hurriedly made, they nonetheless satisfy him. His brother Lindsay has supervised their construction, choosing the style he was most familiar with when employed, years before, as a boatyard apprentice in St. Louis. Flat-bottomed, sharp of prow, and square of stern, they will be riverworthy regardless of the depth of channel and their crude appearance; the latter the result of the lack of certain hand tools, inexperienced helpers, and the perverse nature of their principal building material: nothing more than pine driftwood pushed up the banks during high water and regularly collected by the fort's employees. Excepting the crippled willow groves skirting the river, there is no standing timber of any kind for fifty miles and more, which explains why this bastion, which the Hudson's Bay Company calls its "Gibraltar on the Columbia," is built of adobe brick.

And he is thinking, as he taps his pipe on what's left of his bootheel—for it, like other things, attests to the length of their journey—that it is too bad Burnett and his party beat them to it. For if Ol' Pete had not leased every available *bateau*, they would

Old Fort Walla Walla, the Hudson's Bay Company's "adobe bastion" on the Columbia River, much as it appeared in 1843. (J. M. Stanley sketch)

not have been compelled to build boats in the first place. Now they are two weeks behind the other river travelers, and as the Indians have passed along no news of mishaps, Burnett has surely reached Vancouver safe and sound.

As for the other emigrants who have traded their wagons for pack animals and have taken families and herds on back trails even the Indian eschews, he can only worry for them; especially as they painfully thread their way over the cliffs said to border the southern bank of the river farther down. His own cattle and wagons—he is congratulating himself—will be waiting to be retrieved the following year. What's more, his wife and sister-in-law, both near their term, will be comfortable on their watery road, not overtaxing themselves, and that alone is worth the delay.

Before he turns from the little landing, he takes one last look at the neat line of boats along the graveled strand. In an hour or two, he will help load the mackinaws. Later, after the winds of morning die down, they will shove off—some sixty men, women, and children taking their assigned places.

He has started up the path now, deliberately stopping halfway, for he knows that from this vantage point is afforded a handsome view. Behind him spreads the sloping prairie titted by sandhills and grass-tufted mesas. Even this landscape scarred by too much wind and not enough water is, for a few moments, wondrously transformed, striped by the strident colors of the sunrise. But it is the west that draws his gaze. Brightness breaks more slowly over the waters. And he can see the view that but an half hour before was denied to him: the great Walulla Gap—the river so broad beyond that it seems a vast lake or bay upon which a schooner or steamship could make its way without hindrance.

And in his mind he is imagining the canals, locks, and dams that, years hence, might transform this mighty river, so full of natural obstructions, into the passageway to the Pacific men have so longed and searched for. In the unmade future, he will say how he was thinking of these things even back in '43.

Only now, he is ahead of his time . . . ahead of himself . . . already drifting downriver. His feet strike naught but dust as he ascends the low hill crowned by the fort, within whose walls both stout and formidable someone is now raising two flags: the banner of the Hudson's Bay Company, so long despised by the emigrant,

25

and the red, white, and blue that is not America's but Britain's. If any premonition grips Jesse Applegate as he looks up and sees that Union Jack before he turns once more toward the west and the river waiting there, it will neither be recorded nor remembered.

Two Boys: Elisha and Jesse

Now, when Lindsay Applegate learned that Betsy had finally been delivered of her first baby, he hurried home. It was an occasion on two counts: The child was a boy and, at that time, the only son in any of the three Applegate families. He called him Elisha Lindsay: the Elisha for the child's dead uncle who had succumbed to yellow fever on the long march to the Battle of New Orleans years before; the Lindsay, not because it was his own name, but instead the surname of his mother's people, the Kentucky Lindsays, who traced their lineage to an old and, some said, noble-blooded Scottish clan. All of this sat very well indeed on the proud and sturdy shoulders of young Elisha Applegate.

The second son was called Warren, a name his mother fancied. But by the time the third son came along, Lindsay had his way again. "Betsy, this time I shall honor the living!" Thus the boy was named Jesse Applegate Applegate so that there would be no uncertainty: He was his uncle's namesake! It was then that Betsy sighed, remarking, so the story went, "As if one Applegate in a body's name wasn't enough to live with!" The boy Jesse thought so himself: Yet, on the way to Oregon, he'd come to feel differently: After all, his uncle was the captain of the whole Cow Column, his wagon the biggest, his herds the largest, his very word, law.

Elisha

"What *can't* that youngster do?!" remarked the women. He hauled. He hammered. He knew how to fix a wagon tire or rig a pulley and was a dead-shot to boot! And unlike some of their own, Elisha did not make himself scarce when his mother called upon him to do some simple thing like fetch water or more buffalo chips for the fire. Betsy Applegate was a lucky woman.

And in the makeshift boatyard, jumping out of the sawpit after the jug for his uncle Charley, or helping his daddy plane the boards, and on top of that, knowing where everything fit when it came time to drill the holes for the wooden pegs that would fasten

27

the frames of the mackinaws. And caulk! Why, he was faster than some men.

"Bright as a new penny and reads everything he can get his hands on," his uncle Charley said. "Why, he was reading the *Missouri Republican* by the time he was seven years old, and memorizing whole passages of Scott's *Marmion* was nothing to him!" Whereupon Charley had pulled on his jug and added, his voice full of dote: "I've never seen the like!"

And now and again even his uncle Jesse was not beyond bragging on his nephew, telling how quickly the boy caught on to things, such as using the Burt's Solar Compass, transom and chain, his reckonings reliable.

One day a fellow, watching the boy dress out an antelope all by himself, said, "Well, Lindsay, you could have done worse. You're sure he's just eleven?" and then he winked, speaking up so the boy would be sure to hear: "But you'd better watch out . . . so he don't get all puffed up!"

It was as if some heavenly messenger had delivered Elisha with the word "Promise" stamped on his tiny forehead in glowing letters! But one or two of his near relations thought, as Elisha grew older, that the lad's head had swelled to make more room for all he stuffed into it. Too, he sometimes took on more than was strictly good for him, setting a bad example for the other children.

It had not escaped his aunt Melinda's notice that Elisha frequently twisted the family rules to suit himself. There was the time, for example, some of the boys, including her own Jim, had been discovered up to their necks in the icy Osage. And her sister had switched them—with half a heart surely, for Betsy was not the sort to whale on any child. And the scolding had taken, so far as all the other culprits were concerned, excepting Elisha who, as the eldest of the family boys, should have known better in the first place! No, he'd taken to practicing swimming at the neighbors' farther down the river. Her girls had reported it to her. Diving. Daredeviling. Once, finally, hitting his head on a rock and thereby knocking the wind clear out of himself—was barely able to get back to shore, or so Lucy said to her. And Betsy hadn't known any of it. Didn't know it yet. Elisha had deliberately done what he'd been forbidden to do.

She'd passed all this on to Charley, thinking he might tell Lindsay. But her husband had snorted: "Melinda, any half-grown boy should know how to swim!" He wished, in fact, Jim had some of Elisha's gumption! Besides, Betsy was too timid. Left alone, she would gentle his nephews to death. It was a good thing Lindsay didn't always see eye to eye with Betsy. His brother knew what a boy ought to be: rough-and-ready for anything.

Jesse

Under the high-hung moon, the boy slept—wrapped in a tangle of dream-nets that swung him gently, far to the east, where he visited in sleep the places he would never see again.

In the morning, the memory of his night journey would hover briefly, then disperse like the aromatic smoke of the cookfire. Bad dreams and good would drift away, Missouri would recede, replaced by thoughts of breakfast. The general bustle of the camp, the sight of tents being struck, of his parents packing things, would soon exhilarate him. He'd lead a huzzah for the day then! A whoop for the weather: clear and cool. A cheer for the broad blue river whose back they'd finally ride upon. He'd thought of nothing else for days.

But in his sleep another river was coursing through his dreams and it was not the Columbia. And it was not autumn, either—or nighttime. It was spring under a cloud-pinioned, milk-white Missouri sky. And he was running hard. And Vick and Vine, the greyhounds, and his brothers Elisha and Warren and cousin Jim were all with him, making a beeline for the river, crashing noisily through the green-tipped thickets of sassafras and redbud trees, not caring that they'd set the blue jays screaming and scattered the rabbits. There was only panting and heartbeat and the pleasure of sweating again after a long cold winter, the joyful momentum of their feet striking the red-black earth.

When they'd finally reached the blurred stands of hickories and passed beneath the bare tangled branches of the walnuts, they stopped for a moment, catching their breath next to a solitary gigantic oak, the only landmark of real significance between the corncribs and the beckoning river. Now they could see the thing they had only heard from the house. The Osage, slow, low, and lazy in other seasons, surged and tumbled before them, wondrously transformed, thundering with its glut of melting ice and snow.

And in his dream, the boy cast off his clothes, as he had once done in wakefulness but a season before. He felt the cool ooze of the mud between his toes, the warm new wind of spring moving over him. Laughing, he'd called to his cousin, who held back, glowering, hesitating at the edge of the riverbank. "Hey, Jim! Looky here!" the boy cried, encouraging him. He had taken the plunge then, feet first, into the roiling current, the river rising to meet him with delicious force, almost knocking him down.

Finally, all, even Jim, had given themselves to the turmoil of the current and they cavorted cold and carefree, letting the river pull them down and surge them up again, sputtering, grinning Jacks-in-the-box. Forgetting they were cold and forgetting, too, that one of them had promised to stay on the bank and stand lookout. There was only the power of the river; the heady sense that their sturdy legs and daredevil will would keep them from harm.

Then Vine barked excitedly, her sharp sound overriding their own laughter and the hiss and the agreeable rumble. He had looked up then, scanning the riverbank through the moving curtain of spray and foam. Both dogs were circling in agitation. Vine was barking louder than before. Elisha, closest to him, was walking now, the water whirling around him. And the boy knew from the peculiar expression on his oldest brother's face that something more compelling than the dogs was pulling Elisha toward the riverbank.

Then the boy saw *her*. She stood well above them on the verge of the river. In the dream, she had been unbelievably tall and terrible, an apparition wavering like a ghost in a story. There was a long hickory switch in her right hand. She was striking viciously at the willy-nilly heaps of clothes upon the bank. The pale spring sky darkened suddenly until it was precisely the color of her shawl. She who was a being angry-eyed and frighteningly unfamiliar. She who was their own mother. Almost blue with cold, yet scalding with the shame of being so discovered, they scurried up the slippery bank to meet her, to meet their fate. And the long switch hissed, whizzing above them, coming down hard. He had awakened then, saving himself from his dream and the woman in it. Instead, the bright moon hung serenely above him, a crescent pendant suspended from a bracelet of icy stars. He felt the warmth of his blankets then and soon slipped easily back to sleep; back to

Missouri, wandering over the wooded hills behind his old home, taking his fill of an Osage summer: the sweet wild grapes called Catawba, the green plums with frosted skins, and the June berries.

Within the adobe walls of the fort, oh so very far from Missouri, the boy had awakened to a chill autumn morning. He saw *her*. For some moments, he had watched her soberly until the specter of his dreams receded and was replaced by the kind-eyed slender woman who, leaning down, hugged him, saying cheerfully, "Good morning, Jesse-boy!"

DOWN THE COLUMBIA

Now comes the long-awaited call: Three husky blasts from the old man's trumpet echo over the river and up the hill. Carrying infants or the odd-lot article, the women stream down the pathway, their little ones behind them, trailing like so many kite-tails, their view obscured by the surge of their mammas' skirts, their little ears full of "Get-along-now! Don't dawdle!" Bringing up the rear of this procession, march older sisters and female cousins whose task it is to round up stragglers and keep them from harm.

As they pass the low knoll where the empty wagons form a long mournful line, where the last of the morning winds whimper through the tattered canvas covers and shiver the black chains that link the spoked wheels one after another, no one looks back. All is hurry and purposeful scurry. All is dead ahead.

On the landing below those who are called the "Big Boys" have already deposited their burdens. They have been shooed from the line of mackinaws several times: The men kneeling by the boats are irritable—even the old man, McClellan. Load and reload: Out come the tools, crates, and water kegs one more time and in they go again. For an hour or two the men have been shifting gear around, wedging in Dutch ovens and butter churns, padding everything with quilts and bedticks. All the while, each man is wondering what unexpected stuff that "can't be done without" his woman will haul down the hill at just the last moment. It is leaving Missouri all over again. No one wants his son or some other youngster questioning him at every turn, either. This is why the boys have been instructed to be seen and not heard. Thus they hover about the landing's edges, tired of tag and tossing pebbles into the water.

A few have passed the time by hatching a plan: a simple spectacle to mark the occasion, a homely send-off all their own. The "Big Girls," whom they hope to impress, have not yet arrived at the landing. Lucy Applegate is the oldest. It is her tall form they are awaiting, her pale bonnet.

Elisha has appointed himself signalman. In this, as in everything, he is the captain of the boys. Indeed, he has his own skiff—or so he refers to it. This is his reward for helping the boat builders. McClellan, the skiff's pilot, has permitted Elisha to

33

choose the youngsters who will ride with them in the littlest mackinaw. One spot remains to be filled, and several boys are vying for the privilege. Elisha has promised to reveal his choice when everyone arrives at the landing—just after the "surprise."

So it is that anticipation doubles: Every boy readies himself and when Elisha calls from his post, "Here she comes! I see Lucy!" a lusty huzzah rings out. The air is alive with a flurry of caps and hats and so much jubilation that even a few grown men join in, tossing low-crowned and battered-up beavers high and higher. Their hats are as dark as birds against the autumn sky. Floating down now . . . meeting the glistening beach. But Lucy is stooping at just the wrong moment, being tugged on, listening again to the child, Irene, who leans on her and sniffles into her shawl. What is a combination of question and complaint can barely be heard, for the "Lucy! Where is Mamma?" is muffled and women directly ahead of them are laughing and lifting up little ones. These children are pointing at the sky so excitedly it is as if they have just witnessed an August shower of meteors. Irene is squeezing out a tear or two, still asking for Mamma. Lucy, who all morning has been shepherding around one toddler or another, feels like giving her a good shaking. Instead, she dabs her little sister's nose with the corner of her apron, and when Lucy stands up, the child in her arms, the excitement is already over, has passed her by, she thinks, and sighs.

Suddenly her father's voice rises over the crowd. He has called for attention. Women shush their children and all grows so quiet that even the rhythmic lapping of the current can be heard. Then Charley Applegate is booming again, telling what to do, where to form lines, and in what order the mackinaws will cast off.

Irene is placated. She is as high as a cub in her Lucy-tree, her sturdy little legs twining about her sister's middle. The familiar resonance that is her father reaches out to her like a steady hand. His voice is almost as reassuring as the pump of Lucy's heart beneath the homespun bodice. And when Irene stretches her neck and looks way down in front she sees not only her Pappa but her uncles Lindsay and Jesse, who stand solemnly on either side. The three of them: Here is Safety. They are taller than other men—or so it seems to Irene—and she and Lucy sway to the verge of the path, following the other women and children until they arrive at the landing and are guided to their assigned places. Now Safety is warmed by Comfort, for Irene sees that her mamma is waiting with her aunts Cynthia and Betsy and the littlest children. The friendly tide of faces, the jumble of family voices and gestures tell her she is part of everything again. She is where she belongs.

When the old fellow she calls "Unca" Mac passes by—his stride so vigorous that his greatcoat is slapping against his boot-tops—she has already released her mamma's cool hand. Irene and other little girls are waving to him and Mac waves back.

McClellan is counting noses; everyone must be where he or she ought to be, for the moment is almost at hand; a relief to him, surely, for in the push to get things done, the old man is ruddy. He has overheated himself. Despite this, it has not occurred to him to relieve himself of his coat; nay, it is his second skin, or so he always says. As he moves up and down the seven lines, he is pausing here and there, his coat giving off a faint scent that is as hithercoming to each child he passes as castoreum is to the beaver. Indeed, those children who have sat upon "Uncle" Mac's lap at one time or another, hearing him sing "The Rose Tree," or who have bounced on his knee as one big boot thumps out an accompaniment to "Marching to Old Quebec," or who have spent time hovering in the vicinity of his elbows watching whistles and dolly-men being whittled, or the careful plaiting of horsehair ropes, insist that, even in the darkest dark, they know when the old man is coming by the scent of his greatcoat alone!

The big boots crunch over the blue-gray cobbles and halt. Someone is where he ought not to be. The stout owner of the boots scowls and prepares his admonishments. The culprit fiddles with his buttons, nudges at a stone with one stubby toe, and stares fixedly downward.

The greatcoat is as a wall before him, close enough to touch or stroke. These smells assail the child's nostrils: the odor of pipe tobacco moistened by apple pieces, the tang of green wood shavings, the old man's sweat, of course—for beneath coat-shadow and soiled vest, the yellowed undershirt is unhappily fragrant—and wafting out of the deep pockets comes a pungent whiff of something the boy recognizes well enough, for it has been inflicted upon him countless times in the form of tea, eyewash, and ointment. Uncle Mac, the boy knows, always carries many a tidy packet of noxious weeds, root tendrils, and tiny bitter-tasting flowers. Just thinking of the concoction called "Indian Fizic," the boy's throat constricts as he stands there—so small before the coat. He traces the torn places, the patches, the frayed sleeves with his one good eye. His other is rheumy again: all oozy, for even Uncle Mac's concoctions have not succeeded in curing what scissors had accidentally ruined years before. This is why, as the old man collars the boy to steer him motherward, he is saying to himself, "Poor little lad." This little child, Jesse Applegate, has been known to him since babyhood; since the very day McClellan knocked upon Lindsay Applegate's door, asking if there were need of another hand. The one-eyed "laddie-buck" has remained his favorite, and because of this, though the old man's countenance is stern, his voice is gentle: There is no room in the skiff. No. Not one more boy-body may be added for safety's sake. All has been decided. Besides which, Uncle Mac says kindly, Jesse should be pleased to be in the larger boat—after all, it will hit the water first and take the lead all the way to Fort Vancouver.

Jesse is consoled only a little, for he still feels odd man out. He casts one last stormy look at the three "lucky" ones, who are Elisha, his oldest brother; Warren, who is but a scant year older than Jesse is himself; and his cousin Edward, who is the newest member of the crew. Edward seems sorry for him, and to soften things, his cousin now mumbles how he might consider trading off a time or two later on. This bright prospect is soon snuffed out, however, for after McClellan has delivered him, Jesse's mamma, Betsy Applegate, shakes her head. "No," she says firmly. "Under no circumstances. . . . Why, he is only seven years old," and all the while Jesse's mother is fussing over him, squatting low so she might peer into his bad eye.

McClellan has given a comforting squeeze to the child's thin shoulder, yet in "no wise" does he intercede. Dispute the judgment informed by mother love? Not him! This "Missus" has the full measure of McClellan's devotion and not merely because she is wife to his friend and benefactor. Betsy Applegate's tender sensibilities remind the old man of the sweetheart long ago denied to him. "Where woman resides, so doth kindness dwell"—at least this is his belief; hence McClellan's deference, which is of so deep a grain it is like maple or cherry wood—the very materials he chooses for the little polished boxes he fashions all year long that he quietly offers on Christmastide to every mother and daughter in the family circle where he, too, has found his place.

Nevertheless, McClellan is pleased to see the mother relent a bit and the little boy's face brighten. Jim, a son of Charley Applegate, has beckoned from the front of the line. Jesse soon stands proudly by the young redhead who is his double cousin. These two will have the privilege of being seated before all other youngsters, and McClellan smiles at "Missus" Applegate as he pulls courteously on his hatbrim, for he must complete his duties. The Hudson's Bay Company men are now coming down the path and McClellan has spied them. After farewells, these men will help the emigrants shove off. Now French Canadiens, Scots, and Britishers greet Missouri emigrants like old friends, while little Jesse and Jim are watching the river lick the curved underside of the bow. The boys gaze at the mackinaw with a concentration so complete it is as if they believe that their very avidity will somehow hurry things along.

Thus they do not see the striking-looking woman standing up there upon the hill, but others have noted the opening of the fort gate and watch the stately figure pass the walls of pale adobe and turn down the path which only she and her children are permitted to use.

The woman's cadence is slow, deliberate as a doe or cougar. The seven-point blanket—a fine specimen of the best the trade has to offer—is draped over her shoulders, its stripes brighter than any flame or hollyberry against the desolate hues of the landscape. This woman, Sarah Ogden McKinlay, is from a northern tribe whose domain is as vivid as she is, a land vibrant with wild flowers and greens without number.

Two little figures follow at her heels. Mrs. McKinlay—the chief trader's wife and queen of this lonely bastion—pauses, carefully folding her blanket so that it rides over one arm. Custom dictates that each part of her costume must be seen and admired. Her finery has been passed down from her mother's people or else given by her husband, Archibald McKinlay, as a sign of his respect. And now—when her regalia has been displayed—she will honor the departing ones. For a moment she stands like a finely carved figurehead, the forward slope, her prow. She looks down at her "friends," for she has formed warm ties with a number of emigrant women during this fortnight and shared liberally of her personal stores. Never before has she seen so many female Moving People.

At the bottom of the hill a clot of Company men and emigrant leaders are talking earnestly about the rightful divvying up of cattle, oxen, and spring calves. The Company has agreed to protect the emigrants' livestock until the following year. One or two speak animatedly about suitable camping places and portages farther downriver. They are drawing a map in the dust, their willow sticks scratching. They are the first to hear the jingle of brass bracelets, the faint chiming of tiny bells and thimbles and coins from China, and the more subtle click of narrow strands of bone-white shells—the mollusks that are looped about Mrs. McKinlay's neck and waist. As the men raise their eyes, she lowers her own, gliding past them in the music of her own making.

Now little girls murmur in the lines, gawking and pointing at Mrs. McKinlay's "pretties." Their older sisters glare at them, for their own glances are less direct. Many a half-grown girl is inspired by the Indian woman's haughty carriage, and thus several attempts to improve their posture even though they are self-conscious in their linsey-woolseys and limp ginghams. For what have they on their shawl-dark shoulders? Only that which they have spun and knitted in the poor light of Missouri loghouses candled for winter. And their dresses—unrelievedly plain—are the colors of night or muted mornings, or gray stones or dry dusted creekbeds; and if patterned, the sprigs and florets are so faint it is as if they are seen through a mist, poor girls.

Mrs. McKinlay makes her bright way up and down each line, missing no one. Her glossy-haired children gravely hand out bits of jerky and yampa root. The yampa is what the emigrant boys have been calling "Walla Walla candy." Its very sweetness has made them greedy and caused numerous altercations between emigrant boys and the youths whose parents' lodges dot the surrounding plain. Lest more trouble break out—for both natives and whites have been sorely vexed—all save grown men have been commanded by the chief trader to sleep inside the fort walls. A week has passed since the children have tasted anything so pleasant as yampa. Now the root is hastily wadded in little cheeks and a noisy sucking commences as the dignified chief trader's wife extends her hand to their mothers, for Mrs. McKinlay prides herself on knowing the etiquette of the Moving People.

And these women are thinking, as they touch her brown hand, how they would never exchange their lot for hers. . . . The

noisome winds . . . the bleakness . . . the long months deprived
of worthy company . . . only the local squaws, so tedious in their
familiarity, always haggling and hankering. And at mealtime
would undoubtedly come the loutish trappers, redolent with the
stench of sweat and wild things . . . and the sly-eyed *voyageurs*
and young clerks with baleful looks; and for husband there would
be naught but a Scot of the dour sort . . . a McKinlay or worse.
. . . No, the emigrant women think to themselves, they could not
be this woman who, though handsome and kind, was neither
white nor red, but a half-blood in a border world thick with adobe
walls.

Yet even as the emigrant men arrive at the head of each line
and expectancy rolls over the children, the older girls are still
staring yearningly at Mrs. McKinlay and sighing after her gay shift
of India cloth and the soft leggings of antelope hide. As the
beaded moccasins pad quietly toward the upward path, the air jin-
gling with tribal jewels, the girls look down. Hiding under dirty
hems are their own feet, which are as dusty and bootless as their
brothers'. And soon their skirts and everything they own will be
damp with the chill waters of the Columbia. So it will be all the
way to Fort Vancouver and during a winter that will seem without end.

Jesse Applegate Applegate
Recollections of My Boyhood

I well remember our start down the river, and
how I enjoyed riding in the boat, the movement of
which was like my grapevine swing back home.
Shoving out from the [Fort] Walla Walla canoe landing about the first day of November, our little fleet of
boats began the voyage down the great "River of the
West." Whirlpools looking like deep basins in the
river, the lapping, slashing, and rolling of the waves
crested with foam sometimes when the wind was
strong alarmed me for a day or two. . . .

. . . Often when the current was strong the men

would rest their oars and allow the boats to be swept along by the current.

Children left to themselves and not alarmed by those they look to for protection, do not anticipate danger; as a rule they do not borrow trouble. . . . I soon recovered from my childish fears and as I learned that the motion of the boat became lively and gyratory, rocking from side to side, leaping from wave to wave, or sliding down into a trough and then mounting with perfect ease to the crest of a wave, dashing spray into our faces when we were in rough water, the sound of the rapids and the sight of foam and whitecaps ahead occasioned only pleasant anticipation. . . .

. . . a seven year old boy on pleasant autumn days, who had been travelling all summer barefoot through the desert sands, through sagebrush, grease wood, and cactus, and had often been broken of his rest, mayhap being tortured by prickly pear needles between his toes, now happily enjoyed the ride on the river being rocked as in a cradle at his mother's knee . . . overcome by drowsiness . . . and dreaming of unromantic things, bread and butter for instance. . . .

. . . I [saw] some ugly cliffs of rock, black and forbidding in appearance, along the banks of the river, some high and some not so high, some rough, barren, and precipitous while others were thickly set with timber and brush. Neither did the grown up people seem to be delighted with the scenery along the river. At least I never heard any expressions of admiration. A jaded emigrant, however, might gaze upon the face of a precipice a thousand feet high, with a crack in it from top to bottom, without being struck dumb with awe and admiration.

. . . Occasionally we saw Indians on the river in canoes. Each canoe was wrought of a log cut from fir, pine or cedar. . . . The canoes here on the upper river [above The Dalles] were shapely and neatly finished, but quite plain in appearance and generally large enough for only two or three persons. One day, however, six or seven natives shot out of a cove on the north shore, and passing our bows, slowed up, while the man in the bow of the craft, lifting his hand towards his mouth, spoke and said, "Smoke six!" which literally translated means "Tobacco, friend!" [in the Chinook trade jargon].

The spokesman was a large stout man with more black in his skin than a redman. His eyes were not really black, but looked, at our distance, like burnt holes in a blanket. He was bareheaded . . . [he surely] needed no other covering on his head, for this son of an African sire and a native daughter of a Walla Walla, Cayuse, Klickitat, Chemomichat, Spokane, or Wasco tribe had an immense shock of grizzly, almost curly hair, which grew down to his ears, and to within an inch of his nose making his head appear unnaturally large. Some of our party gave him a little tobacco and passed on.

. . . It was said he was the son of a negro man who came to the coast with Lewis and Clark's expedition as a cook, about forty years before the time I am speaking of . . . a man so petted by the squaws . . . he left many descendents among the Western tribes!

. . . Now of nights, we encamped on the bank of the river, sometimes on the north and sometimes on the south side. I remember especially a camp we made on the south shore. There was a very narrow strip of sand and rock almost level, between the river and a high bluff, with a mountain rising behind it. Here we were, I well remember . . . the broad river before us. We must have landed quite early in the afternoon, for the unusual occurrence which underscored this camping place on memory's tablet took place before the sun was low; for it may have been a nooning place.

Now at a venture I will say that our people for frontiersmen and women of that era, were unusually free from superstitious whims. I had never seen a horse-shoe over our door, they never spoke of looking at a hog's melt for a forecast of the weather, did not be-lieve in lucky or unlucky days, nor that the dropping of a dishrag was sign that the family would have com-

What Belongs to the River. ". . . the event made a lasting impression. The raven . . . flying over all of us . . . heading for the river." (Susan Applegate painting. Photograph courtesy Douglas County Museum)

pany at the house. But mother [Betsy Applegate], meaning to make sport of superstitious notions, no doubt sometimes spoke of a belief among the people that seeing the new moon over the right shoulder was an omen of good luck, and to be candid I must admit that when I know the new moon is out I sometimes put myself to a little trouble to get first sight of it over my right shoulder. That indicates a trace of superstition. Ghost stories, stories of haunted houses, of goblins, of witches and fairies were current among the people of that time but were not told as truths, at least by our folks.

The unusual occurrence referred to was this. Although we had now several days on our voyage down the river, I had not heard anyone complain of the hardships or dangers to be encountered, and for my part I had come to feel as safe on water as on land. But at this camp I heard remarks that renewed my apprehensions.

There was a driftwood campfire burning and the women were doing kitchen work and talking. I don't remember what the rest were saying only that my Aunt Cynthia, Jesse Applegate's wife, said, "There is going to be a death in the family!" She was standing and pointing upwards—a wooden spoon in her hand—and added, "See that raven flying over the camp?" I was lying upon the sand and looked up. I saw the great black bird—a raven or crow, flying about one hundred feet above us . . . and as my aunt's countenance, gesture, and tone of voice bespoke alarm and distress, the event made a lasting impression. The raven . . . flying over all of us . . . heading for the river.

Morning
November 4, 1843

The Indian pilot wore a red bandanna. His black hair hung loose halfway down his leather shirt. Though little Jesse had doubtless seen the pilot's face countless times since they'd started downriver, he could not conjure it as he sat there staring at the Indian. For hour after hour, the fellow looked the same: There was only the dark head slashed with red, the motionless back turned toward them. The Indian was in the bow, standing erect and alone while all others sat; the pilot . . . his unseen eyes ever on the waters, looking out for what might lie before them.

Where the pilot went after they beached at night no one knew. Nor did he sup with them. Yet no matter how early they departed, he awaited them. And the boy would see him, the Indian, already at his place in the lead mackinaw—as if he'd never left it.

The boy had heard his uncle Charley say that the pilot knew the river's every trough and curve. If the winds were bad he and others of his tribe were so accustomed to the channels that traveling at night was nothing to them. Their keen ears—a characteristic of their race—keeping them from harm. And Jesse had thought of his uncle's remarks whenever the waters got rough. He felt relieved that thus far they had only traveled by daylight, which meant the Indian could use both his eyes and his ears, which were somehow better than other men's.

It had not escaped the boy's notice that his father, Lindsay Applegate, was always peering at the pilot and always sat directly behind him, alert and uneasy. Even now the boy's uncle Charley permitted himself to doze, his big head swaying from side to side, though his hand was yet clamped upon the oar. Even so, the boy's father maintained his vigil. His head up. His back almost as straight as the Indian's.

A few days before there had occurred a moment that took everyone by surprise, his father included. The current had chopped with such unexpected force that the mackinaw bounced vigorously and a wave poured over the sides. And this had caused the boy's father to duck quicker than any child. When he'd righted himself again the water was streaming down his hatbrim. His curses were so long and loud that the boy's mother shouted from her back seat, "Lindsay Applegate! There are women and children present!"

Later the grown-ups laughed about the incident, and someone who had been watching the pilot observed that even as the spray and waters broke over all their heads, the Indian had remained upright as a candle in a holder. No, the pilot had neither flinched nor shuddered afterward. Nor was he heard to utter a single oath.

This had prompted someone else to remark that maybe the Indian was a "mute," for, in truth, not one of them had heard him speak. And the boy who had been listening to all of this saw his father frown and heard him say gruffly how he was certain when it came time to haggle over the price for his services, the Indian pilot would find his tongue all right.

But now the boy had given up on thinking and was spending a while counting the grease spots on the back of the Indian's shirt. How dull and drowsy he felt. There was nothing to interest him much on the shoreline.

The previous day had offered exciting diversions, for they'd nooned near a place where some Indians were drying fish on long curing racks, and his parents and others had done some trading, which meant that for the rest of the afternoon the boy and his cousin Jim had dried fish to gnaw upon until there had been nothing left but skins. "Jest skins" hadn't stopped their gnawing, however, for they'd begun to feel hungry all the time. And now the boy ran his tongue over the sore places on the roof of his mouth, for there had been something on the fish skins. He squinted at the river. The sun was but a pale disk, only now and then glinting down on them. He felt more tired, especially when he noted that a faint wheezing had commenced on the boat bottom. He saw that his cousin Jim had made himself a pallet over the tent canvases, curving his scrawny body between the water kegs. An overturned Dutch oven served as his pillow, over which he'd wadded up his jacket.

The boy heard his mother and Aunt Melinda murmuring behind him, the intermittent creak of their plank seat. And his cousin Irene's high pipings lifted over him every so often, his aunt Melinda softly answering. And now, just under everything, came the lulling tune the waters strummed. For "nigh onto an hour" there had been a stretch of calm—or so his father had put it some moments before.

. . . his father. Why, when they finally got to Oregon, there'd be plenty to do! They'd go hunting for bear, his father had said. Yes. And you too, Jesse-boy, for you'll be big enough. And Warren. And Elisha of course. Off we'll go. . . . And these thoughts warmed the boy as he felt the gentle pitch of waves, and by the time someone's infant began squawling in the back, a little song had sounded in the boy's mind, clear as water but seeming to come from some great distance:

Bye baby bunting . . . Daddy's gone a-hunting . . .

The boy shut his eyes. . . . He had succumbed.

Afternoon
November 4, 1843

Now the river swung before them in a great gradual curve that coursed slightly to the north. The current grew lustier by the moment, and even though the waters were yet deeply hued and dully sheened as gunmetal, the oarsmen could see the incomparable agitation that lay in the fast-coming distance, seething and white and gated with rocks where the bend began.

Line after line of breakers were appearing and the men began to prepare themselves, their grips tightening upon the oars, their faces intent and solemn, for the tumult beyond was already rumbling in their ears, announcing its peril, sounding closer and closer until those who had lately been at rest were awakening, each sleeper asking himself: What could it be but thunder? Yet it was not.

Attempting to rouse himself, the boy had stirred a little, but it was as if he were rising from the deep, and his bad eye was sticky—the lashes all crusted together—and the whole of his body felt heavy and thick with sleep.

As the first waves met the mackinaw—the boat rising and falling and rocking—it seemed to the boy that he was still upon the schooner of the prairies that had carried him for thousands of miles, for he was used to the thumping and bumping of their family wagon as it traversed the rutted wastes, and since he was only half awake, the boy forgot he was riding on the undulant back of the river called Columbia, the plank seat of the mackinaw for his bed.

In his mind, the boy was conjuring a thunderstorm and the great lapping he heard was wind to him—not water. If only their horrid bouncing would cease long enough so that he might safely wipe his sleeve across his eyes, the boy was certain he would see the driver; but where was the clatter of wheels, the pounding of hooves, the urgent shouts of the bullwhacker who surely, at any moment, would thrust his stout knee against the wagon brake and stop the affrighted teams?

These sounds did not come—were lost as under thunder. A terrible speed was pulling them along. Even faster now as wind and roar and water broke over him. The boy was lifted from his seat by a force that felt like a punishing hand . . . pushing him down . . . and raising him up again . . . everything heaving now . . . he was lost.

This belief so took hold of the boy that a long time seemed to pass before he dared open his eyes. Yet all this was transpiring in a trembling instant as compressed and violent as the waters that now surged the mackinaw through darkening cliff-lined narrows where the river was twisting and hissing and spilling through a channel braided with rock.

Spray, foam, and motion unceasing: This was the world the boy perceived when he finally raised his head. Only then did he comprehend that he had landed upon the bottom of the boat. If his poor body had not been so wedged between his father's tool crate and several sliding water kegs, who knew what would have become of him? The mackinaw was rearing like a wild horse.

"Starboard!" his father cried. With each mighty exertion, the boy heard the men panting, their oars rattling against the oarlocks. Then came a turning filled with such teetering that it seemed that they must be flying or skidding and the boat was a mere pebble hurled across an expanse of ice. As the air whistled in the boy's ears, the momentum grew more thrilling. No wave reached him. There was a stinging mist, which whipped over his head. Though lightning-fast, their course seemed smoother now, and the boy began to think about righting himself so that he might carefully make his way back to his seat and witness the blurred mysteries they were passing. But just as he had propped his elbows securely under himself and was about to rise up, the odor of wet leather assailed his nostrils, seeming closer than his very breath. Then a pounding roar commenced again, louder than a hundred drumrolls. And through his good eye appeared a sight which made him know that he was not safe at all. Surely some fresh terror was imminent.

The Indian pilot's back was so near the boy might have touched it—the rawhide shirt all dark with water. Then the pilot raised one long arm as though expecting a blow. All this the boy saw clearly; indeed, he was almost upon the Indian as the water churned anew. The spectacle of the Indian's raised arm, and lowered head, filled the boy with an apprehension colder than the currents. The Indian in the bow was squatting low.

But this siege was of short duration and soon the pilot no longer crouched but knelt upon one knee, appearing in control again. Seeing him, the boy took heart and pulled himself up so that he might peer over the sides. Some moments passed before the nearest shoreline grew visible. They sped past rock after rock—each one glistening ominously beneath milk-white froth and rolling vapors. Despite the spew, the pilot must have spied something familiar to him. Suddenly he was gesturing emphatically. The oars rattled imperatively as the oarsmen hurried to do his bidding. Soon the curved shoreline had come so close it seemed they might wreck on the rocks. Finally, the boy saw the Indian nod repeatedly as though satisfied. The men rested at their oars, their shoulders sunk with exertion. The mackinaw had darted through a chute, which had carried them into a little channel. This watery road was glass compared to the fitful, broken course they had known but a moment before.

Even so, the dreadful rumble could still be heard all about them. Whirlpools and great sucking rapids were but yards away. The force of water and motion grew so great and the boat bottom trembled so beneath him that the boy began to worry that the boat might veer or fly to pieces. Lest terror seize him completely, he decided to turn and see how those behind him were faring and whether they were afraid. It was Irene he spied first. She was leaning against his aunt Melinda. Her eyes were wide, yet neither a murmur nor a whimper came from her or any other little person. Indeed, several infants, all swaddled in their coverlets, were sleeping in perfect peace upon their mammas' shoulders. And every mother—including his own—appeared erect and composed. If anything might be read upon the faces of the women, it was not alarm but seriousness. They wore the sort of look he had come to expect at a preach or some other somber occasion.

But the boy's relief was not complete until he had assessed the condition of his cousin Jim, who was similarly stationed upon the boat bottom, though farther back. Jim was wringing out his jacket and quaking from the cold, since the waters had dashed over everything. Something about Jim's gesture—so homely and ordinary as though nothing should be thought about save comfort—made the boy relax. Only then had he returned to his sidelong gazing at the scenery.

At last the mackinaw had cleared the great curve of the river, and in so doing all that had hitherto been behind them swung into sight: The numerous rapids they had passed through curled like a pale wind-trembled plume, with dark rocks beading it here and there. Soon the boy had a fine sweeping view of the bend itself. And oh how glorious it was, for the heavens were bathing everything in a pearl-gray light. Even the horrid cliffs—whose steep sides were raven-black—had a handsome aspect. Their uppermost reaches curved strangely against the sky. Tier upon tier of hills furred with tawny grasses rose behind the rocks, their colors all the more splendid because of their contrast with the morose hues of the shoreline, where the moody bluffs bordered the waters and formed a gloomy corridor. Within the shadowy narrows the river fairly gleamed in its slit.

The boy now heard soft voices in the back of the mackinaw. Everyone, it seemed, was turning slightly upon his seat and gazing across the waters. The pilot was shading his eyes. The oarsmen, too, paused, scanning the currents.

The boy had almost forgotten the other boats, so like their own. Now, however, he concentrated upon them, thinking them worrisome small. Yet sometimes they seemed as fleet as arrows to him, and he almost smiled, imagining how his playmates must be holding on, the wind beating like wings over their heads.

One by one he watched as they entered the bad place, and disappeared in the vapors only to be spat out again a moment later. Each time a boat could be seen skimming over the chute that brought them safely into the main channel, a sighing arose from the women, as if they were of one breath. And now the mackinaw that all day had followed in their wake drew so close that the forms of certain of their comrades could be recognized. Someone could be seen waving and was doubtless calling out, though the voice was drowned by the tumult.

Three. Four. Five. All were counting to themselves. Spirits were so uplifted the boy could feel it. One woman laughed.

But suddenly there fell an awful hush, for now appeared the last boat: the little skiff old McClellan piloted . . . and they saw it angling queerly, pulling away from where it ought to have been . . . and swirling mists exploding over it . . . and round and round it spun until the boy heard his mother's voice. "Dear God!" she said, for the little skiff was disappearing into the powerful maw of the whirlpool and when released again, it hovered eerily—empty of all occupants save one, and this single form was barely visible through the vapors. So that it might have been a ghost or a trick of the mists.

Now a commotion came amidst moan and mournful cry. And their own boat commenced a terrible rocking. So transfixed were the oarsmen that they had forsaken their duties.

A shrill voice could be heard in the rear: "No! They mustn't see it!" And a quilt was thrown over the heads of little children who sat in the back, and all the while the boy could hear his father groaning.

Then the boy saw him struggling to his feet, tearing off his coat, even as the boat lurched; he was ready to dive into the waters and would have done so had the pilot not restrained him.

And the boy grew dizzy. All was happening at once. His father was now leaning over the pilot—gripping him by the shoulders and hissing, "Land! Damn you! Land!" And they struggled in the bow. The Indian's bandanna was as bright as blood.

"Please! Men! Lindsay! You must not!" And this entreaty was so full of anguish, his father quit his attack only to have a new frenzy seize him. Forms could be seen struggling in the waters. "Elisha! Warren!" These names ripped from his father's throat even as rocks were grazing past their own boat; even as the tools slid heavily across the bottom and children cried and women— clutching their babes—shouted again and again until it echoed in the boy's ears: "Men! Men! You must not quit the oars! . . . We'll all be lost—All!"

This lithograph, depicting "the wonderful escape of young [Elisha] Applegate," originally appeared in F. F. Victor's *The River of the West* in 1870.

Jesse Applegate Applegate
Recollections of My Boyhood

The persons in this boat were Uncle Mac [Alexander McClellan], a man of about seventy, William Parker, Aunt Cynthia's brother who was twenty-one, Billy Doak, Uncle Charley's driver, about the same age and three boys: my oldest brother, Elisha Applegate, aged eleven and my brother Warren and my cousin Edward Applegate [Uncle Jesse and Aunt Cynthia's boy], both of whom were then nine years of age. . . .

[William Parker, a strong swimmer, survived. Billy Doak did not drown only because he held on to a feather tick with his *teeth* until he was picked up. Elisha, despite his young age, managed to swim for safety though he was sorely injured. He was stranded on a broken ledge of rock amidst roaring rapids. It is said his bravery helped save Billy Doak, and that the rescue of both was something of a miracle.

Alexander McClellan exhibited unparalleled courage, and when last seen in the currents was holding young Edward in his arms. The old man might have saved himself if he had removed his great-coat and boots, but he did not let go of the boy. Alas, Edward, Warren, and the old man who loved them so well all disappeared in the treacherous waters and were never seen again.]

From the [north] shore of the river there was a level track of ground running back to a hill . . . and extending along the river a considerable distance. Indians were seen to put out after the floating bedding, clothes, and various articles . . . from the foundered boat. It was said the Indians did not make any attempt or show any desire to assist our people in the water . . . [this] may have encouraged the suspicion of treachery against the pilot.

. . . As there was a large village in that vicinity [Wishram/Wu'czam] the appearance of so many Indians was not significant [as first was thought]. A fact favorable to the good faith of the pilot is that only one boat was lost and if that smaller boat had followed the pilot it would have been safe . . . but at the time they entered the rapids their boat was pulled into a strong current bearing towards the south shore [and caught in a whirlpool there].

WILLAMETTE WINDS

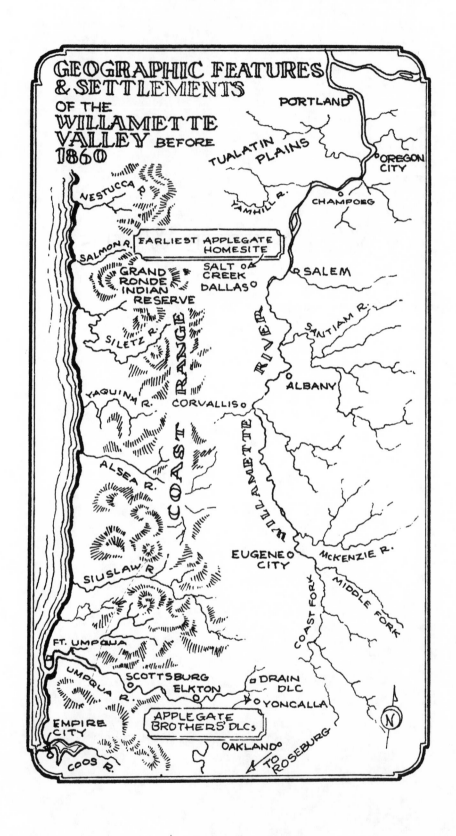

GEOGRAPHIC FEATURES & SETTLEMENTS OF THE WILLAMETTE VALLEY BEFORE 1860

PORTLAND

OREGON CITY

TUALATIN PLAINS

NESTUCCA R.

YAMHILL R.

CHAMPOEG

SALMON R.

EARLIEST APPLEGATE HOMESITE

GRAND RONDE INDIAN RESERVE

SALT CREEK

DALLAS

SALEM

SANTIAM R.

SILETZ R.

YAQUINA R.

CORVALLIS

ALBANY

COAST RANGE

WILLAMETTE RIVER

ALSEA R.

SIUSLAW R.

EUGENE CITY

McKENZIE R.

COAST FORK

MIDDLE FORK

FT. UMPQUA

UMPQUA R.

SCOTTSBURG

ELKTON

DRAIN DLC

YONCALLA

EMPIRE CITY

APPLEGATE BROTHERS' DLCs

OAKLAND

TO ROSEBURG

COOS R.

N

. . . a better road from Fort Hall to the Willamette was both a physical and a psychological necessity. The settlements knew that their increase and trade depended on the establishment of a new route. The emigrants of '46 knew what had happened to their predecessors and the stories had lost nothing on the way to them. . . . If a road could be located it . . . would avoid the Blue Mountains and Columbia River altogether. . . . This [solution] was also important to the War Department which might have to oppose a British occupation of California based on Oregon. . . . The southern Cascades were less formidable than the northern part of that range, and if a good pass through them could be found the terrors of the last stretch of [the old Oregon Trail] would be entirely eliminated.

In May of 1846 the settlements sent out an exploring party to locate the much needed southern entrance to the valley. It was insufficiently equipped, however, and the attempt was repeated in June of 1846 by a party of fifteen men. No more intelligent resolute men could be found . . . all of them the highest type of pioneers including Lindsey [sic] Applegate and his brother Jesse, who was then and long remained the first citizen of Oregon.

Bernard De Voto,
The Year of Decision: 1846

. . . Meanwhile Jessy [sic] Thornton had been filling the columns of Oregon newspapers with diatribes against the Applegates and their trail: the roadbuilders and their defenders retaliated with denunciations of Thornton. By the summer of 1847 the dispute had become a major cause célèbre, culminating when James Nesmith, a champion of the Applegate faction, came to Oregon City vowing to kill

TO THE WORLD!!

J. QUINN THORNTON,

Having resorted to low, cowardly and dishonorable means for the purpose of injuring my character and standing, and having refused honorable satisfaction, which I have demanded; I avail myself of this opportunity of publishing him to the world as a reclaimless liar. an infamous scoundrel, a blackhearted villain, an arrant coward, a worthless vagabond, and an imported miscreant; a disgrace to the profession and a dishonor to his country.

JAMES W. NESMITH.

Oregon City,
June 7, 1847.

Jesse Quinn Thornton refused Nesmith's challenge to a duel, this early Oregon broadside notwithstanding. Nesmith was infuriated over Thornton's alleged misrepresentations concerning the southern emigrant route of 1846, which Thornton derisively referred to as "Applegate's Cut-off."

Thornton. Nesmith challenged Thornton to a duel but the wily Judge—who was walking the streets armed with a revolver and Bowie knife—refused to receive any communications from Nesmith who then sought vengeance by posting a handbill excoriating Thornton.

—John Unruh, Jr.
The Plains Across

The line surveyed by the Scott-Applegate party, somewhat modified, would shortly become the standard route to Oregon. But for the roughly one hundred wagons who took it in 1846 it was the road to near calamity. Jesse [Applegate] had underestimated the distances involved. . . . The settlers' oxen were [already] worn lean. . . . Most important the immigrants were deadly tired by the time they reached Fort Hall, some were sick and almost all were so demoralized they had lost discipline and become lethargic. Urging could not hurry them. . . .

[Jesse Quinn Thornton] had come to Oregon in 1846 [via] . . . the Scott-Applegate Trail. . . . He became and ever after remained convinced that the road hunters were a piratical crew who had deliberately deluded the immigrants to reduce them to want, so as to squeeze a profit from their necessity. And of this company of villains he settled on Jesse Applegate as the most heinous. . . .

—Malcolm Clark, Jr.,
Eden Seekers: The Settlement of Oregon, 1818–1862

TRAILBLAZERS DISCOVER YONCALLA VALLEYS

A Picturesque Description of Attributes— Moving Talk—Family Women Resist— The Bounteous Valley "Willamette"

Charley Applegate stayed home. When the trailblazers returned from their adventures, this is what they told him:

There was no wind. No, no wind to speak of in that serene interior valley they'd happened upon during the third day of their journey.

They had been following a dim trail that an old Indian had described through signs and jargon the previous day. It had not been much of a trail, either—more like a footpath rarely used, with only twisted tops of brush marking it. Now and then the trail meandered over low hills and ridges considerably farther east than the route the trappers used to cut over to the coast. They'd had a devil of a time holding to the Indian trail as they rode over the open country. Finally, the Willamette Valley narrowed perceptibly. The country grew dark and closed after a while. There were corridors of evergreens, thick and deep. They'd almost lost the trail altogether once or twice. At last, it converged with the old trail the trappers had used years before. The pass through the hills known as the "Calapooeys" was more difficult than they'd been led to expect. All were tired when they finally hit the Umpqua River side of the range. After they'd found a nooning place and rested, there came several miles that were more or less easygoing. It was a pure relief to be out of the Willamette. The terrain had a pleasing appearance by then. The foothills were much closer. The very air was warmer. As they'd already mentioned—there was no wind to bite at them as it did all summer long in the Willamette. It was but June in that gentle country they traversed, but the season seemed to have sped along.

As they rode through the first little valley, it was Ol' Jim who alerted them to some special attraction, which evidently lay ahead, for he had nickered, suddenly executing a coltish prance, which had struck all of them as comical, especially since Ol' Jim had so shown his age of late even Jesse avowed that he should have selected another mount. But Jim, jaded or no, had caught the scent of something, by God, and was bound to follow it. Soon all their horses became so lively that it was as if they were beavers "coming to medicine" and Ol' Jim the head beaver, his pace truly astounding.

For a mile or so they'd galloped hard following a winding stream, which had been lustier and wider than any they'd seen that afternoon. Someone then yelled that they ought to rein in and break for camp whether their horses were ready or not. But Jesse shouted back that as their horses appeared to know something they didn't . . . they ought to keep going. The sun grew lower. Their faithful steeds gave no sign of wearying. Thus they continued a little farther until Jim veered off unexpectedly. Not long after, his pell-mell surge came to a halt.

The mystery was immediately resolved as each horse and rider arrived. All knew what had put the grease 'neath Ol' Jim's hooves. Before them rippled the lushest wild pasturage they had ever laid eyes upon. There was acre upon acre of it—so much, in fact, it looked for all the world like some inland sea cupped amidst the hills.

The grass was so high—said the trailblazers—it fairly tickled the sides of their horses. It was heavy-headed stuff; a *mite* bluish—resembling a certain kind of timothy some had known in Kentucky and Tennessee. But the grass surrounding them was coarser and taller. When they'd dismounted and stood in the thick of it a scent assailed them. It was no wonder their horses behaved as if they'd landed in paradise. A man might think so himself. That grass was as aromatic as some old grandmammy's spice chest with the lid raised.

"Yes," they told him, as the cider jug was passed around again, "Charley . . . it's horse heaven down there . . . that's what."

And there was still more to be said for that countryside. In the morning, they'd discovered not just one valley, but a series of them. That long scented grass was everywhere and covered the bottomlands in profusion. The rolling hills gave way to it, and the hills were entirely free of timber and noisome underbrush. The vistas, the very lay of the land itself reminded them of Kentucky.

When they first made camp, they had been much taken by the spectacle those hills provided: Their smooth curved slopes were all aglow, red as June roses. They had supposed those vivid hues to be some trick of light, the sun was setting by then; yet, after the skies grew duskier, the color of the hillsides remained, darkening, of course, but maintaining their peculiar ruddiness.

Upon arising, they'd been surprised to see the gentle slopes even redder than before. What colored them so prettily was wild strawberries, growing in such profusion that the hillsides were absolutely matted with them, and each and every berry was unbelievably sweet, the size of a man's fingertip. They had gorged themselves like boys, and some who were beardless had been in such a hurry that it looked like warpaint had been applied. They filled their tin cups again and again, wishing only for cream. Later on when they had looked at their horses' hooves, it was as though their poor steeds had been wading in wine. God knew hundreds of gallons of the same might have been extracted from those rose-colored hills.

As for water: Why, it abounded. They had seen springs and creeks everywhere. The stream they'd camped beside had been of fair size, cutting through the floor of three interlocking little valleys. But neither that stream nor any other in the vicinity would constitute a threat to human life or property even if swollen with winter rains. Several creeks appeared large enough to provide water power for gristing and milling wood.

The rolling hills were rimmed by lowslung ridges where evergreens were abundant: yellow fir for barns and houses, cedar for rails and shakes, yew wood for gate and fence posts. At the lower elevations they'd seen many a stout white oak, too, and there were little groves of maple closer to the grass-rich flats. The oaks and a few other hardwoods would do well enough if a man needed to manufacture charcoal for the forge. To this last Charley Applegate had attended closely, for he was the family blacksmith.

What of the Indian? This was a question most important. But the trailblazers replied that as far as the Indian went, they'd seen nary a one; not in the vicinity of those little valleys, at least. Oh, there had been signs, of course: ashes from recent cookfires; a snare set in the brush near where they themselves had camped. But the Hudson's Bay trappers they'd consulted earlier, who were the only white sojourners halfway familiar with that country, had never reported any trouble with the Indians there. No, the closest natives known to be troublesome were many miles away, closer to the coast or else along the upper fork of the Umpqua. And those natives were nothing to the tribes the trailblazers had encountered many days farther to the south and east. There they had been met by numerous bands bent on blood and commotion. Yes, they said, those Indians had immediately made themselves known all right, fairly thundering out of the hills and over buttes or slinking through gulleys.

Taken altogether, there was no doubt about it: Ol' Jim had led them to a countryside both drier and more healthful than the upper Willamette. All that grass—unsullied by scrub. Nor was it all eaten over. Livestock would flourish. There would be no need to worry about asking a neighbor "by-your-leave" either. Why should a man bother sticking to the Willamette? Hang raising wheat and putting up fences! They were stockmen. That's why they'd driven their herds clear the plains across. It just didn't make sense holding on where they were on Salt Creek, Jesse said. Not with all that tempting, empty country only three days' ride to the south. It was time to think about selling out at the first opportunity.

Whereupon Lindsay Applegate had taken up the same cant, adding how each year since their arrival they had seen the Clatsop, Yamhill, and Tualatin plains filling up with new emigrants. A man could hardly turn around anymore without rankling his neighbor. In a year or two some enterprising settler making his way north upon the new route they'd just explored would take it into his head to stop short of the Willamette and put up his stake in one of those winsome little valleys. Yes, southern Oregon was bound to appeal to people. It would all boil down to who was the first comer—those who'd seen the country first or some Johnny-come-later.

Yes, Charley's brothers told him, what was needed was a trip south so he could see for himself—after the foul weather broke, of course, and they'd all taken care of rebuilding the fences the snows had buried. Just a little "look-see," they said, so they might confirm their first impression, and show him country worth living in. It was horse heaven. That was all there was to it.

Melinda Applegate grew uneasy. Something was afoot. She'd seen her Charley pulling hard on the jug, with Lindsay and Jesse hunkering there beside him in the blacksmith shed. The tail end of a certain conversation had chanced to reach her ears, for after her girls had failed to rouse their father and uncles with the dinner call, she'd put on her hooded cloak and gone out herself. Though the men had stopped talking and shot her a peculiar look, she'd caught the gist and heard Charley muttering his assent to something. Later, she told Cynthia and Betsy that there was no doubt about it: What she'd overheard was more "moving talk."

And even as she spoke, the seven moves Melinda Applegate had been obliged to make during her life unrolled like a dark-edged scroll. How could it be? she said to the two women closest to her heart. They had only been settled on the Willamette for three short years. Even so, all the signs were there.

But Betsy and Cynthia consoled her and mayhap themselves as well. It was entirely to be expected, they said—yes, men who had spent almost half a year trailblazing and adventuring, taking in vistas both varied and extraordinary, were bound to feel restless for a while after they came home. A body could count on it.

Nor had matters been helped by the winter weather, which had been more vile than any season in memory. Why, even those retired trappers who had lived in their vicinity for a decade and more said so.

It was true the year 1847 had thus far not given a good accounting of itself. No settler had been prepared for the heavy January snows, which had drifted and blown and ramshackled every fence on the Yamhill plain.

Then, too, the game, which had never been abundant, disappeared altogether that season. Even the Indians were suffering—poor pitiful things. And the wolf packs and other predators roaming around at night: Why, the women wondered, didn't they take their fill from the herds of feral Spanish cows that ran all along the foothills? Their frozen carcasses were everywhere. And any wild cow still alive was so reduced it amounted to ready-made dinner. It seemed, however, that the wolves preferred blooded livestock instead. Each night the loathsome howls of the pack grew more distinct.

If only, the women lamented to one another, their men had put by provender instead of filling the barns with wheat. As it was, they, and every other family in the vicinity, had spent December and January watching steers and yearlings lose heft and sicken. How was anyone to know the snow would cover every pasture? And it was remembered by the women that their men had sworn that in Oregon the grass was plentiful all year round and there was no such thing as a bitter winter.

But facts had to be faced, Betsy and Cynthia went on, conditions were as they were, and with their men indoors more than usual, bumping into everything and everybody whilst grumbling about the wolves and the bad weather, there was bound to be talk about places drier and warmer. Talk. Just talk. And they—the family women—would just have to put up with it. But as soon as winter wavered and the snows melted and spring might be smelled upon the wind, surely their men would think about where they were again instead of where they'd been.

"You'll see, Melinda," they said to her, and by the time March was under way and the weeks sped happily forward in a flurry of doing things, it seemed that Betsy and Cynthia were right: Charley, Jesse, and Lindsay had every appearance of taking hold.

Yes—Melinda Applegate sighed to herself—the weather had been no more than a freak, an ill wind that had spent itself—a reminder from the Almighty that they ought to be mindful of their many blessings. One dark season could not snuff out their bright prospects.

Even a restless man bent on finding fault was forced to acknowledge the progress already made. There were many things to be said in favor of life in the broad and bounteous valley known as the Willamette:

The first winter and spring at the abandoned Methodist mission, where they had sustained their families on a diet of boiled wheatberries, dried peas, and a motley selection of what wild game was to be had in that country, had been miserable.

Yet by the summer of '44 what remained of the cattle herds they'd brought from Missouri had been retrieved from Fort Walla Walla. Jesse had then surveyed three locations side by side, where, he assured himself and his brothers, their families, livestock, and crops were bound to thrive as never before. Their cattle, though fewer in number than they had hoped, greatly reduced their financial worries—blooded Missouri stock was yet in demand and never again would there be a shortage of meat on the family tableboard. Indeed, they'd soon grown tired of beef and were pleased to vary their diet with pork as hogs arrived with newer emigrants. The day came when many a finely cured ham emerged from the family smokehouses.

They had been on their Salt Creek farms less than a year when the piddling numbers of milch cows Cynthia insisted on bringing from Missouri had burgeoned to a herd of forty head. Ever after they enjoyed an abundance of fresh milk, cream, and sweet butter. Cynthia's cheese—some of which she spiced with garden sage and other herbs—was in much demand in their neighborhood.

How the family men seemed to thrive on the Salt Creek during those first two years. The prairie rolled under a velvetlike sward of grass. Wild clover abounded in every swale and meadow. The family girls were giddy with the flowers that grew everywhere: the bright blue camas the Indians prized for food, the ivory-colored oxeyes, and the acres of daisies, which could have made a chain clear to Missouri and back again.

And the time came—though undoubtedly they thought it never would—when more than a hundred acres were finally under fence and the tedious backbreaking work of men and boys who had cut timber, hauled logs, and split rails in the course of a half-dozen seasons was over. At last they had transformed the prairies into vast wheatfields—and every bushel was as good as a dollar at Fort Vancouver.

Though the only market for grain was monopolized by the Hudson's Bay Company, the Applegate men had already looked toward another day. Even if the Company withdrew from the region, wheat could still be sold in the form of flour to the hordes of hungry emigrants who arrived every November. Young Elisha had helped his uncle Jesse build a new gristmill right there on Salt Creek. How could they fail? Soon every settler on the Yamhill plain would bring his crop to the gristmill at "Cynthia," for so had Jesse named the site to honor his wife.

What pleasure the women's gardens had given—what bounty. They had made themselves known to the soil—those women— and it had answered, pushing up row upon row of nourishing truck for their families. The milky-green cabbages were as large and perfectly formed as the heads of their own babies, and there were long plump carrots, tender-stocked mustard greens, blue-red beets full of juice, beans-green and beans-speckled, the latter ideal for drying. And potatoes! Why, no one had ever seen specimens of such prodigious proportions. Up they came by the shovelful in any season, firm, finely textured, with no sign of worm or rot.

It was true there was not enough "hot" in the country to grow bumper corn crops like those they had taken for granted in Missouri. Too, they missed the wild grapes, plums, and other native fruits they'd gathered in the southeastern states, for in Oregon, nature had bestowed naught but berries various. But gradually they learned to replace cornmeal with wheat flour, and the tiny seedlings they removed from the abandoned orchards at Mission Bottom were now grown as tall as their oldest sons. Soon apples, pears, and peaches would be there for the picking.

Thus, as the family women set their plank tables that April of 1847, they were for the most part well satisfied. The hard times had passed them by. Their trailblazers had been home for almost a year. The whole of their large family, save for the little souls taken by the Columbia, was gathered safely round. Every trencher piled high, every brimming cup attested to their mutual labors and the goodness of the country where they found themselves.

Their flowering orchards bordered by new fences appeared as white as the snow that had earlier submerged them. And moving talk? The women heard none. They were at long last settled for good and all. No, there seemed nothing to stir things up unless it was the Chinook wind, which, as it grazed the cheek, always brought forth a little longing and restlessness. But that was just a part of spring and the spring feeling, wasn't it? They thought nothing of it.

POOR CHARLEY'S TRIALS AT HOME

A Pint-Sized Army of Harvesters— Worrisome Rumors—The Salt Shortage— Awesome Responsibilities—Homecoming

Their elder brother was not himself. Lindsay Applegate had first noted it in November of '46 after his own exhaustion had abated somewhat. He and Jesse had returned from their arduous trip south in October. For a while they could think of nothing else save the emigrants and the condition of the new road. At length they had considered their own families and farms.

Lindsay's scrutiny of Charley had been natural enough: After all, he had been in Charley's company for the whole of his life. In childhood he and Charley had lived under the same roof. In manhood they had always lived side by side. Thus Charley's every expression and eccentricity was well known to him. Save for Lindsay's five-month exploration of the southern route, the two had rarely been separated. Though once, at age fifteen, Lindsay had taken a notion to run away with Major Ashley's Missouri River expedition, from which illness had necessitated his almost immediate return; and on another occasion he had volunteered to fight in the short-lived war against Chief Black Hawk.

Lindsay noticed these changes in his brother's countenance and habits: Charley's color, usually sanguine in the extreme, was far too pale. His manner was lethargic, verging on depression. Further, though he was attempting to hide the fact from his wife, Charley was tipping the cup more than usual.

Jesse opined that maybe Charley's old condition—which had plagued him during their Missouri days—was bothering him again. Lindsay reserved judgment.

Yet as their weeks back on Salt Creek progressed into months and Charley gradually related to them the full extent of the trials he and the other stay-at-homes had endured, it became apparent that what ailed Charley was more than his old Missouri malady.

The summer and autumn of 1846 had exacted a heavy toll upon him both physically and mentally. One evening Charley related to them that from the time the road-hunting party had left in June until almost August, matters at home proceeded apace without too much confusion, considering he had three farms to oversee and all the livestock. 'Lish (Elisha) had been a great help to him, of course. Given that his nephew was but in his fourteenth year, and had lately discovered the female of the species, Elisha demonstrated himself to be quite dependable. The boy had taken a goodly share of their burdens. Even so, Charley was the only grown man on any of the three places, and 'Lish's shoulder was so crippled up, Charley had been compelled to take on the majority of the heavy work. That had made for long days indeed, and nights seemed "terrible short," he said.

Still and all, he'd survived—felt pretty good, in fact—but then it came time to get the wheat in and the various youths in their neighborhood that he'd lined up to help with the harvest had let him down. Not with malice, of course. It was just that wheat had come on earlier than anyone anticipated. July got hot fast and the able-bodied were all tied up on their own places.

Thus, Charley said, he'd had no choice but to muster all the children into the wheat service—even the littlest one. As there were more girls than boys, they became a regular pint-sized army of female harvesters, though from a distance he supposed they had more closely resembled a horde of grasshoppers: their bright mother-made hats of new oat straw dipping and bobbing amidst the fields as they bound the grain into sheaves. It was a wonder none of them had succumbed to sunstroke, including himself—for they were out day after day. Even so, when all was said and done, they'd somehow managed to get in almost a hundred acres' worth. Why, once they'd had a few days' practice, he had a hard time keeping up with the oldest girls. He couldn't seem to swing the cradle fast enough.

Three quarters of the way through the harvest ordeal—oh, the first week in August maybe—they'd all started back for dinner over at Cynthia's and were surprised to see her halfway down the road, crying and carrying on. Someone had come by with news— and that was but the first of the worrisome rumors they heard concerning the expedition.

"The Applegates and their party are all dead!" They'd been "killed by Indians" or had "perished from thirst in the desert." These tales and others began reaching them with disturbing frequency.

Of course, he'd dismissed these rumors—at least to begin with, Charley said. There were always some people, however, who liked nothing better than to carry bad news even if they had to invent some. Thus, it befell to him to placate Cynthia and Betsy.

Why, if the road builders had been done in as many times as was claimed, they would have had to have as many lives as the proverbial cat, and their capacity to leap wildly from place to place would have been a miracle in and of itself. No, he told the women and older children, it seemed more likely that the stories they heard were the work of people right there in Oregon, such as those farther north who had recently cut the toll road near Mount Hood. So that the women might get mad instead of fearful, he had told them in some detail about other enemies of the enterprise who had no wish to see a southern route discovered, much less used. Many would stop at nothing in their efforts to keep incoming emigrants on the older routes all along the Columbia. For if the emigrants were diverted south, business would drop off at the Hudson's Bay Company's forts and stores. Nor would it be necessary for them to cut over to the Presbyterian mission at Wailaptu. And the worst, as far as Charley was concerned, were all those Oregon City merchants. He'd told the women about them too: How they were fearful because, if the road builders succeeded, Oregon City would not be the terminus of the southern route. Thus the droves of incoming emigrants would no longer winter over there, lining the pockets of those who overcharged them.

Not that anything he passed on to Cynthia or Betsy had the power to diminish their gloom. A bleakness soon settled over them, a hopelessness, too, for the majority of rumors could be neither proved nor disproved and the women refused to believe any Oregonian would deliberately mislead his neighbor especially where matters of life or death were concerned.

Yes, Charley admitted, after a while the whole business had begun to weigh down on him. He kept his worries to himself, though Melinda surely knew. She later told him that for several nights he had thrashed around and moaned in his sleep. One morning, he remembered awakening and the thing had so taken hold of him—a picture so vivid—that he commenced to trembling. It had felt as if a cold hand were squeezing his heart. In his nightmare, he'd seen the lot of them to the last man lying upon some tractless waste—the poisoned arrows of the Digger Indians piercing their flesh, horses included. Yet what could he do save keep these fears to himself? Charley asked. As Charley had related these matters to his brothers, Jesse and Lindsay both looked down upon the ground, for they were full of feeling.

For several days the possibility that they were already dead had gnawed at him, Charley said—the fear pushed its way into his every thought regardless of how busy he kept himself.

The fact was, he was grateful when the salt shortage reared its head—that was the next shortage which fell upon the poor farmers. It gave him an excuse to leave home for a while—though, of course, not for long. When he got up to the store at Fort Vancouver, he discovered that what he'd heard was true. Even the Hudson's Bay Company was almost out of salt. That was a story in itself. According to the Company clerks, it was all on account of some avaricious merchants who, smirked the clerks, had come from New England, not Old England. It seemed these "river pirates" had bought up all the salt so as to corner the salmon-packing markets. Thus the store at Fort Vancouver was charging two dollars per bushel, which Charley at first had refused to pay. The previous year he had got the same for sixty cents, and he hadn't had to go clear to Vancouver to get it, either. But in the end he confessed he'd dug into his britches.

He came home with a third as much salt as he'd gone after, which had caused a great stir. A yammering had gone up, since the women were busy putting by kraut and such, and of course they were worried about what to do with the beef and some fish that had been given to them. Even so, they made do. As for himself, he was calmer after his little trip, for he'd had time to collect his thoughts whilst seated all alone atop his wagon.

It had been on the way home from Vancouver that he'd taken a full accounting of his miseries. Not only was he flustered by the prospect of grieving for the deaths of his only brothers in Oregon, he was absolutely thunderstruck by the responsibilities that might well lie before him in the form of twenty-four children, none older than fifteen years. On top of that he had envisioned what it would entail for him to manage three sizable farms and their combined herds. But the worst of it, Charley said, was the women. There it would be. He would have two sisters-in-law who would doubtless be beside themselves with sorrow, beset with financial worries, and desirous of his support and continual counsel. Instead of one—God help him—he would have three women to answer to, and Cynthia with another baby on the way to boot. From then on he'd carried the knowledge of those awesome responsibilities, wondering whether he had the power to carry on alone and, truth to tell, whether he even wanted to. And as September had dragged on and he tripled the amount of cordwood cut, and as each day found the members of all three families more downcast than the day before, he grew even uneasier and his sleep was broken and that had required "medicine." Not until October did the happy tidings come. Then a week later the women had looked up and seen the familiar horsemen upon the horizon. Charley had confessed that when he first laid eyes upon them they looked almost as bad as they had in his nightmares—save for the arrows maybe. Then he had practically to tie them down to prevent them from going back down there to that hellhole known as the Umpqua Canyon so that they might rescue the poor emigrants still straggling up to the Willamette.

No, Charley told Jesse and Lindsay, his shoulders sagging as though the very act of remembering had exhausted him anew, he would not give two cents for the months just passed—southern route discovered or no.

And so saying, he reached for the jug.

THE CONTROVERSY

Down in the Canyon—
Emigrant Routes Before '46—Fire and Smoke—
Thornton's Revenge—A Road to Hell

A bitterness took root inside the family men in '47 as April ended. It had not been dislodged or dispersed by the Chinook, "the-little-wind-which-runs"; the soft greening rains only fed it; what remained of their winter restlessness only made it grow. Try as they might to ignore it—to keep it well under—that bitterness pushed its way into their daily lives. Life in the Willamette tasted like bad water.

That spring, tales of hardship and suffering on the new southern route were circulating in every Oregon settlement. Many emigrant families who had tried the new route were fanning across the countryside in search of homesteads. Wherever they stopped, they described the tribulations of their recent journey and castigated the men who had blazed and built the so-called road. Some persons considered the name Applegate anathema. Much worse was the trail to which they now affixed the same family's name.

Another name was heard with equal frequency as the perils endured upon that "damnable road" were recounted by the emigrants: It was the name of a place deep in the Umpqua country, located almost one hundred miles south of the settlements of the lower Willamette. Some called the place where the worst of their tragedies had been enacted the Umpqua Canyon; others Canyon Creek. Most, however, simply referred to it as *The Canyon* and would long revile the name.

When the road builders had laid out the trail in the summer and early autumn of 1846 they had faced countless difficulties, not the least of which was a rugged stretch through a portion of the Calapooia Mountains where nature had left them no alternative save to follow a swift and rock-strewn creek through a terrible defile that was the solitary entrance into the country beyond.

Steep canyon walls arose on either side of that creek. The streamed itself, of necessity, became the roadway. Even though the travelers would be obliged to make numerous fordings, the

73

upper reaches of the creek would remain shallow and unobstructed until the rains of autumn arrived.

From the moment the emigrant elected to take the southern route instead of the older route via the Columbia, he had been advised to make as many miles as possible on each day's march. The road builders were confident that should the emigrant make his schedule paramount, all would be well and wagons would arrive in advance of the inclement weather. It was reasoned that after leaving the canyon, the emigrant might then catch his breath and slow his pace somewhat, for he would have only a few more days' traveling until he reached the nearest settlements.

Yet Jesse and Lindsay Applegate and the dozen or so other members of the expedition had not reckoned on the stubbornness and exhaustion of certain factions within the emigrant train. It was, in reality, not one train but several, which had joined at different junctures upon the trail. Many refused to keep up the pace and as a result fell hopelessly behind, losing days and weeks of precious time.

When the going was smooth and water plentiful, so that a man might take advantage and push forward at double speed, there had been those who lingered, seeming almost languid as though on some outing of little consequence.

Others were elderly persons who were troubled by various infirmities. These poor souls were not inclined to hurry and their healthier brethren had failed to inspire them. Each train seemed a slave to contention. A number of the self-appointed emigrant leaders eschewed all manner of plainly stated advice; further, most were incapable of cooperating with their fellows nor had they listened to the small contingent of road builders who had doubled back to implore the stragglers to make haste.

The piteous condition of many families had been portended long days and miles before their tired teams limped into the recesses of the canyon. The Applegates and the rest of their party knew this with certainty, even if the stories being circulated had it otherwise and sought to lay the blame almost exclusively upon the road builders. Could a man be blamed for what he had no control over? No one had known that winter would arrive early and would be the worst in memory, bringing rains so long and heavy that the emigrants in the rear would be forced to lower their wagons with ropes in order to avoid the foaming torrents so newly filled below.

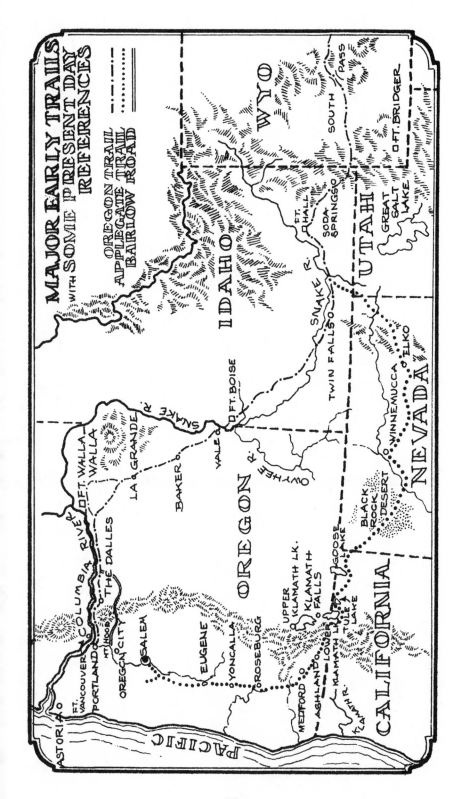

Mud and rockslides resulted from the same cause and extended the emigrants' dreadful passage so that even the wagons at the front made, at most, three miles each day in a stretch that was in actuality no more than ten miles long. Toward the rear, the stragglers endured one hellish week traversing that canyon. All the while their wagons had continually been compelled to halt because repairs were necessary before they could proceed. The road was no sooner made passable when yet another bad place appeared, for the storms rolled boulders and gouged holes all along the way, and the elements raged and poured over them without stint even as hungry children and old folks sickened. A few would die from their exertions.

No, not one road builder doubted that those emigrants had suffered. Nor did they deny that they themselves had sometimes erred in judgment, though they had done the best that might be expected under such trying circumstances. The suffering of the emigrants had been felt so acutely that many in the expedition who had almost reached the Willamette turned south again, and those who had not actually implemented the rescue spent days rounding up provisions and fresh teams that were sent back as expediently as possible.

However, many chose to overlook these facts. There were some who made it sound as if the road builders themselves had decreed an early winter in order that they and their friends might line their pockets selling the provisions that had been rushed to the scene of the disaster.

This had been the twist of the knife as far as the wives of those who had volunteered to explore and build the road were concerned. Their men, however, struggled to keep their peace on the theory that "lest said was best said"—after all, sooner or later, the men insisted, the talk was bound to exhaust itself. Yes, the matter would blow over. Soon the disgruntled newcomer and his vociferous mate would be absorbed with the rigors of frontier life. In the meantime, their own skins were thick enough to sustain such barbs, and if mistakes had been made they had already been admitted. But regardless of the indifference their men feigned, the women knew better.

Jesse's and Lindsay's bitterness was evident even though they kept mum about it. Not one of the original road party had been recompensed in currency or otherwise for the five months each had given of his life in order to do service to his fellow citizens. And when Jesse and Lindsay returned home quaking from exhaustion, their immediate concern had been to aid the emigrants stranded below. Melinda, Betsy, and Cynthia had themselves helped load the pack animals. Potatoes. Flour. Countless other provisions. Charley had donated a half-herd of beef and had ridden around the neighborhood for two days encouraging other settlers to do likewise. Those that had it shared it. Some who didn't have much at all shared anyway. That was the unwritten rule of the settlements, for everyone in Oregon at one time or another found himself beholden to his neighbor. Nor was there ever talk of repayment or obligation, especially when people were up against it. It was in this spirit that the majority of settlers had rallied to assist their fellows. To a large extent it was the Applegate families who had spearheaded the effort.

"You'd think," the family women said among themselves, "that people would have the sense to be grateful. . . ." Did the families who'd tried the new southern route imagine they were the only emigrants to suffer miseries and hardships on the way to Oregon? Suffering! What of the people right there on the Yamhill—women they knew and had talked with who'd taken Stephen Meek's terrible cutoff in 1845. Because their husbands had wanted to save themselves one hundred and fifty miles of traveling, those women and children had staggered over the rough country around the Malheur River and then gone cross-lots to Crooked River, where the fording had been a calamity. By the time they got to the Deschutes country, most of their animals had starved and the carcasses were strewn everywhere across the desert for fifty miles and more. What a horrible thing it must have been to watch friends and loved ones dying before their very eyes. And toward the last had come hunger and some peculiar fever. Every bit of provision was already devoured. Some poor souls had hung on to life by eating grass stew, sprinkled with coarse salt—which, of course, had only worsened their thirst and made their pitiful children retch. They'd been half dead by the time they reached Reverend Perkin's mission on the Columbia River.

What waited for those exhausted travelers then?—the women said to one another as their indignation mounted. What waited for every emigrant who struggled into the Oregon country by way of the Columbia? Nothing more than a long perilous ride to Fort

Vancouver upon log rafts that had been hastily lashed together—the lucky ones with their wagon beds and canopies over the whole affair—not that the rain and wind didn't get in anyway. There came so many thousands of emigrants in recent years that wood for both rafts and campfires was much diminished, and most were obliged to endure the elements without protection. They shivered as the winds howled through the gorge and their stomachs growled. Their sufferings were acute until transport could be had.

Even so, the people waiting for *bateaux* from the Hudson's Bay Company or renting Indian canoes were more fortunate than those who took to the waters alone, risking life and limb . . . but there was no need to speak of the rest. In their minds, the terrible waters seemed to rise for a moment. The maw of the great river opening again. And the family women fought the currents, holding them back—memories best left alone.

While their men had been exploring the southern route, Betsy and Cynthia Applegate told themselves that if the expedition succeeded in finding a new trail into Oregon—a way that meant no man, woman, or child need ever throw themselves on the mercy of that monster river again—they would thank God most humbly.

Yet the emigrant who'd used the new southern route did not tender thanks. Matters grew worse. In April the talk had but irritated. By May a gentleman very new to the country, whose name was Jesse Quinn Thornton, had dipped his quill pen in venom. In language "most intemperate" he made his accusations public in the form of letters to the newspapers. The results of his campaign against the Applegates and their friends would soon be almost as unsettling as the weather itself.

It was hardly the rain-kissed May people had come to expect in Oregon. The weather grew unusually hot and dry, pushing ill and speedy winds over the foothills and carrying shrouds of acrid smoke, which hovered so close to the valley floor that the vistas seemed to shimmer. The sky, when it could be seen at all, was stained with a terrible beauty. Above the burning forests and blackened fields, the yellow-pink hazes tumbled and rolled. Higher still hung a silvered sun, which, when stinging eyes could bear to look at it, was surrounded by a wavering, incandescent aureole as blue as a bird's wing.

Some newcomers blamed the Indians for the fires, but they were wrong. The Calapooia people never set their harvest fires until later in the season—at which time the wild sunflower seeds could be easily shaken from the scorched stubble in the meadows.

The majority of settlers blamed the weather itself, and it was not a good augury for the seasons that lay ahead. The grasses that had looked so promising were disappearing before their very eyes. Mumbling through their neckerchief masks—unsatisfactory barriers between their nostrils and the lung-searing smoke—those who had wheat crops to protect set themselves to digging ditches in the event the winds changed and carried the fires homeward to their own fields.

That smoky May, Melinda Applegate was carrying her eleventh child. The fires licking their way to the edges of the western hills were visible from the family farms. The child, who would one day grow to be a burly man indeed, was pushing inside her so hard she could hardly breathe. This discomfort had been worsened by the vexations of heat and smoke. Each evening Melinda stood upon the porch of her loghouse, pressing her hands on the small of her back—watching the hellish glitter of the distant fires. Her younger children looked forward to the darkness, and welcomed the great eerie glow that lit up the western sky, but she, like all settlers, had a horror of fires. When she went to bed, she was unable to sleep. Each night she wondered and worried: What if the winds were suddenly to shift and what if all those acres of wheat they'd planted and were counting on were acres of nothing come morning.

What she especially remembered about May of '47, she said years later, were the fires and waiting for Tom. After Tom had arrived and the fires had spent themselves—no harm coming to their wheatfields after all—she was herself again. Which was a good thing, for June had come along.

How could any family member forget? June of '47 was a dreadful month, "the Thornton business" almost entirely taking it up. Various men who'd explored the route with Jesse and Lindsay came and went continually. Lindsay seemed angry all the time. Charley was half sick and blustery, any little thing seeming to set him off. Jesse grew more and more close-mouthed. There was little that could be done to induce him to leave his place. Thus the women had relied on one another for company more than ever. Cynthia, particularly, needed someone to talk to. She, like many others, thought Jesse ought to give Ol' Thornton some of his own medicine and it had been all Cynthia could manage to keep herself quiet on the subject.

The things that Thornton kept writing and sending to the *Oregon Spectator* hit Cynthia hard. It was all the worse for her, since she could barely read herself and was obliged to have some other family member read Thornton's lambastings aloud to her. In private, of course, Jesse had strictly forbidden the subject to be brought up at home. If he followed the controversy in print, no one knew. No family member, at least, caught him reading the newspaper.

As for the rest of the populace—why, they had devoured every word and with evident relish, too. A few emigrants backed Thornton publicly but most—if her memory served—sat back watching the judge get his licks in on their behalf.

Friends of the road builders, including one or two who had been on the expedition, wrote letters in defense of the enterprise. They attested to Jesse's indefatigable courage, high character, and so forth, for Thornton's personal attacks on Jesse had been scurrilous in the extreme. Yet Jesse refused to defend himself, at least directly, even as Charley and Lindsay and others of his old comrades began to hammer on him to do so.

No, Jesse would not "lower himself" to respond. Nevertheless, the whole business was surely painful for him. Melinda Applegate had watched him grow drawn and pale during this time and had overheard him make little remarks to Cynthia. He was beginning to despise the country, he said, especially all the damned fools who were moving into it. This, of course, had disturbed Cynthia—and all of the women for that matter, for they began to think the moving talk would soon start again.

Yet who could not sympathize with Jesse? No man appreciated being drawn and quartered and hung on a public meathook so that all might sniff at him and turn up their noses.

Then an old friend of their family, who'd crossed the plains with them in '43, decided he'd had enough. Nesmith—"Nes" they all called him in those days—had married one of the road builders' daughters. He began writing letters to the newspaper, but for some reason signed his father-in-law's name instead of his own. It was generally known that David Goff could neither read nor write. Most people assumed that Nes was the real spokesman and defender of the new road. Every time Nesmith came down hard on

81

Thornton, Thornton followed suit. Each letter written to the newspaper was more abusive than the one preceding it. Before anyone could induce either Thornton or Nesmith to stop the whole affair, word reached Salt Creek that their old friend Nes had challenged Thornton to a pistol match. Thornton ducked out of the duel at the earliest opportunity, though for a while afterward some people claimed they'd seen him wearing a "sidearm" when he went anywhere. He was evidently scared to death, for Nes was not only flamboyant and outspoken, he was volatile, too. Though Jesse had no love for Thornton, he had been beside himself when he heard about the pistol match. He considered there was no such thing as "gentlemanly" violence, and when he had served in the legislature of the provisional government, it was he who had pushed through the law against dueling. Then Nes started putting up handbills in prominent locations in which Thornton was called every imaginable name fit for print. Everyone wondered what on earth would happen next.

But nothing had come of it. The terrible news about the Donner party distracted people. Suddenly there had been all manner of reports, not to mention the dreadful rumors. Everyone was talking about how the Donners had taken an untried cutoff to get to California and got caught in the bad snows in the Sierras. That winter, the winter of '46–'47, was the same one that had brought blizzards to the Willamette Valley. Word concerning the Donners was a long time reaching anyone in Oregon. Some people, doubtless, wished it had never arrived at all. It had been hard explaining to children why folks would commence to eating one another.

When Lindsay learned what had happened to the Donner party, he remembered a group of emigrants he had passed in the desert. These people had been determined to take an untested cutoff without the aid of an experienced guide or anything save a poorly prepared map. The road builders had begged them to reconsider. Lindsay had done his best to convince them to head for Oregon instead of California. There had been a strong-minded individual in the train, however, who was absolutely adamant about taking the Hastings cutoff. In the end, he had persuaded the others.

Later, it was rumored that Jesse Quinn Thornton had known some of the families who had ended up with Donner and his party. It had given Melinda cause to wonder as years went on:

Thornton had made it safely to his destination via the southern route. The rescuers had come to his aid before further disasters assailed him or his wife and that dog they'd brought. What *was* its name? Charley had laughed about it, she remembered. Prince Draco or Darco, or something of the sort. And what had piqued Thornton the most was that some fellow in the rescue party had bartered for Thornton's broadcloth suit. That was what fired Thornton up all right. But what had Thornton lost in the end? Naught but earthly goods: his fine-appointed wagon, his library bound in Moroccan leather, his oxteam. Some people who had come to Oregon had lost far more. How well she knew. Yet the outcry Thornton raised in the newspaper and the common gossip it stirred up brought discomfort and humiliation to the brave men who had cut the southern route, not to mention their families.

Who knew? If Thornton had not sought to avenge himself, Jesse, Lindsay, and Charley might not have turned so sour on life in the Willamette Valley, and instead of moving down to Yoncalla everyone might have stayed put. Of course, all manner of other things were to intervene before the move to Yoncalla actually occurred. Nevertheless, the women felt the change coming. It had been as a shadow falling. Thornton had played his part in it all, whether he knew it or not.

No, Melinda Applegate told her granddaughters—for they were interested in such things—Thornton had never relented in later years or reconsidered even one of his accusations. He caviled and ranted without stint, continuing to rake things up at every opportunity. He even wrote a book. Whether he ever bothered to thank his God, she didn't know. After all, he had not been with the Donners back in '46. The way Thornton took was easier, but where his friends had gone was down a road surely paved to hell.

Open Doors

The Deadly Flux—A Hairshirt—
Massacre Most Cruel—
Mere Slips of Girls—War

When the autumn of '47 arrived on rain-soaked winds, the distant ridges were glazed bone-white. So soon? people asked themselves glumly as they hurried on with their cutting and stacking. Each man pondered the size of his woodpile: October was bitter and November would surely be no better. Though the faint tender green covering scorched fields held promise, the new grasses would never make it under a cold blanket of snow; nor would livestock survive another terrible winter. The cattle appeared neither fat nor healthy. The fires and the long summer drought had seen to that.

Then November came and droves of emigrants arrived again, trying to find friends or old associates with whom they might lay over until spring. If they had no ties in Oregon, or people to call upon, they traveled—desperate and hungry—on foot or in ramshackle wagons, to the very doors of those reported to be kind-hearted.

"Go to the Methodists," they were directed. "Go to the Math-enys, or the Waldoes, or the Nesmiths," they were told. "Go to the Applegates." What had at first felt half humiliating soon was replaced by gratitude for the open door, the warm fire, and the Dutch oven filled with meat and potatoes. But more than any-thing, they had appreciated the good sympathetic company of people who understood what that long journey had exacted from them—who had plucked miserable children from their mothers' aching arms and said simply, "There . . . there . . . now. Soon things will right themselves with you and yours."

But that autumn those who were inclined to make room for others in loghouses that were already crowded had welcomed the weary fearfully.

Tom was four months old when Melinda Applegate looked out her tiny window and saw the first of the sojourners coming down the road. Their faces looked hopeful. Charley and her boys, who

85

had been busy hauling wood to the porch, called out a greeting. How did she feel as she looked down at little Tom and then around the room where her other small children were laughing or squabbling—their homely playthings scattered all across the puncheon floor?

She and everyone else had heard the rumors that had followed the great river, and cut through the hills as surely as the wagon trains themselves. The emigrants of '47 brought sickness with them—terrible sickness. Not only did they carry measles of the most virulent variety to Whitman's mission and the surrounding country where the Indians were dying in untold numbers, but it was said they had brought something even more dreadful to Oregon. Some people called it "cholera." Others referred to it as the "deadly flux."

Melinda surely struggled for a moment as she peered through her window, weighing the well-being of her own little ones against the pinched, hollow-eyed countenances of those children outside who she could see were shyly reaching for the strips of jerky her older boys were proferring. Their mothers, fathers, and big brothers and sisters were gathered behind them, looking for all the world like a congregation of the woebegone.

Then perhaps she turned to Betsy, who had passed the afternoon with her sewing and who now arose to replace the water kettle upon the crane over the fire. Their eyes—worried, troubled eyes—met and held for a moment even as the voices drew ever closer; even as the footfall reached the other side of the door where they could hear people politely stamping the mud off their shoes; now murmuring, now lifting the wooden latch . . .

Nevertheless, Melinda took them in. She believed then what she believed throughout her life: Any child—she always told Lucy and her other daughters—*must* have what it needed and be cared for like any other, sharing bed, cup, and trencher with a person's own. And any grown person who could not find it in his or her heart to behave in exactly that fashion was only a partly grown person after all.

That distressing autumn, she, Cynthia, and Betsy had moved from one straw tick to another, coaxing the ailing children of the travelers, as well as their own, to sip soothing teas concocted from the flowers of the feverfew and Solomon's seal brought from Missouri. And if the coughs worsened they resorted to remedies the

Calapooia Indians on Salt Creek had told them about. Down unwilling little throats were poured concoctions made from the needles of Douglas fir and the bark of the chokecherry tree.

Each time Melinda, Betsy, and Cynthia touched those children or emptied the dented basins or aired the pee-soaked bedding, they had said to themselves, "Never mind"—even though the very thought made them quake. "Never mind," they'd said again and again. "Never mind about the cholery."

But cholera had not visited their place after all, although measles and whooping cough came, and later an exhausting round of intermittent fevers accompanied by stomach miseries. It seemed to the women that a child no sooner got back its color and humor when it was stricken again. Some little ones—Melinda's daughter Susie among them—jerked and then stiffened most painfully with "complications." After such a siege the victim could not walk or even turn upon his pallet without someone's help for days on end.

As the weather turned bitter and blew great gusts down the mud-brick chimneys so that tanged smoke hovered over the fitful little sleepers and those who watched over them, the nights became tribulations mixed with cough and moan.

Just under the wind had come a new sound so utterly desolate and so unexpected that even if heard again and again it never failed to evince a shudder from the lonely woman hearing it: those beasts . . . calling to one another from the hillsides . . . traveling together . . . yellow eyes glinting . . . the stealthy bodies gliding onto the prairies. Closer now . . . readying for bloody rounds of plunder. A woman awake heard them howl as she sat rocking her child, and at such times she wondered how it was that she had come to such a country.

When had the idea first come to her? Was it when some proud family marksman brought his booty home one frosty morning? Did he say, "Looky here, Melindy. Look at the size of this critter"? There on the ground lay one of those who howled in the night, the blood of the cow or steer it had killed still sticky on its muzzle. Yet the creature's fur must have attracted her, for it was as thick and gray as a rain cloud and each strand was as long as her little finger. How warm the wily wolf beneath its winter coat—which was more than might be said of Charley and her boys who worked outdoors regardless of the weather. As the winds grew colder she had mulled over the matter. Her mother had always told her that, above all, the chest must be kept warm. Unless it was protected, chills and fever were bound to follow. She, Betsy, and Cynthia had often said to one another that what they needed in Oregon was new sweaters, jumpers, and warmers of the sort that they had knitted for their families in Missouri. Unfortunately they had herded neither ewe, lamb, nor daddy-buck across the plains, and though some of the newer emigrants had brought sheep into the territory, their numbers were still too small to meet the demand. During their five years in Oregon, they'd had little to spin and their old woolens had been cycled and recycled until they were "no more."

Winters had been mild the first few years. Their boys wore odd-looking capotes which Betsy had fashioned from old tents and canvas wagon covers. When lined with fur scraps, the hooded cape proved quite warm and kept off the rain to some extent—but only if an embarrassed youngster could be induced to wear it and didn't leave it on a branch or fence rail as soon as he was out of sight.

But the winter of '47 turned colder and colder until nothing any woman could come up with truly protected goose-bumped boy-flesh, especially when the heavens brindled with snow clouds and heaved white upon the land. The layers of buckskin clothes grew so clammy and damp that no woman could stand the stench, particularly in close quarters.

Charley had told her it was an idea that would never work. That was why she had called for the help of the other hunters in the neighborhood. She had a spinning wheel made for her, since everything in that line save her wool cards had sunk in the Burnt River when they'd had that rough fording coming "acrosst." Soon she had quite a heap of wolfskins to work with, but the task she had set for herself was frustrating because the pelt from one largish wolf or coyote yielded only enough "wool" to make a pair of child's slippers. The work was slow and tedious, she told her granddaughters—who, in turn, had told their granddaughters— because the hairs broke in the spindle and were not quite long enough. Even so, before abandoning the project, Melinda knit her Charley a fine sleeveless "jumper," which, it was claimed, wore like iron and kept the chest wonderfully warm. . . .

Yet it cannot be said that the long hours Melinda Applegate spent spinning very much altered the discomforts of anyone else.

Nothing short of the miraculous could have taken the cruel bite out of the winter of '47.

What tired rider brought the word? He'd come to see Jesse, his horse's hooves crackling over the frozen trail to Salt Creek, where he'd avoided the groves of hardwoods whose heavy branches glistened and dangled in spiked curtains of ice.

His tidings bore heavily upon him, and as he spoke to Jesse, who was working outside, the messenger's words hazed and congealed in the atmosphere, as if their import demanded some more tangible form.

The messenger entered the house and was given coffee for his trouble. He stood worrying his half-frozen hands by the hearth, not speaking to anyone for some moments, so that the oldest of the family daughters, Lucy, Rozelle, and Susie, who sat there sewing, grew uneasy and pulled their shawls more tightly about their shoulders, as though protecting themselves from words that had not yet been spoken.

Cynthia was called in and all who were in the room silently waited her arrival. They could hear the dried peas rattling in her basket before they saw her, for she'd been in the provision room. She'd been about to greet their visitor, about to ask if he might take supper with them, but her husband's odd look stopped the words in her throat. When the messenger began, she saw Jesse shut his eyes.

Soon she lifted her apron to her own eyes and buried her face in it, murmuring brokenly, "No . . . no . . . Doctor Whitman? Surely not Whitman." She had looked up at Jesse, awaiting his confirmation, and he had nodded bleakly while the man described the dreadful happenings on the Walla Walla until what he reported seemed to reel about the room, staining the air with pictures most horrid.

One tired rider after another rode over the countryside that December carrying the word. And the word was *massacre*. Then the news seemed to pass by some power all its own, moving with astonishing speed, like wind or fire—sweeping over the lonely farms on the icy sway-backed prairies, and up onto the snowy ridges, reaching the most remote fir-shadowed cabin where the trappers and their women had been holed up for months or years; until, it seemed, there was no one in Oregon who did not know that Marcus Whitman had been felled on his mission doorstep, a

Cayuse "tommyhawk" cleft mortally between his shoulders.

And it was reported that his male helpers had lain all around him in bloody disarray, and for long moments their shouts kept ringing out until their strength gave out; until neither curse nor prayer could be heard; until all, like poor Whitman himself, had given up the ghost.

The passage of days and weeks had added countless details, each one more lurid than the last. In the villages of Portland, Salem, and Astoria, women carrying parcels and guiding children across the frozen, mudded streets stopped in their tracks and wept openly.

In their minds, they saw the brown hands gripping Narcissa Whitman's golden hair, the bright coils wrapped around the Indian's fingers. And this was all the worse because many of them had met Narcissa Whitman and supped with her or taken comfort beneath her roof when they'd been on their way to the Willamette years before. And to think of her proud face lashed by the Indian's whip made them feel sick, and when they looked down at their own mud-mired skirts they knew that hers had been drenched with blood from her numerous wounds, that she had died entreating her God in the slippery darkness of the irrigation ditch that in happier times had carried water to her flowers and fields.

When the news of the Whitmans' sufferings had dulled somewhat, people turned their thoughts to the forty captives the Cayuse still held hostage. Hundreds of outraged settlers grabbed their rifles and rode hell-bent for Oregon City, where a ragtag army of volunteers mustered on Christmas Day.

Lucy Applegate was almost eighteen that winter of Whitman and war. The horses of the young men from the neighboring farms made muffled thunder past her door, and it had frightened her. Yet her fear had been mixed up with some peculiar excitement, which might have been almost pleasurable, she confessed later, had she not been forced to look into the eyes of several of those new recruits.

They had come to bid her pappa good-bye before galloping on to the rendezvous at Oregon City. They stood in the doorway, all gangle and gawk, their battered hats in hand. One or two of them had no cloak or any outer garment whatever except for a Hudson's Bay blanket. They owned nothing else that was fit to take on the cold campaign ahead, they told her. Then they asked if they might see "Mister Applegate," their voices serious and low.

"Mister" Applegate. This had struck her strangely. These were the same young men who, in less troubled times, called her pappa "Charley," or even "Uncle Charley." These were boys she'd known since Missouri times or since they'd come across the plains together in '43—friends of the family. She would not have called them "beaux," however, for during those Willamette years her pappa had made it known that he intended to be the only rooster in his henyard for some time to come. Nevertheless, the young men who stood in the doorway that cold December afternoon had, more than once, cheerfully put their backs into whatever needed doing. Never had she known any of them to turn down an invitation to noonday dinner. Some of those boys had come west without families and as a consequence enjoyed the hospitality "over to the Applegates'." Her mother treated them as kinsmen, too.

While they had waited, they muttered how no woman or child was any longer truly safe in Oregon. She had heard her father and uncles say similar things, of course, but until that moment she had felt perfectly safe herself. No, she had never feared an Indian, yet now all was brought home: A war against the Cayuse . . . people she knew might be hurt and even killed because of it.

Then her father came in and she overheard things she wished she hadn't. It was rumored that the Cayuse had spirited away a number of female hostages and that they were to become "wives for the heathens." Some who had been stolen, the boys said in lowered voices, had been "no more than slips of girls."

When her mother came out of the backroom the boys had looked at her meaningfully, with a tenderness that was almost fierce. And, Lucy supposed, similar looks had been cast in the direction of Ellen, Susie, and herself. She at least had her eyes fixed on the floorboards. Her embarrassment was acute.

"No more than slips of girls . . ." She'd repeated the words to herself and shuddered; for she was finally old enough to realize the precise nature of what were called "conjugal obligations." What was worse, she knew that those boys—her former playmates—knew also.

Then the boys had hugged her mother so hard that she dipped like a sapling, declaring, as she righted her stringed cap, that she would never be the same again—hugged, as she'd been, by so many a bear. There had been tears in her eyes.

91

Some people, Lucy supposed, had almost enjoyed that war, or at least the idea of it. In places like Portland the female population was all astir and thought it romantic. Why, young women her own age had written letters to the *Spectator*, doubtless thrilled at the prospect that everyone should admire their fine sentiments. In these letters they had vowed that no man's attentions would be accepted unless he enlisted on behalf of God, Home, and Virtuous Woman.

That anyone should ask another to risk his life had seemed incomprehensible to her.

That winter on Salt Creek they'd stitched clothes, taking apart some of their own garments to do so. She had helped make a banner for the 1st Oregon. Her brothers and male cousins melted down a little toy cannon Elisha had made for them so that her father might manufacture balls for percussion rifles out of the metal. These sacrifices, they knew, had been puny enough, but people at home wanted to do something. The "army" had been short on everything, and people would have done anything at all that might help those boys on the fields of battle. Mostly, however, they'd just worried, especially after her uncle Jesse was called away that January. Aunt Cynthia would not permit herself to be comforted, which had not been good for her nor for the baby she was carrying. And every time they heard anything about the war, both false report and true, Lucy, Ellen, and Susie had wished fervently—though it was not to be—that they would never again have to say good-bye to people they cared for, or wonder whether they were alive or dead on some godforsaken field of war.

Oh, how she'd waved and wept on that long-ago day, watching the young horsemen—those brothers of their hearts—disappear, mayhap forever, in the gloomy curve of the distant oaks.

AMERICANS ALONE

The Governor's Plan—
Cynthia's Character—Jesse's Derring-do—
Snows in the Siskiyou—A Man Marked—
Spring Beauty

This was a matter of gravest concern to the settlers: What if the Cayuse, joined by the tribes known as Walla Walla, Wasco, Klickitat, and Nez Percé, arose "as one"—their fury directed toward all the settlements? Who knew? More peaceable tribes, such as the Calapooia, Mollala, Tillamook, and Clatsop—whose peoples mingled freely with the whites living in the Willamette Valley as well as on the seacoast—might also turn against the settlers.

Eventually, it would be representatives of the much-maligned Hudson's Bay Company who would help defuse the war. If they had not, the war might have been as grisly as the one the terrified populace waged in its imagination. As matters stood, things were bad enough.

The people of Oregon were inflamed. In but two years' time only the hanging of a group of Cayuse perpetrators would satisfy them. Even so, a deep suspicion concerning any Indian would linger. But in December of 1847 and January of 1848, the struggle had just begun and Oregon's provisional government was beset with difficulties. Jesse Applegate had personally taken a request for a "war" loan to the British at Fort Vancouver. The unhappy fact was that there were, on the verge of the continent, fewer than two thousand American settlers whose existence their national government had not yet seen fit formally to acknowledge and whose temporary governing body had less than fifty dollars in its coffers.

In the end, Jesse Applegate succeeded in talking the Hudson's Bay Company out of five thousand dollars—a sum of which was set aside for war materials. Yet that paltry amount would not go far to wage a bona fide campaign against the "savage"—or so believed the provisional government.

Thus, the governor, Abernethy, came up with a plan: If a

small overland party could make it to California, Oregon could better cope with the expected uprisings. Such a party might conceivably reach the garrisons in Sacramento who could, in turn, relay the dreadful news of the Whitmans' massacre and the threat of all-out war along the Columbia to the U. S. naval commandant at Yerba Buena, California. Surely, the governor reasoned, the commandant would come to the aid of the settlers in Oregon, perhaps dispatching a warship, guns, ammunition, and such trained troops as could be spared.

First, however, the governor was obliged to find men brave enough, or foolish enough, to attempt such a journey in the dead of winter. Joe Meek, a retired but still indomitable mountain man, was the first choice. Meek had already volunteered to make a breakneck ride across the whole of the continent, hand-carrying Oregon's petition for help to Washington, but he had refused when Abernethy suggested that he go via California. Most of the valleys south of the Willamette all the way to the mountainous verge of California were nothing more than mudded corridors besieged by rains fully as thick and relentless as those that had stranded emigrants two years previous in the dread canyon of the Umpqua. Even a party of experienced men familiar with the route would have difficulty, Meek argued. If they should somehow be able to pick their way over the drenched trail, if they succeeded in fording the half-dozen weather-glutted rivers between themselves and California, the Bobtailed Mountain Range (Siskiyous) would yet lie before them, where they would find the worst the winter had to offer. The mountain passes were heaped with snow drifts, horse-high. And if they weren't already buried in that cold oblivion, the great white wind that blew continually would make it impossible for any sojourner to see his own hand before his face. No, Joe Meek said, any man who felt compelled to push over the Siskiyous in January would find himself stopped dead in his tracks, or half dead if he was lucky. Joe Meek was right.

How the family women must have quaked up on Salt Creek when word reached them that Jesse had volunteered his services to the governor and was already on his way to California. Under the captaincy of his friend Levi Scott, Jesse had induced eleven men to accompany them. He was almost in the Umpqua country by the time his wife had learned of his departure. That Jesse knew the

94

route was but cold comfort to her despite the assurances of her brothers-in-law. If anyone could make it through, they said, it would be Jesse. There was much they avoided telling her, however. Cynthia was expecting her ninth child at any moment. Neither Charley nor Lindsay told her that her husband intended to avoid the worst of the California mountains by attempting Donner's treacherous shortcut. Any attempt to lift Cynthia out of her doldrums was manifestly futile. She refused to be comforted. All thoughts had flown from Cynthia Applegate's head save one: Where was Jesse? Lord, where was Jesse now?

Jesse's "plump Dutchy" was a simple countrywoman. Yet though Cynthia could barely read or write, she was hardly simpleminded. Indeed, those who loved her valued her intelligence and called her "canny." Her powers of intuition were acute. She rarely misjudged anyone's character or motives, her relatives said, although her husband's reasons for doing things must have sometimes perplexed her.

She was a woman who hated to travel and found her husband's perpetual comings and goings troublesome and sometimes painful. In later years, she adjusted somewhat and appeared to be quite an "independent little woman." She managed the farm, children, and various business affairs virtually singlehandedly when Jesse was away.

But this had not been what Cynthia—especially during the first decade of her marriage—wanted. She would have been satisfied to remain with Jesse Applegate on the edge of the serene hickory forests of their Missouri homeland "just always," she told her daughters, where she had once held the lantern for him at the prow of the canoe whilst he adjusted his hooks and lines waiting for the catfish to "come to medicine" and where she had stood at the bottom of the ladder handing him up the boards for their first frame house on the Osage. If she'd had her way, he would have always been close at hand—seated beside her and their children before a plain plank table laden with the foods she'd relished since childhood: roasted 'possum, fried catfish, sweet potatoes, collards, and cornbread. Yes, she always said, with the family gathered round itself as it ought to be, the common comforts . . . that was all she had ever wanted and not new land after new, nor a double-storied house; nor had she hankered for Brussels carpets or high-backed rosewood chairs, much less for an alpaca cape. Unlike her husband, she had not needed a melodeon, books, or distinguished company to make her happy.

No one knew whether she ever wondered why Destiny (or Providence) had tied her so inextricably to a scholarly, stubborn, exceedingly complex, itchy-footed frontiersman like Jesse Applegate. Yet her marriage knot held even when circumstance seemed to encourage its undoing. That winter, as Jesse made his perilous way down to California, was no exception. Cynthia Applegate sent incessant prayers to the God her husband only half believed in.

Jesse was then thirty-nine years old. He was not yet prepared to accept the old man enthroned in his wife's sky—that Heavenly Father who supposedly regularly interceded in the affairs of men. Instead, Jesse placed his faith in himself, for he was convinced that any man who acknowledged Nature's Immutable Laws, and who exercised self-discipline, could accomplish virtually anything.

". . . Training, simply training, in a life constantly surrounded by danger and death, will so strengthen the nerve, and the will, to meet and resist them, as to amount to heroism of the highest order recorded in the annals of the past." Years later Jesse Applegate would write these words to a young friend. In 1848 he himself had ample opportunity to prove his assertion. Indeed, the Oregon wilderness provided a perfect stage for enacting the myth of Hero for any who had pluck enough. Some men, however, contented themselves with mere heroics. Jesse Applegate was not one of them.

Time after time, he pitched himself against the nature whose laws he respected but refused to be intimidated by. In 1848 Jesse still believed that men made history and that history, by and large, did not make them. Oh, an "Imponderable Destiny" might nudge a man now and again; a "Creative Force," a "Supreme Lawmaker" might witness the soar and plummet of humanity, but men, Jesse told his sons, still had the power to exert change in their world because they had been endowed with Free Will. It was through exercising this faculty that a man might prevail. All a man needed was to keep his self-confidence, and never should he let tested principles desert him. Above all, the "worthy" man dared not permit debasing self-interests to distract him regardless of the circumstance.

How differently he would feel later in his life when history at last rolled over him, leaving him to contemplate a future over-whelmed by paucities, a past filled with regret, and a present which, for a time, would quite literally make him take leave of his senses. Only then would he—almost pathetically—hold out hope that Divine Justice would somehow be served in the same Here-after his wife believed in.

But in January of '48 Jesse Applegate was an "uncouth Inde-pendent" who thought he could do anything. Doubtless he truly wanted to be of service to his fellow Oregonians; but there was another matter: If he and Scott succeeded in reaching the Califor-nia garrisons, the sheen upon their reputations might be renewed. Let the governor eat his words.

That Governor Abernethy now found it necessary to depend on Jesse Applegate and Levi Scott was not without irony. Aber-nethy had so detested the "damnable" road that he had sent hand-bills to the emigrants arriving at Fort Hall in 1847, giving dire warnings concerning the Applegate cutoff and stating not so roundaboutly that any individual connected with the road or hav-ing the gall to offer his services as guide was reprehensible and then some.

Abernethy had openly sided with Jesse Quinn Thornton dur-ing the controversy. The governor had first taken out his spleen on Jesse Applegate and then turned on poor Levi Scott despite the fact that by 1847 Scott had greatly improved the southern route. Even the most long-suffering emigrant found little to condemn Levi Scott for. Nevertheless, he had taken his lumps along with the other members of the southern route expedition. It had cut him to the quick. He had hastened to defend Jesse Applegate as well as himself.

To be vindicated and lauded as heroes: Were these the forces that pushed Jesse and Levi Scott forward as they and the eleven other volunteers hurried down the southern route on a journey that was every bit as difficult as Joe Meek had claimed it would be? Or had things been more pure or simple in 1848, without "debas-ing self-interest"?

How distant seem the motivations of men like Jesse Applegate; obscured, as if wrapped within a snow cloud, their tracks too far behind in time, barely discernible over the deepening drifts where, that terrible January, pack animals were abandoned or put out of their misery, and half-frostbitten hands bent the icy willows low to fashion crude snowshoes.

At length Levi Scott felt compelled to call it quits, and was making camp even as Jesse, leading six others, who thought they could accomplish their desperate mission on foot, struck out alone. With fifty-pound packs on their backs and banks of wolf-gray nimbus rolling over their heads, they struggled through the rock-slashed passes of the Siskiyous. Jesse pushed them on mile after mile, stopping just short of death.

His companions, their beards glittering with ice, implored him to turn back. They had tried. They could not make it.

The failure hit Jesse hard; failure was then, and would always be, even more difficult for him to endure than criticism. They took only what they still had the strength to carry and limped north.

It was to be Jesse's fourth trip through the dreaded canyon of the Umpqua. The rains were almost as thick as they had been two years earlier. The day after he and his companions had waded through the canyon's gullet, they saw Levi Scott and the other half of the party camped in the distance. There was a noisy re-union. Levi Scott allowed he hadn't thought there would be one at all and he'd given up hoping.

The sojourners' spirits rose as they continued north. They soon came to the edges of the same secluded little valleys that had so impressed Jesse in 1846. The fact that the bottomlands were neither high with grass nor the hillsides ruddy with wild strawberries did not disguise either the beauty or potential of the place, Jesse said later. The meadows and swales were wet. Thus for comfort's sake he'd veered a little, cutting over a low ridge on what appeared to be a well-used Indian trail. This route was a few miles farther west than the one he'd followed previously. From a considerable distance he saw the high hump of the hill he would eventually name Mount Yoncalla. As he admired the vista, especially the way "his" hill rose so singularly out of the heart of the nearby valleys, he'd known with certainty he would return to the spot. He was as "a man marked," he said. He even envisioned the house he would one day build for his wife.

Cynthia was overjoyed to have him home again. The baby appeared robust, though Jesse's "plump Dutchy" looked tired. It was no wonder: She had just endured yet another variation of the salt-tanged worry and wait so peculiar to her sex. She'd felt even more drained as Jesse recounted his tribulations in the mountains. She could feel, she said, that Death had breathed hard on him.

No record says Jesse told her about the slopes of Mount Yoncalla downed with feathery and misted greens, and the house he had envisioned on the southern exposure. It is unlikely, too, that he described the intense lodens and rich emerald hues of the bottomlands where the wild grasses would tickle a man's chin by June. Or the "old man's hair"—the silvery mosses—swaying from the gnarled oaks, or the lusty stream, which sang with its winterfill while a faint breeze—for there was no wind, no, no wind at all—whispered an accompaniment in pleasant sibilance.

Even though it was early February, there had been wildflowers blooming here and there: the minuscule pink, spring beauty, and something shaped like a star and very low to the ground. The chilly Willamette would not be so enlivened for long weeks to come.

Perhaps Jesse considered that it was just as well if he kept his thoughts and his hopes to himself. What cared Cynthia for distant and sunnier climes? She'd stay where she was—thank you very much—and if she wanted to see spring beauties she had but to wait a little.

A READY-MADE HOMESTEAD

Destiny's Golden Steed—The 48'ers—
Lindsay Tries His Luck—
"A Mint in Hell"—Moving Fever

How perverse it is that when one finally releases something, firmly decides to let it go, good fortune or beneficent forces shine on what was about to be abandoned, altering it unexpectedly, making it tolerable, or even desirable, precisely when one has already reached the crossroads, no longer cares, and has entirely committed oneself to some different path and destination.

There are people, at such times, who will not permit themselves to reconsider; because of plain stubbornness, or mental exhaustion, they feel compelled to proceed. Reason is no longer their master. The course has been fixed, they may no longer veer from it. The silver needle of their soul swings to the new direction and sticks inexplicably.

So it must have been for Jesse Applegate.

That fecund and gentle July of 1848, other men felt entirely satisfied. In a pacific sky, Old Sol swam benignly, occasionally accompanied by a fleet of harmless sail-white cumulus, which dispensed trembling veils of soft, warm rains whose effects—the farmers said—were "most salubrious."

Nothing, they fancied, could go wrong now. Why, it was the best growing season yet. The vast pale wheatfields were nudged by soothing westerlies. The heat did not feel excessive; on the contrary, it comforted, and it was remarked by people who had been disheartened by deep snows, droughts, fires, shortages, epidemics, and Indian scares for two terrible years that it appeared—blessedly—that Oregon was God's own country after all.

But the bonhomie that had settled over people and made them content to immerse themselves in the steady but unhurried stream of their labors was not brought on by fair weather and the prospect of a whopping harvest alone.

No longer did the possibility of an all-out Indian war darken their futures. Hostages had been retrieved—humiliated but alive. The 1st Oregon, in a brief, fitful, disorganized series of skirmishes, considered that they had "whupped" the Cayuse "good enough." If ever again the settlers faced similar troubles, they would not have to meet them alone. Joe Meek—rumor had it—had made it across the continent clear to the nation's capital, and had received certain secret assurances from the president. Polk promised that soon the orphan Oregon would find itself under the protective arm of the United States and be acknowledged a territory. This welcome news filtered to every village and farm. Thus settlers felt relatively secure. All that was demanded was to concentrate upon what was good for themselves and their families. Larger events no longer distracted or agitated them.

But while Jesse's neighbors seemed to be burrowing their taproots ever more deeply into the productive earth of the valley Willamette, Jesse set about pulling his out as painlessly as possible.

He had learned a galling lesson since coming to Oregon. When he'd hurried out of Missouri in 1843 neither he nor his brothers had bothered to sell their farms or otherwise wrap up various business affairs. They'd trusted others to "settle up" on their behalf. Six years had passed with neither penny nor promise forthcoming. Thus prudence demanded that Jesse must somehow keep the wild horse inside him well hitched, even though, God knew, it was contrary to his natural impulse. He no longer cared how long it took him to disengage from the Willamette Valley and its droves of "new people." In his mind he had already deserted.

Ever since he returned from his failed expedition to the mountains, Jesse had been obviously and irascibly discontented. At length it had occurred to his wife—and how disturbing the knowledge—that if her husband appeared to take fleeting pleasure in their hundreds of acres of ripening grain, their thriving orchards and gardens, the commodious loghouse with its newly added wing and porches, or his gristmill—which everyone declared would make them well-to-do after the coming harvest—it was only because with things in such fine fettle, he was bound to find a buyer.

Cynthia could not bring herself to think about it. She almost preferred that disaster would strike, she said, or that the weather would be miserable and the crops poor, so she could convince herself that he was right and they ought to pack up. An unhappy vision had come to her: Fall would bring more people again—and on one incoming wagon or another there would sit an emigrant whose money belt was fat. Sooner or later he would hear about their place on the Salt Creek and bring his wife to look it over. What woman could fail to be pleased? Why, what awaited her was a fine ready-made homestead. And all the woman's husband would have to do would be to plunk his money down, maybe throwing in his rickety wagon for good measure, whereupon Jesse, doubtless, would solemnly shake the extended hand. From that moment on, as Cynthia saw it, she and her children would only have "starting over" to look forward to!

When Jesse wanted to talk of the forthcoming move he found a more appreciative audience in his brothers. Charley and Lindsay were considering that trip down south again—the "little look-see" they'd promised themselves for two years and more—before a swarm of circumstances and the attendant sting of responsibilities had ruined everything. With a little luck—they were overheard to mutter—after the wheat was in, but before the gristing and the autumn rains, they'd do what they wanted for a week or so, pack up their gear, and ride down to those valleys where the grass was as high as the sides of their horses.

What did Melinda say when Charley got back from his trip, all fired up and full of talk about the blue wild rye, red fescue, cheat-grass, brome, timothy, and clover in that country?

How did she feel when she saw the dreams of his Kentucky boyhood rearing in his eyes—those glossy-flanked stallions, mares, and geldings bred so thoroughly?

But Destiny's steed is a queer creature and can thunder out of nowhere, trampling the plans of men. It kicked up dust all the way from Cal-i-for-ni-a. In the end, the family women had a brief reprieve. Destiny's dust was of an unexpected color.

A hardworking, moody former Oregonian named James Marshall found it first. The peculiar little lump glinting in the shimmer of Sutter's millrace was shaped like a smallish pea; at first glance, hardly impressive, resembling—as someone said later—"a piece of spruce gum just out of a schoolgirl's mouth"—though slightly more yellow in color. Marshall found it soft when he bit it, the taste unpleasant and metallic. Soon he'd gathered numerous similar specimens, which he carried in his white slouch hat back to camp. There he and the other carpenters working on the millrace conducted a series of on-the-spot experiments. The decision was unanimous: All those little lumps were, indeed, what the Californios called "oro."

Marshall made his momentous discovery on a crisp, clear morning in January of 1848. Had Jesse, Levi Scott, and their companions made it through the mountains they might have learned of Marshall's find long before other men but not bothered to come home to tell about it. The not-too-well-guarded secret—for few men, once they had a glimmer of it, could contain themselves—was not revealed to Oregonians until August. Farmers were sweating under the sun and beginning their grain harvest; but how pale the gold of wheat compared to the stuff they'd heard about down Sutter's way.

By the time the pulse raced in the Willamette Valley, Jim Marshall was already beginning to reconsider the worth of his discovery. Had he brought fortune or misfortune to the beloved pastoral quiet of his new homeland?

When September turned its tawny face upon the landscape around the American, Yuba, Feather, and Bear rivers and the sun had leached every bit of green away, Marshall saw so many familiar Oregon faces amid those scrabbling beside the California miners that he was said to have wondered aloud whether there were any Webfoots left in the Willamette Valley.

Jesse's old friend Peter Burnett was among the first to drop everything and clamber down to California. Burnett told Marshall that he estimated two thirds of the grown men in all of Oregon had come south to try their luck. Further, it was rumored that in the settlement of Salem there were only five grown men and they, Burnett said, had stayed home only because they were either too old or too sick to travel.

Burnett hadn't needed to twist anyone's arm in order to form a sizable expedition of would-be miners. The wagons and pack animals of his one hundred fifty comrades soon clotted the southern route, which some men called the "Applegate Trail." Even the "respectable" could not resist the prospect of longer pockets: Oregon's physicians, merchants, schoolmasters, lawyers, and clergymen jostled shoulder to shoulder beside the ne'er-do-wells and just-plain-loafers all the way to the gold fields.

Lindsay, who seemed especially restless, the women noted, lost no time. He immediately cast his lot with Burnett's contingent and helped organize the expedition by riding up and down the Willamette gathering recruits and supplies. Many men found "Captain Applegate's" presence in the enterprise reassuring: After all, Lindsay was well acquainted with the trail south. By proceeding ahead of the main caravan with a few hand-picked men, Lindsay intended to ascertain the temper of the Indians and, more important, to find the least rugged ascents for the four dozen wagons following him. The Indians had been peaceable enough—only later would they constitute a threat to the throngs of gold-seekers—but though Lindsay tried, he was unable to discover a less strenuous route for the gold-seekers' supply wagons. When the teamsters complained, Lindsay defended himself by reminding them that the road builders had originally cut the trail so that wagons could get into the Willamette and not out of it.

Neither he nor any other man, he said, had foreseen that anyone except an occasional driver and his pack animals would need to leave Oregon! Now the territory was draining more quickly than an unplugged fat vat.

The heavier rigs, which had been laden with provisions and tools, were of necessity pulled by triple teams over the rough inclines in the Umpqua country. The thought of abandoning these wagons was repugnant. The stubborn struggled on, lurching up the precipitous eastern spur of the Siskiyous, and rattling down and across the grueling basin and range terrain of the Klamath region. By the time the rugged arid plateaus skirting the marshlands were reached, a few men considered doing Lindsay harm, but fortunately "Captain Applegate" mollified his detractors. He and other scouts were eventually to discover a far less difficult trail into the Pitt River Valley, the terminus of which lay upon the very border of the gold country. When all was said and done, Lindsay was congratulated for his efforts.

The gold-seekers congratulated themselves as well. How fortunate the Webfoot was to find himself already on the Pacific Coast before the rest of the country—or the rest of the world, for that matter—heard what twinkled in the streams of California. Except for the local settlers, their Indian helpers, a crowd of Mexicans, and a few Mormons, the Oregonians had found it first.

It was said that any man who did not find between twenty to forty dollars' worth of gold a day was not working hard enough and had better "get a leg up" before the pickings became slimmer. He had only himself to blame if he did not become rich in a few months' time.

Gold fever not only fired the soul, a heavy toll was exacted

105

upon the body as well. Lindsay and every other miner noted that soon there came a certain weakness in the knees and the bowels would loosen at unexpected times. Worse was the heat, which sent spears through a man's battered hat whilst he stood for uncountable hours in the chilblain-producing streams of El Dorado. And all the while his brow beaded, his head ached, and he was assailed with dizzy spells that played havoc with the equilibrium as his body waged an exhausting war against the unhealthy and perpetual mix of hot and cold. Nor did a diet composed of frizzled salt pork and underdone biscuits eaten at irregular intervals do much to keep up his strength. Married gold-seekers like Lindsay who had arrived well padded and robust were to suffer most. Back home a man depended on his wife to serve up his "victuals" at the appointed hour, and to remind him that cleanliness was next to godliness. After a few months in California, only makeshift suspenders or hemp belts guaranteed that trousers would remain where they ought to be. The formerly smooth-cheeked hid gaunt faces behind matted beards that served to accentuate a certain wildness of eye. Twitches and tics developed in the most sanguine: Prospecting for gold, it seemed, brought forth a St. Vitus's dance of the spirit, compounded by a nervousness and unabated restlessness.

No, Lindsay said later, there had been nothing "romantic" about a stint in the mines. Backache and heartache for most. Eternal vigilance. Almost immediately California had teemed with untrustworthy fellows whose bad habits or bad luck had reduced them to thievery. His own poke was always secured in the clasped-leather safety of his money belt. His hand—even in sleep—remained close to his gun.

At night, under the spangled heavens, as his nostrils filled with the stirring smells of balsam and the curiously bittersweet tang of tan oak and madrone, though dead tired he'd stayed maddeningly awake, imagining that other things were murmuring besides the wind and the nearby stream. He resisted sleep until the last possible moment, he said. Beneath the pine boughs sharp stones prodded. The thin, unwashed bedroll stank with the thousand hours of his own sweat. He slept in his clothes, of course, ready for anything.

Lindsay never talked much about the sense of satisfaction that must surely have stolen over him as his eyes shut out the stars. He had done quite well for himself—he slept with six thousand dollars' worth of gold dust in his belt. From this amount Lindsay extracted a share for the return trip home. He and several other Oregon miners chartered a ship, which embarked from San Francisco's infamous Barbary Coast. The vessel was supposedly bound for the mouth of the Columbia via the most direct route possible. The captain had been paid "liberally." Lindsay and his friends looked forward to a brief sea voyage wherein they might refresh themselves and collect their wits after an exhausting interlude in the mines.

Instead, they found themselves organizing a Webfoot mutiny. It was soon noted that the ship's captain was guiding their vessel south rather than north. The seven Oregonians on board were then told that they must go on short rations. Thus, Lindsay later related to his sons, as they were evidently to be starved as well as robbed, there remained no remedy save to corner the reprehensible captain in his cabin. Six revolvers and one double shotgun were aimed at his head. "Turn her north, now!" demanded the Webfoots. The captain complied. For the remainder of the voyage, the landlubbing mutineers from Oregon watched the wheel and quarterdeck night and day.

One afternoon, even though they had been close enough to the mouth of the Columbia to make it in before sunset, the captain refused to so instruct his crew. His excuse was that the breakers were too high. Lindsay and his comrades were not disposed to wait. "Go in now or you'll go to the bottom," they told him, "and if we go too, there's a mint in hell and at least we'll have our gold when we arrive."

The vessel pitched and shivered and the galley was a wreck. Crossing the bar at Astoria was never easy. Nevertheless, the passage was safely made and in the end the captain pressed hands with the mutineers and a toast was made. Bygones were bygones.

Lindsay's story outlasted the gold dust he brought home. His poke was quickly depleted because of poor investments. The trip to the mines had nearly cost him his life, not to mention the succession of muscle-stiffening days that stretched close to a year, which he spent with his partner, rocking an awkward wood and canvas cradle way down in that California valley rich with lode and lodens, some nine hundred miles from his wife and home.

Rocking the cradle: While Lindsay was away, Betsy Applegate

was in the man-short Willamette, spending much of her time rocking a cradle of a different and far noisier variety. What she and a few thousand other mine-widows found deposited in the frayed, dingy, continually recycled diapers of their infants were not nuggets.

It was as if some woman-hating shaman had shaken his rattle over Oregon. His incantation was simple enough and but four letters long. Even so, women and children watched helplessly as husbands and fathers vanished before their very eyes. G-O-L-D preempted any consideration of those at H-O-M-E.

In July of '48, before the gold spell ruined family life, Oregon women had been feeling almost smug about their improved lot, the forthcoming harvest, and the security it would bring. The same month, some of their female contemporaries back east in Seneca Falls, New York, had been airing certain grievances. At the world's first women's rights convention, a soft-spoken Quaker named Lucretia Mott delivered a moving keynote address. "Man," she said, "cannot fulfill his Destiny alone, he cannot redeem his race unaided. . . ."

Had she known of the plight of the gentler sex in Oregon, Mrs. Mott surely would have added that the reverse was also true: Women left unaided and alone, particularly along the desolate frontiers of the continent, were equally incapable of fulfilling their destiny when deprived of their men.

By autumn the barns of the Willamette Valley had not brimmed with neat bundles of grain as they should have. How distressing was life to those left at home. They had had no choice save to watch and sigh as hogs snorted and rooted over the wheatfields, taking their greedy fill of what had been intended for the long, curved wooden teeth of yet another variety of cradle. What the hogs hadn't ravaged was flattened by the rains and winds. The women and children of Oregon had tried to salvage what they could: Theirs had been a desperate and haphazard harvest, made all the more difficult because the would-be miners had absconded with every horse and mule fit for travel.

Where was the cordwood usually piled high around the loghouses or inside the sheds by October? the women asked one another. Was winter not going to make its chilly rounds in Oregon that year just because some fool in California had discovered gold and other fools had felt compelled to find it?

Betsy Applegate was luckier than most: She had seventeen-year-old Elisha to depend upon while Lindsay was in California. Elisha hadn't much liked the idea of staying at home, of course, but his father had insisted.

Neither Charley nor Jesse had been bitten by the gold bug, and the grain harvest over at the Applegates'—other women in the neighborhood noted enviously—commenced as usual, and due to short supply had fetched a pretty sum indeed.

But Melinda and Cynthia soon realized that even though Charley and Jesse seemed healthy and appeared to keep their wits as the wheat money piled up, a variant strain of miner's fever had assailed them after all. Jesse succumbed first. By the spring of 1849, he had packed his family up. Charley and Lindsay followed his lead within the year. They wanted not gold but the green of newer pastures to call their own.

A DIVIDED HOUSE

Yoncalla, Oregon
May 13, 1861

Dear Theresa,
I think now is the time for women to assert their rights, for they should all have the right to fight. If the southern women are embroidering flags and rattlesnakes why can't the northern ones have spunk enough to tear them down!! We heard that when Jo. Lane landed he raised the secession flag and began to make a speech. The women broke loose, tore down the flag and burnt it in the street, and beat him out with rotten eggs. . . . There has been talk of Jo. Lane trying to raise [his flag] at Roseburg, but if old Jo does, there will be a fight in Umpqua, for our Republican men there say that they will not bear it!!! If they do stick it up, I hope their women will tear it down. . . . How I would glory in burning their treacherous rattlesnake. Their emblem is well chosen! . . . The South is sinking and the sooner it is down, the better. Our President has come under many difficulties and he is showing himself worthy of his office. I am not afraid for our Union for I know the just God will not give the power into hands of these oppressors of the human race.

Your Cousin,
Harriet Applegate

P. S. to Letter from Harriet Applegate to Theresa Applegate, May 13, 1861 written by J. T. Miller (nephew of Melinda Applegate)

113

It is a fact that old Jo Lane accidentally shot himself and was taken to the Charles Drain home for nursing and care. The ball entered his left breast pretty low down coming nearly out a little below the top of the shoulder blade. If his blood is in good condition he will *recover*. He has been visited on by a good Republican, Uncle Jesse, who has invited him to his home.

JTM

Yoncalla, Oregon
February 12, 1862

Dear Theresa,

What an awful state this continent is in now. His Satanic Majesty is certainly loosed upon it, and has, for the time, undisputed sway. How do you stand on the War? . . . I am the only "peace man" in the family. I think I would vote for a compromise, anything to stop, anything I say, to stop the shedding of blood. I am eager in the cause of liberty, I would like to see every slave free, yet to gain this effect the country will have to be steeped in debt that we shall never see ended in this life, yea, in many more lives to come. I would rather be at quits. Don't blame me for such sentiments, I am but a woman with a woman's weak brain and soft heart. I am a deep "sympathizer" but not a sympathizer of rebels but with the widows and the orphans, the desolate home circle, the famine and the misery, *that* is why I would compromise. I can but see the utter folly of it. For when the "storm dieth not, and the fire be not quenched" as long as slavery exists this war will go on and on and this generation will expiate the sin of it as will other generations to come.

Your cousin,
Gertrude Applegate

A Yoncalla Home

Even in the earliest days, when its new paint still shone whitely in the distance unstained by rain or other inclemencies, when its square-pillared porches and broad balcony were yet unweighted by vines both lush and serpentine, and its locust and walnut trees were hardly higher than a grown man, casting no shadow across its commodious front, only the Indians had wondered at its luminous presence upon the *illahee*. No other passerby was truly surprised to see it as he or she traversed the rutted trail. From the beginning Charley Applegate's house had seemed as much a part of the country as any solitary cedar, darkly rocked hillside, or other natural thing. It was as if the house had been inwardly sensed, seen, and even remembered by them. These feelings reached back and back, long before 1851, the year the grandfather firs had been hauled down from the ridges and made into posts, beams, and boards as heavily scented as the old forest itself.

From the Historic American Buildings Survey. (Library of Congress)

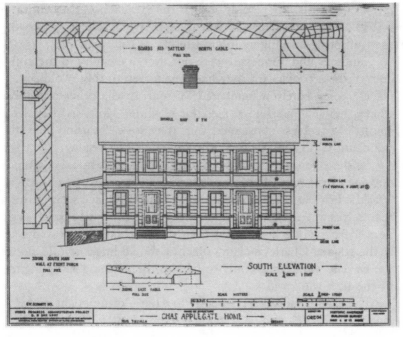

115

The big white house rising at the hazy heart of the fields. The gentle roll of the hills behind. When the moody light was right, and roans and bays could be seen grazing upon the heavy-headed grasses, there were some who regularly paused along their route, beguiled by the vista. For a moment they could almost convince themselves they were once again in their places of origin and childhood. Though there were other landscapes they had more lately left, those regions exerted no such tug upon their hearts. Missouri and Indiana, Ohio and Ioway—the settings for their most recent disappointments—had merely intervened before Oregon beckoned. It was Kentucky and Tennessee that these people had tucked away in their memories. As surely as they had brought their great-grand-so-and-so's red-lettered Bibles and far homelier family relics clear across the plains, so they carried their nostalgia for those "old-time" places. It was no wonder then that when they found themselves musing and gazing at the big white house, Kentucky and Tennessee returned to them like some rediscovered keepsake that had the power to mist the eye.

In the year 1857, these men and women were of middle age. They were thought of—and thought of themselves—as older, for upon reaching forty, most were in reality far closer to death than life. Despite this, the records of their time reveal how they continued to "beget and begat," even though their prime had passed, their offspring arriving as intermittently as the rains.

Kentucky and Tennessee were not even a memory to the children of these people, for they had never been to those "old-time" places. Some barely remembered Missouri or the other midlands where their parents had paused for a while. Most, as they said among themselves, considered that they were "growing up with the country" in the territory whose name was Oregon.

To these younger persons, Charley Applegate's house conjured nothing of the past. They saw it for no more or less than what it was: the first bona fide house in many a mile, a place such as they themselves might aspire to. And as they had no choice but to pass near the big white house—for their damp schoolhouse cabin was at the edge of Charley's claim—if they should linger awhile along the way, it was perhaps only to admire the morning sun clinging to the new windowglass.

The glass itself was a testimony to what Oregon might do for a man. It had been shipped 'round the Horn at no little expense, via the new city of San Francisco. Thence, it had been transported by coastwise schooner to the thriving settlement of Scottsburg, which was near the mouth of the Umpqua River. Charley and his boys picked it up and packed it off. The glass had been carted a full forty miles home—all, the story went, without either crack or mishap. Charley Applegate led a charmed life, or so thought those who had settled more recently in his vicinity.

Pane by pane, the glass had been carefully inserted into the numerous upper and lower window frames. Only in the autumn of '56 had Charley permitted his wife, Melinda, and those of their fifteen children who were not yet married off to remove from the dim loghouse adjacent, where they had lived for a half a decade.

Even so, the big house had not been truly "warmed" by the neighborhood until the following February. By then the weather had improved and white rosebuds could be gathered in substantial numbers. Many of these flowers were used to decorate the big front rooms. The choicest specimens found their place in the glossy dark hair of Mary Applegate, who on the occasion of her wedding had indeed appeared as "merry as any marriage bell."

In addition to her own large immediate family, her uncles, aunts, and at least twenty first and double first cousins attended Mary's wedding. Those persons who were referred to as "married-ins," and the ones who were "shirttail" relatives, either because of distant connection or pure fondness, arrived by the score all day long. The front rooms and porches brimmed with them. Other well-wishers had felt compelled to cut short their visit because of the sheer number.

Whatever long-remembered chord was plucked inside people as they gazed at the outside of Charley Applegate's big white house grew still when they stepped over the threshold of either front door. No mirror-hung hall greeted them—there was, in fact, no hall at all. No planter's chandelier cast candleglow or flashed glassy sparks upon polished hardwood floor or patterned carpet.

The ceilings were surprisingly low, more reminiscent of the farmhouses they had visited or lived in before arriving in Oregon. Thus women unaccustomed to the finer things immediately took their ease as they surveyed the western front room of Charley's new house, where strings of peppers and apple rings and onion braids dangled from the sturdy beams.

Why, they might have been standing in some enlarged version

117

of their own cabins, they said to themselves. Even the light from the numerous windows did not flood the room because the unfinished handiwork upon the suspended quilting frames curtained it somewhat. The dim air was softly hazed with kettle steam and smoke pushed downward. The Dutch ovens hooked over the fireplace emitted aromas stronger and more comforting than the tanged undersmell of cedar-faced walls, fresh paint, and new firwood floors. They noted, too, that neither mantel clock, pewter tea service, framed picture, nor any other object better than common met the eye. Though bookshelves in the big east room were lined with hundreds of volumes that Charley had "sent back east for," these editions from Harper's Young People's Library were of such uniform size and so darkly bound that they had an unobtrusive appearance. Doubtless the books had been expensive, yet they might be expected in the home of the man who had donated the site for the first schoolhouse.

Generally, a visitor selected a straight-backed chair to light upon, adjusting his or her backside to the uncushioned rawhide webbing upon the seat, which was only slightly more accommodating to the body's shape than a stump or some upended wood round. In both front rooms the furniture was plain—all of it handmade by various Applegate sons, or maybe by some hired man who had a knack for building cabinets and other useful articles. In the whole of Charley Applegate's house there was nothing so large or elegant that it could not simply be shoved aside if a gathering of neighbors was under way. A fiddle had but to be unwrapped from beneath its homely cover to inspire an impromptu dance, whereupon Charley would call to his wife that the quilting frames should be immediately taken down and the hooked rugs rolled up.

The master of ceremonies could be expected to dispense something better than soft cider, coarsely ground coffee, or yerba buena tea at such times. Indeed, certain of Charley's male guests had come to anticipate it, special occasion or no. If he had taken a liking to them, almost anytime was suitable for refreshment of the kind Charley liked best. He had known how to imbibe, he always said, since his earliest years. How could it be otherwise? After all, he grew up in Kentucky.

Those who had been Charley's friends since way-back-when observed that neither his Missouri years nor his time in Oregon had done much to slacken his thirst. Charley Applegate might be the Blackest Republican in the whole of their vicinity, they laughed, but unlike some of that ilk, Charley had never let his politics get mixed up with "the damned temperance" business! Nor was he stingy when he unplugged that certain little barrel he'd stationed on a corner of his new porch. It was said that any man who had been privy to the warming contents of that little barrel at least once had never found it empty when he came again.

Most people agreed that Charley had all the expansive characteristics necessary to any good host. From the very first, his home had become a center for young people in the neighborhood. This situation seemed natural enough, since a full two thirds of the school population carried the name Applegate. Yet Charley's open-handed hospitality extended far beyond his kin. It was a regular come one, come all situation over at the big white house. Related or not, a young person made himself at home.

Charley sponsored all manner of lighthearted comminglings beneath his commodious roof, and he made no secret of his fondness for the "gentler sex"—women young, old, and in-between were always present. This had caused some consternation among a group of newcomers known as "hard-shell Baptists." Not only was he likely to encourage parlor games, dancing, and other unelevating pastimes; his liberality, it was said, included corruption of the innocent: More than once he had been known to offer wine or a cordial to a female guest.

His views on "universal education" were especially repugnant to those who believed they understood their Creator's plan for womankind. Charley was inclined to agree that a woman's place might indeed be near home and hearth with her offspring gathered round her, but he thought it was precisely because of a woman's important sphere of influence that she should know how to read, write, and think. He was, therefore, apt to admonish any father who denied education to his daughters. His own daughters, he always said, would know of a world of literature larger than the tales that the Bible offered up. He would rather that his girls spent their Sundays reading Dickens or Harriet Beecher Stowe or even a romance by Sir Walter Scott if it spared them from nightmares caused by some wild-eyed preacher's tirades concerning hellfire and brimstone.

Yet despite Charley's apparent openmindedness, love of sociability, and belief that the gentler sex had certain rights, he had done something which truly perplexed people. Why, it seemed contrary to his very nature! Some of his friends opined to one another that even a hard-shell Baptist would not have gone so far. His friends were not the only ones who wondered why Charley had seen fit to divide his house right down the middle.

In effect, he had built not one house, but two, though the same roof covered both. It was a double house, laid out in an old-time style some of them had seen or heard about years before back in Tennessee. All was perfectly symmetrical, or almost, each room having its twin on the opposite side of the main interior wall. But what had Charley Applegate needed a double house for? they asked themselves. As far as anyone knew, he had never intended to live with any family save his own. No other relatives shared his roof except for short stints. Daughters who had married immediately relocated in their own places, where they raised their own families. Further, his oldest friends had heard him say more than once that the surest way to make everyone miserable was to have more than one family under the same roof. As close as he was to his brothers Jesse and Lindsay, and though they lived side by side, each had maintained his own residence.

Each sex, it was true, sometimes needed privacy to carry out the duties distinct to its gender. Charley's "domain"—as he called it—was the east front room. His wife Melinda's was the big room to the west. These two rooms had individual entrances from without. This, people agreed, bore a certain logic, since there was no main entry hall in the house and Charley or his wife might occasionally wish to be sequestered in the event of callers, sickness, and so forth. But once inside the house, whether the visitor entered the west or east front room, it was noted that something was amiss. No amount of scrutiny proved it otherwise: No door existed between Charley's room and that of his wife. Thus direct intercourse between the two was impossible, for if either wished to have access to the domain of the other, there was nothing for it but to leave the house and enter through the appropriate outside door—just the way everyone else did.

Almost from the beginning people began referring to these two front rooms as the men's side and the women's side. This appellation seemed even more fitting when it was learned that a similar arrangement existed on the upper floor. Charley had even troubled to build two separate little staircases, each equally narrow and

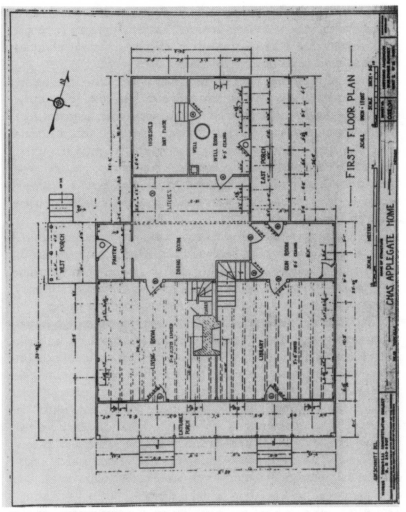

From the Historic American Buildings Survey. (Library of Congress)

steep. These rose from the back of each front room on opposite sides of the main wall and opened on separate landings. No doors, save for two on the balcony, each of which was usually locked, allowed passage between the sleeping quarters.

It appeared that only the smoke was permitted to mingle as it passed through the bedrooms over at Charley Applegate's, people said, shaking their heads, for there was but a single chimney thrusting dead center from the cedar-shaked roof.

There were no fireplaces upstairs, and it was some time before Charley ordered a little cast-iron stove for the girls' dormitory, which, his daughters complained, did no more than keep the edge off. Downstairs, there was but a single fireplace with a double front that opened toward both big front rooms. No mutual warmth was forthcoming from this big fireplace, however, for it, too, had been divided in twain. Each half had its own firebox made of sandstone blocks; thus fires were laid separately, obliged to blaze alone on separate hearths.

For a year or so all the indoor cooking was done in the fireplace on the women's side. Since Charley liked to have the family and whatever guests were present gather around the big plank table in his room, the cooks were forced to haul their culinary efforts roundabout at no little inconvenience to themselves.

The opening of the fireplace in the west room, though somewhat deeper than that of its mate on the other side of the wall, was relatively small and low. Adjustable cooking cranes of the sort the family women had been used to back in Missouri could not be accommodated. Instead, Charley had fashioned a series of iron hooks in his smithing shed. These hung by a stout rod, which he had bored into the sandstone of his wife's fireplace. As a limited number of Dutch ovens and kettles could be suspended at any given time, if a crowd appeared at dinner the women had to struggle to have enough hot food to go around. At such times, the meal progressed in a series of separate sittings, the cooks finishing last. After traipsing back and forth for an hour or more, outside and then in again, ofttimes all the women received for their trouble was whatever remained on the cold platters, for whatever was hot was gone. All this caused so much dissatisfaction that at length Charley agreed to build an addition on the back of the house.

Several seasons passed before the new kitchen and dining

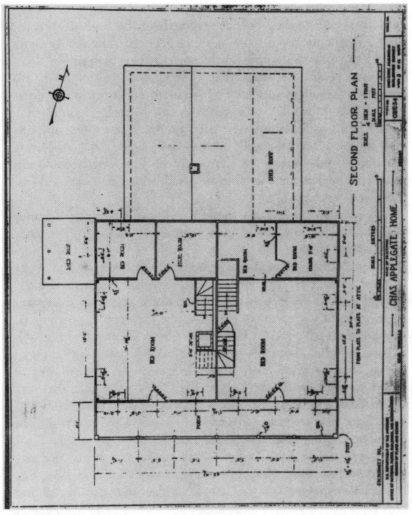

From the Historic American Buildings Survey. (Library of Congress)

room were completed to his wife's and daughters' satisfaction. To appease the disgruntled, he sent for a big cookstove. To please himself, he built a little gun room, which could be entered from the dining room, the men's side, or the long kitchen porch. The women, too, could pass from a door in the back of their room to the dining room and thence to the kitchen. The big new kitchen had two doors leading outside. From them the vegetable garden and springhouse could more easily be reached. The family cooks found these circumstances much more to their liking.

Some people speculated that while Charley was improving his premises, he might just take a notion to cut a few other doors where they might do some good. A few discreet inquiries were made about whether any new entryway had been added upstairs. But nothing had changed in the main house, the Applegate daughters said—either upstairs or down. The long north–south wall remained as impenetrable as it had before: East was still east and west was west.

A number of Charley's friends concluded that either Charley had overridden any complainer, or that no one of consequence had complained.

Certain matrons in the neighborhood, however, had gradually formed their own opinions concerning the "peculiar arrangements" over at the Applegates'. When taken altogether their speculations went something like this: Maybe the separate apartments, double staircases, and so forth hadn't been Charley's idea at all. Marriage—they avowed—was a mansion containing many a room, some of which were hidden from view and known only to the man and woman who lived inside. Who really ruled the roost over there? Oh, they had all heard Charley snap, bark, and even roar from time to time, especially when one of his sons had done some little thing which displeased him; yet these eruptions did not necessarily mean that Charley's word was law, for he did not play the despot for long, they noted, if his wife was in earshot. No, Melinda Applegate was the sort of mother who considered that any child's feelings were more important than a chore half done or a gate left open. In this, she differed from her husband.

When the women had gone over there to quilt, or to pick up peaches, or to spend a day helping stuff sausages in return for apples they were allowed to pick, they had been obliged to alter their initial impressions concerning Melinda Applegate. More than once, they had seen her turn the lion into a lamb—or a sheep maybe, for Charley usually had a sheepish look after his wife had made her feelings known. Sometimes all that was necessary was for her to stiffen and stare coldly at him. Even if he'd been tippling, Charley seemed to read her disapproval from clear across the room.

While Melinda Applegate might seem meek to those who didn't know her—for rarely did she push herself forward in any gathering, including the ones in her own home—those who counted her as friend never doubted that *she* was the mistress of her own house. Some of them had been present when she unbraided a certain Virginian bachelor who had made the mistake of bringing up slavery while he helped himself to more cobbler. Others had heard her express her opinions on common gossip and those who indulged it, or had arrived to find her delivering admonishments because she would not tolerate any child of hers picking upon a helpless creature, even if it were only a yellow jacket or housefly. Yes, they knew all these things about Melinda Applegate and suspicioned even more. After all, like Melinda, they were somewhat older than numerous of the "poor young things" more lately come to the country who had not yet learned to stand up to the bluster of their husbands—Charley Applegate wasn't the only man who liked to "lord it over."

Thus it seemed to them that Melinda might very well have designed her own house. There had been nothing for it but for Charley to build her way. Thirty years of marriage and fifteen children surely counted for something.

It was observed by a matron in their midst, who had known the Applegates since Missouri days, that one thing was certain: Even a man in his cups, dead set on funny business with his wife, would have trouble walking through a wall. In this, Melinda Applegate enjoyed an advantage over those whose dwellings were more ordinary.

As time went by, other advantages were noted. The older Applegate daughters grew to appreciate the sanctuary afforded by their separate living quarters. While they might yet overhear the goings on on the other side of the wall, they were at least spared the sight of them. On evenings when their father invited one sojourner or another to lay over, the din was apt to be considerable. His guests, like as not were of the garrulous sort, inclined to

125

hoot and belch, occasionally bursting into song or expletive. These unpleasantries were even more likely when the weather was bad, and their pappa permitted the guests to billet in front of the east-room fireplace, in which case little oaken kegs called Blue Bulls were conveniently located beside their bedrolls so that they might gradually swig themselves into oblivion. This state was looked forward to by the women and children, for it meant a blessed quiet descended.

If the sojourners happened to be returning miners, and their clothes and boots were caked with mud, the older daughters felt somewhat compensated for their broken sleep. When morning came, and they had finished dispensing mush, sourdough biscuits, and coffee black as the dirt beneath certain fingernails, the keen-eyed young women entered the vacated room to clean. Often the dirt they swept into the dust shovel had a pretty glitter to it. In this manner, treasure was gleaned from the tailings in the east room, for they sifted as carefully as any Chinaman, or so they laughingly said.

In a few seasons they had filled their mother's biggest blue sugar-bowl with gold dust. They placed it on the mantel in plain sight on the theory that like attracted like. They were not disappointed. Those miners who had learned of their scheme to fund finery when next "the peddler came through" took pity on them. Other men who had reason to be grateful for the family's hospitality dug into the little pouches they carried on their belts. Sometimes more than one pinch of "Oregon money" found its way into the bank upon the mantel whose contents were far sweeter than sugar.

Why—people wondered—didn't Charley just turn his place into a roadhouse and be done with it? He and his family could have made a good living from the hospitality he offered up for free.

"Charley," his friends told him, "you ought to charge regular rates."

And they went on about how it was rumored that the stage line was finally going to pass through Yoncalla; how he might just as well make a bid to be the stage stop. After all, he had but to improve that little bit of wagon road that angled right through his back fields. That done, he had only to apply for the contract. How could the company refuse him? He already had himself a fine big house.

But Charley snorted at such suggestions, for he was not about to rearrange his family's affairs around some stage driver's bugle call, day in and day out. He had cattle and sheep to raise. Nor was his wife in favor of it. Let old man Ambrose down the road make his bid and put up with whatever characters chance had deemed foolish or solvent enough to ride the six-horse-limited and company mud wagons. Charley preferred to pick and choose his wayfarers. Ever since the gold strikes had hit closer to home, and the diggings at Starveout, Coyote, and Barton's Ravine were opened up, the Big Road had been clotted with men whose company and proslavery sentiments he'd just as soon do without. Nor would it be long before they would be followed by plungers and speculators, until Roseburg, doubtless, would be as full of them as Jacksonville. Why, he said, shaking his head, it was as inevitable as a gold mine petering out.

His friends came to expect such talk from Charley Applegate. The country was changing but he wasn't. He complained that they went after any wild goose that honked loud enough to attract their attention. They averred that as long as the goose was golden, they might just as well stop what they were doing long enough to collect a stray egg or two.

Charley, they knew, was a "mite" opinionated. If he happened to ride by and saw one of his neighbors plowing, or overheard people arguing about whether they ought to plant wheat or oats to take advantage of the new markets, he was certain to scowl and say his piece: *His* sod would not be so disturbed. No, he always said, he would not plant anything unless he was forced to put in feed and seed for his own livestock. Plow it up and watch it go to ruin, after which the topsoil would end up in the nearest creek. In the end, the plowman would have neither wild pasturage nor grain. Yoncalla was stock country. So certain was he about the country's rightful use that men of the meeker sort found themselves uncomfortable and even embarrassed that they should have thought otherwise. After all, Charley had done well for himself. Maybe he was right.

Other men reminded Charley that he had been among the first to shift from cattle to sheep with an eye to better profits. Why shouldn't they adjust themselves to the markets, too?

But sheep were just another kind of livestock, Charley argued. The country was ideally suited to them. Grain was another matter

127

entirely. It had to be imposed upon the country; besides which, if they were not careful, they would find all the goody sucked right out of the ground, just as the wheat farmers in the upper Willamette had. Whether the miner came or went, a man could always count upon selling his wool. No, he wasn't about to tie up time and acreage trying to turn good grazing land into a bread-basket. A man was better off to leave well enough alone.

Leave well enough alone. How many times had they heard him say so? And on more than one subject, too. Charley Applegate stood on his six-inch sod as immoveable as any hundred-year white oak, his taproot sunk just as deep, as firmly imbedded as his opinions. Opportunities were passing him by. Or so some thought. These were the same men who wondered how Charley could remain so thick with his brothers and yet have such a different outlook on life. It was evident that neither Jesse nor Lindsay Applegate was averse to taking advantage of the times. Jesse, in particular, was what was known as a forward thinker. There was always something new going on near the sunny southern slope of Mount Yoncalla where Jesse had staked his claim. Unlike Charley, Jesse believed that man could apply his ingenuity toward the betterment of anything, nature included.

Jesse's ingenuity was well known. As were certain of his peculiarities. It was a case of too much mind over matter as far as some of his neighbors were concerned, but then they were less meticulous than he was. That they had got their fences up at all was enough for them. Sturdiness was the important thing, never mind how they appeared or whether the posts had been set first or if the fence line veered a little into another man's property. Jesse was mathematically inclined and order reigned not only in his computations but in his eye. Thus he'd employed compass and chain laying out each and every fence. There would be, he said, no slovenly parallels nor would any corner project where it ought not to.

This had been quite an undertaking, for Jesse had not been content to take his square-mile square. Instead, he'd carefully surveyed his claim so that its contours resembled some gigantic arrowhead—the point of which was aimed due west. As his was the first claim in the district, those who came later had been obliged to work around him. When the mapmakers came through in '55, trying to make sense of things, it was rumored that one had

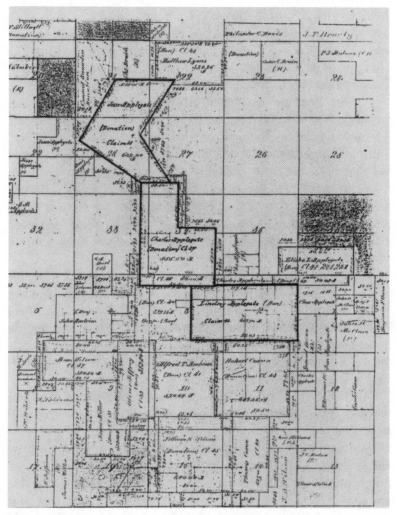

". . . it appeared that Jesse Applegate had 'let his arrow loose upon the land,' and it was a mighty big one, too." (Office of the County Clerk, Douglas County, Oregon)

laughed, saying that it appeared that Jesse Applegate had "let his arrow loose upon the land," and it was a mighty big one, too.

Several little brooks and springs meandered through Jesse's bottomlands, which were choice as far as growing things. Yet even these bountiful natural waterways did not find favor with their master. Over a period of time, he had pushed them into submission. More than one stream had been entirely rerouted from its "dilatory" way. Carefully, Jesse redirected them through the perfectly straight little ditches that crisscrossed his lower acreage.

A less exacting cultivator might have found himself any number of satisfactory garden spots, but not Jesse Applegate. Whenever possible, he commandeered an evacuated streambed, refilling it with rotten wood, straw, and dried brush. He always had plenty of the latter, as he was forever waging war upon the "immortal fern" and the other wild plants he considered obnoxious. He layered the old streambed according to a formula of his own devising, after which he mounded it over with "improved soil," which was so pungent with steer and chicken manure that it stung the nostrils of any bypasser.

People said they had never seen anyone go to so much trouble to grow vegetables and melons; yet even those who poked fun at his methods were forced to concede the results. No one could beat Jesse Applegate when it came to garden truck. In a bad year he alone managed to have a surplus, which meant, of course, that he got top dollar when he shipped his produce to the mines on his own freight wagons.

And apples? Why, he had successfully grafted varieties that had not yet occurred to other men. His vast orchard was so well kept that gophers and insects avoided it, taking up residence somewhere farther down the road. Or so it was said. Although he was a teetotaler, he made cider whose potency was celebrated for miles around. It alone would have provided a tolerable income had he not given it away. But then he could afford to be generous: Every apple he freighted to the mines was worth a pinch of gold dust upon arrival.

If he had a fault when it came to doing business, it was a tendency to extend credit to those who were not likely to repay him. This, however, was a fault his customers could live with. When a man wanted help in springing some new enterprise, he knew where to go. No, Jesse was not timid; he was a forward thinker, all right. He did his thinking with the best of them, too. More than one important "feller" sought him out and tried to shake him loose from his roost on Mount Yoncalla, but politics, especially with the Democratic bunch up in Salem running things, Jesse said, was not for him. He'd stay home and watch "the sod grow" and remain in the company of other Free-Soilers like himself. By which it was supposed he meant his brothers.

Politics: On that subject, the Applegate brothers were of like mind. It was an unfortunate man who tried to take them on. Together they were as formidable as a stout stone wall where even a piece of straw could not have found a chink.

Yet it had not escaped notice that the old triumvirate was not all that it had been in former times. One of their number had made himself scarce. Lindsay Applegate was out of the country more than he was in it.

Naturally, conjectures abounded, for the three brothers had been fixtures in the neighborhood since its earliest days, living side by side. Jesse kept mum on the subject. Anyone who asked Charley what Lindsay was up to was likely to be answered by no more than a shrug and maybe a remark about how he supposed that his brother was just off seeing the world. Lindsay, after all, had never been one to let on everything, nor was he much for writing letters.

But this much was generally known: After the southbound wagons known as "freighters" could be counted upon to bring flour through Yoncalla and to points beyond, Lindsay had closed his little gristmill. He had only operated it for the convenience of his neighbors, he said. Those who were considering growing grain for the mine market had tried without success to convince him to reopen it. But Lindsay declared he was finished with gristing for good and all. They'd be better off to take their business down to the town of Oakland, or Roseburg even. The new mills were bigger than his had been, and the millers were more interested in their work.

His oldest friends thought that Lindsay was acting like a man who had something on his mind, but then again it was characteristic of him to prefer to do things that kept him on the move. Work on the military road, a little surveying or bridge building when the opportunity presented itself, these stints seemed to enliven him and fit with his philosophy that a man ought to stay light on his feet. There was a prancing horse inside Lindsay Applegate, all right.

Then Charley had talked him into sheep. Lindsay invested heavily in a sizable flock. For a time he was seen in their neighborhood as much as in previous years. Still, this endeavor seemed halfhearted after a while, and Lindsay was heard to mutter that he didn't know whether to continue to shoot the eagles preying on his lambs or to shoot his whole damn flock and be done with it. He'd never had to spend so much time with animals so short on brains, he said.

It was not too long before they heard that Lindsay had left some of his sons to manage things at home whilst he took off with his oldest boy to find some more agreeable venture.

Several months passed before Lindsay returned. It was rumored that he had found himself a little toll road to buy and that neither of his brothers was happy about it. What his wife thought about the toll road no one knew. She had lost a little boy earlier that year, and people said she had more or less holed up at home, and that she was as low as she had been years before when she lost that other little boy who'd gone down in the Columbia River.

It was not hard to understand why Lindsay's family was not excited about the toll road. For one thing, it was situated atop the Siskiyou Mountains, so deep in southern Oregon that a man had but to crane his neck a little to peer into California. Thus it was ten days' hard traveling from Yoncalla, too far away to make family life easy.

Other people thought it peculiar that Lindsay had gone so far afield to spend his money. Further, the toll road's former owner had wanted a pretty penny and Lindsay was short on cash. But this had not dampened his enthusiasm. He had apparently decided that if his brothers did not recognize a good investment, he would find someone who did. For a while he made the rounds in Yoncalla talking up the toll road, which he claimed was already a going concern, for not only did the stage take the cutoff over the summit, but so did packers, freighters, and all manner of other travelers. New quartz leads had just been discovered near Jacksonville. Thus it looked like another mining boom. Southern Oregon would be bustling again, just like the border towns on the California side. It was the ideal time to invest in the southernmost localities, and he had found the perfect investment.

To those who inquired how Lindsay planned to oversee the toll road and keep his ranch in Yoncalla going, too, he responded that he intended to stay home after he had got his foothold on the mountain and had overseen a few little repairs on the road itself. His boys needed something to occupy themselves, he said, and as they were finally old enough to be useful, he would do his utmost to entertain them. In any case, there was work needed on the tollhouse, and of course there was the upkeep on the road. Further, his workers would stay out of marital trouble for a while longer, for they were not likely to be distracted. The country was high and wild, and female travelers few and far between.

Lindsay had said other things while going around trying to scare up money. When taken altogether, it sounded as though he were considering moving more than just his boys. Some opined that the fact was Lindsay Applegate was just plain sour on Yoncalla.

And it might be that he liked the mountains, where the air was clear and bright and had a little bite to it.

And it might be that his Yoncalla claim had too much bottomland to suit him and that the "wet" brought on congestion that would not leave him.

And it might be that Lindsay Applegate's feet itched something awful after the seventh year doing anything in any one place.

Those who knew him best put their money on the third "might." They were convinced it was just a matter of time before they would hear that Lindsay was selling out entirely.

The year 1859 had come and gone, and so had Lindsay Applegate more times than the seasons had turned. Poor old Charley. It seemed as if he was just too stubborn to read the signs. It was no-such-a-thing, Charley insisted. Lindsay was not foolish enough to throw everything over for some half-baked enterprise. While it was true that his brother more and more had been obliged to travel back and forth to see to his business on the mountain, it was only because Lindsay's boys could not induce certain "roughs" to pay the toll when their father was not there to back them up.

There were evidently other troubles, too, in the form of claim jumpers, desperadoes, and long-haired Democrats of dubious vocation. These formed the majority of Lindsay's so-called customers. But soon, Charley predicted, his brother would surely call a halt.

Lindsay Applegate. (Applegate family photograph. Courtesy Douglas County Museum)

Yes, he was bound to come home for good, and if they should hear rumors that Lindsay was selling something, it would be the g_____ d_____ toll road—or so it was hoped, and Charley was hoping.

Doubtless Lindsay's wife was hoping, too, for she and her children had passed a dreadful winter, suffering from an illness that resembled a regular old Missouri attack and the worst kind of Oregon pleurisy all mixed together.

Why, poor Betsy Applegate had been almost dead when Lindsay last arrived home. The women in the neighborhood who'd heard the story from Charley's older daughters avowed that Lindsay should have got down on his knees by her bedside right then and there and promised his family that he would never leave

Elizabeth "Betsy" Miller Applegate, wife of Lindsay, sister of Melinda
Miller Applegate. (Applegate family photograph. Courtesy Douglas
County Museum)

them again to fend for themselves. Yet what had he done instead?! Shortly after Betsy Applegate recovered and he at last tended to what had nearly gone to ruin around the place whilst he'd been away, he struck out anew for the Siskiyous. And taken another boy with him, too! And if Betsy thought he'd rushed off to wrap things up so he might hurry home to her again, she soon learned she was mistaken. Before six weeks were out, Lindsay wrote, advising her to begin packing. He could not abide another season with her struggling on, he said, and him worrying about how things were in Yoncalla. Logic suggested a solution! They would all live on the mountain together. Just as soon as the weather could be counted upon, he and some of the boys would come back to load up the wagons and head out. They would find a caretaker to stay on their Yoncalla place until more permanent arrangements could be made.

As far as anyone knew, there the matter rested. All Betsy had to look forward to, it seemed, was life on a lonely mountaintop, with her only neighbors maybe an Indian family on the next ridge over, not to mention a grizzly bear or two. Yes, it looked like it was "whither thou goest" all over again for Betsy Applegate, all right; and so saying, more than one woman looked hard at her husband, for there was a certain strain of restlessness more to be dreaded than the ague or the worst kind of pleurisy.

Many a husband agreed that it was a shame all around. Lindsay and his family would be sorely missed, they said solemnly to their wives. Such sentiments, once expressed, quickly passed away, however, for it came to certain men that as there could no longer be any doubt about Lindsay's intentions, there could be no harm in making certain inquiries. How much, they wondered, would Applegate want for his place? After all, if the stage company decided upon the route that cut through a portion of Lindsay's acreage, any man who succeeded in buying the place might soon find that what he'd bought was worth twice what he had paid for it with no improvements necessary. . . . Yet what if Charley had the same idea? Not on account of the stage route, of course, for Charley avowed he had no interest in it; but because his brother's property met his own south border, Charley might wish to keep things in the family and enlarge his holdings somewhat.

These were the very questions that were put to a number of

136

Charley's longtime associates, old compadres all. So a friendly little delegation was formed from their midst, and these men rode over to the big white house on a certain spring evening in 1860, in order to discover what was what and whether one man or another might profit from it.

If any neighborhood speculator had been waiting to make his move subsequent to that interview, he was disappointed, for the report was terse indeed. Some thought that the old compadres made poor emissaries. They seemed almost as closemouthed as they claimed Charley had been.

All that was relayed was this: While Charley had admitted that things looked bad, he insisted that Lindsay still had time to change his mind. In the meanwhile, Charley declared, the whole matter should be left alone. And, no, Charley had absolutely refused to entertain any more questions upon the topic, whereupon—according to his old compadres—Charley had put his big head down and commenced shaking it from side to side like some old bull ox resisting a new yoke—a sure sign, they said, that the subject was closed.

As to what other subjects might have extended the discussion so far into the night, no one was saying. Several wives had been overheard to complain about the lateness of the hour their husbands had returned. None laid the blame on libations, however, for their men had appeared as sober as preachers on the circuit when they arrived home, and twice as grim. When the women inquired whether something of import had happened over at the Applegates' or some unexpected problem arisen, not one of the old compadres owned up to anything. No wife, it seemed, had been taken into her husband's confidence.

In the weeks that followed, the new men in the vicinity noted that the old compadres were keeping strictly to themselves, unless of course some good Republican happened along, in which case that individual was taken aside and talked to earnestly. But these goings-on had only been witnessed from some distance, for whenever a good Democrat appeared it was as if Medusa's head had been displayed.

A Good Republican Calls on His Uncle Charley

June 1860

Their cousin Elisha had appeared unexpectedly. He reported that first he had stopped to see his own family and found them much agitated about the impending move. He had taken his supper there and his mother had consulted with him about one thing and another, especially upon the condition of the tollhouse, where she would soon find herself living. His younger brothers and sisters had pestered him with similar though more childish questions, and kept him up late. They had awakened him early the next morning with more of the same. After which he'd spent the better part of three hours tracking down a ram and an old ewe who had deserted her lambies. He'd got the ram back but not without a fight. Some of the Indians helped him. The ewe had expired, as it turned out; her bloated body was discovered in the abandoned millrace.

"Ah," he said, plucking at the bright thing in his pocket, "the mundane concerns of a rancher's life. Exhausting, too!"

Elisha then swiped at his brow with what was obviously a brand-new neckerchief, emblazoned with white stars upon a blue field. It had been given to him by a certain "patriotic miss," he said proudly, a regular Union maid, who dwelled in the fair city of Eugene. But after several questions regarding the identity of this 'Union maid,' he grinned mysteriously and announced that he was in an all-fired hurry.

Yet it did not seem so, for he lingered on the side porch with his little female cousins, who were shelling peas; and when they sighed, saying their task amounted to a mountain—for great was the green heap before them—Elisha squatted amiably beside them as if he had nothing better to do, tearing the seams off "neat" and inserting several "strays" into his mouth. All the while he spoke most entertainingly.

Harriet had been cutting out biscuits on the far side of the kitchen. She had not seen the rider or heard the gay greetings of her sisters. In truth, she had been "woolgathering," as her mother sometimes put it. She had been wandering with her thoughts. Yet,

Charles Applegate. (Applegate family photograph. Courtesy Douglas County Museum)

at length, the deep familiar voice penetrated. It took her a moment to identify its owner, whom she had not seen for some time. With her long apron on and her nose daubed with flour, she fairly flew through the door.

"Why, 'Lish!" she cried, "it's you!"

Elisha responded by standing up and saying, "Hark! The cook approacheth, for it can be no other judging by the flour on her nose!"

As the little girls giggled, he added, "Harriet! Why, you've grown tall and taller!"

Embarrassed, she quickly drew up her apron to hide from his gaze, which was most appraising indeed. At which point a cloud had arisen from the apron so thick and white she had sneezed twice. Then all laughed. Fanny's sharp little voice piping, "The mousie is out! The mousie is out."

When calm had been restored, Harriet was herself again. Her first act was to shake her finger at her cousin: Where had he been so long, with only one letter home to show for it, too? she demanded pertly. Shame on him.

Elisha's handsome face reddened slightly—for his pretty relative's charge was true. Doubtless Harriet was not the first to make him feel guilty on the subject. She sat down beside the pea shellers. All were now awaiting 'Lish's rejoinder, which, if they knew their cousin, was likely to be neither brief nor short on color.

He did not disappoint them.

In the first place, Elisha said, he had been a-traveling somewhat more than usual. He had been obliged to attend both the Democratic and Republican conventions on behalf of his newspaper. Old man Pengra, the owner of the *People's Press*, had sent him hither and thither. As to writing: Why, he'd written so much of late he supposed that he'd plumb written himself out. Of necessity, he'd become a veritable machine of prose, much to the distaste of the Democrats—he added with a decided air of importance—who were mightily displeased with him indeed. Nor were they happy when he intruded himself at their convention so that he might report the dubious manner in which they had conducted their affairs.

For the fact was, though the news might not hitherto have reached the remote hills and vales of Yoncalla, Elisha had acquired himself a reputation. Yes, he had become a well-known

Melinda Miller Applegate. (Applegate family photograph. Courtesy Douglas County Museum)

Republican of late. For that matter, he had played his part in getting the new party rolling, and had won many an old Whig over in the process. The ranks were swelling.

Nor had he restricted himself to needling the Democrats solely through the auspices of the newspaper, for though his pen was mighty, his voice was even mightier. Or so he'd been told.

To bring this point home, Elisha cleared his throat, his posture deliberately droll, his thumbs tucked under his suspenders, his voice ringing forth until all who were gathered on the porch laughed again so heartily that Harriet gasped and breathlessly begged him to desist.

When the oratorical blizzard finally ceased, Elisha seemed so stimulated by the warmth of his audience that he was inspired to go on. An incident had been brought to mind, he said, which might interest them further. Yes, he told them, seeing Harriet and her two pea shellers made him think of three other young ladies, who had not been nearly as pretty.

At this compliment, little Jane flushed so rosily her numerous freckles had given every appearance of fading away. But they soon returned. Her eyes were fastened upon Elisha as if he were one of the Seven Wonders.

After clearing his throat, 'Lish launched his story: It seemed that many months before, he had been invited to speak in Albany on the subject of slavery and its heinous economic effects. On the afternoon before the lecture, he was walking past the new courthouse, where he was to speak later that same evening. He stopped dead in his tracks. What had caught his eye was a large sign affixed to the billboard near the place. He was amazed to find himself standing before a crudely drawn caricature of sizable proportions. Above him loomed a depiction of a giant, perhaps eight feet tall—which, as it was woolly-headed and as black as soot save for a set of grotesque, staring eyes, he immediately took to be some Democrat's depiction of a Negro.

Beneath this poor black monster a caption had been written in letters very large indeed: THE GENTLEMAN WHO ADDRESSES YOU TONIGHT.

For some moments he stood there gazing up at the lugubrious Negro, who, it seemed, was intended to represent none other than Elisha's own personage. In the midst of his contemplation, three schoolgirls sallied by and—the black giant accosting their vision also—paused to ogle it.

He heard the first girl declare upon reading the caption: "Why, that ain't so. My father says he knows Elisha Applegate, and he's as white as I am."

The second girl, he was pleased to note, agreed with the first, for she added to his defense by saying, "Yes. My pappa is attending the lecture tonight and I heard him say that Mr. Applegate is an able white man, too!"

Before Elisha related the remarks of the third girl, he extended his neck to a haughty length, so there would be no mistake concerning the nature of the speaker. Lifting his voice as high as his nose, he said disdainfully, "Well, my goodness, what difference does it make whether he's white or no? My parents say all them abolitionists are amalgamationists and *do* want to marry 'niggers.' They're *horrid* people!

"Thus," 'Lish added, "you young Yoncalla damsels will now know something about your counterparts in the Willamette Valley, and that great moral courage is required upon the part of anyone who wishes to become and stay a Republican, for we are slandered and vilified at every turn. No, we are not popular 'fellers' in what we are now pleased to call our spanking new state of Oregon."

This said, he took his leave, for he was off to find their mother, whom he referred to as his "goodly" aunt Melinda. For 'Lish, as Harriet had so often noted, never liked to put things plain if there were the slightest possibility for embellishment.

Before his audience had the opportunity to comment upon his "yarn," Elisha returned to stand briefly in the kitchen doorway. He wondered whether anyone would be kind enough to hasten fieldward in search of their pappa? He had grave matters to discuss with his uncle Charley. Alas, his own visit was destined to be brief.

Whereupon, Harriet immediately dispatched Jane—or tried to. Giving her older sister a saucy look, Jane flounced off, her red braids swinging and not entirely because of hurrying, either. Well out of sight now, Jane spied her little brother Buck, who, she noted with irritation, "seemed to have nothing better to do than fritter away his time playing with little Milt by the creek." Exactly so did she put it to him; Harriet commanded him to go find Pappa quick as anything, for 'Lish was waiting, Jane said importantly.

She saw her brother take off over the pastures, Milt on his heels, struggling mightily to keep up. And the lie hadn't bothered her a bit, she thought; it had not bothered her very much at all. For she had had quite enough of Harriet's telling her to do this and do that. Besides, it doubtless had made Buck feel important, as 'Lish was a great favorite of his.

A lie didn't count—Jane told herself—when everything turned out right.

Nevertheless, the second lie had made it hard for Jane to look Harriet in the eye when the little girl returned to find her in the kitchen.

Buck had volunteered, Jane reported, her crossed fingers enveloped in the folds of her dress. To make up for stretching things, Jane promised herself a forfeit and made it good. Obediently she hauled forth yet another heaped-up wooden bowl, all the while wishing their mamma wasn't so set on having things fresh. Other mothers, she knew, left all their peas to dry upon the vines, pods and all.

When Jane saw her little sister Fanny wrinkle her nose at the new batch of peas and start to say something unpleasant, she said to her, bell-clear, "Now, Fanny, don't whine. Mamma wants them and we all have our jobs to do."

Harriet overheard Jane, as she was intended to. But if Harriet wondered at the reformed little redheaded worker commencing so very amiably to shell peas again, she did not say.

Jane, at least, was at peace with her conscience. She'd made up for things. Though it might have been nice if Harriet had complimented her some. Instead, Harriet wore a distracted look, which everyone complained was lately all too characteristic of her.

It wasn't long before Charley Applegate appeared in the yard. He was quite red of face. Even more so than usual. The mighty barrel that was his chest heaved. He'd ducked his head under the pump spout, cranking the pump handle as if exasperated. But when he stood up again, his look was jovial.

"I have risen," he said.

When 'Lish had arrived upon the scene, a great deal of manly shoulder thumping took place. If Elisha's shoulder bothered him, as it had off and on since his childhood, he showed no sign. Yet Harriet knew—for she'd heard her mother say it—that for all

Elisha's apparent robustness, his poor body had never wholly recovered from the beating it had taken when he was almost drowned in the cold Columbia. The currents had dashed him against the rocks again and again as he bravely swam for his life. Many bones had been broken and some had but improperly mended.

As Harriet watched her pappa and 'Lish, she recognized something special between the two men. 'Lish was more son than nephew. Now the uncle tugged at the bond, saying that of course Elisha would be staying for dinner. For doubtless all that was yanking him back to Eugene City so hurriedly was one pretty face or another; in which case, Charley said with a somewhat wicked leer, Elisha needed victuals to sustain him in whatever might lay ahead.

The inference had not been lost on Lucy, who upon hearing the activity on the porch had hastened outside. Lucy looked extremely disapproving, but Harriet was far more interested in Elisha's reply. He protested that it was duty that had brought him to Yoncalla, and 'twas duty, equally, that made time of the essence. For he had messages of import: matters he considered his uncle and every other good Republican in the district should know about. And even though Elisha's countenance had been suitably grave as he spoke, it was clear that the master of the house was not swayed.

Charley was adamant: If 'Lish had important news to pass along, it would be better heard on a full stomach. Thus sayeth the Lord.

Lucy appeared resigned to what she and Harriet must accomplish next. Already she was squinting, her one good eye darting about the kitchen and cupboards as if she might organize everything even as she stood still.

Harriet, however, was not resigned at all. She felt herself grow cross and crosser. There was no way around what now lay before them. Women and girls alike would be compelled to scurry in the hurry to get dinner ready. After short work had been made of the meal, and men and boys heard news which was bound to be more enlivening than any of the humdrum happenings of Yoncalla, those exiled in the hot kitchen would still face a stint of cleaning up. Half the afternoon would be gone and so would any chance for sociability. This, then, was Harriet's dread and in part explained her sour look.

Lucy, the eldest of all the Applegate daughters, was all business: They would need deer-tongue lettuce from the garden and watercress, which maybe Buck would gather near the creek. No, she would be better off to get it herself, Lucy murmured. And there were new potatoes to be dug up, which at least would not have to be peeled, which would save time. The peas, blessedly, were shelled . . . thin-sliced venison with gravy and the two spotted trout the hired man had caught that morning. Harriet could fry them, though Lucy would make the gravy and white sauce for the peas and potatoes herself. There was the leftover gold-dust pudding, which they might stretch with currants and nuts, though it wouldn't be quite right without more kidney suet. All the same, it would have to do. Their pappa would frown at the sight of dried-apple pie again, especially with 'Lish at the table, who deserved better fare. But the pie was already made, though Lucy supposed if Harriet wanted to, she might double up on the sourdough biscuits—in 'Lish's honor. To go with the biscuits there was quince jelly, and red currant preserves, which Harriet should have Jane get out of the pantry. Both varieties tasted especially good, Lucy commented as she paced about, that ought to keep 'Lish happy, as he always claimed to dote on them.

Harriet was dizzy. The rag between her legs was sticky. She felt a wreck. She wanted to go upstairs and right herself, yet she couldn't seem to get the words out. Lucy rolled on:

"Now, Harriet, you *must* be vigilant about biscuits this time. Keep your mind on your work. I'm going to see whether Irene is feeling well enough to come down and make the bacon dressing and chop the eggs, though you'll have the onions to do. The fumes aggravate Irene so."

She hated it. She hated it. If only Lucy would stop talking. If only they had known 'Lish was coming. If only their pappa had not come back from the fields earlier than usual, expecting dinner nevertheless. Never mind what it meant to those in the kitchen, he kept to no schedule save his own. . . . If only Lisbon had not fallen down again, which meant their mamma was now required to station herself by his downstairs bed lest he do harm to himself. . . . If only Jane were older and not so snippy, so that she could be more help. . . . If only Irene had not been in the middle of yet another one of her "sick spells."

Harriet took a long draught of cold water. Well, she could feel

147

her own headache coming on. Or almost. She had half a mind to kick the stove, too, even though they were all glad to have it . . . at long last.

Lucy had been quite oblivious to all this, of course. Harriet watched her doff her old hat and set out toward the garden. So intent was Lucy on her mission that she forgot about summoning Irene. Which was just as well, thought Harriet, her head now abuzz with Lucy's latest instructions. For it would not do to have Irene at her elbow, sighing over the cooking smells, her eyes baleful, her palm periodically pressed to her brow. Irene: the very epitome of martyrdom.

It was evident that Harriet was to struggle on alone. Thus the hour passed, full of nothing except her duties. Harriet dared not drift. Even so, when she remembered the biscuits, she was dismayed to find their bottoms overbrown.

Dinner, it turned out, passed pleasantly enough, though Harriet and Lucy hopped up and down so much 'Lish had called them regular Jacks-in-the-box. Engrossed in what lay before him, Elisha had little else to say. His uncle Charley, however, who had curtly refused the dried-apple pie, had gone on for some time about his new Merino lambs. Somehow this eventually led him to the subject of the toll road.

Harriet lingered for a moment, waiting to hear what her pappa might say next about her uncle Lindsay and, more important, what Elisha might say in defense of his own father in response. But nothing much came of it. 'Lish had merely nodded as the older man droned on. When Harriet saw him reach for yet another piece of pie, she decided to remove herself and boil the dishwater. She heard her father say that after the dessert he and Elisha would soon adjourn to the porch, which meant the serious talking would begin. Harriet's curiosity was as sharp as the old knife she used to slice the venison. She did not intend to miss a word if she could help it.

Irene had not appeared at dinner. Her messenger, little Jane, lisped that "'Rene's head was still a'throbbin'," but she might just try just "a little something"—whenever Harriet found the time to send up a tray.

Lucy was sitting with Lisbon so that their mamma might take dessert at the table.

The little girls traipsed back and forth, carrying the good willowware dishes.

So solemn were their expressions and sedate their cadence that Harriet was compelled to smile a little. Each had carefully stationed herself on either side of the heavy ironstone platter. The remains of the trout were gently laid to rest upon the counter. Harriet could see that her little sisters had heeded Lucy's warning—for she had told them she would skin them alive if anything whatever "got broke."

Lucy had followed the men to the porch, eavesdropping for a while, but when she returned she offered no report, only declaring how hot the kitchen was and how cool the porch. Standing over the steamy dishwater, Harriet could feel the dampness growing across her back. Yet other matters interested her more.

"Well, what do you suppose they're talking about?" Lucy had snorted. "Politics and more politics. And naturally, 'Lish's doings are at the center of it, according to him anyway. Though I'm sure working for that newspaper has brought him attention, I do wish he wasn't always so full of himself. Now Uncle Jesse has come by and the men are all out front. 'Lish is getting his second wind and says he may lay over after all."

After which, Lucy noted crossly that Harriet was not rinsing all the soap off the tableware. Lucy could see it. Her finger skidded down the surface of the big white platter. The leftovers had not been covered either; there were flies everywhere.

But after Lucy read the unhappiness upon her sister's face, she softened. If it made such a difference to Harriet, she might as well be the one to take out the coffee, Lucy said. Their pappa and 'Lish might stay out of the whiskey barrel a little longer—if Harriet were prompt.

And Lucy observed that her younger sister could be quite expeditious and even efficient, if the situation suited her.

It occurred to Harriet, not for the first time, that Lucy was awfully hard on 'Lish. As Harriet had grown older—and she felt much older than her mere fourteen and one half years—she had sometimes wondered whether Lucy mightn't just be a little jealous of 'Lish. Lucy and Elisha were the oldest children of all three Applegate families. Though they were not especially close any longer, they had been great chums as children. Lucy was thirty and so was 'Lish, or almost. Yet Elisha, despite his age and the slight portliness he had acquired after a year or two in town, still had liveliness and a boy's fun about him. It was said, too, that while a certain Miss Marshall had lately monopolized him up in Eugene City, several other ladies had made their interest in him known, in the event his interest in the demure Isabel should flag.

Lucy was another matter. She spurned all comers. When viewed from a distance, especially as she wielded her hoe, wearing her raggedy-edged old straw hat crookedly atop her head, Lucy might easily have passed for forty or even older. The only subjects that seemed to animate their eldest sister were her vegetables, her ducklings, or maybe the condition of her roses. She exhibited not the slightest curiosity about the numerous young strangers who passed so tantalizingly to and fro along the road. And never did she lift a book or bother to sew anything for herself that was not strictly "useful." Who knew how Lucy would end up?

"Old maid": But even as the hateful expression arose in Harriet's mind, she attempted to wipe it out. Nevertheless, it lingered for a moment as school words sometimes did upon her slate, though she might rub and rub.

No. "Old maid" was too harsh. The words were cruel. They put dear Lucy in a box that was, somehow, not entirely of her own making. For Harriet knew that no one, except their dear mother, worked harder than Lucy for their mutual good. And how would their poor mamma have survived all those years having baby after baby if it had not been for the steadfastness of her eldest? Lucy: upon whom they all depended; who always put others first.

And Harriet promised herself that she would never—not even secretly—inflict the words "old maid" upon her sister, for words had power.

It came to her, as she reached for the mugs upon the open shelf and then cranked the coffee beans so hard that they rattled in the grinder, that there, at the back of her thoughts, was another expression, one which Elisha had used earlier that afternoon—an appellation even more to be despised than "old maid."

Doubtless 'Lish had meant no harm. He only repeated the expression to add verisimilitude to his "yarn," she said to herself. Yet the little girls had been there, all eyes and ears. For what was Elisha? No less than the family hero. Some blame must be placed upon him, Harriet decided. He might have stopped and thought and put things differently. She herself had winced when she heard it.

Why, only the evening before she had encountered the same loathsome word. She had been reading aloud to her younger brothers and sisters; quite stirringly, too, she thought, for who would not find the words of Mrs. Stowe full of power and inspiration? Even a poor reader must of necessity rise to the occasion, so full of life seemed the voice of each character. But there had come that unfortunate little passage, and considering the age of her audience, Harriet had felt compelled to skip over it. The hated word it contained had seemed to jump out at her. Then Jane, who had been looking over her shoulder (for Jane claimed the book was never turned around long enough for her to get a good look at the illustrations) had piped up, "You've missed some words. Why, Harriet, you've left out two whole sentences—see." Whereupon Jane's pudgy finger had landed heavily on the passage in question. Had the word been a fly, she would have squashed it flat. Harriet had almost given her little sister a good pinch, but just then their mother passed through the room. Jane was bound to do it, it seemed. She had lisped out the words for all to hear: "'And he was dreadfully angry. The little *nigger* boys had thought it grand.'"

Harriet had tried to compose herself and told Jane and all of the children how they must never, never use that despicable word. It was common. It was an insult to those who were struggling in the very pages they were reading from. Yes, it was as bad as cursing. Worse even.

Then she'd read on, thinking the matter finished. She'd quite lost herself following Eliza over the icy floes: During the moments that ensued, it seemed to Harriet that her own shoes were gone; her stockings sliced from her feet by the hard, glittering edge of the winter river; the half-frozen baby boy whimpered in her tired arms as the hounds barked menacingly behind her, every desperate step marked by drops of her own blood.

Jane had appeared to be listening dutifully, yet it soon became clear the other matter was not forgotten. Why, Harriet had no sooner carefully inserted the little scrap of lace and closed the book, the marker dangling so limply as if it, too, were exhausted from the tragedies inflicted upon Uncle Tom and those who loved him, when she heard Jane say, her freckled face mischievous, "Harriet, if Mrs. Stowe *writes* the word, can we? Even if we can't speak it, I mean."

To which Harriet had replied coldly, though her cheeks were hot, "Jane, Mrs. Stowe is an author, and you are not. It is as I've already said, no decent person should let that ugly word pass through her lips and if I catch you writing it, nothing but the switch will do."

Even this threat had not prevented Jane from wondering aloud whether Harriet herself might sometime write the word n-i-g-g-e-r. After all, hadn't Harriet said she wanted to become an author? Giving Jane's bottom a quick little swat, Harriet had then dispatched the girls up to bed and sent the little boys to their pappa's room so they might say good night and trundle up their own private stairs.

Harriet thought of all this as she poured the coffee and readied the plank tray. If only Elisha had not used the word himself. Jane, at least, would be sure to bring it up all over again. For the fact was, and how well Harriet knew it, Jane took as much pleasure needling her sometimes as Elisha did his Democrats.

But these vexations faded. Already Harriet could hear the deep voices of the men as she moved slowly through the kitchen, the dining room, the little gun room, and finally into her father's lair, where the air was yet trailed with pipe smoke. She stood for a moment in the open doorway, balancing the burden she had welcomed and breathing in the pleasant aroma of coffee. The steaming mugs cast warmth and color upon her face. Or was it instead the heat of the afternoon? The pink of her own anticipation.

She felt all eyes upon her. She stepped carefully onto the porch, fearful of spills, of tripping over the catch in her unmended hem. Yet these things had not happened. Her honey hair tendriled charmingly around her ears, the rest coursing in waves all down her back. The restraining blue ribbon so indifferently tied earlier that morning had loosened from her exertions. She dipped again and again, offering her wares, trying to keep the tray steady as one or another of her "customers" spooned out sugar. Nor had she raised her own eyes, seeing only the big hands reaching forth as she made her rounds. How tall she felt. More awkward and long-waisted than Lucy even.

Yet she was as a child born on a Tuesday—yes, Tuesday's child, and, hence, full of grace. Everyone thought so, only Harriet did not know.

•   •   •

The previous year Elisha had declared himself a Seward man. Senator Seward, 'Lish claimed, was unquestionably the ablest and most conspicuous statesman of the Republican party and would make a fine president.

Yet all this changed. By his next visit to Yoncalla, Elisha had found Seward lacking and had shifted his support to a Missourian named Edward Bates. Several of Oregon's convention delegates, he told his uncles, intended to vote for Bates on the first ballot. This news was well received. From the outset, Bates had found favor with the older members of the three Applegate families, especially with Jesse Applegate.

Years before, Edward Bates had exerted a powerful influence on him. Jesse had once worked in the same building where Bates maintained his St. Louis law offices. Jesse had been but a struggling young surveyor then. So much interest did Edward Bates exhibit in the younger man's education that he had frequently lent him valuable books. Too, Bates deliberately initiated debates on the contents of these volumes. His own rigorous intellect liked to match wits with his protégé, especially on topics pertaining to the formation of the Republic. In this manner Bates did much to elevate a "backward youth," for so Jesse referred to himself whenever he reflected upon that period of his early life. So great was the esteem that Jesse conferred upon Mr. Bates that a child had been named in his honor. This boy was Harriet's cousin Edward Bates Applegate, whom she had never met, for he had died in the chill waters of the Columbia on the way to Oregon, as had little Warren, another cousin. Harriet could never think about these events without feeling tears well up, for these were the sufferings of her own family. In their way, they seemed as pitiable and dramatic as any of the sad circumstances Mrs. Stowe wrote about.

Thus while it yet appeared that Edward Bates might indeed receive the nomination for president from the Republican party, Harriet had felt very pleased. Justice, she thought, might at last be served in some small measure. Her aunt Cynthia and uncle Jesse had grieved for so long over their own lost son, and wouldn't it be wonderful, she said to her sisters, if the name Edward Bates would be remembered by every citizen? When Bates became president, the names of both the man and the little drowned boy would be uttered in the same breath.

Harriet's hopes were soon dashed, for one afternoon her uncle

Jesse had ridden over, bringing various newspapers. Bates's political star had fallen. A man named Abraham Lincoln had won the Republican nomination.

It was then that Harriet learned about an old-time family connection with this same "Mister" Lincoln, which so stirred her imagination that she had soon forgot about "poor Mister Bates."

Her uncle Jesse said that her uncle Lindsay had served with Lincoln in the Black Hawk War. This fact, though titillating, paled before the story she heard next, which was later confirmed and details added to by her uncle Lindsay himself. When next he returned from the Siskiyous and had called on them, Harriet hung on every word of his narrative, for Abraham Lincoln had become her especial hero.

Lindsay related that when he was a boy, he'd been sent off to stay awhile with a great-aunt—one Letitia Applegate, who had married a good Dutchman named Lanterman. The Lantermans lived in the Sangamon country of Illinois. Now, this aunt Lettie was a religious sort of a woman who could not abide either work or play on the Lord's Day. Even so, that hadn't much prevented the young people in her charge from having fun. . . . Here, her uncle Lindsay had paused, saying he would continue only if Harriet would fetch him another piece of her blackberry pie. She had obliged. It seemed there had been a tall older youth in the vicinity whom Aunt Lettie had claimed as some sort of shirttail relation. This fellow had come every now and again to entertain the younger boys. He arrived one Sunday and, on some pretense or another, managed to spirit away a group of youngsters, who were mighty pleased indeed to be away from the lectures and hawkeyed glare of Aunt Lettie for a while.

When some distance from the Lanterman farm, the boys commenced to hunting coon, for their pet hounds had accompanied them. In time, the dog pack treed some game in a big hollow oak, which had several broken limbs. Some had evidently voted in favor of cutting down the oak tree, but in the end the tree was preserved because, if left alone, it would continue to harbor other critters at some future time. Their leader, the older youth, suggested that the coons be "smudged" out. A fire was built at the base of the tree for that purpose.

When the smoke grew strong enough, three small heads had peeped down at the hunters, the ringed eyes wide, as though astonished at the cleverness of those below. That set up a big laugh. . . . It was at this point in the story that Lindsay Applegate himself had laughed, and this interruption was of such duration Harriet became a little impatient. . . . But eventually her uncle continued, saying how the older youth had then pretended to be stern with the hunters and shaken his finger at them. He declared in a credible imitation of that voice they had so often heard before: "Boys! We oughtn't to have such *levity* on the Lord's Day!!"

Yes, her uncle assured her, it had been none other: The older boy was Abraham Lincoln, all right, although he had been known simply as "Abe" in those days—a name, her uncle added, that was as homely as he was. And when Harriet had inquired whether *"Mister"* Lincoln's appearance had improved with age (for she refused to refer to her hero by so undistinguished a nickname as "Abe"), Uncle Lindsay replied that the passage of years had not done much to improve things. When he had seen Lincoln next it was during the campaign against Black Hawk's Indians. He had spent only a brief time with Lincoln; yet even so, they reminisced a little. Lincoln had seemed every bit as droll, honest, and forthright as he was formerly.

Her uncle Lindsay had then winked at her, saying that since these were the very qualities absent in most politicians, he supposed if they couldn't have Edward Bates, they might as well *all* become Lincoln men. Who knew? It might be—in the end—that Lincoln was the best man after all!

Charley Applegate had come over to Lincoln almost at once. Jesse, however, hesitated. Two years earlier, when Jesse had walked out of the state constitutional convention, he had declared disgustedly that politics was a mercenary and selfish game which he, henceforth, would eschew. For quite a while he had held himself aloof. His support of Edward Bates had been an endorsement of a most informal nature. Eventually, however, he had roused himself on behalf of Abraham Lincoln.

Too much was at stake, he told his family, for him to stand idly by. When the time was right he intended to go on the canvass up north, and if necessary would ride to every farmstead, regardless of how remote. In this manner he hoped he would convince those he called "loyal" Democrats that the indivisibility of the great Union of States had become more important than whether a man had a right to own slaves.

155

"The Union forever . . . severance never. . . ." These words had asserted themselves one morning while Harriet stood all alone in the dark coolness of the springhouse, where she'd been sent very early to bring back butter. As was so often the case, Harriet had commenced to dawdle. Instead of the plain serviceable mound she intended to lop off the larger round, Harriet spent some moments rather absently sculpting pale butter geese, roses, and other fanciful shapes. Meanwhile the rhyme reverberated in her mind. Yet the poem she was certain the words portended refused to arrive. In the end, she had tucked the phrase away for future use, much as her mother had put by the individually wrapped apples and pears whose heavy sweetness permeated the air inside the springhouse.

Harriet had been so lost in thought when she closed the little door that the flood of light which met her eyes quite stunned her. It was then that an image had come to her mind which was somehow related to the words. In her imagining a tall, dark manly figure held a lantern. So benevolent was this presence she knew it must be Lincoln. And the steady, blinding brightness emanating from his lantern was the light of the dear Union itself, she said to herself. It came to her that only Lincoln could show the way out of their troubles. Perhaps the words portended a picture she was to make, and not a poem at all.

The words "the Union forever, severance never" seemed to keep time with each step she took. She could almost hear them— only just then Lucy had come upon the porch, calling Harriet's name, and Harriet knew it was because Lucy was fretting about the butter, and the milking yet to be done.

After her father broke with the newly elected school board over political matters, it had come to pass that Harriet, like her cousin Gertrude across the valley, had found herself assigned to play professor at home. While this had had the advantage of excluding her from certain chores, Harriet sorely missed the daily companionship of her female school chums.

Thus only those girls who had regularly called on her that spring were privy to the story about her uncle Lindsay's old-time connection with *Abraham Lincoln*.

Charmed by the coon-hunting tale, Harriet's friends declared her most fortunate indeed to be so picturesquely connected to persons of importance. Unfortunately, Lucy overheard this remark and later accused Harriet of putting on airs and bragging.

The *real* braggarts in their neighborhood, Harriet insisted, were the supporters of Ol' Jo. Lane, Oregon's senator. These persons said awful things about Lincoln and the Union, too. No! Harriet said hotly, Lucy did not know what bragging was until she heard some of the daughters of turncoat Democrats right there in Yoncalla. At this, the unflappable Lucy had yawned, for truly she had grown quite tired of the subject of politics.

How dismayed Harriet was as she gradually learned that more of their neighbors than she'd ever imagined were not only Democrats but sympathizers with the South and the cause of slavery. But more shocking was the news that Senator Lane was an avowed secessionist, or so Elisha said. Under the guise of serving the people of Oregon, Lane had kept bad company in Washington with men who were southern slavocrats all. These men had liked nothing better than to have a prominent politician from the Far West "in their clutches."

Lane and his cronies had actually refused to support Stephen Douglas, their own party's presidential nominee. They, and other Democrats whom her pappa referred to as being of the "ultra" cast, had gone against what the people of Oregon wanted and broken away from the Democratic party in the process. Now, it was said, the new wing, which called itself the Southern Democrats, was about to hold its own national convention. These Democrats would nominate their candidates on a platform designed to undermine the Union of States.

This was what had the Democrats in the Applegates' neighborhood abuzz and smug. Lane was certain to be put up for the presidency of the United States, they claimed, and failing that, Lane would at the very least become the "second man"—the vice-president.

Harriet explained these matters to Lucy at some length until their mother had looked up from her quilting and said firmly, "That's quite enough, Harriet. I daresay Mr. Lincoln and Senator Lane will fight their own battles. What the schoolgirls in Yoncalla think about it won't make a whit of difference and bragging is bragging as far as that goes, no matter who does it."

The truth was, of course, that Harriet too had wished that she might take pride in the fact that a man from their very own state, whose family lived not thirty miles away, aspired to the highest office in the nation. Harriet's uncle Jesse had had many satisfactory associations with the "General," as Lane was then called. When Lane had been appointed Oregon's first governor, he had served the new territory well. As a child, whenever Harriet heard of Lane at all, she had heard only good. As she grew older, she had not thought much about Joseph Lane save to have the feeling he'd "always been there." A politician forever. Oregon's own.

People were saying that Joseph Lane was the better-known candidate, and better liked into the bargain. Joseph Lane would have his way, and so would the South!

It must not happen.

How Harriet wished to know more so she might better defend her "cause"; for "cause" it had become.

THE PORCH CONGRESS

It was no wonder that she attempted to linger after the coffee had gone round a second time. The porch congress was obviously well under way. No one could draw and quarter a man with words better than Elisha, and Harriet had the feeling he was just getting started on the subject of Ol' Jo. Lane. She was curious, too, about what her uncle Jesse might say. As she was about to sit down upon a chair on the far side of the porch, she heard her mother tapping on the window. Harriet was to go inside again. It was evidently her turn to watch Lisbon for a while.

Though Harriet had opened the west front door so that the voices of the men might still be overheard as she sat in her mother's room, this proved unsatisfactory. The geese in the side yard had commenced honking at intervals, and poor Lisbon moaned in his slumbers. Several times Harriet had been obliged to leave her listening post in the doorway so she could stroke her brother's head and murmur soothingly to him. Although Lisbon was twenty-three, a few years older than Harriet's sister Irene, his demeanor was exceedingly childlike. In sleep he looked as rosy as a boy.

When her mother finally returned, Harriet spoke up as brightly as Little Eva or some other obedient heroine. If only she might take her work out on the porch, Harriet said sweetly, she would be pleased to do some mending. To emphasize the utter necessity of the task, Harriet lifted the lid of the big mending basket, peering gravely at the contents therein.

All this, of course, had not fooled her mamma.

On more than one occasion her mother had wondered aloud how it was that Harriet might so minutely render a likeness of a person or a flower, yet be so slipshod when it came to plying needle and thread. Why, even little Jane could do better; nor did Jane complain, as Harriet always did.

This, alas, was perfectly true; Harriet had no use for what *Harper's* magazine called the "womanly arts." In moments of frankness Harriet confessed to her girlfriends that she would rather sketch than stitch or knit or—heaven help her—embroider, though sometimes she could be induced to draw intricate designs upon the borders of the pillow slips or hand towels that her sisters fashioned and fussed over.

159

Knowing her daughter's shortcoming, the mother did not immediately give consent. The following instructions were given in a
firm voice: Harriet must "stick to the socks," whose wearers would
not care how the stitches looked as long as the holes were gone.
So saying, she plucked several specimens out of the basket and
handed them over to Harriet, who upon receiving them sighed.
She dared not inhale, she said to herself, because a certain masculine odor could always be whiffed by any sensitive darner regardless of how numerous or stiff the launderings.

With the accoutrements necessary to her task stowed deeply in
her apron pockets, Harriet stole quietly onto the porch. The chair
closest to the railing on her mother's side was to be her station. A
moment passed before she was certain she had not drawn attention to herself. She wished particularly to avoid her pappa's notice. If she were spied by him, it was all too possible some errand
or other would be commissioned. She dared not look up. She was
like a child who, not seeing, believes that it remains unseen.

On any other afternoon Harriet could not have resisted gazing
out across the fields, for often she had sat in the selfsame spot,
wishing she could paint what her eyes beheld: the countless greens
and the endless undulance of the spring grasses; the lambent light
striping the neat lanes of the orchard just beyond; the fluffy clots
of grazing sheep, so white and blurred in the distant pastures they
seemed as clouds come to earth. Instead, she squinted intently at
the darning egg upon her lap until her poor neck felt quite cricked
indeed; for she wished to convey the impression, should her presence be eventually noted, that nothing save the sad condition of
her pappa's old wool sock was of the slightest interest to her.

It was soon obvious that a different mood had descended upon
the porch congress. Gone was Elisha's former animation. Some
subject of concern was evidently under consideration, for each
man's voice seemed grave and unnaturally low. Nor was the discussion fluent but, instead, ponderously slow, as if too heavy to
achieve momentum. All this might have been more bearable,
Harriet decided, if only she had known the subject at hand. There
was nothing for it but to sit very still.

At last relief came, or so it seemed at first, for she heard her
father snort impatiently and say, "Well, out with it then. You
have alluded to rumors. You have spoken of treason. But what are
the particulars? You have given us the hook without the fish."

But even this curious remark did not appear to hurry things along. Someone's fingers drummed softly upon the railing, her uncle Jesse's perhaps, for it was his voice which came next but only after a considerable pause.

And names were given, none of which were recognizable to Harriet, but certain men, Californians all, she heard her uncle say, were his "informants," and as if to buttress whatever else he intended, he spent some moments attesting to the staunch character of these individuals and providing other details—with her father and Elisha interjecting every now and then. Her uncle Jesse's voice, Harriet decided, was most unpleasant. Higher and less resonant than either Elisha's or her pappa's, it was further marred by peculiar and unexpected inflections. It seemed, too, that he was at an effort to speak even more quietly than usual.

Though Harriet had strained to overhear until her ears hummed with the effort, she was not rewarded. The tantalizing and fleeting words "rumor" and "treason" seemed lost. The warm drowse of the afternoon pressed down on her.

And that was why Harriet had risked a fast furtive look upward. So engrossed were the talkers a ruminant curtain seemed drawn around them. One look was followed by another, until at length Harriet succumbed to undisguised gazing. In this way, Harriet hoped to keep from dozing, for surely her eyes would entertain her until such time as the elusive topic might again leap out of the dreary thickets of her uncles' discourse.

Her pappa and Elisha were seated, their chairs situated on either side of her uncle Jesse, whose tall form stood between them in almost perfect triangulation.

Three: three manly and familiar figures. How benign was this little tableau to Harriet. Her eyes saw it. Her heart took it in. So it had always been. The love which resounded in the depths of her childhood memories coursed steadily forward. She had never had the need to think of it, only to feel it. Three. They were there.

It was an entirely satisfying composition, she decided, and the extremes of light lent it drama. Such was the very stuff depicted in the lithographs she had sighed over in *Harper's*, or else in some old book. Two figures in the dusky shade, the third illumined in a portal of unbroken light, as if to emphasize his importance.

Only now an apprehension tugged a little, even as Harriet admired the alternating rays of sun and pillar-shadow that played

Departure. Little Milton cries as the Lindsay Applegates leave Yoncalla in the summer of 1860, bound for the tollhouse in Siskiyou Summit, their new home. (Susan Applegate painting. Photograph courtesy Douglas County Museum)

across the length of the porch, as though deliberately directing her eyes to those convened at its easternmost verge.

A realization saddened Harriet—it was Elisha who took his father's spot in the old triumvirate that afternoon. More and more Lindsay Applegate had pulled away from Yoncalla life. And soon others near and dear to her, she knew, would follow him to the remote and lofty summit of the Siskiyous. Dear Theresa, dear Oliver, and Ivan and Lucien and little Frank and Ann. Aunt Betsy most of all. Her cousin Jesse A. had long since left the valleys of his youth, as had Elisha. Her family had already been divided by the knife of distance. Even so, to see her aunt and uncle's home lived in by others . . . Ashland seemed so far away. Briefly, these thoughts tormented Harriet, but she told herself that she must not dwell upon such matters. She dared not, lest her eyes become as full as her heart. She felt her worries pass, quick and dark, as she molded herself to the present moment. The men droned on; her eyes became her pencil as she gave her uncle Jesse a long, appraising look. How unfortunate it was that what Elisha often referred to as the "nobility" of their uncle's mind was no-where manifested in his appearance.

Jesse Applegate's head, she noted, so full of ideas, seemed no larger than that of a half-grown boy's, especially perched atop such a lengthy and loose-boned body. Often, at closer range, Harriet had wondered how she might render her uncle's face. His brow— as Mrs. Stowe and others were wont to put it—was extremely beetled; and the same gray-wired hair that overhung his eyes grew in a profuse thatch kept so uncommonly short that it looked as if he had hurriedly shorn his head with the sheep clippers, without the counsel of a looking glass, much less his wife's. His nose was distinctly hooked. This feature was not of itself particularly displeasing. Indeed, Harriet had had the occasion to draw just such a nose, for it could be found on numerous of her male cousins. But in her uncle's case she thought—and almost laughed aloud on account of it—the size of his face made it seem that a big beak had been fastened on a very small bird indeed.

But by far the worst were his ears. How grateful were his daughters not to have inherited them. The ears themselves were long-lobed and defiant as well, so adamantly did they refuse to lie flat. Even at a distance they attracted notice, nor did he ever bother to clip the renegade hairs sprouting therein. Yet might not an artist reduce their size a little for posterity's sake, Harriet mused, since how unflattering the portrait if rendered true. It would not do. . . .

Her survey was at last interrupted, for her own ears bade her attend. Her uncle employed a new tone, to convey anger or pain she could not decide. His bony fingers flexed. Now the spear was flung. "It is Joseph Lane who has helped hatch this plan."

Whereupon her father uttered an ugly oath and Elisha expelled a great breath as though putting out a candle.

Black was Jesse Applegate's look. Blacker still was the scheme he now revealed to them, until the fair hand which held the darning needle trembled with the knowledge, for what was at stake was nothing less than the dear Union itself.

But in the end Harriet's father said it best, his voice thick with distress: "Oh, how can this be? How can Ol' Joseph have sunk so low?"

WADING IN BLOOD UP TO THEIR KNEES

Let us glance quickly about the room where Harriet sat that June evening after her uncle and cousin had ridden away, each in his own direction: The west front room bore an aspect of the purest homeliness; the brightly laden quilting frame dangled from the ceiling like a happy banner in lantern light; the cast-iron kettle, as yet unfilled, hung on its hook over the hearth; the simple furnishings were all in their customary positions, except for the narrow bed, which temporarily occupied a quiet corner of the big room.

All was in readiness according to the hour—around the single rocking chair had been arranged a crescent of low wooden stools suitable to the size of those who would soon sit upon them, for the nightly reading was about to commence.

Harriet surveyed the room. "Come here, children," she said with a weariness that was mixed with crossness.

Buck brought the book. Night, now fully descended, was filled with the patter of a gentle rain that could be heard from within.

"I don't care if it was June today, it's March tonight," Irene said peevishly. "Since Pappa has a fire on his side, I don't know why *we* can't!"

With this declaration, the reading was delayed. Buck protested because it was his duty to get the wood and set the fire.

"Never mind, Buck, we won't begin without you," Harriet said consolingly. But since she did not feel what her older sister called the "dankness of the room," her own irritation grew, especially as Jane and Fanny mounted yet another protest, beginning to bicker noisily about who should sit closest to her.

This flurry caused Harriet to look anxiously at Lisbon. She had no wish to disturb the invalid. Her older brother seemed perfectly calm, and even listless, as he lay propped against his pillows. During his recent attack he had broken several bones. An angel fallen, he. But now he rested. It was as though his poor mind had taken pity on him and had led him away to some country that was altogether more peaceable.

Harriet sighed. Then she shushed the little girls for her own sake, and bade Milt to sit in the coveted spot, which was nearest her and in closest proximity to the hearth. Thus little Milt would soon be warmed by a good story and a cheery blaze as well.

165

Keeping her promise, she waited, the unopened book upon her lap, her look pensive and distracted, her fingers plucking nervously at the marker.

After some moments the first exuberant crackle resounded in the room and Buck slid gratefully onto "his" little stool. He liked nothing better than to gaze upward at his favorite sister. Harriet's sweet face, lively eyes, and expressive voice always perfectly conveyed the mood of the characters she spoke for. Buck, she treated with especial tenderness, even letting him use her precious drawing pencil at times. After her drawing he liked her reading best. He waited for her to begin, looking rapt and holding on to his knees.

But this was an evening when Harriet's heart was not in it. Even as she opened the book she feared that Mrs. Stowe, vivid and engrossing as she was, would not have the power to lift her out of the doldrums where she had resided since afternoon.

How appropriate were the first words to meet Harriet's eyes. It was almost as if Mrs. Stowe had known exactly what weighed upon the mind of her reader in faraway Oregon: "Chapter IX" . . . and then, in bold capitals, the words that introduced the topic "IN WHICH IT APPEARS THAT A SENATOR IS BUT A MAN."

These words suddenly seemed shaded with a new and unexpected significance. Harriet had read *Uncle Tom's Cabin* several times. She knew full well that Mrs. Stowe was referring to a kindly gentleman—Senator Bird of Ohio. Even so, the image of quite another senator arose in Harriet's mind. This visage was far from kindly; indeed, it seemed as if Senator Joseph Lane now cast the ominous shadow of his intentions upon the very pages in front of her.

Oh, how Harriet wished she might blurt out all that she had overheard that afternoon, for her need was great. Yet she knew, and how lonely the knowledge, that she must keep her unhappy silence. For how could she speak of what her ears had not been intended to overhear?

Often, when troubled, Harriet had sought out her mother—a ready and sympathetic listener. But Harriet sensed that she must now eschew any childish need for comfort. That afternoon, in the somber wood called Maturity, Harriet had glimpsed a tangle of motives and schemes that quite literally stretched over her poor head. What she'd overheard was not the stuff of some novel but a tragedy of real life. How upsetting was the knowledge that a once good man might seek to overthrow the very things he had promised to uphold, and in the process jeopardize his fellows. And this he had not even done in the light of day but covertly, in concert with a skulking group of men who would doubtless spread their calumny even to the remote reaches of her own neighborhood. She could not bear it.

Yet she must, for the woman Harriet was soon to become felt compelled to keep a secret: Had she not heard her uncle say that all he had relayed must be held in closest confidence? Only the most loyal Republican men in their district would be privy to the knowledge upon which their fate might ultimately depend.

Before she chanced to hear serious men speak worriedly of serious things, the child in Harriet, so eternally curious, had been delighted and even thrilled by any thread that connected the lives of herself and her kin to a larger world. Until that afternoon, Harriet's imagination had waxed shinily, if not deeply, on events more complicated than she knew, until she had all but covered them with a patina of sentiment. Now the child grew fearful.

Poor Harriet. She felt quite sick, she realized. And tired. To the dismay of the gathered children, she shut the book. It lay upon her lap. There was nothing for it save to press Irene into service.

"Why, Harriet, I've not felt good all day long. You know that," her sister protested. Nevertheless, Irene reluctantly came forward and, after settling herself upon the rocker, allowed that she simply could not read aloud—for her eyes bothered her so— but she might just muster one little story.

Harriet's skirts, full and frayed, whispered upward. The stairs she climbed were narrow and steep. The candle in her hand hissed and gave but a faint and wavering light. If she fancied that once in her bed she would feel safe and sound, she was mistaken.

But what had the power so to unnerve our girl upstairs? What deeds did her uncle and other thoughtful men suspect were being plotted by Senator Lane and certain of his cronies?

The hook has been provided, now comes the fish: It was a grandiose scheme. Had it succeeded, Harriet, and all who called Oregon their home, would have known it by a different name. Oregon, California, and Washington were to be joined together, forming an entity which would henceforth be known as the Pacific Coast Republic. As such, it was to be forever severed from the great Union of States.

The sponsors of this treason, who it was rumored had held countless clandestine meetings, had played fast and loose with the word "republic"; not in the least would this so-called republic resemble the species so near and dear to the hearts of America's founding fathers.

Their "republic" better reflected the oligarchies of the ancient Venetians, for it was exactly that form of government which had inspired certain of the conspirators. In reality, what they wished to establish was an empire which, while providing for an elected executive, deposited all real power in the hands of a hereditary nobility.

These self-appointed nobles, of course, would in no account stoop to common labor. For this purpose, a servile class was to be procured in the form of imported Negro slaves, South Sea Islanders, and Chinese "coolies," the latter already being present in abundant numbers, especially in California. And Indians, too, would be taken from their recently acquired reservations and trained instead for menial tasks; for why should Indians be allowed their own lands and a privileged status that set them above other colored folk?

With the principles of universal suffrage so cavalierly discarded, so too would disappear the real equality of most white persons living within the new "republic's" boundaries. The majority would occupy the middle or even the lower rungs of society. Without representation, their lives would be dictated by the decisions of a chosen few. How abhorrent must this proposition have seemed to self-reliant men such as Jesse Applegate and other independent thinkers who valued their liberties.

This, then, encapsulates the principal characteristics of the so-called republic as it was envisioned by certain California extremists in the year 1860. Yet it must not be imagined these persons were merely malcontents on the fringes of their society. Some wielded great political and pecuniary power.

One Senator Gwin—every inch a slavocrat and an avowed supporter of the would-be secessionists—was said to be the principal architect of the plan. And with Gwin's name was linked that of Joseph Lane. Not only was Ol' Jo. reported to be a friend and colleague of the senator from California, Lane had also become the darling of the radical wing of the national Democratic party, whose members openly spoke of secession in the event their cause was ignored. In not-so-secret conclaves these men who were Ol' Jo.'s cronies discussed the formation of a string of far-flung "republics," which would extend from the Gulf Coast to the Pacific, and would become sympathetic partners in the event of war. While this new party had, as even Harriet knew, been ready to offer Lane the position of first or second man, none seriously imagined a national election would be won. They planned instead for other contingencies, with powerful sympathizers like Joseph Lane doing their bidding openly or secretly. This was especially crucial in the westernmost verge of the continent, with its trove of gold.

War: Harriet had not truly grasped this possibility. Nor did she understand the bitterness of many Californians and Oregonians who had long considered that the millions of dollars' worth of gold dust pouring into the federal coffers in the form of taxes, duties, and customs were bringing them little good. Where was the great railroad connecting East and West so long promised them? When would wealth be distributed in the very region where it was produced? And was this wealth—their wealth—to be turned upon the southern states by being transformed into guns, powder, and armaments in the event the secessionists so exercised their right and the Union seek to punish them?

Never! Already those of southern extraction residing on the Pacific Coast knew they would not be party to such fratricide—for so they considered it.

What, thoughtful men asked, was the way out of this terrible dilemma? How could any loyal Oregon men feel secure? Whether he lost or won, Ol' Jo.'s influence at home would doubtless remain. For lo, his countless supporters, especially in southern Oregon, would follow him to the ends of the earth, to the end of the Union. And who knew? perhaps to the founding shore of a Pacific Coast Republic as well.

This last was of the deepest concern. Jesse Applegate's California informants had spoken too of the secret societies, which, they claimed, were not only springing up in their own state but in portions of Oregon as well. With sinister picturesqueness these societies called themselves the "Knights of the Golden Circle." Initially they had taken their name from the so-called golden circle of the Caribbean, for there were many who believed that Cuba must be taken over, its wealth and strategic value fastened to the interests of the South. The avowed purpose of all the societies was to support the southern cause. So widespread were these groups that they were already well established in many border states, including Ohio.

To join, a secret oath was required. Reportedly, it declared that an initiate's body was to be severed in four parts if he betrayed his "brothers"; and in some "castles"—for so the groups referred to themselves—it was vowed that each adherent would wade in blood up to his knees and would not sleep or rest in the event Lincoln were elected, until he were removed from the presidential chair one way or another.

It was no wonder that Harriet quaked inwardly and could not seem to get warm no matter how high she piled the quilts. What a curse, ofttimes, is a vivid imagination. She had scarcely closed her eyes when it seemed as if boatload after boatload of colored persons were arriving. Her mind had even conjured the heavy chains that linked them, and these chains rattled upon the groaning decks. Or was it the groans of the miserable chattels themselves? Orientals, soft brown Sandwich Islanders, and Indians; but in Harriet's nightmarish vision, it was the poor Negroes she saw the most clearly. They were the saddest of all.

Now, queer to say, Harriet herself had never seen a Negro, for Oregon's laws had long excluded them. Even so, it was claimed that a certain Mr. Eads, whom Harriet had met once or twice, was half Negro. He lived on Thief Creek and was occasionally employed as a farmhand by Mr. Wilson—an old family friend. But Mr. Wilson was very close-mouthed concerning Eads's background. Even Wilson's daughters, who were Harriet's especial confidantes, could shed no light upon the mystery, though like Harriet they speculated that Mr. Eads was a runaway slave whose coloring was pale enough to let him "pass." More interesting to Harriet was the full-blooded Negro who was reported to work as a barber in Roseburg. Though Harriet had longed to see him, the occasion had never presented itself. Even so, she felt great empathy for the Negro, for her father had predicted the barber would soon be run off or worse. Roseburg, after all, was Jo. Lane's homeground—and so full of slavocrats that the elder Applegates had lately avoided the place.

What the poor barber thought he might accomplish in such a place she did not know. He was a freeman, or so he claimed. For Harriet, the figure of the barber merged with that of George Harris, the father of Eliza's baby, in *Uncle Tom's Cabin*. In the whole dark and troubled race which now populated her distress she seemed to see variants of Uncle Tom, Cassy, Topsy, and Sambo. Mrs. Stowe had made them real for her. As Harriet tossed upon her bed, they clutched the rails of her nightmarish vision. Their heavy chains seemed to drag across her heart.

Oh, how she ached for that black tide of humanity. For if the designers of the Pacific Coast Republic had their hideous way, the groaning boatloads of persons of color would dock even in little Scottsburg, where evil men would auction off flesh to the farmers of the Umpqua.

No, it must never happen. Good men would surely prevent it. This conviction so gripped her that she had roused herself and sat bolt upright. Whereupon she'd risen, for Nature, the Great Interrupter, not infrequently calls us down from the most lofty pinnacles of thought. Whereupon the blue and white chamber pot was snatched from the gloomy recess beneath the bed.

"Wading in blood up to their knees." The words of the disgusting vow made by those who called themselves the Knights of the Golden Circle came back to her as Harriet carefully replaced the rag between her legs and tied her "drawer" string. Her own blood, alas, had stained her waters, which meant she must immediately dispose of the evidence, for Harriet's little sisters did not yet know what it meant to turn into a woman.

So our girl padded unhappily toward the balcony door, cradling the chamber pot and its womanly contents under her arm, whilst her free hand maneuvered the lock and latch.

She had no sooner succeeded in this endeavor and felt the cool air upon her face when she was startled by a sound as distinct as the distant beating of a drum. Beyond and below could be heard the rhythmic thud of horses' hooves approaching nearer and nearer until where the road curved toward the house their imperative prance shattered the surface of the low puddles.

Who were these riders come so late in the dank and moonless night? It was no wonder Harriet's heart beat wildly for a moment. Her head was still thick with ominous dreams.

Yet despite her tremors, her curiosity ran even deeper. After the chamber pot was silently laid down, she glided onto the balcony. There was no upstairs light to give her away. A pillar further shielded her from view. Her hands felt of the chill wood. Her socked feet were quite damp now.

How spectral seemed the approaching horsemen. Mists hovered over the fields. They cut stealthily closer, as if to catch her household unawares. No command could be heard. Four men. Five. Now the horses were silently tethered.

Then she heard her father open his downstairs door, his voice deep and wary: "Who goes there!!"

Came a rejoinder in the form of a low manly laugh and the words "It's Wilson, Charley! And some other callers—old compadres all!"

The presence of these good Republicans was as a cool cloth applied to a feverish brow. Even the sound of several sets of boots thumping upon the porch steps and, thence, into her father's lair brought comfort. Harriet could easily envision the familiar aspect of those who flanked either side of the glowing hearth downstairs, her pappa's big chair in the middle.

And surely these were the very men—loyal and reliable—whom her uncle Jesse had intended should be alerted. Mr. Wilson and the rest *were* old compadres all. Her father would entrust them with the knowledge. Together, they would press their broad shoulders against treachery's wheels and shove treason out of Oregon. So Harriet told herself as she shut the door. The loyal men of the Umpqua would never go down without a fight: No schemer would deprive good men of their liberties even if it meant . . . and a shudder passed over Harriet. This was followed by a thought so engrossing that she was oblivious to the creak of the downstairs door opening again and her father's noisy ministrations at the spigot of his whiskey barrel. For the first time Harriet permitted herself to dwell upon the unthinkable: war. And there were loyal men everywhere.

This knowledge filled her up so that she stood straight and unafraid in the darkness as a new rain droned without.

She had need of a lamp, but in the end she settled for her candle and wrote hurriedly, a torrent of words streaming forth under its wavering light.

How glad she was for the little lap desk she kept upstairs, the homely scraps of paper, the inkpot, and the new steel quill she'd purchased when last the peddler came through.

She sped. She flew. Later she would go back. Go forward, she commanded her mind and fingers.

And before her sleepy sisters had trundled up the stairs, the thing was done, bringing her release and happy tears:

May the Union Stand Forever
—1860—

May our Union stand forever
And down with the traitor hand
That once in wrath shall try to sever
That holy heaven blest hand.

May our Union stand forever
May our states be parted never
Woe to the hand that dares to sever
The ties that bind our once blest land.

    Though the trump' of war is sounding
    We will onward to the fight
    Hearts of bravery abounding
    Our Name shall yet be bright.
There'll be many a night of sorrow
Many a day of bloody horror
We'll be led by freedom's light
Though we may yet be near the battle
And ere many days are gone
We may hear the cannon's rattle
And the dying soldier's groan
Though these clouds of battle o'er us
And the gloom of death before us
We've freedom's star there to cheer us
We'll not disgrace our *Oregon.*

Sighing, she paused, signing her name. Not the plain Harriet her parents had bestowed upon her, but something better, worthy of the poem: Miss Harriette Applegate. Daughter of Oregon.

173

WE MEET A MELODEON'S PRETTY OWNER

June 1861

A year has passed: How easily this simple declaration slips upon the page, for so may any author pluck time out of reality, choosing but one apple to turn in hand, while other apples are left to dangle. Yet so it must be, for a book is not the world.

Yes. A year has passed . . . it is another June, as ripe with promise and pain as was its predecessor. But now we are in a different part of the valley, a place equally soft and green, which is somewhat west by a mile or two from Harriet and her family's residence.

The house of Jesse Applegate is but newly made, set prettily against the southern slope of a rather singular-appearing hill. This hill is both high and round. Some call it "Old Baldy," but those who love it know it by a more stately name, Mount Yoncalla.

The handsome structure, so close to the mountain's grassy bosom, boasts no balcony, yet it is a fine house just the same. On this spring day, numerous windows in the upper parlor have been flung wide so that music, reedy, sweet, and tinged with melancholy, drifts out and down, attracting the attention of a lone figure toiling in the garden. The assiduous scratching of the hoe has stopped for a moment. As the gardener looks down at the fresh-turned earth, the sound of the old hymn is still fingering his heart.

Death has but recently touched this place. Only a fortnight ago a grown daughter had passed quietly away in a sunny upper room, the bed encircled by many who loved her, just as her mother had enfolded her in a last embrace.

Rozelle Applegate Putnam had been brought home to die as the dread consumption made its final inroads. She was not yet thirty years old.

Thus in a little meadow behind the house, near the neat lanes of the apple orchards, may now be seen several of Rozelle's orphans playing and picnicking, with several of their young uncles and aunts looking on.

The eighth orphan, a toddler, nestles in his grandmammy's

A sketch of Jesse Applegate as remembered by his nephew George "Buck" Applegate. Self-conscious about his appearance, Jesse Applegate refused to have his photograph taken. (Original in collection of Oregon Historical Society. Photograph courtesy Douglas County Museum)

arms, his little face impressed with an expression older than his years. Not faraway is a low knoll crowned by drooping firs. Here lies this poor babe's mamma, the grave yet mounded with the dried remains of once bright bouquets and wreaths purple-flowered, fashioned from the wild vine known as the sweetpea. These offerings were gathered by Harriet Applegate, her sisters, and other sad maidens to serve an even sadder purpose.

Cynthia Parker Applegate, wife of Jesse Applegate. (Applegate family photograph. Courtesy Douglas County Museum)

Yet among all those relatives and neighbors too numerous to name, who cried unabashedly at the simple service on the knoll, it was the father, Jesse Applegate, who was the saddest of all. It is he who now resolutely drags his hoe across the earth again.

However, it is, just as Mrs. E.D.E.N. Southworth has put it, whose writings are much admired by the young woman playing the melodeon upstairs:

Sweet and beautiful and lovely as is the deathbed of a Christian, we will not linger too long beside it.

The melodeon, which occupies an airy corner of the well-appointed parlor, like the house it graces is brand-new. The best that could be obtained, this melodeon has journeyed round the Horn by clipper ship and thus has seen far more of the world than the moody musician who, whether out of sorrow or boredom, has just laid her hands upon her lap.

Made in an East Coast manufacturing center, the melodeon is but one of the objects in this attractive room that are products from some distant shore. Surrounding the young woman are several exquisitely patterned Brussels carpets and a splendid panel of French mirrors. There are as well many interesting clocks in this home, but one of the most charming specimens occupies a special niche in this parlor, where it is shown to advantage. Made in Hamburg by Old World craftsmen, this clock has delicate hands, which encircle a gleaming face resplendent with handpainted roses and pansies of every shade.

Jesse Applegate has taken great care in selecting these and other furnishings. His tastes are somewhat more cosmopolitan than either of his brothers'. Though Charley is in reality the most well-to-do of the three, for the time being, Jesse's numerous enterprises would seem to be on the way to making him a most wealthy man indeed. He likes the finer things, especially those which, like the clock, have been carefully wrought in places "a-way-far-off."

Places a-way-far-off: ofttimes the melodeon's owner—for it was bought especially for her pleasure—has dreamed of such places. Yet Gertrude—that is her name—has lately longed, not for the cities of the Old World, but instead for a bustling, largish settlement in her own state that is some one hundred miles north of her family home.

An ocean or two might as well intervene, she thinks, for her father will have her home from now on. How fleeting was her excursion into the wider world, where she attended an upper-level school. The parties, the outings, the cultivated company—or what passed for it in Oregon—now seems forever out of reach.

And Salem, the capital, where laws are made, and a lady might obtain decent millinery! How Gertrude languishes for that place in particular. Yet, in truth, it is not the stimulus of politics that pulls at her heart, for, unlike her cousin Harriet, she has no deep interest in such things. Instead, she sighs after one who practices the law—a charmingly brash young man whom she has met sometime back at a party given by a girlfriend.

About this liaison—and oh how ill-fated it is—little will be said at present save that the whole business has been kept secret.

As to why Gertrude, the epitome of downcastness, now stares out the window, we will be charitable and assume she is not preoccupied with her own troubles but instead with mourning. Surely Gertrude's dark deer eyes are brimming with sisterly sorrow. Poor Rozelle. She will brighten the world nevermore.

Rozelle: Jesse Applegate's much-beloved firstborn. Even though she was a daughter, her father did not mind. He had doted on her and tutored her in all manner of things from her earliest years.

Yet despite her tutoring, Rozelle's eloquence came from deep within, as was amply demonstrated in her personal correspondence, some of which has but recently been returned to her family. These letters, tied with a blood-red ribbon, will doubtless bring a bittersweet pleasure to any who linger over them in days to come.

Bright and independent, Rozelle had married a struggling young printer named Charles Putnam. This Charley Putnam was the same young man who had helped her father blaze the southern route in 1846. Rozelle had made it a point to be a constant companion to her husband, helping him set type and otherwise assisting him in the printshop. Even when the children began to arrive and Charley headed for the mines, she remained close to her husband in spirit—a wife who knew the meaning of her vows.

Yet never did Rozelle forsake her father. She and her husband came with him, leaving the Willamette settlements to live at the lonely base of Mount Yoncalla even before her uncles and their

179

families arrived. The surrounding valleys in those days had been remote indeed, and for a while the simplest necessities had been denied to her.

Later, when she and Putnam had taken their own claim some fifteen miles distant from Yoncalla, and when even more babes had been born, one after the other, she maintained her close relationship to her parents, for always she was an example of the purest filial devotion.

It is no wonder that in these weeks following her passing, Jesse Applegate has often found the need to dab his eyes. His manly heart constricts each time he sees one or the other of the sweet-faced orphans who are now assigned to his care.

And Gertrude? On her comely shoulders has fallen the mantle of eldest daughter. Prior to the sad event, Gertrude had felt one of the youngest, with several older brothers catering to her every whim. The fact is that for most of her eighteen years, Gertrude has had naught but her own needs to think of. The care of four younger siblings has never much taxed her, since Gertrude's mother has always been healthy and capable. In plain words, "Gert," as she is known, is somewhat spoiled.

But now the youthful ranks have burgeoned. Eight little orphans have been added who have need of many things. Thus Gertrude's father has recently declared that she must devote herself to others and put her fine education to use. Her Lord, has given long enough and now he wants something in return: She can teach at home if she wishes, but a schoolmarm she will be, and perhaps a cook, too.

Stern his words, and unbending his manner. Nevertheless, Jesse Applegate has his soft side, hence the new melodeon.

Torn between her duties and her heart's desires, Gertrude does her best. But if Rozelle was naturally as placid and deep as a mountain lake, this cannot be said of Gertrude. Great is her struggle to be all her father wishes her to be. Yes, Gert wants to be good. She is sensitive, too, and knows full well how her pappa misses his firstborn.

But the sad truth is that each and every human family is as a constellation in the firmament, which, whether clustered or farflung, contains both brighter and lesser lights. When one star dies, pity the others, for they may never fill the darkened place, no matter how hard they try.

A MOST SINGULAR HOUSEGUEST

Now something must be told of a certain room downstairs in Gertrude's house, which is her father's study. The mate to the Hamburg clock in the upper parlor reigns here; upon its face march colorful depictions of the royalty seen on playing cards. The chimes do not tinkle musically, but are bold and imperative, so they may be heard in virtually any quarter of the lower floor.

Other furnishings, too, impart an intensely masculine atmosphere to this master's den—for indeed this is what it is. The walls are lined with books. Multicolored maps, both large and small, are everywhere pinned up. Over the surface of the big desk and library tables drift papers and periodicals of every description. More of the same may be seen littering the floor, especially at the base of the largest of the two oversized leather chairs.

The tall windows in this room are numerous though narrow. The desk faces east so that the owner of the room while doing his paperwork may, without inconvenience to himself, gaze through the window, which affords a fine view of the Big Road beyond, as well as of the short branch road that leads toward his own premises.

Since Gertrude's father does not relish his duties as a storekeeper, he prefers this scholarly outpost, where he may remain until the last possible moment; not until he sees his customer reach the second gate is he obliged to rouse himself and walk the short distance to his place of business. If he is not in his garden, or orchards, or woodcutting "up the mountain," he will surely be found at his desk in ordinary times.

But these are not ordinary times. For several weeks Jesse Applegate has hardly lifted a pen, even though he is a faithful correspondent to at least a dozen influential persons both near and far.

Volumes concerning ancient history, horticulture, geography, and astronomy lie open here and there, but of late they have only been glanced at; nor has their owner made notes upon these works or on other subjects of interest as is his usual practice.

His calculations tracing the transit of Venus, for example, were almost completed before Rozelle was brought home to die. These papers are now buried under other papers, and the new telescope, which stands upon a tripod near the largest window, is both dusty and unadjusted.

181

Yet we would be wrong to assume that this unusual state of affairs is solely the result of a daughter's death and a father's grief. In no event will he permit himself to drown in his sorrows.

Something, nevertheless, has had the power to steer him from the familiar course of his intellectual pursuits. The reason may be found in this room: Against the western wall there is a somber-colored couch, which is not immediately noticeable from the doorway. A long, fully dressed figure reclines upon it—boots and all. The leonine head is elevated somewhat; the eyes are closed. The corpselike aspect of this supine presence is dispelled only by the sound of breathing; yet so heavily and deeply does this sleeper sleep, it is doubtful that melodeon, clock chime, or even gunshot would have the power to disturb him.

On closer inspection, it may be seen that this gentleman, who is perhaps sixty years of age, has a well-made broadcloth coat draped over his shoulders. His linen shirt is worn loose and is but partially buttoned. Around his chest and over one shoulder has been wrapped a wide dressing, which covers two wounds.

These wounds are the result of a single pistol shot: The first marks the entrance of the pistol ball just beneath the heart, and the second marks the spot where the ball was removed by a local doctor from behind the left shoulder blade. Though these wounds are now ten days old, the patient must still occasionally resort to pain-killers. The tincture of opium the physician brought by has been eschewed, however. The patient prefers a more manly potion. So a tumbler of whiskey sits half empty upon the low table beside the couch.

Now Jesse Applegate has quietly entered his study and stands at the foot of the couch for a moment, apparently contemplating the condition of this most singular houseguest. For almost a week every comfort has been provided that is within the family's means.

On several occasions Jesse has found himself staring at his sleeping visitor with as much fixity and fascination as a child might direct toward a campfire or the passage of some crawling thing: Who could have foreseen such a turn of events? There upon the couch of a good Republican had landed an arch-Democrat—the man whose admirers in better days had called the "Marion of Oregon" and the "Andrew Jackson of the Far West." General, governor, senator—these are the dignified titles that have been conferred upon the sleeper in his lifetime. Yet how weak and dispirited seems the wintry-haired figure who now coughs roughly in his slumber. It seems that the senator is but a man.

His host stoops to lightly swat a fly, which has landed on the senator's care-lined forehead. Compassion may be detected. Indeed, who would not pity Joseph Lane a little? Of his last acrimonious months in the United States Senate something must now be relayed:

As has been said elsewhere, Joseph or Jo. (for we will henceforth refer to Lane by the familiar name Jesse Applegate uses when conversing with him) had never really expected to win his bid for the vice-presidency. In the end, he had had the honor—if "honor" it may be called—of running and losing, as well as helping split his own national party. But Joseph had gladly gone down with his fellow "ultras," and during his last days in the Senate, he had given the rousing speeches that caused one of his colleagues to remark that the senator from Oregon was more southern than the South itself.

Enemies Jo. had made aplenty. Fearful that those states which had lately seceded from the Union would not be respectfully recognized, Joseph had hastened preparations for his journey back to Oregon. As he packed, he had been filled with foreboding. Lincoln would surely march upon the secessionists at any moment. Jo. had refused to attend the inauguration, for he viewed the new president not only with distaste but with alarm.

Oh, how Ancient Joseph wished to distance himself from any potential conflict. Regardless of what his detractors said, he had no heart for war. He left a son back east—a lively youth who stayed with an old family friend by the name of Jefferson Davis. Gratefully, Jo. boarded a sailing vessel bound for the distant western shore, where the very name of the waters meant peace. Doubtless he breathed deep.

His personal effects were safely stowed belowdecks. Among the odd-lot pieces of luggage and trunks were several stout wooden crates whose presence would soon bring him much trouble.

Joseph has not seen fit to disclose either the nature of his thoughts or his intentions as he made his long voyage home. Jesse Applegate is still left with unanswered questions. Had Jo. left for home with the express intent of implementing certain plans concerning Oregon's withdrawal from the Union? Had he been ready to commit treasonable acts or to encourage such acts overtly or covertly on the part of others? And when his sailing vessel reached the Bay of San Francisco, had he conferred with California schemers while awaiting the steamer that would take him north to Oregon? Last but not least, for whom were Jo.'s stout crates really destined?

Not a day has passed without Joseph Lane protesting his innocence as concerns these and other matters. Jesse Applegate has listened most carefully, drawing his own conclusions, which he has thus far kept strictly to himself.

Joseph has been glad for a "willing ear," for he feels much wronged: It is the newspapers who are to blame, he insists, the "scavenger press" of Oregon, which printed unfounded rumors and scurrilous lies that even his staunchest supporters had grown to believe after a while.

And this, he says, was quite enough for a loyal man to face as his steamer arrived home. Even so, given half a chance he might have swayed his detractors and rekindled the affection of his supporters, as he had done on countless other occasions, for it had not been the first time he'd thought to drown in political waters.

Destiny, however, had denied him any opportunity to transform an unpleasant homecoming into a semblance of the hero's welcome to which he had been accustomed in happier days.

Poor Ol' Joseph. It is perfectly true that the timing of his arrival could not have been worse. No sooner had he found himself and all his personal effects upon the Oregon docks when the steamship's captain announced the momentous news he'd kept secret all the way from San Francisco.

Oh, how all who were gathered had hushed and shuddered in unison. "Fort Sumter," the captain said, "has been fired upon by the Carolinian secessionists. If we are not at war already we soon will be."

After this announcement Joseph noted an angry hum. There stood Oregon's most eminent espouser of the Southern Cause, calling vainly for a drayman to take him and his personal effects to the hotel.

How humiliating it had been when several men boldly refused him. Why should they aid an *old* secessionist?! they taunted. Besides, shouted one particularly threatening-looking individual, what did the "General" have in those stout wooden crates? Rifles? With which to supply the Knights and other Copperheads? Let Ol'

Jo. find his own way down to the Umpqua country, they jeered, he was not in the "secesh"-sympathizing sewers of southern Oregon, but in the stronghold of Union men, where no honest man would provide a wagon to haul him home.

Eventually, however, an Irishman quietly came forward and this fellow had immediately been hired. And oh what a miserable journey it had turned out to be. Men he had known for years snubbed him as he passed through their communities. Many who had been vociferous supporters of states' rights behaved as if nothing save the Union's desires mattered, even if it meant that a gallant and chivalrous people must be struck harshly down.

When he passed through the villages dotting the Willamette, schoolchildren pelted him with eggs or called him names as their parents cheered them on. In one formerly hospitable community, he awakened to see an effigy swinging from a tree visible from his hotel window. Humiliation had been heaped upon humiliation all the rest of the way home, and Joseph has outlined each one to his host. Was a man to betray his conscience and principles? Joseph sometimes asks in a tormented voice. Was he to turn against his own kind? The South and its institutions had been bred into his very bones.

He and Jesse Applegate have talked long and deeply, each espousing his own beliefs, each trying to find the place where the other might bend. By mutual agreement the two men have always spoken in private. Thus no one has overheard these debates, not even the Black Republican's good wife, who regularly pads in and out bringing victuals and pitchers of cool spring water. Now she is entering the room, prepared to exchange old bandages for new.

Cynthia Applegate is surprised to see her husband standing so quietly at the foot of the Roman couch. Jesse turns toward her and, glowering a little, raises a finger to his lips: Let the sleeper sleep. And to this end Jesse Applegate follows the sprightly steps of his wife and carefully shuts the door behind them.

Here, as the sleeper sighs—for though his brain has bidden him to turn for comfort's sake, his shoulder has signaled otherwise—certain facts must be relayed.

Thus far, several important questions have remained unanswered: Principal of these is whose hand inflicted these wounds upon poor Joseph? Did some miscreant—such as an infuriated Union man—hide behind a roadside boulder, waiting to lay Jo.

low? This is but one of the numerous theories that have found adherents in this district. Naturally, the population is abuzz. Back-east happenings and even the news of troops gathering have been eclipsed temporarily, for there is something to "chew on" much closer to home.

Many have been dissatisfied with the simple and somewhat improbable tale that Ol' Jo. himself has told, which Jesse Applegate has dutifully related to a certain Salem newspaper correspondent:

It seems that no miscreant may be blamed for the shooting, for it is Joseph's own hand that has pulled the trigger. And with his own pistol, too! The story goes that after traveling all day and passing into the northern reaches of the Umpqua country, Joseph and his Irish teamster had grown much fatigued. When they were nearing the home of Jesse Applegate's nearest neighbor—a Mr. Snowden—it came to Joseph he might arrange for a night's lodging there. This done, Joseph returned to the wagon where he was helping the teamster unload the luggage. At this point, Joseph's pistol somehow fell from where he was carrying it and immediately discharged upon hitting the ground. The result of this mischance was the wound in his left breast. The Irish teamster, who was the only eyewitness to the accident, attempted to run away lest he himself be blamed. Fortunately, an unnamed passerby arrived moments later. He carefully loaded Joseph into a wagon borrowed for the purpose and drove him five miles back up the road to the home of a Mr. John C. Drain. After Joseph's wounds were tended by Mr. Drain and a local doctor, word was sent to his family in Roseburg that Joseph intended to remain at Drain's place until sufficiently recovered to travel home.

When it was inquired as to why the senator has instead ended up here, in Jesse Applegate's study, this answer was given: A few days after the episode Jesse and his sons had ridden over to John Drain's and extended an invitation. The senator accepted. To this terse report Jesse has added only that he would have come sooner had there not been a death in the family.

Still, people are saying, there must be something more to this affair. John Drain is the principal secesh in the whole vicinity and a good friend to other secessionists. Thus many wonder why Joseph has forsaken the household of such a doting admirer and accepted Jesse's invitation. Applegate's home is an unlikely sanctuary, to say the least.

Further, it has not been explained why a man who the doctor has admitted was bleeding profusely nevertheless permitted himself to be hauled a dangerous distance up a long and rutted road. Why hadn't the Snowdens taken him in instead? They might easily have sent for the same doctor.

Some are wondering, too, whether Joseph was carrying his pistol in the usual manner. If so, how had he managed to drop it so easily? Even if his gun had fallen upon a rock or a wagon tire, causing the hammer to strike hard enough so that the trigger was engaged, it was hard to imagine how the pistol could take such neat aim in the process. No, it seemed entirely too peculiar "an accident" for an experienced old soldier like the "Marion of Oregon"! Lane surely shared the habit of any good military man. For safety's sake the pistol hammer was always kept deliberately down with an empty chamber beneath it. This precaution made an "accidental" firing almost impossible.

How tantalizing are these speculations!

Oh, what certain individuals would give to interview the wounded lion in Applegate's den.

And if it is true that the stout boxes he has shipped home from Washington contain Sharpe's rifles—where are the rifles now? Some are concerned that the rifles were taken to John Drain's place.

These same individuals have offered their own explanation concerning Joseph's troubles. The "General"—they say—never made it to the Snowdens' at all, but instead was waylaid at the dark curve just before the road forked between the Snowdens' and the Applegates'. Beleaguered as he had been all the way to the Umpqua country, he certainly would have balked at anyone who tried to pull him over. Yet what if someone had demanded the right to search Ol' Jo.'s luggage? Even Joseph's detractors admit that he is stouthearted and when cornered, as touchy as a fighting cock.

"Nay!" he would have shouted. And if pressed further, Joseph would have drawn his pistol and stood ready to deliver. A scuffle might have then ensued. Who knew whose hand actually pulled the trigger? In the end the result was the same: Upon the ground lay one of the most famous men in all of Oregon. And if—as the saying went—the hottest heads were Copperheads, wouldn't a mortally wounded Joseph Lane make a fine rallying point for those who wished to further divide public sentiment in Oregon for their own ends?

It is no wonder, say these theorists, that Jesse Applegate hastened to John Drain's and spirited away the King Bee before his "workers" could take it in their heads to swarm. Let Ol' Jess calm things down. If the right words are said in the right spirit—they believe—maybe Joseph will go home a wiser man, content to live out his retirement peaceably. And in the event Joseph should become truly repentant—for now that Fort Sumter has been attacked, even he must concede that it is not Lincoln who has brought matters to a head—perhaps the Pacific Republicans and other traitors will no longer find a friend in him.

One thing, at least, is certain: If Lincoln has need of Oregon's troops so that short work might be made of the seceding states, the Union's cause will not be served if men are fighting among themselves in the western states. Thus farsighted Yoncalla men are saying: Let Oregon's old fathers alone so that they can try to patch things up.

And let Oregon's old mothers comfort them in the process. Just as Cynthia Applegate does now. Carefully balancing her tray, she has reentered the room. Softly she calls the name of Senator Lane, whereupon the supine figure on the Roman couch gradually shudders into wakefulness. The white head raises up.

Yes, it is as close to Carolina stew as she can come. "And there's a saucer full of chard and mustard greens, too," she is saying.

The big napkin is pulled away and a hearty fragrance wafts from the blue and white bowl. This aroma of greens and scallions is, in its way, as pungent as the whiff of barn manure which the little breeze has carried into the room. One of the tall windows has just been opened. The patient smiles and declares it "bracing." In a moment Ancient Joseph will lift his spoon like a happy boy.

Surely, it is the innermost desire of every human heart to envelop itself in harmony and restorative peace. The older the heart, it seems, the greater the need.

Yet the young languish in the prospect of too much calm. They prefer what wildly beats. They cannot help themselves. Nature drives them to it. It is their lot to stir things up and their elders' lot to live through it.

THE AFRICAN AIR PLANT

Two painful partings await us up ahead, but let us delay a little. Instead of grief or history, we shall devote ourselves to love, or at least to the sort of *Love* which is experienced by the young.

This *Love* we are speaking of is rather like the exotic growth known to inhabit the tropical reaches of the subcontinents. Its characteristics are queer indeed. It flourishes impossibly high up; it has no need whatever for even the slightest nourishment from the soil and, as a consequence, does not establish roots. Commonly it affixes itself to the most unlikely and unexpected objects—a wind-swept and barren rock, for example, or some remote stony lintel upon a ruined temple. As for feeding itself, it merely inhales its requirements from the atmosphere.

It produces nothing save the continuation of itself. It gives nothing, only a brief green exuberance. Even if forcibly removed from its home environment the plant continues to survive, and will exist in unhospitable surroundings without accommodation of any sort for months or even years. And when it expires it gives no sign before times; it dies as mysteriously as it has lived.

Harriet and Gertrude would have enjoyed the preceding. Such analogies were the lifeblood of their favorite novelists.

The mothers of Harriet and Gertrude, Melinda and Cynthia Applegate, grew impatient with such stuff. They considered that the young were entirely too given over to romanticism. What did any mother care for the "rootless" *Love* that occupied the impossible heights of their daughters' imaginations? What mothers hoped for, and what seemed to elude their comely daughters, was Sensible Love; a love of Duration and Consequence. This sort of love was not easily obtained in those years. The countryside was rife with unsuitable suitors.

Here, history will briefly insinuate itself.

What the discovery of gold hath spawned! From 1849 onward bachelors of every description and point-of-origin poured into Oregon. Lured away from more humdrum destinies, they had determined to stay in the West.

Some drifted up the Big Road from the mines of California. Others arrived later from the southernmost parts of the territory— for territory it was until 1859—on the heels of numerous smaller

189

"rushes." Whenever they had come, few of these young miners boasted pokes full of nuggets or dust. Most brought only resourcefulness and loneliness, hoping to pause for a while at one or another of the farflung farmhouses that studded either side of the main wagon route between Eugene City and Jacksonville. And as the middle-aged farmer's wife responded to the knock upon her door, perhaps glowering a little, even the most principled young stranger was not beyond hanging his head if he felt it might soften her up! Thus his demeanor, if not his words, conveyed the impression of that most pitiful of creatures: THE HOMELESS BOY.

What matron, who was herself perhaps the mother of grown sons, could resist the subsequent look of entreaty, the shower of compliments, the gusto with which a "plain ol' cup of coffee" was drunk and a slab of her berry cobbler devoured? And oh how indispensable became these grateful youths: No task was too large or small.

Many of Oregon's mothers had only themselves to blame for their daughters' troubles. Into their houses slipped the fox, his way made easy by the grease of flattery.

Yet Oregon's fathers must not be overlooked. They too shared the blame: If his farm was large, and his sons too young, too few, or off on farms of their own, Pappa was inclined to take advantage of any so-called volunteer appearing at his door. Let the young drifter "look" all he wanted, reasoned Pappa, and flatter every female in the household, too. As long as the "volunteer" continued to put his back into his labors, a farmer could tolerate almost anything.

Some of these young drifters were quite cunning indeed. Quietly they commenced to "courtin'" in the most *serious* way with neither Pappa nor Mamma wise to it. Alas, Oregon had been full of sweet and trusting maidens in those years.

"I shall return," swore the departing swain, whose restlessness had bested him again.

"I shall wait," promised the object of his unscrupulous desires. And so she did, sometimes forever.

But this situation, however painful, was preferable to another, wherein the drifter had his marriage vows forced upon him for reasons as old as time itself. Such ill-founded alliances and their little "issues" were all too common in the rural localities. A son-in-law acquired in such a manner often showed interest in one task only: that of milking his father-in-law's pockets.

Many a harebrained business enterprise was begun as a result, for Pappa was usually willing to do almost anything if it meant his home might again be peaceful and his daughters' needs off his conscience.

Such troubles had not yet been visited upon Jesse or Charley Applegate, however. They were pappas who considered themselves vigilant. Jesse's single son-in-law, Charley Putnam, had seemed more "son," especially as time passed. After Rozelle's death, Putnam, as much as his eight motherless young ones, made Jesse Applegate's his home.

Of Jesse's four remaining daughters only Gertrude had reached marriageable age. Yet Gertrude, her father noted, seemed to hold herself aloof from neighborhood and wandering swain alike. If Jesse ever wondered why his doe-eyed and stately daughter appeared to eschew the entanglements so common to her age and sex he kept it to himself. In any event, he was a busy man. He had no need to tolerate young drifters: He had strapping sons of his own.

Charley's case, however, was somewhat different. In the beginning he'd been blessed with more daughters than sons. Though Lucy, his eldest, yet remained at home, he'd married off the next three oldest girls. In each case he'd been in no hurry, however. His pearls would not be cast willy-nilly among the swine, he said. That he had himself wooed his wife when she was but fourteen made no difference. His own daughters, he declared, would reach the ripe age of twenty before marrying. As for the pleasures of "courting" without responsibility, more than one lovestruck aspirant had been run off Charley's place. Some few who had respectfully pressed their suit for month after month, imagining that they might eventually pass muster, were disappointed. Charley liked nothing better than to pick a fight with them. Thus, down the road they'd go, almost as teary-eyed as those who gazed from the windows after them.

It should be said that two of Charley's sons-in-law had themselves been gold-seekers; yet there their resemblance to that other breed of drifter so common in the early '60s, and despised by Charley, stopped.

George Burt and J. W. P. Huntington had arrived at Charley's doors in the 1850s, asking for work and a place to lay over. A pair of Connecticut Yankees, they were not only "Whiggish" in their politics but industrious. They'd voyaged to the Pacific Coast with a group of Masonic lodge brothers. A stint in the mines had actually lined their pockets. After they'd worked for Charley awhile, they'd bought their own places. Charley hadn't minded in the least when after long and careful courtships Ellen and Mary had married them. Even better was the fact that they'd moved to nearby farms, so that now and again Charley might prevail on them for help.

But where were the young men of substance "nowadays"? Charley and other fathers of comely daughters were heard to lament. For the '60s brought dreamers and get-rich-quickers. These sojourners, barely past their teens, showed untimely signs of dissipation; their hands were often tremulant, their complexions sallow, their eyes hooded and dull; unless, of course, someone declared, "How about a cardgame, boys!" or, "Let's have a jolt!"

Public-mindedness? They had none. Old-time patriotism? They knew not the meaning of it. And when the subject of what some were calling "Mr. Lincoln's War" came up, there was a certain sort of insolent character who, when interrogated by his elders, freely admitted that he was "mighty pleased" to find himself in the Far West, where a man could do as he d———d well wanted. And if at some point Honest Abe should take a notion to call for Oregon volunteers—said these same young men—he'd be disappointed to find many so peaceably disposed. Picking apples, or even a louse off a comrade, was preferable to picking up an army rifle.

These "peace-at-any-price-boys" were derided by the loyal men of Yoncalla. Many a staunch Democrat, too, was similarly offended. No, their party and even their principles had not prevailed. Nor had their own man been elected. Despite this, the Union deserved their allegiance—they said—such was the responsibility of any son of the Revolution, by which they meant of course the war their fathers had fought.

Many of the "peace men," however, proclaimed themselves indifferent to the cause of Unionists and secessionists alike. Because it was believed that their indifference would ultimately abet the South, these men were ignominiously referred to as "Coppertails," the hind part of that symbol of Dixie, the copperhead. That a representative from either end of that infamous serpent should have slithered into the home of any good Union man was unthinkable. Nevertheless, though many a door was firmly shut, certain hearts were open.

NEVER DID HE LAY HIS FIDDLE DOWN

There is, perhaps, nothing so alluringly alive as the gentle throb of a young woman's pulse witnessed unexpectedly after she has exerted herself. It may be that she has in all innocence pulled back her dress collar a little to fan herself, or that a sudden breeze has done the same. If she is fair-complexioned the merest glimpse of the speckled rosiness that is her heated flesh can cause the most jaded man to catch his breath.

The gaudily half-clad belle of the town, mining camp, or road-house, who has indiscriminately displayed her most sacred parts to drunken, yearning men of every sort, is no real match for an authentic beauty of the rural localities.

This surely occurred to the dark young man who watched the object of his desires lifting the ladle again and again. The bright faces of the waiting children before her were as sun-drenched hollyhocks, all in a row.

He stood quietly by, content to remain unnoticed. Indeed, he savored the moment, for it is the way of lovers sometimes to delight in observing each other unawares—to appreciate the familiar anew, as a stranger might.

Thus he watched her and put away his lust. How pure she appeared in her pale summer dress. She was a pillar of light amidst the cool and somber gray-green of the oaks. Graciously she reigned over the low makeshift table from whence she dispensed refreshments to her little subjects.

But by degrees his pleasure in the spectacle slipped away. Her very kindliness, the gentle remarks so sweetly given to each and every one of the small persons arriving before her, disturbed him. The young woman was, herself, not quite sixteen. Even so, before his eyes he saw her transformed into that most empathetic aspect of her gender: that of Mother.

He could not help himself. He imagined her long tapered fingers smoothing his hair, her soft palm pressed against his brow, or brushing his cheek with so much love he felt it sing all down his spine and his whole being buoyed up. And these sensations—for they were not thoughts—made him feel what he had not felt for years. All his life he had been bereft of tenderness, neither giving it nor receiving it. Such feelings were almost as remote to him as the ocean-edged Nova Scotian village of his childhood. But even as a brand-new babe comprehends the nearness of his nurturer though his milky eyes do not yet see her, and knows equally when she has left him to fend for himself, so did he now recognize his lack.

Here came yet another child. He saw the hand of the young queen mother ruffle the boy's hair. His own body—nay, his very soul—was filled with longing, which was all the more unbearable because it would *never* be assuaged.

Some instinct bade him step out of that shadowy Oregon grove. He did not advance toward her; yet suddenly he had need for her to know. He was there.

Scented and sultry, the air of Independence Day trembled over the blanket-dotted meadow where a satisfied people lounged and laughed, full of fellowship, cake, and roasted beef. The breeze was languid against his cheek, smelling faintly of mint and flowering clover. When the air grew still, a musty aroma rich with life and death arose from the moss-rocked waters where the creek grew low.

Earlier that afternoon there had been the smell of horses everywhere. When all the races had been run for a while, there had lingered the odor of man-sweat, too. The crowd, composed of Indians and whites, had been considerable, and none had taken either win or loss calmly.

His own clothes were saturated with smoke. How could he help it? He had been assigned to be tender of the fires: Master of the Roasted Beef.

This meant that he and his helpers had dug pits, set in the sidepoles, and erected spits for several days, along with choosing the choicest steers and preparing the carcasses. He had found himself up half the night as well, for if his offerings were to be enjoyed by afternoon the cooking must be well under way by morning.

His eyes appeared as if he had wept without stint. In truth, their sanguine tint could be blamed upon the combination of overlate hours and too much smoke and water—or at least too much of that variety of *fire* water that is found in jugs on festive occasions.

Before posting himself in the grove so that he might "spy" on his beloved, he had given some thought to his appearance. His comrades yet congregated in the vicinity of the horse corral, but he had taken himself "up the creek a ways," headed for the place where boys of middle size often frolicked and swam.

The bend was obscured by a curtain of willows. No soul save his own was there. He shaved his lean face, taking special care around his jaw, which was squarish and somewhat oversized. He felt of it with his big hands. It was to be a "blind man's" shave, as he had no fancy mirror like certain San Francisco "gents" he'd known. He then gave himself a good dunking. A half-breed woman had once shown him a plant called "Indian soap." It grew profusely along the creek. He plucked generously of it and rubbed its blossoms hard until a little foam appeared. He scrubbed and scrubbed as if he might not only remove the stains of his labors but of a life lived too hard.

On his way back to the meadow he had passed a steamy marsh where redwing blackbirds dipped amidst the sawtoothed grass and cattails. Farther on appeared a spectacle even more pleasing to his eye. Out of the reeds drifted pair after pair of dragonflies. Vibrating and iridescent, they hovered one over the other until they seemed to pause in midair quite deliberately, or so it seemed. For some moments he watched as the male of the species gracefully exercised his conjugal right. To the dragonfly, nature had bestowed the truest blue of all, save for the blue of certain eyes. . . .

This unexpected sentiment, arising as it did from the nether regions of his own mind, caused him to smile rather sardonically. Was he a sentimental fool when all was said and done? He immediately gave his thick dark hair a good houndlike shaking until the water flew and he felt himself again.

When once again he strode into the crowd on the meadow it was as a man refreshed, a man baptized in the knowledge of his love.

Now he must speak out. But something bade him to quiet himself and hang back. Thus for a while he had sequestered himself in the oaks, content to "worship from afar." Then had come the moment when he felt compelled to make himself known, to stand in the light.

How was it that she did not see him? She lifted the ladle up and down, the children coming and going, her dewy brow creased with seeming concentration.

Many times he had seen her similarly absorbed, her head bent down, the honey hair brushing the page of a book whilst she read

195

or else scribbled words, or better yet—for this she herself considered the acme of her endeavors—with a paintbrush held in hand, her little "daubpots" neatly arranged before her in the order of colors she used most. At such times, she had once shyly confided to him, she "heard not," though her mother and older sisters believed it to be otherwise. Her eyes attended only to that which was directly before her. Like the little ships she often painted, she sailed away.

Yet ladling apple juice was surely not nearly so transporting a task. He drew closer. No acknowledging glance was forthcoming. This made him bold.

On the ground lay an abandoned cup. He stooped to claim it, and when he stood up again, he was the tallest "boy" in line—for so did he feel. He'd commenced to flicking his fingernail against the side of his tin cup as if impatient for his turn.

Even this brought nothing from his queen, save a slight and fleeting smile. This smile, he thought with no little irritation, might have been meant for the child who had most recently lisped its thanks. He had been about to call out her name, since as another moment passed, the little game, if that was what it was, made his impatience real.

How young and oblivious she suddenly seemed to him. And yet he stayed . . . a tin cup in his hand. And he a man who had seen his thirtieth year! Even so, the softness in his heart might still have been read upon his face if only she had looked up.

No matter. It was too late. A bitterness as old as he was took command. He would not do it: To *need* something from another made a man appear small in his own eyes. There had been nothing for it then but to turn upon his heel and wordlessly take his leave.

When dusk arrived, out had come his fiddle to keep company with the rest, while others packed their picnic gear and saw to it the meadow was made right again. Wagon after wagon rolled away until only the Indians remained. Sometime later when he had mounted his horse, bound across the fields for Ambrose's place, Old Halo, the Indian headman, and his relatives could still be seen beneath the spreading oaks, finishing off the beef. The pies were long gone.

Old man Ambrose's front field—their dancing ground that night—twinkled with many a camphene lantern slung from the trees. The house looked festive, too. As he dismounted he noted it had been expanded somewhat and painted, doubtless in honor of its new status as the stage stop.

Puffed up from pride and whiskey, Ambrose jovially welcomed the revelers. No secessionist had arrived, he said, to mar the festivities.

Ambrose and his boys had even built a little platform for the music makers. "Yankee Doodle," at Mrs. Ambrose's request, was the first tune to be played. Some said later they'd never known a better Independence Day or heard better music. After a jolt or two from the jug Ambrose had left for their convenience on the platform, he'd thought so himself.

He watched her grow rosy with dancing; yet, he was pleased to observe from his perch, she favored no particular partner and many times she looked up and waved gaily at him.

The music makers had been the first to enjoy the breeze which wafted sweetly over the platform after a while until even the bunting swung back and forth a little.

Oh, how he wished he might draw his long arm about her narrow waist and lift her off her feet with Love. Yet never did he lay his fiddle down.

A SYMPATHIZER IS REVEALED

His name was Henry Lane. He'd doubtless thought his surname fortunate. It was rumored that when he first arrived in Oregon he'd hired out to one of Senator Lane's sons for a while. He had even passed himself off as some distant relation for convenience' sake.

It had not escaped his notice, however, that of late Yoncalla had become a stronghold of well-to-do Union men with comely daughters. He, therefore, took pains to renounce any kinship with the Lanes of Roseburg. He was no secesh, he snorted. Some suspected he was no patriot, either.

The account he gave concerning his background was terse: He was one of the "Canadian" Lanes, he said, which—or so his tone implied—was evidently a connection of consequence. Some thought this explained the origin of the handsome fiddle he brought to nearly every gathering. Surely, it was a family heirloom.

The violin—Harriet had refused to refer to such an exquisite and obviously venerable object as a fiddle—had frequently been left in her brother John's care when its owner was away. John, according to his promise, carefully "stashed" the instrument, for he had sworn no hand save his own would touch Lane's fiddle. It was no wonder Henry Lane guarded his treasure so jealously. Instead of a common scroll, the end of the violin's neck boasted a cunningly carved head—that of a man with a flowing beard and hair; his nose, aquiline; each and every detail of his features rendered expressively by an obviously expert hand.

On the violin's back, beautifully inlaid in delicate particolored slivers of wood, was a depiction of an Old World scene, complete with turreted buildings and crenellated walls. On a yellowed strip of paper glued to the inside the following inscription was clearly visible:

Duffy Prugagr Bohomentis Anno 1517

For this spidery inscription to be read, the instrument first had to be lifted up and held at just the right angle. This is exactly what Harriet had done, for unbeknownst to her brother, she had several times gone to the hiding place and lifted it down. Carefully she had removed the violin from its case. She could not help herself. She was drawn to it. As she held it, it seemed she felt something of the refinement and even elegance that she had sometimes glimpsed in its owner. This impression she kept to herself, however, for Lucy and Irene would have surely scoffed.

Henry Lane, they charged, was "rough as a cob." They disliked the influence he had on their younger brothers. There was something altogether too "dark" about him, they avowed. It went beyond his looks.

But Harriet's mother had been somewhat more tolerant. There was nothing *too very much* wrong with Hen, she said. It was simply that he was a rough-and-ready sort—a proverbial man of men.

"A man's man." Perhaps this explained why Charley Applegate had taken such a liking to the younger man. In the beginning, at least. For several years, Henry Lane had come in and out of their district according to his whim. Sometimes he had tales to tell about his wanderings, sometimes not. When he could be induced to linger he was a fine worker. Though rarely one to pay for what he hoped to get for free, even Charley Applegate had not objected to parting with a little money, for Lane was a useful man to have around, particularly when some especial task was under way, such as building the big new barn.

Nor had it hurt Charley's feelings any when he learned that Hen Lane knew how to drink with the best of them. Libations never interfered with Lane's labors, however. Moreover, he was always ready with a good story when the work was done. Unlike some men, Hen Lane did not easily capitulate to slumber, which meant if Charley felt the need for company in the "wee hours," Hen could be counted on.

Of course, Charley knew other "young bounders" who regularly drifted up and down the Big Road exhibiting similar qualities. Hen Lane, however, had talent in the bargain. This made him irresistible to any music lover; and Charley Applegate, who had a fine tenor voice and played a mellifluous flute when the mood struck, was that, all right.

Even Lucy and Irene had been forced to concede that no one could play the fiddle quite the way Hen Lane did.

When of an evening he picked up his bow and commenced to

rubbing it across the amber-colored rosin, sometimes a sigh went up and little children quieted.

What would it be? A gay *chanson* à la Montreal? A seafarer's hornpipe? But, oh, those moody Highland airs which sank lower than the sea itself only to arise again like a songbird soaring over waters.

Was it any wonder that Harriet went into "raptures"? She confessed as much to her cousin Gertrude one afternoon. It was not only Hen Lane's music that uplifted her. There was also the grace of his long body, which, she allowed, swayed like a willow branch when he walked. And oh how tenderly he cradled his violin before he tucked it beneath his manly chin. As he played, his expression was transfigured by so much joy and release she could scarce bear to witness it! But before Harriet could further rhapsodize, Gertrude intervened, begging her younger cousin to desist; Gertrude had come to disapprove of Henry Lane.

In the first place, Gertrude said, Hen Lane was singularly lacking in ambition, and though he would soon be past his prime, this had not lessened his restlessness a whit.

But his worst quality, Gertrude claimed, could be summed up in a word: arrogance.

As Harriet listened, perhaps she thought in regards to this last indictment that in life it is often true that we are quick to condemn in others the very qualities we suspect in ourselves.

Poor Gertrude!

If only she could have chattered as innocently about the matters nearest her heart as Harriet did. But Gertrude dared not. It was no wonder her soul was troubled.

Perhaps her worst moment had come at the Fourth of July celebration. Her father had selected her to read the Declaration of Independence before the assembly of patriots lining the picnic grove.

How lovely all the maidens of her neighborhood had appeared as they carried their emblems, for they fairly floated onto the green, their full dresses whispering over the dry grasses, the name of one or another of the so-called loyal states beautifully embroidered upon each banner. A circle was formed and she walked to the center. She quaked. There she stood: the only "peace man" in the whole of her large family or, who knew? in the whole of Yoncalla perhaps. Yet why inflame her family and neighbors by exposing such sentiments? This at least was what she told herself. No, it was not hypocrisy, it was only "keeping the peace." At great expense to her conscience, she had gone on. She knew the words by heart. She spoke them clearly. When she was done the patriots cheered 'til they were hoarse:

Three cheers for the Union!
Three cheers for Mr. Lincoln, too!

She had stood in their midst, feeling ashamed; yet angry, too. She was doubtless a "sympathizer," but not a sympathizer of rebels. Or so she claimed. It was the orphans, widows, and their desolate home circles that she pitied, as well as those who, with them, faced the prospect of famine and misery. Any sort of compromise, she thought, would be better than the shedding of blood, even if it meant the slaves did not go free.

Yet had she dared to admit such sentiments, surrounded as she was by antisecessionists and brothers and cousins who spoke openly of running off to help the Union win its war . . .

Only by writing to her cousin Theresa in Ashland had Gertrude found relief in the expression of certain beliefs. But she had been unable to bring herself to confide all and everything, for she knew that Theresa would be distressed in the extreme by the shadowy presence of such an unsuitable suitor in Gertrude's life. In an effort to protect Gertrude from herself, who knew what Theresa might do?

So it was that Gertrude had only two real confidants; one was a young woman who resided a few miles up the road. Of pretty Mary Drain, the daughter of the neighborhood's best known secesh, only a little need be said. Her father, John Drain, it may be remembered, had given shelter to Senator Joseph Lane before Jesse Applegate intervened. As concerns Gertrude's second confidant, the suitor himself, a whole tome might be easily written.

For our purposes the following will suffice: James D. Fay was his name and, though much younger in years than Senator Lane and Charles Drain, Fay too had been born in the Carolinas.

A precocious if impulsive youth, James Fay had left his homeland, friends, and family very early in his teens. He crossed the plains to Oregon virtually alone and would not have lived to tell about it had various wagoners and their families not taken pity on him.

Upon arriving in the Willamette Valley the boy wandered from one frontier settlement to another enduring a life of hardship and uncertain supply. When he was fifteen years old fate at last smiled upon him.

Fay's benefactor was an influential Democrat who had served as an Oregon legislator. So impressed was this gentleman by Fay's cleverness that he sponsored the youth in the study of the law. After his "schooling" Fay gained increasing respect from Democrats, especially those in the so-called ultra wing.

Endowed with what even his friends would have called an unctuous charm, Fay ingratiated himself to numerous powerful individuals. Rather quickly, he found himself quite gainfully employed as the city attorney of Corvallis. By 1860 Corvallis had gained a reputation as a secessionist hotbed. Soon it was proudly acknowledged that Jimmy Fay had become one of Corvallis's hottest heads.

Time and time again, men would follow Fay's lead, even as they referred to him, sometimes derisively, as the "little bantam," for Fay's physical stature was not impressive. In 1861 his backers urged him to try his luck in politics. To that end he removed to the gold-mining settlement of Jacksonville, which was only some twelve miles from where Lindsay Applegate operated his mountain toll road. Jacksonville, with even more secesh among its citizenry than Corvallis, turned out to be the perfect place for an ambitious young office-seeker like Jimmy Fay.

During the July which had brought so much patriotic pleasure to the good citizens of Yoncalla and so much pain to Gertrude, Jimmy Fay made regular trips between Corvallis and Jacksonville via the newly extended stage line: At Pass Creek, located only a few miles north of the home of Gertrude's chum, Mary Drain, the stage driver laid over. This place was the quaint hostelry known as the Spotted Horse. There Gertrude would meet Jimmy Fay.

These clandestine meetings, which would have been impossible were it not for the complicity of Mary Drain and her family, ran a predictable course. Whilst other passengers stepped down from the six-horse-limited and made their way to a fine spread at the Spotted Horse, Fay made his way to a waiting buckboard and thence to the home of John Drain.

How expectantly the proud head turns at the sound of the horses in the drive. Only a moment is lost. The dark eyes are luminous. The sallow cheeks blush. Her skirts billowing, she runs toward her paramour.

How outraged would the father be to see the secessionist "runt" plant his kiss! But Jesse Applegate has been spared this and other spectacles.

If only he had known what awaited his Gert at the gates of higher learning. For it was while she was away at school that she had met the young radical who would take her down and down. But it is too late now. She is fixed upon him. For two years she has managed to deceive. So it will be for two years more.

And why? Fay's ambitions have fired her. The tales of his former hardships never fail to invoke her sympathy. What she ought to have written to Theresa, had she dared, was: Yes! She was a "sympathizer," and the opinions and politics of the object of her sympathies had gradually become her own.

Just like one little leaf in autumn, Gertrude's will blows hither and thither. Gust by gust she drifts from her family and friends.

In the end, poor soul, even she will admit that it was an ill wind indeed. But it is not autumn yet. . . .

A WEATHER BREEDER

Much as Romany women read tea leaves, there are some who through long practice read the natural things. As August slipped away, the omens were not good: The wild grasses and pastures were but half as high as in former years, for the weather had turned exceedingly cool and dry.

About this time an old friend of the Applegate brothers who had crossed the plains with them in '43 passed through the neighborhood, bringing tidings that no Union man relished. Word had at last reached Oregon that General Lyon had died in battle. Though he and his troops had fought bravely, his campaign against the Confederate troops was lost. The southern part of the state of Missouri was all "torn up" in more ways than one. This setback, coming as it did so early in the war, had been as disturbing to some men as had the news of the Union army's defeat at Bull Run. Charley Applegate and other men who had spent long years in Missouri were especially downcast. They imagined their old neighborhoods, and many an old neighbor, too, who had been forced to choose up sides. Doubtless some of these same men had already lost their lives or would in days to come.

Quite naturally Charley's thoughts had turned toward his older brother, Lisbon, who, alone of the four surviving Applegate brothers, had remained in Missouri. More than a year had passed since any letter had been received from Lisbon or his immediate family. Nor had any recent Missouri emigrant brought news concerning him, as had often been the case in former years.

An influential and respected judge who long years before had performed the marriage between Charley and his wife, Lisbon had never had any love for Black Republicans. He shared the convictions of the majority of his colleagues in Missouri, which was to say he was a Democrat of the Jefferson and Jackson school.

A townsman instead of a countryman, Lisbon had never understood his brothers' abhorrence of slavery. He had never been forced to compete with the Missouri slaveholders' glut of cheap labor and land, whilst the farmers of middle size struggled to work their own land and get goods to market at prices that they and their families could live with. In the '30s Charley and Lindsay had especially been frustrated in this regard. This was one of the principal reasons they had emigrated to Oregon. In the early '40s, Jesse, too, experienced the hardships of the agriculturist.

For all Charley knew, in the almost twenty years since he and his brothers had last seen Lisbon, Lisbon's views concerning states' rights and other matters remained. Surely, if the choice were forced Lisbon would side with the Confederacy; and as he had always been a man true to his convictions, it seemed likely that he and his sons might actually take up arms against the Union.

These speculations were extremely painful to Charley, Union man that he was. Nor did Charley forget that Lisbon had been his boyhood defender, and in other ways was a most laudable brother before certain misunderstandings, having nothing whatever to do with politics, had arisen. Now, it came to Charley that his brother might be killed before amends could be made, and what other men already knew, Charley felt, too: Oh, how dreadful is war. It divideth both border and blood. And of the poor Union, Charley thought long and hard. General Lyon had already sacrificed himself for the Union's sake. Who knew whether a man's own sons might not go?

Upon learning of Lyon's death, Charley and Jesse had made certain that the large new flag was lowered to half-mast. In the midst of this grave and symbolic act, no one forgot that elsewhere in Oregon there were men waiting to rip down the Stars and Stripes so that they might replace it with the Stars and Bars of the Confederacy. In a few Willamette Valley hamlets, it was said, that deed had already been accomplished. Those who had so impudently flown the Stars and Bars were cranks and loyal neighbors had quickly torn the hated standard down. The Union had far worse enemies in Oregon.

While it was true that Joseph Lane had sequestered himself in a cabin in the high hills outside of Roseburg, and had publicly avowed that he and politics were forever parted, his "retirement" had not scotched the plans of certain secesh plotters. Lesser lights in the region schemed in Lane's stead. According to rumor, one of Lane's sons-in-law had become a prominent leader in the organization of the Oregon Knights. This same son-in-law was known to be a close associate of an aspiring young politician but lately moved to Jacksonville, one James D. Fay.

Ten "castles" of the Knights of the Golden Circle were believed to be flourishing in the state. It was generally understood that their principal work was the systemic plundering of arsenals, both public and private. Through this tactic they hoped eventually to deplete the resources of their adversaries as well as arm themselves. Each and every defeat of the Union army, they supposed, brought them closer to the time when their goal for a separate "republic" could be realized. They had but to wait, undermine what they could, and rehearse the particulars of their takeover. It was assumed by loyal men that such training maneuvers were already taking place in the remote localities of the state. As most of Oregon remained utterly wild and untrammeled, there was no dearth of "rebel" training grounds.

There was, however, a far greater concern shared by Charley Applegate and every other Union man. It was feared that during such troubled times, the Indians—especially those along the eastern frontiers—would seek to press their advantage. Who knew whether the secesh would deliberately incite them? Though the majority of natives had been removed to reservations, their unhappiness was well known. Thus loyal Oregonians might very well find themselves fighting on two fronts: against the Knights who undermined from within whilst the Indians warred without.

President Lincoln had at last made a formal call for Oregon volunteers. The prospect of plucking able-bodied men out of Oregon so that they might fight on distant battlegrounds was not attractive, considering that Oregon herself might well need protecting. Thus it had been decided that if Oregon was to survive as an outpost of the Union, the majority of her loyal men should stay in the Northwest.

To counterbalance the threat of the Knights of the Golden Circle as well as the indifference of "peace men" and "shirkers," those who were devoted to the Union formed secret organizations called "Loyal Leagues." By October these leagues had adherents all over the state. Yoncalla's chapter, it was said proudly, was among the very first. When the roll was called, there was many a young man named Applegate present. Yet matters of defense and loyalty were not the only things bothering Oregon. The sad truth was, Oregon was failing.

In a few short seasons, the prices of her livestock, produce, orchards, farmlands, and homes had plummeted. Some desperate men, unable to sell out, had merely walked out, headed for God knew where. The controversies agitating the rest of the continent had made money "terrible" scarce in the West. In Oregon one hard-to-get dollar equaled what three had been worth before. Yet soon people asked—where was a man to lay hands on even one dollar?

At the very acme of this almost universal depletion, along came news of the sort that was bound to test the character of even the most responsible young man: The story went that a loose mule had got itself stuck in a mudhole up in the Salmon River country of "I-de-ho." After remaining there for a time, it decided it ought to go home so as to track down its feedbag. Pretty soon it found its owner, who had then looked the animal over with some astonishment. It seemed that Mr. Mule had "yaller stuff" all over its legs, which, when scraped off, had amounted to several ounces of the purest dust. All a "fella" had to do—or so claimed the tired, broke, and desperate—was to leave the disasters of Oregon and "hightail it" a little north and east.

But this temptation did not immediately amount to a "siren's call"! Early that October other serious distractions had commenced, which left most of Oregon's men too preoccupied to think about packing up just yet. Were their other problems not enough? The weather, it seemed, had turned on them, too.

The first "howler" of the season, aside from arriving prematurely, had brought winds of such ferocious force that people claimed their houses had literally rocked upon their foundations all night long. Some said they had been put in mind of Missouri storms endured years before, though in Yoncalla, at least, the skies had not turned green.

But this storm passed quickly. Thirsty from its summer lack, the ground soaked up the rain. The morning after had had a pure and dazzling look. The Applegate women and their counterparts all over the valley built fires under their big black kettles. When the waters were hot they washed their clothes and hung them out, doubtless enjoying the apple-scented air and the smell of moist earth.

By afternoon Old Sol had cast a most comforting warmth. At Charley's place his visiting daughters had brought their babies out on the big side porch, where they basked and dozed as their mothers gathered squashes, dug potatoes, or sat talking whilst making onion braids.

Melinda Applegate and other older women said later that they had seen it all coming. About dusk they noted how the clouds had gathered so queerly until they were piled up in one corner of the sky like so many dirty fleeces. What their mothers had told them years before came back to them. The sun had shone far too brightly. The storm had been more than a storm. It was a weather breeder.

That night came thunder, lightning, and sleet. In the wee hours, mothers taking their infants to teat had reason to pull their shawls more tightly about their shoulders as they padded back to bed. Through their windows the vistas gleamed as if pale with moonlight. It was snowing. It was October. It was just the beginning.

PROSPECTS

On the morning following the first snow, Harriet liked the smooth look of the back hills, the frosting upon the dark and distant firs, the bright yellow of the single heart-shaped catalpa leaf captured under the sheath of puddle-ice that she had passed on the way to the milking barn.

As she didn't own a pair of mittens, she'd commandeered an unmatched pair of Milton's socks. Little Milt himself wore no mitts whatever, but he cheerfully carried the milk pail behind her, taking the tracks she made in the snow for his own, and, of course, chattering without pause. For in the whole of his life, Milt had never seen snow—"leastaways" not right there in their own pasture so thick that the grass did not stick up through it.

It was a new world. Harriet laughed.

Across the virginal whiteness of the farthest field a lone figure now made its way toward them. Milt waved his arm, delivering a sharp sound which though intended to be a whistle—an "art" he'd but recently learned—was more a squeak.

How glad Harriet was when she recognized the graceful lope of Henry Lane—for it could be no other.

And when he'd reached her she saw that he had the look of robust good health; his brown eyes were uncommonly deep and clear, and his glance was steady. How big-shouldered he seemed looking down at her. He took her hands in his own as if his sole purpose were to examine and mock her little mitts! She flushed and pulled away, or tried to, for Milt was there, his eyes fastened upon Hen, who was one of his heroes.

But Hen would not release her. He shook his head a little and grinned down at her. His long, cool fingers nudged at the woolen edge of the socks and probed gently for the warm wrists beneath. This gesture brought on such pleasurable and unexpected sensations that Harriet was certain he could feel her pulse, for it raced, keeping time with her heart. Indeed, she felt his thumbs bear down a little. She was quite captured now. She could not bear to return his yearning gaze, lest her knees give way altogether and reduce her to a snow angel such as the little girls were making out in the yard that morning.

Whereupon she heard Hen say—his voice uncommonly soft—

that she might at least wish him luck, for if all went well within the hour he would be a man with "prospects." At which point he stepped back, withdrawing his hands and shoving them into the pockets of his greatcoat, which was heavy, gray-blue as gunmetal, and which she had never seen before. This, he said, was his Canada coat. Just to have it on made him feel better. And the weather lifted him too, steady and cold. After manufacturing a little snow flurry all his own by delivering a quick playful kick in Milt's direction, Hen grinned at both of them. They saw him make his way toward the blacksmith shed, where he supposed he would find Harriet's pappa.

Now Charley, it has already been noted, was a circumspect man when it came to money. Hitherto, he had restricted himself to the modest backing of one son or another and from time to time, maybe of a son-in-law. Henry Lane was neither.

That morning Charley had not yet made it outside. His body was stiff with rheumatism. Thus he was lingering awhile. Despite the fact that he'd fed the fire half the night, his room seemed unusually chilly. So it and he would remain for long months to come.

Since his brother Lindsay had left the valley, Charley seemed more disposed than ever before to spend time alone in his big front room. There he could be found at unexpected hours with his tumbler in one "paw"—for so did his young granddaughters refer to his hairy hand—and with one big booted foot propped up on the special andiron which he reserved for that purpose. More frequently, too, did the mood which his wife called "broody" descend upon him. Sometimes he stared into the fire for moments on end, fingering the place midpoint across the sandstone lintel where a crack had appeared not long after the fireplace was put into regular use. Gradually, what at first amounted to no more than a hairline had widened into a place wherein a grown man might insert his fingertip. It had taken some months for Charley to take full note of the change. After that it seemed that the little cleft in the sandstone was a source of fascination to him. In the same way that some men pull repeatedly upon one earlobe, jingle the coins in their pocket, or drum their pipe stem on any surface handy, Charley seemed compelled to run his thumb all along the jagged edge, exploring the places where the stones no longer met. It was like a crack in the heart of things. . . . And money was short. And the weather was bad. And, it seemed, there wasn't much in the good old world that was dependable anymore. Not even what a man's own brothers would do.

Hen had stomped hard upon the porch, trying to give Charley a little warning before he knocked. Charley was the sort who hated to be caught unawares. The weather still glistened upon Hen's greatcoat when he neared the porch, for Buck had ambushed him. As soon as Charley opened the door and Hen set boot in his employer's lair, he found himself infused with the shifty alertness peculiar to gambling men, especially when the cards are about to be dealt.

Almost immediately Hen noted that Charley was exhibiting only a trace of his usual joviality. Charley allowed that he had had to put a little "medicine" in his coffee but he didn't offer Hen any. So dour did Charley appear, in fact, Hen reconsidered his own mission. What he thought he wanted was to purchase some of Charley's surplus sheep, for Lindsay Applegate had left all his flocks behind. Hen, however, was as usual "much reduced." He had scraped together what he could to offer Charley a down payment that was paltry indeed.

But Ol' Charley surprised him. He confessed that he had something on his mind that he was anxious to get settled. The winter might not be quite as far away as a man would like it to be, he said, and his flock had burgeoned to almost two thousand head. Thus, he continued, before Hen came down with "mine fever" and bolted the country altogether, Charley was prepared to offer Hen six hundred sheep on shares. No money need change hands. They could settle up after the spring shearing.

Astonished that he had had neither to steer the conversation in the desired direction nor wheedle his case, Hen had stood dumbstruck for a moment. But Charley mistook the meaning of this intermission. Thus he had begun talking up the sheep business: "Why, Henry, sheep will make a man money even while he sleeps." All that needed to be done, Charley said, was for Hen to drive the flock up into the mountains, where, if he were vigilant, the animals would winter and have plenty to eat. Charley, it seemed, was short on grazing land. Who knew, Charley continued, Hen might well find himself with enough capital to "prove up" some place and settle down. After which, he had given Hen a most knowing look.

It seemed to Hen, after he'd shaken Charley's big hairy hand and found himself in the cold again, that the only sounds he could hear for some time were the ringing of his ears and the crunch of snow beneath his boots. Slowly he'd angled toward the back pastures where Fortune awaited him.

A descendant of Nova Scotian seafaring men, he was now drifting toward respectability. But something weighed him down that seemed heavier than his coat. All the way to the fields he puzzled over it. He couldn't make himself out.

By November's end enough rain had fallen all over Oregon to justify several autumns all strung together. When the rains, which had descended in great inundating curtains as opaque as a widow's veil, at last paused for a while, it was only so that sleet and snow might come instead. So the landscape was not only engorged, but half frozen under a "motionated" membrane of muck and ice that crept over rocks, roads, bridges, and whole towns—some of which would never be used again.

By what landmark did they any longer know the place? a despairing and sodden populace asked itself. The whole of the Willamette Valley looked like an inland sea, said travelers who were forced to turn back. The hilltops appeared like islands poking up at intervals. Creeks, streams, and rivers seemed to seek one another out all across the valley floor, as if they desired to converge as one and wash away every handiwork of man. Blessed was the farmer who'd had the sense to build high up.

Farther south, in the hundred valleys of the Umpqua drainage, the river and all its forks and tributaries surged across the lowlands and fingered the foothills.

It seemed impossible that the waters kept rising, even in places like Yoncalla, where only Elk Creek and lesser streams meandered. Yet little waters became big waters that November. Wider, deeper, and more dangerous than any settler had ever seen. As the rains fell, and the snows froze and then thawed in what seemed a succession unending, even little Elk Creek thundered and reached across the land.

In the *ahnkuttie laly*—the little-long-ago—Chief Halo and other Yoncallas remembered a flood so great that when the waters at last receded, huge canoes could be found dangling in even the highest treetops. The Indians were much afraid. Maybe Worldmaker had decided to drown The People after all, said Halo, for it seemed to him that over the years the Yoncalla had fallen ever further from grace.

But perhaps no man had been more alarmed than a certain ship's captain named Hall. What he saw was almost enough to convince him that the whole of Oregon was being swept out into the sea.

On December 8, 1861, Captain Hall had been headed for the mouth of the Umpqua. From there he had intended to continue passage upriver to Scottsburg, where he periodically delivered cargo to the merchants. From these same merchants, it should be said, Jesse Applegate and other inland storekeepers purchased the majority of their goods. Briefly, Jesse had owned his own business there.

While still some miles out to sea, Captain Hall had been astonished to see a vast expanse of what were obviously fresh, though mudded, waters. He immediately took it for a flood, for he'd seen floods before, but never had he seen one of such magnitude. In its currents appeared barns, sheds, and even a two-storied log cabin. Bobbing chicken coops (with chickens still roosting upon them or anything handy), fences and posts, and even haystacks passed by. Then came the careening drowned herds of sheep and cattle, not to mention bloated pigs, their troughs, and every other structure of agricultural life.

When he finally got upriver, he found that, save for one or two houses built on much higher ground, Scottsburg's main district was no more. So much for the city which but a few years before had aspired to become San Francisco's rival!

San Francisco! It was a place that had been much on Hen Lane's mind during the icy cycle of bad days and worse nights that followed, as he and his shivering flocks picked their way up and down the snow-blown ridges. San Francisco: More the haven envisioned by every bona fide gambling man and less the bitter scene of some of his most costly carousals.

Down in the valleys Charley and his oldest boys fought off the rains and the perpetual seep. So waterlogged were the sheep's fleeces that some ewes could scarcely make it to the hay piles Charley set out for them, for their bellies dragged in their tracks. That winter, Charley would feed his livestock over seven hundred bushels of grain, most of which was devoured by his thirteen hundred head of sheep. When that was gone he and every other rancher in the neighborhood had resorted to apple brush and even the moss that dangled from the oaks, for there was nothing else worth having on the flooded stubble that had once been fine pasturage.

In December the snows fell again. So glad were people to be free from the "wet," they said, that they welcomed the cold. But a little digging beneath the snow soon revealed there would be no new grass to look forward to for a long time to come. What lay under the blanket of white was rotten and black. The fastest-moving creek had frozen solid, and cattle, their hides dusted with hoarfrost, waited in miserable clots as men with pickaxes hacked at the ice so their herds might drink.

Since wagons were useless, many a homemade sleigh was hastily constructed. But even if the weather had been fit for wagons, few of the old roads remained. The November floods had ruined them, and any bridge that hadn't yet been washed away would not survive the spring freshets.

And Henry, poor Henry, up in the hills, alone with his six hundred sheep. Unlike Charley, he had no grain to feed the bleating flocks. After the storms buried the wild pasturage in the high meadows, any hazel or willow branch sticking out of a snowdrift was what passed for "feed" in those miserable mountains. He watched his sheep stagger and fall.

Every day there was nothing for it but for Hen to carry the breaking-down strays back into line. Each evening, as the winds came whipping through the draws and screaming through the high hollows, he wondered at the sorry bargain he'd made with Charley Applegate.

As his deprivations mounted, even the honey-haired girl beside her parents' hearth in the valley below seemed to fade away.

At night he sat in his greatcoat, staring into a sputtering fire. Icicles hung from the huge old firs and wolves howled. In the end, more than anything, he wished for the sound of his fiddle. The fact was, try as he might, he didn't have it in him to be a rancher, either wet or dry. He drove the sheep back down the mountains, leaving them to wander in the low hills behind Charley Applegate's.

None of this had "set very well" with their pappa, who had cursed and cursed and then cursed some more. Yes, the worm had finally turned on Henry Lane as far as their pappa was concerned.

Or so reported Irene, for she had "chanced" to overhear all that had transpired, she said. Nor had this stormy interview been extended. After John gave back the fiddle, off Hen had gone, she knew not where.

Whereupon, wondering at the commotion, Harriet had come downstairs. For some moments afterward, Irene noted, Harriet was very quiet indeed.

CABIN FEVER'S CURE

Is it pluck or desperation that compels humankind "to make merry" when little testifies to any condition save misery?

Whichever the answer, the good citizens of Yoncalla were tired of their troubles and more than ready to give a hale and boisterous welcome to the New Year, 1862, if only such a celebration might find suitable quarters and other obstacles be overcome.

The obstacles were these: Since Scottsburg for all intents and purposes had floated out to sea, most everyone had been on short rations. "Boughten" things, such as coffee, tea, sugar, hard liquor, and cake flour, which most considered indispensable to merrymaking, were no longer available. Roads to the north and south as well as to the coastal settlements had been flooded anew, for only a few days after Christmas the rainstorms had arrived to replace the snows again. Anyone who needed to travel stuck to the older packing and Indian trails that followed the hilltops and ridges. Any journey took twice as long, for there was nothing for it but to go the "long way" around!

The miserable weather had done much to undermine the community's health. Many had become bedridden, nursing one ailment or another. Terrible outbreaks of boils, pleurisy, colds, and stomach miseries were commonplace. Even those who remained relatively healthy pined away, for there were men, women, and children who had not been off their homeplaces for months and who, as a consequence, developed that condition quaintly known as "cabin fever."

No one knew exactly why it was the Cowans decided to break the evil spell cast by the old year—or so, at least, it was to be hoped. Ol' Mr. Cowan was a Scot, one of the very earliest settlers in the valley. He was not especially given to frivolity. Never before and never again would he host such a party—but a party it was in every sense of the word, such as to live forever in the annals of his neighborhood.

Most had set aside several hours for traveling so as to allow time for any inconvenience or delay. To miss the Cowans' ball would be unthinkable, especially for the numerous younger members in the vicinity. Sick persons recovered with astonishing speed, and in the short wet week between Christmas and the New

Year, many a matron had found something in her trunk she just might "make over" after all.

Swaddled in any homely wrap or covering that might conceivably prevent the elements from ruining their finery, the partygoers arrived in carriages, wagons, on horseback, and even on foot.

Never mind that the voluminous rims of hoopskirts and hand-edged petticoats grew heavy with the red mud so prevalent in the country as their owners picked their way up to the hillside home. Inevitably, the Godey's Lady's Book "coiffures" so labored over by certain girls were windblown and in some cases drenched by the time "an entrance" was to be made. "Where are the women?" the young men asked, as an hour or more elapsed between a maiden's arrival and her actual appearance in the makeshift ballroom. This, too, became a portion of the festivities, while girls and women laughed and "combed one another out" in front of the narrow mirror in an upstairs bedroom. Mr. and Mrs. Cowan surely used all their "reserves" that night, for they had turned their new gabled house into a palace of sparkling lights. The rooms were graced by dozens of camphene lanterns and what seemed hundreds of candles.

During those long and stormy months, there had been an unusual abundance of wild fowl. Migrating geese and ducks, as well as grouse, quail and, other birds, flocked to the farmyards in search of food. Young boys practiced their shooting and "picked off" supper for their mothers.

Thus plenty of stuffed grouse, mountain quail, and other delectable fowl were to be found on the Cowans' oaken tables that evening. Various guests had brought along other main dishes, such as miniature chicken pies which some called "coach wheels." "Thoroughbraces" of pork and "porcupine sausage" and side dishes, including sliced head cheese, buttered parsnips, and lye-hominy with hogs' head, were also enjoyed. Yet the most tantalizing offerings of that "groaning board" were what housewives called "dainties." This was the fare that had been secreted in cupboards until some especial occasion. Arrayed before the hungry guests were the culinary treasures of the neighborhood: gem-colored jellies and preserves made of quince, gooseberry, salmonberry, and currants; hazelnuts and chinquapins (which had been shelled and roasted and dipped in honey); not to mention sugared plums, candied and minted pears, and brandied peaches. As these and other offerings were nibbled on plain or else spread over hunks of fresh bread, oven jewels, or sour biscuits, an ecstatic expression could be witnessed upon the face of the consumer.

Even those who as a general rule "did not touch the stuff" could be seen sipping wild strawberry wine, cherry bounce, and a concoction known by the unattractive name of "metheglin." In reality, this beverage was an extremely light and honeyed wine whose ingredients included spring water, eggs, and bruised Jamaican ginger, the latter having been brought to Scottsburg via the coastwise schooners.

Poor Scottsburg. This was a subject much on people's minds. For so long they had been deprived of one another's society it was natural that some portion of the evening was taken up with passing along news concerning their recent sufferings and those of others they'd "heard-tell-of." Some spoke of hair-raising escapes in the currents; others reported the names of persons feared drowned, and told tales of barn-high snowdrifts and of a certain grandmother in particular who, it was claimed, had lain ill and alone until she finally froze to death with two inches of snow upon her bedclothes—with every door and window closed in her cabin, too.

Yet this tendency to relive the recent past soon seemed to disperse, leaving the heart less heavy. How much better it felt to dwell on the new dress a neighbor wore, or to bow to one's partner. Following the bounteous supper, and after young ones had been carried to doze all "comfy" under quilts and coats, even ol' married men were light on their feet again and seen to wink at their wives.

"Rosin' the Bow" and other lively tunes, some of which reached back even to their parents' parents' times, like the lanterns themselves seemed to brighten up the rooms. Of fine musicians, in general, there was no shortage. Fifes, flutes, and fiddles had all been well represented. Yet later when this happy occasion would be relished and remembered, not once but many times it would be said that of all the music makers the best had been the "Fiddlers Three": John Applegate, Alexander Applegate, and Henry Lane.

When the witching hour almost arrived, Mr. Cowan, who was after all a Scot, shouted for the toast to be raised and for "Auld

Lang Syne" to be played. Yet for this purpose the most accomplished of the three fiddlers could not be located. He had evidently slipped out the door some moments before. An informant who had observed this surreptitious act reported that the fiddler had seemed intent on "fiddling," for his arm was looped about the narrow waist of a lovely blue-eyed girl dressed in green delaine.

However, no one saw the fiddler finger a stray golden curl, and brush it back as tenderly as a father might wipe away a child's tear, for he and the girl had taken pains to stay deep in the shadows of the porch. Who knew whether her flushed face was cradled in his hands when he bent for his kiss, since any person standing near a spouse or sweetheart at that moment was similarly occupied.

Then from behind the house had come the sound of the anvil being fired, followed by some random hoots and rifle shots. Jigs and Schottisches of feverish tempo replaced the sentimental strains of "Auld Lang Syne." With only a few hours left before dawn, the revelers reeled about the room with an almost desperate vigor. Just under their gaiety resided the knowledge that winter was far from over. There would be lonesome days ahead.

THE NEW YEAR'S SAD PORTENTS

Harriet's parents had stayed home, but her brothers John and Al had been instructed to keep "the bevy" in tow. They had, accordingly, driven over a wagonful of their sisters and a few female cousins, of whom proud Gertrude was but one.

At length, the time arrived when every driver had need to summon his passengers. The large crowd had begun to disperse. Half a dozen young bachelors, who had ridden over the ridges all the way from the little village of Oakland, gratefully pumped the hands of their host and hostess. Then, a little tipsy, these same gentlemen had quite deliberately and rather noisily surrounded Gertrude and Harriet. Standing at the center of that manly swarm, only the girls' hoopskirts, it seemed, were keeping the "bees" at bay. Even the appearance of John and Al, who had arrived with the girls' wraps—for the teams were hitched—had not discouraged the attentions of these same young men. They followed Harriet and Gertrude outside to the waiting wagon, gallantly offering to lift the "lovely damsels" up onto their seats.

Harriet had been mortified, or so she put it later, for a moment came when one of the Oakland bachelors—the tallest of their number—had dramatically lowered himself to one knee. He had then begged permission to call upon her as the weather permitted, not caring who overheard. While he was in the very midst of his performance, Gertrude had come up behind him and administered a little shove. The poor fellow had sprawled. By then, Gertrude had been lifted up and was reigning from her wagon seat and, of course, laughing gaily at the poor fellow's expense.

No, she did not feel sorry that he'd got his new britches muddy, she said to Harriet as their wagon pulled away at last, and if Harriet felt pity she was a "goose," just as the bachelor was an "ass."

Now Gertrude, it must be admitted, had led at least two of these Oakland admirers on that evening. Though several of her kinswomen suspected that Gertrude had long since promised her heart to another, she sometimes made a great show of flirtation. In the year just passed, more than one young man in the district had been dismayed to be played with so coolly.

Somewhat younger than Gert, and perhaps because she had

known no world save little Yoncalla's, Harriet had always been quite taken with her cousin's wit and the artful airs and coquetries that Gertrude had developed "up at school." Nevertheless, Harriet was not disposed to imitate Gertrude or any other mortal. Harriet's heroines breathed only in the pages of her favorite books. Innocence yet exuded from Harriet just as little mists sometimes arise from a morning lake. It was only her acute intelligence that made Harriet seem older than her years. In a family of "quick studies" no one, excepting her cousin Oliver—so dear to her heart—could sketch or write half so well. Nevertheless, these qualities, so extravagantly admired by her kinsmen, had failed to enthuse even one young man her own age. This bothered her, for she did not think much of her looks. The fact was, when she was not distracted, she responded with an astonishing and disarming directness. She grew convinced that she "scared men off."

It had taken a fully grown man, knowledgeable in the ways of the world, to appreciate Harriet. Henry Lane had watched, waited, and coveted. The qualities that disconcerted others were like gold to him. Yet could the cost be borne?

As the revelers sighed and a certain tiredness had stolen over them much as the new year had stolen over the old, Hen felt engulfed by helplessness. Before him had transpired the very thing he had come to dread. For in his own way he was an astute observer, which was, of course, one of the things that lent him a certain power over others. He perceived what Harriet as yet did not: Despite the vapors of metheglin and cherry bounce, the Oakland bachelors had at last seen the light. Nor was it merely the dark and scornful Gertrude who, with her swelling bosom and musical laugh, had attracted them.

Poor Hen! He had been quite taken aback at long last to experience jealousy. His swaggering confidence was in reality a sham.

How lovely Harriet had appeared that eve: The rich wintergreen of her low-necked gown set off the glinting lights in her tawny hair, her eyes, her skin; but even so, it was not these things that imparted an angel's glow. About her the very air seemed to stir with freshness and hope. She was strong and warm. It was no wonder the bachelors drew closer, or that the "feckless swain," with Gertrude's help, had quite literally fallen all over himself to please.

From the porch steps, still holding his fiddle case, Henry had watched Harriet cover her mouth with her hand as the fellow went down. What young woman would not have been flattered by such an episode? Hen asked himself. Though ringed by laughter on every side, Harriet instead had bestowed a concerned and compassionate look, and as her young gallant, his hat in hand, had shakily arisen from his mudbath in order to bow to her, not once but twice, she had blushed prettily. The wagon lurched forward. Hen saw Harriet turning in her seat as if looking for someone in the crowd.

He was a proud man. It pained him not to know for whom she had intended her little wave and a smile so sweet it stung the heart. The rosy streak that had first appeared on the mottled horizon had given way, he noted. The morning had broken all silver and gray and colder than he'd thought.

Something bade Henry to make forthwith the acquaintance of a certain Oakland bachelor. This he had done only a few moments after Harriet's wagon disappeared over the rise. Hen strode over with his saddlebag flask. As the young man "put one back," Hen sized him up. Now, some will say there is no choicer range for one man to gauge another than that which is afforded when a flask is passed. Henry had not found the fellow harmless.

The bed feather-snow floated down. Hen was oblivious to it. He had taken to recounting his failures one by one. There was almost a peculiar pleasure in it. At length, the whiskey slipped down his throat almost as easily as his self-recriminations.

An hour passed. Mrs. Cowan, looking "all worn out" indeed, had waved the last of the Yoncalla revelers off. The bachelors, too, had ridden away. At which point Hen retrieved his own horse from the barn and with some difficulty replaced and cinched the saddle. He strapped the fiddle case into the leather sheath he'd made for it, which hung just below his rifle. He decided not to return his flask to his saddlebag. In truth, he had not decided at all; 'twas long habit which instructed him and he obeyed.

As he rode away, it came to him how tired he was of Yoncalla and all the people in it. He thought of other places farther south such as Roseburg and Canyonville, where he was well liked. He discounted these destinations, however, on account of the terrible weather.

Then he dwelled awhile more on his troubles, his various resentments, old and new, rising up like something bad got eaten.

225

Charley Applegate came to mind. Hen knew he'd failed him; but then again it seemed, as Hen took another swig, that Charley had somehow failed him. He slumped forward a little. The young bachelor's pappy, it was said, had just bought himself a sawmill.

Now, Hen's horse was a good ol' horse. It had picked its way up Cowan's hill without any advice from its master, and as Hen himself seemed to have no preference, the horse followed a trail familiar to it.

Halfway to Oakland there was an old man who lived with his sister. Over the years, whenever Hen returned from his intermittent wandering, he had frequently laid over there. Time was when he'd preferred the old man's company to that of any of the Applegate brothers. When he had need to hire on someplace for a while, in the past Hen had always checked with the old man first. Now this seemed as good a place as any to light until the weather got better.

The horse seemed in favor, too, for Hen noted with some relief that they were already following the right ridge line. The snow fell thick and soft amidst the firs. He spied the red-brown of a bounding deer and heard the blue jays prattling. The wind stung his face.

He took deep draughts of his elixir for warmth's sake, and had been on the verge of another when he discovered the flask had somehow been drained.

It was then that a good idea had come to him. It was not a new idea really, but more like an old idea that had been laying in wait. Nevertheless, it had the glow of novelty. Hen spent some moments thinking of Idaho. He thought of a poke bulging with prospects even more golden than her hair. He didn't need sheep, he said to himself. Charley had too much respect for money to turn a rich man down. Nothing could stop him. When the weather got better.

And knowing that all was not lost, he tried to straighten up in the saddle. In this confident state he finally made it to the place known as "Red Hill." Upon seeing the familiar figure and his horse, the old man had gone straight to the cowshed, for he had "a little something" he knew Hen would appreciate hidden in the rafters there.

DRAUGHTY AND CROWDED QUARTERS

Up in the snowblown Siskiyous that same and dreadful winter of '62, Lindsay and Betsy Applegate and their sons and daughters anxiously awaited word concerning the valleys that had formerly been their home. The task of letter writing fell mostly to the younger Applegates who, unlike their parents, enthusiastically took pen in hand. It came to pass that, along with reading and music making, "scribbling" to one cousin or another constituted an important part of an evening's entertainment. Even the most laconic had been known to pour his heart onto paper at least once during the rainy season. That winter, as the cold winds whinnied down the chimneys, and rattled the windows, and the country wore no color save white, writing letters became even more important. Never mind that it might be weeks or months until the roads were clear and the mails could be counted on again to deliver them to their destinations.

Often a correspondent was afforded more satisfaction through letter writing than he or she received from conversing with some person closer at hand. Day in, day out, they had known no company save one another in crowded and draughty quarters. Blessed was the world of pen and ink.

Alas, unlike one of Mrs. Warner's characters in *The Wide Wide World*, which had been read aloud over the course of that unhappy season, neither Harriet nor any other family "scribbler" owned select papers large and small with matching envelopes and note-sheets. Personalized seals and sealing waxes in red, green, blue, and yellow, ivory letter knives, neat silver pencils, and other elegant accoutrements such as those favored by fastidious back-east correspondents were not to be found in Yoncalla, where the writing desks, if there were to be found at all, weren't apt to be mahogany.

Oregon's letter paper tended to be of scanty weight and blue. After the Scottsburg mercantiles had been flooded out, steel and quill pens were even more jealously guarded by their owners, for who knew from whence would come more?

Gertrude could often be heard complaining about the "horrid" shortage of one thing or another. Harriet and her sisters, who had

227

not been blessed with a quite so generous pappa, "made do," as they said.

Nevertheless, there was one lack which Harriet felt quite keenly. During those gloomy months less and less was she satisfied with her lot in life.

She had read several novels in whose pages lived "lovely young sensitives" of "an artistic bent." Upon these attractive heroines had been bestowed items that Harriet could not help but covet. What she would have given for a French easel and watercolors, she sighed, or for oil paints, fine egg temperas, and even just one good drawing pad of vellum.

For she had no paints at all, save diluted ink and the homely tints she concocted. The red from her pokeberries was nothing to the crimson called "alizarin." How could blackberries, walnut shells, and alder bark produce the "ever vibrant" hues she read about? Nor could she boast a sketchbook bound in fine Moroccan leather. All she had was an old school atlas wherein she was forced to work upon the blank backsides of maps. When made moody by such "lacks" Harriet would find fault in each and every of her former efforts, calling even the drawings she had once taken pride in childish and silly.

This had been especially disturbing to her brother Buck, who loved to watch her sketch. One evening, saying disgustedly that she would draw no more until she had something better with which to accomplish her work, she had put away her sketchbook and given Buck the only pencil she owned. Their mother was quite surprised to see him with it and queried him. In the end, Melinda blamed Harriet's "humors" on the illness both Harriet and Irene had come down with just after New Year's.

Harriet's strain had been the most severe, accompanied by intermittent fevers and headaches. Before February's end, she had taken to her bed and had not attempted to sit up for a whole week. It was no wonder, her mother averred, that when March arrived Harriet was not entirely "herself." About her clung a dispirited air, sad to witness in one formerly so full of life. No longer could Harriet be spied working on "her Romantic novel"—or so Jane referred to it. At length even letter writing failed to interest Harriet. She could think of nothing to say, she told her older sisters. Then she allowed that maybe the old general they'd all read about was right: The comet had given the earth a push toward the North Pole. Nevermore, Harriet sighed, would there be another spring.

The old "dreaminess" they had always noted in her deep blue eyes was gone. More and more she sat by the window and fingered the quilt upon her lap, for she was always cold, she said.

About this time Charley Applegate's newborn lambs had begun to die in great numbers. Even though he and his sons daily braved the cold, sleighing hay and such grain as remained to the upper fields, the ewes continued to abandon their trembling babes, leaving them to fend for themselves in the snow or else never owning them at all, even as the lambkins had dropped sticky and new from their bodies.

So nearly forty of these "little bummers" had in the course of weeks been kept warm in the house, for the barn was too cold. Harriet's sympathies had been awakened by these poor creatures. With the whole of her heart she addressed herself to their care. These "bummers," whose housebound number was rarely less than a dozen, could be heard bleating at all hours, especially during the wee hours prior to feeding. They sucked cow's milk from the little nippled bottle Harriet and her sisters struggled to insert into their mouths. Four times each day did this exasperating feeding commence.

Sometimes, a little before dawn, Charley Applegate would arrive, thinking to check upon the lambs and quench his thirst. He never got used to finding Harriet already there.

What a startling picture she had made with her pale hair streaming down, an old black shawl covering the bedraggled white nightdress. There, at the center of her miserable retinue, she would stand, holding yet another dead baby lamb in her arms. Despite the family's tender ministrations during those wretched weeks, every lamb save two died. Each time its pathetic bleat ceased, Harriet had hugged the wretched orphan to her chest as if she might will it to live again. There, under the incessant sound of its brothers, Harriet might be heard crying, too.

What unsavory fragrances stirred in those gloomy country rooms where damp laundry dangled. The air was sour with the smell of spilled milk and lamb scourings. And when the lambs were gone, the odor of old chickens stewing on the cookstove might regularly be inhaled, for since no eggs were to be had, it was reasoned that certain hens might just as well be eaten before they froze to death.

And tempers grew short and shorter yet. And the girls got coughs whilst their brothers got boils, and some of the boys—out of their mamma's hearing—bragged that they hadn't changed underclothes all winter long and that when they were forced to the basin, they had only washed their faces and maybe "up" to their elbows.

But comet or no, signs of spring eventually arrived. Most of the snows melted. Once again the waters rose to cover the lowlands until, as Gertrude put it, her pappa's and Uncle Charley's pastures looked like "sheets of gliding silver."

GONE AWAY

If the path were on higher ground and followed carefully, a restless young woman might hope to make her way across the little valley to her cousins' home where she had not been for "ever so long."

So it was, on a certain March afternoon, that Gertrude Applegate, in her oldest clothes and boots, had undertaken the adventure.

Who was it stomping on their porch, gaily hallooing?! The door flew open. Harriet, resurrected at last, had thrown her arms about Gertrude's waist and spun her about the room. Whereupon even the invalid Lisbon, who'd been brought downstairs to sit awhile, followed the example of his sisters and began to laugh as if he'd never known sorrow.

And of news Gertrude brought plenty, though she teased them awhile. How she relished putting them off with descriptions of the rotting carcasses she'd seen strewn everywhere en route until Irene, tired of hearing about the disagreeable look and smell of the countryside, avowed she'd just as soon stay home. Although Harriet had "died" to know of certain matters and persons, she did not have the nerve to inquire in front of her sisters.

At length, however, Gert had "sprung" her news. It seemed that her brother Alex and Henry Lane had started to the Idaho mines. Her father, she said, though not entirely approving, had given them each two hundred dollars so they might buy such supplies as they needed. Gertrude's other brothers and her brother-in-law, Charley Putnam, too, would head out as soon as possible, intending to catch up with Alex and Hen.

Harriet gripped the edge of her mother's little round table and turned as if to look out the window. She wished no one to see what was surely written upon her face. Her worst fear, it seemed, had already been accomplished: Hen Lane had gone back to the sort of life he'd known before. He'd gone away, and who knew whether he would ever return.

Irene saw her turn. Had Gertrude not been so entertaining, Irene might at long last have put two and two together.

Gert was enjoying the expression of disapproval on her cousin Lucy's face. Gert had "half a mind," she said, to don some of her brothers' clothes, a big ol' hat, and head off to Idaho herself. For surely, when all was said and done, it was a better thing to be a man. And any man who did not go off to Idaho to make his fortune was a fool.

At which point Lucy, declaring herself quite pleased to be a female, had inquired with considerable heat whether Gert thought John, Al, and Tom were fools. For Lucy was quite certain her father would not permit her brothers to take off for Idaho, much less "grease" their way with two hundred dollars each as her uncle Jesse had. The mines themselves were a humbug and an abomination, Lucy continued, attractive only to secessionists and those who wished to ignore their responsibilities at home. Having thus spoken, she abruptly sat down, as if surprised by her outburst.

Gertrude, until that unhappy moment, had intended no harm. She had only been busy being Gertrude. But suddenly she threw her proud head back. She would come down hard on Lucy, or so Irene thought. Thus 'Rene had wrung her hands, not knowing whom to placate first. In the end, all she had been able to muster were several "Oh dear, oh dears!" Something else came to her: It would not do to get Lisbon stirred up, she said. All now peered into the invalid's corner. His mouth hung open. He had commenced to rocking a little, his big hands clamped in his lap.

Gertrude, whose conscience had been plucked, hastened to her cousin. "Poor dear Lis!" she said aloud. Then, kneeling down so she might look directly in his eyes, she sweetly whispered something meant for his ears alone. The smile these remarks elicited had a good effect on everyone, including herself.

Another family storm had passed. The love shone again. Gert declared Lucy's dried-apple pie wonderfully spicy, and they all drank some tea made from the wild yerba buena vine, for there was no coffee yet. Yes, all were quite happy, save one whose name was Harriet.

John came in. Upon seeing him, Gert remembered a message she was supposed to have delivered: It seemed that Hen Lane had left his fiddle in her care with instructions to give it to John. John was to keep it until Hen returned to fetch it—his pockets full of nuggets. For Hen, Gert said laughing, had sworn to become the richest man in Yoncalla, sheep be d———d.

At this, even Lucy smiled a little. During Gertrude's visit the sky had filled with clouds. John offered to ride Gert home.

This plan was gratefully adopted.

John led his horse to the front yard. After Gertrude had been hugged all around, she took her place behind John, arranging her skirts accordingly. The sound of the big horse prancing through the puddles was almost pleasant. Gert waved and gave a lusty "war whoop," to the especial amusement of Fannie and Jane, who wondered along with Lucy, "Now just what will Gert do next?"

All save Lisbon lingered on the porch for a few moments until John and Gertrude receded from view, for the low ridge they traveled was thick with oaks.

Harriet insisted on lingering outside awhile. As she had on her warmest shawl, what could be the harm, Harriet asked. Whereupon Lucy had clucked at her. Yet how cheerful Harriet looked. Lucy was glad for it and shut the door.

The air was fresh and sweet. The sky was Harriet's entertainment. The wispy clouds thickened and shifted in mystic shapes— now dark, now light. He had gone away. Nevertheless, he intended to return.

Then something giddy nudged her. Off came her house moccasins and her high woolen socks, after which she hitched up her skirts in the manner of some mining-camp dancer. These acts at once chilled and delighted her. Her feet sank into the clover-rich sod, which gurgled a little as if to protest. The ground, though very wet, had a pleasant springy feel. As Harriet turned into the side yard, Lucy's geese honked companionably on the other side of the fence. They glided, gray and white, over the green-brown glassiness of the lower pastures.

Her outing was soon cut short, however. Just after she had paused and looked west so that she might admire the snow-streaked slopes of Mount Yoncalla in the near distance, an emphatic rain commenced. The little breeze, which at first had felt mild and springlike against her cheek, whipped over the water-bound fields.

Sighing, Harriet ducked under the dripping eaves and made her way to the front porch. As she passed the dining room window, she fully expected to see Lucy glowering at her. How different the world inside. Her mother's room was silent and dim. Lisbon had been left to doze in his chair. His big handsome head drooped to his chest, his hands were clamped together. Harriet sighed again. It made her feel sad to see him all alone in his corner.

She padded toward the chair nearest the fire. As she pulled up her stockings, she was glad no one was there to chide her.

An even stormier month would lie ahead. The weather that people feared most—the silver thaw—would cover the valley with ice, never mind that the calendar said April. The following morning, in fact, Harriet would arise and find the landscape white again.

But as she sat in the chair closest to the fireplace that afternoon, Harriet gave no thought to the weather, save perhaps to hope that John and Gert had found comfortable shelter in which to wait out the storm.

The rain quickened, pelting the windows while distant thunder rolled. How tired she felt. She closed her eyes a moment, her hair was damp under her fingers. Her mind presented picture after picture. Suddenly the lean figure of Henry Lane seemed to appear on a lovely meadow. He was carrying something. He drew closer. She was amazed to see a baby lambkin in his arms. This image faded, to be replaced by another. Vainly, she tried to call him back.

At length her conscience prevailed on her. She arose from her chair intending to find her duties before they found her. The deep, manly voice startled her, for less and less did Lisbon speak. He sat straight in his chair, his hands moving. Finally, she made out the word. He was saying, "Gert! Gert!"

Gertrude, she explained, hurrying to him, had gone home, "Gert" had gone away. Whereupon the invalid had grabbed her wrist, looking up at her beseechingly. Slowly he scanned the room, finding it empty of all those he loved save herself.

He did not say "Gert" anymore. Now came two words, which he repeated several times. His full lips quivered: Lisbon's refrain seemed to echo in the room. The thunder rumbled without. "Gone away," he said. "Gone away." And he would not let go of her hand.

Gertrude's Dream

If only it might be said that spring—for it finally arrived—had transformed all it touched, bringing contentment and calm to the stormiest heart.

It was true that as certain young men sowed wheat and mended weather-broken fences, they could not help but occasionally admire the undulant verdure of their homeground. So many iris and Indian camas bloomed upon the swales and bottomlands that the flowers appeared like little lakes of celestial blue amidst the returning grasses. The grasses themselves, though slow to start, seemed unusually lush. The awful thrall of winter had apparently loosened at last. Great numbers of fruit trees had survived and indeed appeared to thrive. All boded well for the honest tiller of the soil.

In less peculiar times vigorous young men had followed the example of other species who, like the red-throated grouse sequestered in copses of alder and vine maple upon the lower hills, chortled and drummed in courtship. Similarly inspired, the ring doves cooed their plaintive song in mistletoe chapels clumped high in the oaks. And everywhere upon the ridges, beneath the kingly shadows of the great fir trees, countless birds trilled and warbled as the fecund steam of life and the promise of life arose from the mossy forest floor. Resting on cedar snags, darting beneath the bright canopies of ferns, flitting through the cloudlike white dogwoods—these birds might be heard day or night.

They sang of loneliness. They sang of need that transcended mere desire. They sang as nature had intended them to sing.

Yet it was neither loneliness nor lust that made the young men of Yoncalla restless on spring evenings. When they finished the tedious tasks that were part and parcel of any farmer's life, if they sang at all, they sang of distances, not females. For it seemed to them that the rest of humanity was passing them by. How hard it was to "sit tight" at home when they might witness the Idaho-bound streaming up the Big Road at all hours of the day.

Many of these sojourners could be seen leading mules laden with supplies and tools. Others setting out for the northern mines traveled on foot, their meager foods strapped to their backs, their ill-mannered mongrels yipping at their heels and worrying such livestock as they passed along the route.

It was not these dogs that caused so many chickens to disappear from Yoncalla's henhouses that spring, but the two-legged "varmints" who owned the dogs, or so said the housewives of the locality.

Many of these would-be miners had camped carelessly along the roadside, leaving refuse of all kinds. They gathered up fence rails which the floods had carried away from nearby farms. Though the rails might have been reused, thus sparing the farmer the effort of splitting rails anew, the Idaho-bound thoughtlessly burned the rails in their campfires.

No man in the whole of Yoncalla was more against these men than Charley Applegate. Even his wife declared that he had become quite unreasonable on the subject, for at every opportunity he ridiculed not only those who were bound for the mines but those who supported them, his own brother Jesse included.

Through March and April Charley remained as irritable as his sons were wistful. It seemed that Charley had "got wind of" a certain invitation extended by his nephews, who believed that gold mining ought to become a family enterprise. John, Al, and Tom, the nephews urged, should pack up forthwith and join their expedition. Hen Lane and their brother Alex had already staked the perfect claim and were awaiting them. By going shares they could all be rich men. At which point Charley had flown into a high dudgeon indeed. Henry Lane was at the bottom of it all, he told his nephews. They would be better off to place their trust in the Devil than to follow Henry Lane. Charley had harangued even longer and harder when he discovered his own brother was providing more capital for the scheme.

Jesse complained of being short on money, Charley thundered, and yet he was throwing it away and leaving himself bereft of farmhands in the bargain. And worse than that was said, for Charley had been tippling at the time.

The nephews as they left Charley's house were much annoyed. But Charley was still not done. He then bellowed at his wife, all the while hammering his big fist upon the wooden mantel. If any of his "own" should "elope" to Idaho, those who had stayed home would find themselves wealthier when he died.

During the days that followed, Jesse Applegate looked better and better to his three nephews. John, Tom, and Al grumbled to one another as they split new fence rails and otherwise did Charley's bidding. It was not so much that they wished to go off to the mines, they complained, but to go "just any place at all." This was not to be, however, for Charley's sons were like certain of his horses: They were securely hitched to his plow.

Thus on the day that their cousins left for the mines, neither John, Tom, nor Al had been there for the send-off. They had been dispatched up into the hills to cut wood for their father. As it happened, Gertrude herself did not bid her brothers farewell, for she had gone to spend a day at her friend Mary Drain's, and from there had sent word that she intended to stay for a while with Harriet, who had taken a little sick again.

Sometimes it seemed to the offspring of Charley and Jesse that their families might just as well live across the country as across the valley from one another. Their fathers, of late, seemed estranged, and Uncle Lindsay was long gone from the neighborhood. Was nothing to remain the same even in the midst of one's own? Where was the old-time closeness? These were the very topics which had caused Gertrude to dab her eyes, not once but several times in the course of her visit to Harriet.

As she dramatically uttered these sentiments, she took Harriet's hands into her own for a moment. The upper porch, bathed in an oblique and misted April light, was Gertrude's stage. She had then paced back and forth, complaining of her life, which so suddenly, she said, had changed her into a grown and unhappy woman.

"No," Gert had exclaimed, "good-bye" was a word she could no longer abide. "Partings . . . farewells . . . misunderstandings." Surely, Lucy said later that same evening to Irene, Gert was not going "on and on" about partings and so on merely because her brothers were off to the mines! Something was afoot, Lucy opined. And what had Gert been doing of late passing so much time with Mary Drain? Had she nothing better to do than to befriend the daughter of a "sympathizer"?

But an occurrence in the wee hours of the following morning put off further consideration of these questions.

Harriet and Gert had been sleeping in different beds. Then the onset of one of Harriet's "spells" had come. At such times it seemed to Harriet that something immense and weighty had been

237

placed upon her chest. She could not breathe. Gertrude came to her bed and propped Harriet up against the headboard.

In a little while, save for the intermittent flutterings in her chest and a lingering sense of tiredness, Harriet was able to sleep soundly. She said later that she had felt Gertrude climb in bed and curl up beside her. A contented feeling was the last thing Harriet remembered.

Yet what a start she received a few hours later. Her eyes had flown open. Sobbing filled the room. Was it dawn or candlelight? Lucy had been standing at the foot of the big bed. And Gert? She was gone. It took Harriet a moment to understand. The figure weeping in the corner of the room was Gertrude, her face buried in her hands. At length Gertrude managed to say, "Oh, girls, I am so sorry to have awakened you."

Then Gertrude had padded to the westernmost window and plucked back the curtain a little as if, despite the faint light, she might see clear across the valley to her own home. "The boys are starting out for the mines this morning and I am not there to say good-bye," she said brokenly. Then she turned toward Lucy and Harriet, her voice seeming to row against the stream of her tears. "I dreamed . . ." Gertrude began and then beginning anew—for she was much wrought-up—she said again, "I dreamed . . . that there are some of us who will never, in this life, meet again."

After this startling announcement, Lucy shook her head and said rather horribly that if Gert truly felt the need to see her brothers off, she should bundle up, take John's horse, and gallop homeward. This, in Lucy's opinion, would have made far more sense than standing barefoot in the middle of the room crying. Of course, Gert didn't do anything of the kind, as Lucy was quick to point out later, for Gert stayed over two whole days more.

Nevertheless, Gertrude's dream had made everyone feel uneasy. Word of this dream was soon relayed to the young miners, for Gertrude had written them a letter, passed along to them by another Yoncalla man who had headed in the same direction and had made better time.

A few weeks later a returning miner brought a reply. Gertrude's brother Bob had written her the following: "We set out on Sunday after bidding all good-bye except yourself. We parted with many tears as your dream foretold. We parted when there was a probability that there were those of us that would never meet again in life. . . ." With these portentous words began the opening chapter of the little book that Gertrude commissioned, for she had demanded her brothers regularly send home an entertaining record of their observations, successes, and failures. Since the poor women on the planet, she complained, were permitted few of their own, secondhand adventures would be better than none "a'tall."

WHAT THE WEBFOOTS WRITE

Let us linger a moment on the broad front porch, since has it not been said there are partings up ahead? What day is it? It does not matter. Suffice to say that the special clover which Lucy had planted in the front and side yards is blooming in riotous purple-reds and imparting a remarkable sweetness to the summery air.

What an attractive figure Gertrude has become! Her olive skin is flushed. Her overslender look, which lent her a certain sharpness, has rounded charmingly. But beauty is indeed in the beholder's eye, and all who see her now, tripping gaily toward them, love her more with each day that passes.

And Harriet? There is a bluish cast beneath her eyes. She has grown thin and thinner. Yet today her look is alert and her sketchbook is upon her lap again. Buck, his little chin to her shoulder, has been watching the June rose she paints bloom upon the page. But now Buck runs and Harriet puts down her paintbrush. Gertrude has come. She is waving the long-awaited installment in her hand and merrily shouting her halloos.

Just before Gertrude's arrival all had been discussing the abundance of wild strawberries growing upon the hills, so many that year that the southern slopes, especially on the netherside of Mount Yoncalla, seemed startlingly hued in pink—or so a neighbor who recently called on Charley has told them. And so succulent and heavenly sweet grow these wild strawberries in the minds of those gathered upon the porch that an expedition to the hills might have been organized on the spot. Only Gertrude has appeared, driving her pappa's smallest buckboard.

"Gert! Gert!" Buck and Milt have now waylaid her as if she were the deer and they a pair of young hunting dogs.

And Irene and Lucy—for they are the gardening women—are rounding the corner, wearing their wide oat-straw hats, carrying their spades or hoes. But even Lucy will stop her work when Gert appears. For it is Gertrude who brings the Salmon River and all its colorful happenings to their very door, so that miles shrink and even beloved and absent voices seem to sound in their ears for a moment. And when the spirit moves her, for Gertrude is not the

241

least shy when she reads aloud to them, her droll interjections are apt to be almost as comical as the narratives themselves.

Indeed, all save Charley Applegate have been much amused by the installments the sojourners continue to send home, each "author" making contributions in his own style. Irene, especially, has been taken with the title of the book, which is as follows:

Ventures and Adventures of a Party of Webfoot Miners on Their Way to and in the Poly Region of the Northern Mines . . .

Written and composed by Alex, Mr. Robt. S., and Wm. H. H. Applegate, C. F. and Chas. Putnam, and Henry Lane.

Even Mr. Dickens's serial *Great Expectations,* which she has followed avidly in *Harper's* magazine, has taken second fiddle to the adventures of their own Webfoots.

John, Al, and, Tom, who had spied Gert and her buckboard from a vantage point in the upper fields, have hastened down and have now stationed themselves on the shadiest portion of the porch. John is working on making yet another dulcimer, and Tom and Al are mending tack. All three have a relaxed look, for their taskmaster has taken himself off the premises for the afternoon.

And their mamma, seated nearby, has a peaceful look, too, as she spoons Lisbon his favorite sort of soup, for even the invalid has been hauled outdoors for a while.

Fanny and Jane are playing quite amiably, their dolls' quilts hanging on the railing. They have taken hollyhocks from the side yard and transformed them into water-dancers, whose flared petal skirts now whirl across the surface of a filled waterpail.

If only Ellen, Mary, Susie, and Jim and their spouses and little ones might be here, too, Melinda Applegate thinks: The family— all gathered round itself. But let them be happy at their own homes today or else all would be far less peaceful.

Gertrude opens the packet and begins. Now, all will hear how a d———d old secesh has been met on the road to Idaho and what he has had to say about Charley Applegate and the cattle he sells. And John, who has been to Salem only once, will learn how loose change is lured from an unsuspecting "feller's" pockets as he

walks down the lonely gaslit streets of the new metropolis of Portland. And Tom will laugh long and hard at a certain silly conversation that transpired between French Jo, a boatman, and of a
rough, wet ride up the Columbia. Irene will shake her head over
reports of "poor" blistered feet and "measle" attacks.

But of all the anecdotes that Gertrude has relayed from these
first chapters, one Webfoot adventure has special significance for
Melinda Applegate—so much so that she has actually interrupted
the reading. It seems that the young family miners have visited a
tumbledown adobe ruin located at the confluence of the Columbia
River and the Walla Walla River. This place was once called Old
Nez Percé, or Fort Walla Walla, which is the name known by the
older Applegates.

Oh, how vividly this old fortification stands out in Melinda
Applegate's memory. "Can it be almost twenty years?" she asks
aloud as she scans the faces of her children. And Gertrude, she
points out, was but a year old at most when her father and uncles
began building the family boats while laying over at this same old
Fort Walla Walla.

Gertrude continues reading aloud. The young Applegates have
disparaged the old bastion of the Hudson's Bay Company. They
have compared it unfavorably with Fort Sumter and other mod-
ern-day military establishments they have read about, noting, disdainfully, the doubtless even in its heyday, old Fort Walla Walla
could not have withstood the firing of so much as one Union
cannonball. It seems that even Idaho and the prospect of making
a fortune in such a wild and remote area of the continent have no
power to make young men forget. The distant war pulls on their
imaginations even as they write of reaching the canvas-sided city
of Lewiston, Idaho.

When next heard from, the Webfoots will report about how
they have spent their last dime on bread and will admit that the
Salmon River country is not all that they had hoped for. At new
"hunting grounds" near Crooked River they will be scrabbling for
venison instead of gold. Even so, they will brag about their culinary triumphs, preparing Idaho grouse, elk, rabbit, curlew, and
woodcock. They will even go so far as to express perfect contentment. In their "log pen" with but a canvas roof they'll say
how pleasant it is to eat bachelor's bread made in a frying pan

with no one to please but themselves. Yet no one will be fooled at home, for even John, Al, and Tom will read between the lines. Oh, what the Webfoot miner wouldn't exchange for even the smallest taste of the wild strawberries of Yoncalla and for the sweet company of those who picked them, too.

FATEFUL STRAWBERRIES

Later it would be said that Harriet ought to have been *made* to stay home, for the fact was, she had just gotten over another "spell." Yet who had had the heart to keep her from going? "Strawberries!" she had exclaimed as jubilantly as any child. "Why, of course I'm going."

George Burt, her sister Ellen's husband, came to fetch them. Who knew why? Perhaps he'd wanted to show off his new spring wagon or hoped to please his children or himself. It was no secret that Burt was a lover of jams and preserves. As the strawberries were of dainty size, vast quantities were needed for such treats as his sweet tooth required. All pickers, large and small, would be welcome, he said when he climbed down from the wagon. The more, the merrier. And this surprised his sisters-in-law, of whom there were many, for George Burt was not known to have much "fun" in him. In general, his disposition was as heavy as his hams—or so it was said secretly.

Harriet's "spell" had been peculiar indeed, for it did not resemble any other. One morning she awoke to find her feet so swollen that her shoes would not fit. Even her house moccasins hurt her, and everyone could see how her ankles puffed clear over their tops. Her knees had been similarly swollen. After a few days this remarkable condition passed, but only after her mamma had put her strictly to bed.

Some thought later the episode had heralded the decline, even though Harriet herself had insisted she was completely improved and no longer sick but "only tired." As if to prove this statement Harriet had taken on more of her old duties at home. While a look of effort could always be seen upon her face, something of her former vitality appeared restored. Appearances were deceiving on that June afternoon.

The persons arriving in Burt's wagon were Burt himself and two of Harriet's older sisters, Ellen and Mary, who were accompanied by numerous offspring. To this gleefully noisy crowd were to be added Harriet, Lucy, Fanny, Jane, and Irene.

As all prepared to climb aboard Burt's wagon, Irene's comfort became everyone's concern. She too had been ill throughout the winter. Earlier she had announced that she was afraid she might catch cold again. On that basis she had threatened to stay home. To which Harriet, seeming her old self, had responded with somewhat exaggerated sisterly devotion, "'Rene, 'Rene, you must come, for never has there been a more glorious day." After which, Harriet had avowed that should a wind come up, she herself would shield Irene from it.

This was why Harriet deliberately sat in the outermost seat all the way to old Mount Yoncalla. The weather was good. There was not so much as a breath of a breeze.

At length Irene looked almost cheerful and confessed herself glad to be "off the place," for she'd been no farther than her garden since the new year. June ripened all around them. It almost seemed as if nature were compensating for former devastations. Everything they passed shimmered with goodness and green.

Birdsong hovered above the easy slope they climbed. How often Harriet would think of this in the long weeks to come. More memorable still would be the delicious scent of wild strawberries ripening in the sun. To Harriet, only the low and lovely violet produced a perfume that was more beguiling.

The particular slope Burt had chosen that afternoon was less than a mile from Jesse Applegate's home on what was known as the Hayhurst side of Mount Yoncalla. Gertrude, not one to be left out of any fun, had suspended her little "school" for the day. With her younger sisters Sally, Alena, and Flora bringing along extra pails and five of Rozelle Applegate Putnam's orphans, she had trooped over to the picking place. The sixth Putnam orphan, Charley Jr., was with his uncles and his father, "Big" Charley, trying to find gold in Idaho.

At first the clouds had merely feathered the eastern horizon. Then, more pale than ominous, they arranged themselves into low, pretty pillars—the distinctive formations the local people called "thunderheads." The younger children, not knowing the cause of their excitement, began to fret and prance quite wildly just as horses and other animals sometimes do before a storm.

"Oh dear," Irene was heard to say worriedly, for it was she who first pointed out the darkening horizon. From that moment forward, her pleasure in the outing had been entirely "spoilt."

Now, George Burt could be a scoffing sort of man, but sensing his sister-in-law's distress (and because his wife had urged him to it), he took Irene aside and assured her that the storm was yet a long ways off. Indeed, it might never reach Yoncalla at all, he said.

Nevertheless, 'Rene had been the first to head down the slope to the waiting wagon. Others were quick to follow. Grumbling, for he had yet to feel a drop of rain, Burt "did as he was told." After which, he commanded his wife to place the Indian basket, which contained the fattest strawberries, right there beside him on the wagon seat.

He had, however, been much mistaken about the storm. For it came to pass that he could not move his team fast enough. The wind whipped mightily down the valley. The willows they passed were half bent over. Heavy and warm, the rains poured over them.

Gertrude, her sisters, and all their little charges had also been crammed into Burt's wagon. Holding out their voluminous skirts as windbreaks, Gertrude and Harriet stationed themselves on either side of Irene. Even though this endeavor proved largely successful, Irene was still heard to moan intermittently. Once or twice, as though with great effort, she leaned over and patted the soaked shoulder of one or the other of her bodyguards, commending them for their sacrifice.

Although exceedingly wet, neither Gertrude nor Harriet appeared any the worse for the experience. On the contrary, later that evening Gert declared the rain had been as pleasant as bathwater, adding that it left her hair feeling softer than any baby's.

Why, it had been just the thing, Harriet said. Just the sort of excitement she had craved all winter long! And she laughed then and recounted how, as the wagon lurched, Burt had cursed and popped strawberries into his mouth whilst the children squealed anew at each clap of thunder. Irene, however, had declared it no adventure at all. She had been chilled to the bone, she said. Indeed, Irene had appeared quite miserable and distraught.

Thus when the pickers arrived at Gertrude's home, where they had been invited to lay over until the storm should pass, it was little wonder that Gertrude's mother took care of Irene's discomforts first: poor pitiful thing.

At length most of the other pickers found themselves warm and dry, for Cynthia Applegate and Gertrude dragged out many an old thing from "hamper and cupboard." At Gertrude's insistence, Harriet finally accepted a loose-fitting shirtwaist whilst her dress dried by the fire. Harriet said nothing, however, about the condition of her petticoats and underclothes, which were damp in the extreme. This failure to make herself more comfortable was later blamed on her acute modesty.

The storm was in reality a series of little tempests following in rapid succession until, finally, even Burt agreed there was nothing for it but to stay overnight. Their hostess's hasty supper was enjoyed by all. Indeed, theirs was a festive if impromptu gathering. How happy they were to be in a "family way" again. Cynthia Applegate declared the storm a blessing. Yet throughout the evening, even as others enjoyed themselves, Harriet had been terribly chilled. Only after the incident did they learn that she had shivered all night long and not removed her damp underthings until she'd again reached the privacy of her own room. As Irene was subsequently to describe the episode, it almost seemed as if Harriet's damp petticoats in and of themselves had brought on the sickness that was so painful to witness.

Nothing could shake Irene's belief that she was somehow to blame, for whilst at their aunt's and uncle's, she said, with nothing under her save a thin rush mattress, poor Harriet had lain upon the draughty floor in front of the fireplace. Irene, at her Aunt Cynthia's urgings, had been warm and dry in a feather bed upstairs. "No," Irene would say over and over, "I will never *ever* forgive myself."

Oh, remorse! Is anything quite so painful or futile? Remorse for that which cannot be changed; for that which is past and done and will never, by human hand, be made right again. Who in Harriet's household did not feel it? Even Jane heaped imprecations upon her own little head, ashamed that she had imitated Harriet at almost every opportunity. For Jane had come to resent the sight of Harriet "drooping" around. More and more of Harriet's chores had been assigned to her. Thus, playing on Harriet's conscience, Jane had deliberately whimpered over her "extry" duties, adding that the *least* Harriet might do, since she could not do anything else, was to read aloud to them more or less on demand, and Jane could be most demanding.

Yet what reason to think that the little cold that Harriet had contracted after their strawberry outing should amount to anything more than what had gone on and on all winter long? Why, Jane herself, though indifferently treated, had the "snuffles," too.

Thus whenever Harriet had been asked to read and she demurred—pleading tiredness—Jane had nagged without mercy, with Fanny, Milt, and Buck following her example. Harriet, exhibiting none of her former firmness, quickly gave in. Yet even the littlest among them noted that Harriet seemed increasingly taxed by reading aloud. So a compromise was struck. For several days she had simply "told" them a story of her own devising.

One afternoon, at a particularly suspenseful point in Harriet's narrative, Gertrude arrived. Gertrude brought a letter from Elisha, so entertaining, she said, that Harriet must read it "at once." With this command, Queen Gertrude had gaily dropped the letter into Harriet's lap.

The truth was Gertrude was not gay but worried. She had not, until calling on the household that afternoon, known of her cousin's relapse. Harriet's bright hair was dull and limp. Her look was gray. But would Jane let Harriet read her letter? She would not. Harriet must keep her promise, Jane whined. 'Lish's old letter could wait.

Gertrude glared long and hard at little Jane, but in the end Jane won, for Harriet allowed she must "finish up." Her voice quavered a little. Gertrude had gone into the kitchen to say hello to Lucy while Harriet brought an end to her chapter. Jane didn't much like what had happened to the heroine and said so, too.

Jane then watched her sister pick up the letter, which had been lying upon her lap throughout. The letter was carefully unfolded, and Jane saw Harriet lift it ever closer to her eyes as if trying to make it out—whereupon a great and sudden sob could be heard. The letter was flung down, its numerous pages fluttering to the floor.

At this very moment Gertrude returned, saying to Jane, who stood astonished and motionless, "What on earth have you done you, selfish child?!"

These were words to scald any spirit, but worse were forthcoming: "Oh, Gert," cried Harriet who, her head in her hands, sat weeping inconsolably. "My head aches so! I might as well be blind and be done with it for I can no longer read at all. Oh, Gert! What's to become of me!"

And after this confession had been made—for none had suspected the true extent of her suffering—Harriet's sobs had grown deeper and deeper until she was gasping for breath and clutching at Gertrude's slim waist as if her very life depended upon it. Try as she might, Gertrude did not succeed in comforting her.

The color had quite drained from Harriet's face and she commenced wheezing and twisting in her chair, as though trying to loosen invisible bonds. "Quick! Jane," Gert cried, "go get your mother!"

How Jane came to hate the memory of it. Harriet had been shouting words that made no sense at all. She flung back her head. She fought Gertrude. She fought her distraught mother. In the end, it had taken both John and Al to carry her up the steep little staircase from which she was to descend no more.

So agitated did Harriet remain that at length they had even removed her from the big front bedroom she had always shared with her younger sisters. Neither Jane nor any other child was permitted to visit her in the little spare room. Harriet would not "know them," their mother told them sadly. Yet they sometimes heard their sister moaning. And once, quite clearly, she'd shouted, "Can I not die?" Then, much more softly, in a voice filled with such resignation that tears rose in the eyes of all who overheard, Harriet prayed, "Oh Father. Dear Father in Heaven. Thy will be done."

And Gertrude had not gone home after all, for she feared Harriet's days were drawing nigh. She and Lucy maintained an almost constant vigil behind the closed door. At length Harriet raved no more. Breathing came too dearly to her. She seemed in danger of suffocating even as she lay still. Nor would the fever leave her. It was at this point that Melinda Applegate became utterly desperate. She resorted to some little pills the old Dutch doctor in her neighborhood had given her.

It should be said that Harriet's mother had long been experienced in the care of the sick. All winter long she had administered from her considerable store of homegrown "yarbs" and "simples" that had so often given comfort to Harriet in the past. As time went on, and Harriet had rallied only to fail again, Melinda Applegate had at last sought advice from a kindly older man known as Doctor Dagan. He, too, placed great stock in what he called nature's own medicines, most of which he had transported from the Old World. He had prescribed certain tonics and pills and evil-smelling poultices, all of which Harriet had, for reasons known only to herself, refused quite adamantly. Let him try his "cures" on someone else, she had said.

Thus only desperation now forced Melinda Applegate to impose Dr. Dagan's medicine upon her daughter. Yet what else was a mother to do? A short time after the medicine had been given, Harriet was beset with tremors. Fearful that her daughter would expire on the spot, it came to her mother that the destructive medicine which had evidently instigated the tremors must immediately be purged from the patient's system. To that end Melinda Applegate had given a dose of the emetic known as ipecac.

Oh, how she rued the day. The act of vomiting had itself used Harriet up, or so her poor mamma believed. And though all remorse is painful, is any to be compared with that experienced by a heartbroken mother? There had been no hope whatever after that. They waited and knew what they waited for.

The weather was hot. The hills had turned tawny. The hay had been reaped. Lucy and Gertrude watched the light disappearing. Each of the two little windows grew dark. Just as the candle was lit, the crickets started up in earnest, or so it seemed to the two women stationed by Harriet's bed.

Unlike Lucy, Gertrude was not disposed merely to sit with folded hands gazing mutely at Harriet. Surely, thought Gertrude, an evening so oddly sweet was not meant to be borne entirely in such an unrelieved and stoical silence.

It was the third of July. But a year had passed since Harriet had visited Gertrude and they had spent the day making gay preparations for the grand and glorious Fourth! And as the memories of this event rose in Gertrude's mind, she recounted them in a soft though expressive voice, only half aware at first that she was not so much addressing Lucy as her poor cousin upon the low bed. The lone little candle illuminated Harriet's face; her sunny hair spread loosely over the pale pillow. As Gertrude murmured on, it seemed to her that Harriet bore the aspect of some trance-ridden maiden in a fairy tale.

But something sad and sharp rose unexpectedly in Gertrude even as she continued to speak. How could it be? Rozelle had already been taken and now, it appeared, so would another. Why did God take the young and kindhearted? Surely the Creator would relent.

Gertrude went on, as if her eloquence might somehow penetrate the sleeper and make things right again. She described the meadows, the cool shadowed oak groves, the pony races, the fiddlers upon the green. At last her voice trailed off, and Gertrude rose as if to depart. Surely relief would arrive soon in the form of Irene and her mother, Lucy said, for she too was ready to leave the room for a while. At which point Gert sat down again and Lucy, in a rather flat voice, began to recollect aloud.

It was like Lucy to describe each and every banner that had been made for the previous Fourth of July. So lackluster was her recounting that Gertrude, thinking to herself that silence would have been better, was unable to suppress a yawn.

It was then that Lucy, perhaps to ensure Gertrude's attention, had spoken for some moments about the raising of the new flag and about Gertrude's portion in that ceremony.

Alas, no subject could have been more sore to Gertrude. She saw herself as she had been but a year and a day before. Her heart then had been heavy with the knowledge of her hypocrisy. She was no "Union maid." She had merely wished to bring her father pleasure. Yet it was not the man's cause she loved, but the man himself. It came to pass that the man she loved most was no longer her pappa but, instead, James D. Fay.

Of all Gertrude's kin only one had gradually become privy to the innermost secrets of her heart: Harriet, who had not judged her but only loved her. Whereupon so lonely and lost had Gertrude felt suddenly that she knelt beside her sweet cousin's bed as if comfort might be forthcoming even in such a hour of extremity. And when once again Gert stood up wearily, she felt herself tremble, for she knew what she must do with her life.

It was then that Gertrude heard Lucy gasp. There had been no sound save that. And the crickets. And the footsteps creaking upward upon the little stairs.

Silence hung over the narrow bed in the narrow room.

She had given up the ghost. She had slipped away. Harriet, free at last, breathed no more.

A Sad Afterword

Now, years later, many things must be related. Those who believe in the next world may perhaps take heart from the following account, which concerns a strange episode that occurred on the night that Harriet died.

After Gertrude and Lucy had quietly closed the door behind them, the tears coursing down Gertrude's cheeks conveyed all that Melinda Applegate needed to know. Their hands joined, Melinda, Irene, Gertrude, and Lucy stood silently in the dark hall together. The chiming of the new downstairs clock could be heard. They stood there prayerfully as it struck ten times. Only then did all enter the narrow room. The candle they had left lit was out. The time of Harriet's death, then, was placed at about three minutes to ten o'clock on July 3, 1862. She was but halfway through her sixteenth year.

Each of Melinda Applegate's eight daughters had been under her roof on that melancholy night so long ago. It was assumed that poor Harriet might pass away at any moment, thus all had arrived to be of assistance to their mother as well as to one another when the sad time came. About eight o'clock Buck, Milt, Fanny, Jane, and numerous of their little nephews and nieces, who were in some cases nearly their age, had been dispatched upstairs to the bedtime quarters appropriate to their gender.

But here we will let Irene Applegate take up the particulars, using her own words. On July 21, sitting in the same room where Harriet had died but weeks before, Irene wrote the following to her "dear dear Aunt Betsy" in Ashland.

    . . . All the time Harriet was sick Buck and Milt would beg to see her but after she got so bad that she hardly knew anybody they were kept away. About nine o'clock on the evening of her passing Buck came down and told Mama he heard Harriet calling him.

He was sent back to bed, and, as is the habit of healthy children, slept throughout the night, no one disturbing him.

In the morning he got up early and came into Mama's big room and said to her: "Mama, where is Harriet? I want to see her."

253

And Mama told him, Harriet died last night at ten o'clock. "She is not here anymore."

"No, no," cried Buck, "I saw her last night and she said she was well. She came in where Milt and me was sleeping and I saw her plain."

It was only when Buck saw her lying dead upon her narrow bed could he be convinced that it was so.

Did ever a young woman's death sadden a family more! How full of dread were the sons and daughters of Lindsay Applegate when Irene's letter arrived, sealed ominously with black sealing wax. At first all had been certain it was Melinda Applegate who had been taken from them. Yet even before the seal was broken and its gloomy contents revealed, Oliver Applegate was heard to say: "No . . . no . . . it is not the mother but the daughter. . . . It is dear Harriet! Oh, that it were not true!"

This same cousin, Oliver, or O.C. as some called him, had been closer than any brother to Harriet. So shaken was he by her passing that he wished in some small way to commemorate her life. A few years later, while exploring the wilderness of the Sis-kiyous, Oliver happened upon a tiny gemlike mountain lake known only to the Indians. To this lake he bestowed the name Harriette, spelled deliberately with two t's and an e, for he knew she had always wished it to be thus.

Harriet's funeral was a simple affair attended by countless friends and neighbors. Some pious persons regarded it as a genuine Independence Day, for it fell on the Fourth of July. Very little was seen of Gertrude afterward. At length, however, as the summer waned, there came a September twilight when a lithe form could be seen coming across the fields. As so often had been the case, Gertrude was carrying a letter. Though addressed to her, the letter contained "special messages for Uncle Charley's family" from those who yet toiled in the distant mines.

"Your dream that some of us who parted last spring would no longer meet again in this life has been fulfilled. . . . You were right in supposing that we had heard of Harriet's death and there were but few dry eyes in the camp. . . ." So did Gertrude's brother Alexander Applegate put it. And all who listened so quietly on the porch as Gertrude continued reading the letter envisioned the

254

somber young miners seated around a campfire, where sparks shot upward into the spangled Idaho night just as surely as human souls soar toward their Maker. What Alex wrote next had even pulled Charley Applegate's heartstrings a little, and went a long way indeed toward putting a resentment to rest at last. For Alex wrote that: "Poor Henry Lane seemed to take Harriet's passing harder than any of the rest of us. After we had all calmed down enough to get to sleep we awoke far into the night only to see him sitting by the fire with his face in his hands."

It is reported that Henry Lane did not come back to Yoncalla for many a year, and that when he did his intervening dissipations and the rough-and-tumble life he'd led showed plainly upon his countenance. He had become a serious gambling man, six-shooter, studded cowhide vest, and all. His fiddle remained with his old friend John Applegate.

But at a more venerable age Henry Lane is reported to have foresworn his long affair with liquor and cards. Always he'd thought affectionately of the Applegates, and from time to time in those later years he made a point to call upon various members of the family. It should be added that when Irene and Lucy saw him, they had been much chagrined and had refused to entertain any conversation with him pertaining to their beloved Harriet. For Love, coming as it did from the "likes of him," could not be understood by them even though it had endured, spanning decades.

Love: As the reader was forewarned, *two* painful partings were to sadden these pages. The second parting must now be described in the briefest manner possible, for we have already lingered too long.

Gertrude's liaisons with Mr. Fay, which were chaste though passionate in spirit, continued until October of 1864. Shortly after Harriet's death Gertrude tried desperately to bring the whole affair out into the open. She confessed her affection for Fay to her family and tried to portray her lover in the best possible light. She had quite understandably grown tired of the need for deception and hoped, indeed prayed, that Mr. Fay might eventually win acceptance from those she loved.

This cause was hopeless. Her father refused to let Fay set foot over his threshold. At every opportunity Jesse Applegate disparaged the politics of the young secesh, vainly attempting to apply logic where feelings reigned. It came to pass that though they continued to live in the same household, Jesse Applegate and his daughter spoke but rarely.

Sometime during this period several of Gertrude's cousins moved quite close to the mining settlement of Jacksonville, where James D. Fay had taken up residence. These cousins were outspoken men. Their mistrust of Fay extended beyond political questions and into the realm of morals and personal conduct. A feud of sorts developed. It was claimed by Fay that Ivan Applegate had been the perpetrator, though, as might be expected, there were countercharges.

Suffice it to say that Gertrude was furious to find her lover the subject of so much unfair controversy, for in those days Fay could yet do little wrong in her eyes. By the summer of 1864, Gertrude turned upon her kinsmen to such a degree, even upon her staunchest supporters, that they ceased to defend her.

These personal and political disputes were in many ways exacerbated by the generalized fear that then gripped the Union men of Oregon. Although the turning point in the Great Rebellion

Gertrude Applegate Fay, circa 1867. (Courtesy Southern Oregon Historical Society)

Henry Lane, Harriet's suitor, circa 1870. (Applegate family photograph. Courtesy Douglas County Museum)

had been reached near Gettysburg, Pennsylvania, in the summer of 1863, Oregonians still had good reason to be concerned with their future, especially as the concept of the Pacific Republic had found increasing acceptance. James Fay was said to be in cahoots with many of the would-be organizers. Most certainly, he was an active Knight.

In the years 1865 and 1866, many of the Applegates had volunteered to serve their state and country. They did not look kindly upon "shirkers" like James D. Fay, especially when they found themselves assigned to the lonely outposts of eastern Oregon whilst Fay and other secesh stayed home doing more or less as they pleased.

Thus far the portrait of Mr. Fay has been unflattering, to say the least. Yet some attractive quality or qualities must have existed in him. After all, Gertrude was an intelligent young woman and she remained steadfast in her loyalty to him—and he, it is supposed, to her—for some seven years. However brash he may have been, Fay was evidently admired. His law practice thrived and his political star was obviously on the rise. Several times he would be elected to state office.

As to why Gertrude waited so long to escape to what she surely must have seen as the permanent security of her lover's arms, it will be remembered that her mother, Cynthia Applegate, had inherited no less than eight little orphans. Year after year Gertrude was her mamma's helpmate. Regardless of her headstrong ways, she was a conscientious daughter. In the end, even concern for her mother was not enough to keep Gertrude home.

Early one October evening in 1864 Gertrude was seen to board the southbound stagecoach. She carried a single valise of medium size. Her lover waited within. He said later that she cried without stint all the way to Roseburg. There, they disembarked. The papers were prepared and ready for signature. The vows were exchanged in the sterile atmosphere of a court. This not especially happy union lasted about three years more.

Her poor family, some will say. Yes, it is true they were crushed and that her father, especially, could find no comfort for months to come. At the time of her elopement Gertrude had left not even a note! Only a few words were scrawled on her bedroom wall, saying that her little sister Flora should have her things.

And Gertrude herself? Thinking that since the deed had been

accomplished, her father might relent, Gertrude wrote regularly to her family. No answer came.

Surely, her pappa would acknowledge the birth announcement she forwarded to Yoncalla soon after little Jimmy Fay was born, she thought. But no good wishes for her baby boy or inquiries concerning him or any other matter were forthcoming.

Poor Gert. Though almost two years had passed since her marriage, she was not merely disapproved of but *shunned*. When he could no longer stand his fatherly pain, Jesse Applegate had simply killed his daughter off. This act, though symbolic, was tragic all the same. Gertrude's name would never again be uttered under his roof, he said. He had forbidden it. Further, he had made certain that everyone was apprised of his displeasure. Gertrude had betrayed not only her family but the cause they all stood for. Should she have the audacity to call upon them, Jesse wrote to numerous friends and relatives, he urged them to turn her away.

The cord had been forever cut, he said. With his sharpest penknife he methodically scratched Gertrude's name from the big family Bible, leaving only the smallest trace. It was as if she had never been born.

Oh, what harm we do when we cut ourselves off from our kindred, whether their wrongs are imagined or real. Who is to say the true cause of Gertrude's illness. It is the spirit that weakens first.

Sometime in 1865 Gertrude took sick. Her cough. Her thinness and unnatural brightness of eye. No Jacksonville physician cared to relay his suspicion to the passionate Mr. Fay. At length, it was Gertrude herself who dared speak the truth: it was the same Dread Consumption that had taken the life of her dear sister Rozelle. And so saying, she told her husband that she wished to return to her parents' house so she might be reunited with those she loved before she wasted away altogether.

This idea suited Fay very well. After all, he was an extremely busy man who seemed inclined to travel at every opportunity. Even with a housekeeper to help with their little boy, it was surely not easy for a man of his disposition to abide a continually ailing wife. The truth was, in his way, he loved her. As the months passed and his "Gert" grew worse instead of better, he took matters in his own hands.

From Jacksonville, then, came letters stating his wife's desires

258

and the sad condition of her health. For some time his entreaties went unanswered. Gertrude's mother pleaded without stint so that at last the father relented somewhat. Gertrude might return with her babe, but the man who despoiled her, "that contemptible and cocky traitor," would under no circumstances set boot on Mount Yoncalla.

This answer was relayed to Gertrude when a relative called upon her in 1867. "Gert" felt compelled to make her painful choice all over again. She meant her marriage vows. If her husband could not bring her and her baby home, she would not go.

But there came a desperate day, not long after, when Fay, distraught over Gertrude's decline, packed her and their boy into their family carriage and set out for Yoncalla. She would have her deepest wish, decided Fay. If, after delivering her safely, the door remained closed to him, he determined within himself that he would go quietly away. He led his wife to believe amends had already been made.

It is said that for many miles Gertrude did not seem entirely sensible of her surroundings: Nevertheless, instinct guiding her for some reason, she partially rose from her improvised bed. They had reached the point where the schoolhouse could be seen.

"It is all the same," she said, sighing. Then, lying back on her pillows, "Only I have changed."

As the carriage stopped in front of the big house, her brothers, overjoyed to see her, hastened to help Fay lift her down. Yet Gertrude would not permit them to take her up the steps. "Not until I am sure my husband is welcome! I cannot go in if he does not."

By then her mother had flung open the door and rushed down to them, embracing the little grandson, who still held on to his daddy's hand. "Come in," said Cynthia Applegate. "All of you, please come in! And take my girl upstairs to her old room."

Only then was the tall form of Jesse Applegate evident. "Pappa," said Gertrude as they carried her past him. "I have come home to die."

"You have only come home to be nursed back to health by your good mother," her father told her sternly. "That is all you have come for." Nor did he call upon her as she lay in her sickbed on that day or for many days to come.

One evening, after a fitful afternoon, she asked for her husband. Her younger sisters and nieces had gathered around her bed.

259

Gertrude begged for a favorite hymn "unheard," she said, "for far too long."

Fay, standing at her feet, listened to the little choir. "Who taught them to sing like that?" he asked, dabbing his eyes.

"I did," said Gertrude.

On the next morning Gertrude asked her mother to fetch her father immediately. After some moments Jesse Applegate responded to this pathetic summons. No one save himself ever knew what he said to his child or she to him. Afterward he strode out to his orchard alone. Even as Gertrude's life "flickered out," the figure in the orchard could be seen working with his hoe up and down the rows.

Then, true to her prediction, Gertrude, whilst snug in her "dear ol' bed" in her "dear ol' room" like Harriet and Rozelle before her, bade good-bye to the "dear ol' world."

It is said that one of Gertrude's young sisters learned to play her melodeon, and that for years to come its sweet notes continued to drift out of the high windows and down to the gardens below. If this is so, let us rejoice that certain things are never lost and may indeed be passed along. Nevertheless, as has been said before, the sad truth is that each and every human family is as a constellation in the firmament, which, whether clustered or farflung, contains both brighter and lesser lights. When one star dies, pity the others, for they may never fill the darkened place, no matter how hard they try.

PART TWO

PORTRAITS AND MEDITATIONS

THE MARROW

Melinda Miller Applegate

Pioneer Wife and Mother
Born Clay County, Tennessee
Growing to Womanhood in Missouri
Came to the Oregon Territory
Wife of Charles Applegate

1879

. . . To be strong but to be tired and have no one know about it. To be worried and worrisome and to have no one know about that, either. An old woman . . . you're an old woman, Melinda.

"I'm gonna go upstairs and sit on the balcony for a bit, 'Rene. Call me if he awakens." The daughter watched her walk to the doorway. She was skin and bones, her mother, drab, large-framed, like most of the women in the family. She could not remember a time when her mother had not looked exhausted, uneven pallor and deep lines in her face despite the slenderness. And yet she appeared no more or less tired than usual this morning, though she had not slept once in three days of caring for the sick man. Her everyday voice, the same determined look, the pinch-lipped composure that never seemed to give way to pain or joy. The long sickroom vigil left no mark. But then she was a woman long experienced in the care of the sick. Used to birth and death. She was a midwife, and not only for her many married daughters and daughters-in-law. At times her big white house functioned almost as a hospital for her community. She doctored her large family with the concoctions and extractions she made from the "yarbs" she grew in her special garden, or the roots and wild things gathered on the hills and meadowlands. During epidemics of measles, whooping cough, diphtheria, and influenza more than one anxious mother had been given the advice "Go to Mrs. Applegate's, she'll know what to do." But this man, whose forehead she now dabbed with cool, sweet-smelling compresses, whose bedding she smoothed so carefully, was her husband of fifty years, Charley Applegate.

The girl, Irene, was high-strung, they said. Short of steadiness. A good girl—or woman really—but missing the strong will of her mother and older sister, Lucy, and given to maladies. On that first

The Last Apple of Winter. Melinda Applegate and
four of her grandchildren are depicted as they gather
wild herbs in the fields behind the Charles
Applegate house. (Susan Applegate painting.
Photograph courtesy Douglas County Museum)

evening the father's face had turned a deep and nasty yellow.
Irene had blanched, was visibly shaken, and had to leave the
room for a while. Perhaps more than her brothers and sisters, she
felt a special affection for their father, a loyalty that had not
wavered even in the face of what her uncle Jimmy Miller, a Methodist lay preacher, referred to in sepulchral tones as "the family's
humiliation." She watched her father's once robust body, so
strangely still now and empty of its bluster or flashes of mirth. It
was bloated, her mother said, from "bile." "It's not just the old
sickness, mind you, it's the liquor that puffs him up so. All those
years of John Barleycorn."

Irene thought of one morning during the past winter, just before the trouble had come to a head. It was early. Maybe four
o'clock. She had come to the kitchen, feeling bad herself. She saw
him through the kitchen window. He stood on the porch, with
the fog swirling all around him like a moving wall. He was dipping
into the whiskey barrel with the white porcelain cup he always
used. Once, twice, tilting back his head to meet the whiskey. He
came through the door, wiping his mouth on his shirtsleeve.

266

"Well, 'Little,' up pretty early, ain't ya? Spying on your pappa, eh?" He laughed. "Well, I've been up all night doin' the thing everybody nags me on, that's all. Writing my memoirs. 'The exploits of the plains.' A man needs some juice for a task such as that." He laughed again and hugged her.

She thought at the time how much she loved him and how familiar that smell of whiskey was on him, along with the day-old clothes and sweat. *He was their pappa!* No matter what had happened with that other woman, no matter what pain it had caused and would cause them yet. No matter what the sisters' husbands and the brothers' wives said about it. She and Lucy, the "old maids," they were being called, still lived at home and had seen it happen. They'd been there when the woman came with her hateful papers and put her fancy hat on an upstairs bed. Even so, though sad to see their mamma look so glum, neither she nor Lucy had ever said a word against their pappa. And those who had would change their minds when it came time to divide up the things their pappa had worked so hard to get.

The old house was filling up again: noises of children and women; men outside, finishing up the harvest and feeding stock; some of her brothers and brothers-in-law, helping themselves to the contents of the little barrel on the porch, using the measuring ladle in the flour sack instead of her pappa's white cup. All these things came to her as she tried to keep her eyes open, but the darkness of the room, the summer warmth let sleep take her.

Her mother, Melinda, leaned against the pillar on the balcony. The valley spread beneath her with its hazed summer golds. She did not see the vistas really, but stared silently at her grandson. The boy was rolling a wagon wheel around the horse turnaround. He prodded it with a stick, sometimes spinning it in a circle or pushing it across the slope of the yard. Forward and backward, backward and forward. She watched the wagon wheel as if hypnotized. She did not hear the boy say, "Looky here, Grandmammy," when he spun the wheel like some gigantic top. She was thinking that the boy looked like most of her other grandsons, except he was special in his way. He was the child of the son she had carried in her belly all the way to Oregon.

She breathed deeply, taking in air that was not stale with sick and sour smells; cooled by a faint breeze that rustled the tops of the walnut and locust trees beneath her. They had brought the seeds with them from Missouri. Now the trees had nearly reached the level of the balcony railing, and she thought deep within herself:

> It was the indifference. That was what she had objected to the most. There were no words for it; she had simply felt it pressing down on her all those years, like a child yet formless; swelling inside her.

It was the day of leaving; of their slow departure by wagon from the Missouri countryside she loved so well. The day she saw her father for the last time. He had ridden his powerful gray horse alongside the party as far as the river. It was comforting to see the old man on the horse beside them. He didn't say much. It was his way.

She had been feeling queer and half lightheaded and wondering whether or not to tell Charles she was expecting another child. There were already eight little ones to contend with.

But Charles was busy with his two brothers and some of the other emigrant men, organizing the wagons and stock. She felt the distance between herself and her husband. She felt cut off from her duties, her children, her will. How cumbersome would be this expedition of men, women, and children, and animals. Their wagons and herds streamed into the rendezvous place from all directions. She heard the nearly deafening accumulation of their sounds. Then, she remembered, she felt nothing except the certainty that she would soon vomit. She loosened her neckerchief, already dreading the pitch and jerk of the journey before her without yet having climbed atop the wagon.

Young Billy Doak was to be their teamster. Charles had been somewhere nearer to the front, meeting with some other men. At length he had made his way back to her, pausing briefly, brusquely relaying the plans of the day. Upon seeing him, the children had begun wailing, "Pappa, why cain't we take Ellis? Uncle Lindsay is taking Vick and Vine. Oh, please, Pappa!"

They had, of course, been through all the business about the dogs before. Charley, like Jesse, had been convinced no dog, regardless of how well behaved, belonged on such an extended trek as theirs. Lindsay and his beloved greyhounds, however, would not be parted. Charley was disapproving and made it plain. Charley glowered at the children, who had brought up a sore subject.

At that time Charley had not been particularly stout. He'd been a solid block of a man. She watched him set his jaw. The sweat glistened down the thick column of his neck as he turned to leave them. He said sharply, "Melinda!," his way of telling her the children were her precinct on this day, that he was tired, concerned with matters far more important than the family dog.

Tears welling, Lucy, the eldest, looked at her beseechingly. "Oh, please, Mamma, it's so hard to leave just *everything.*" Tears in her own eyes, she replied, "Your pa has said not, children. Leave him be now!" Oh, and leave me be, too, she said to herself, feeling her throat constrict, ready to heave up its cornbread and black breakfast coffee.

When they first pulled away from the two-storied log cabin that had been her home, she remembered how the orchard had looked, the cowshed, the pigs snorting noisily in their trough beside the road. Lisbon Applegate, the oldest of the Applegate brothers, was to sell all their holdings for them. It hurt her to roll right past them. Money didn't matter to her. It had hurt even more when she took her last look at the three rosebushes her mother had given her from Tennessee cuttings.

And this place on the Osage was her true home. Leaving it made no sense. The sassafras trees slid by in a dream, gray-green, their pungent odor filling her nostrils. She felt the tug of the oxen on the wagon pulling her away, tearing her from the things she knew.

Oh Soft Missouri—thickening with low green
Flickering scarlet of your Red-Bud trees
This early May!

Why? Why were they going? All the years since then—the poor ones and the bountiful ones in their new country, Oregon— she had often asked herself the same question. Why had they ever left Missouri?

Yes, there had been hard times, but by 1841 and '42, things had got better. During the bad, severe years the price of pork and every other kind of stock had fallen so low a man could not sell a thing he'd raised, much less get it to market. Nor could anyone trust the currency that was then changing hands. Her brother-in-law Jesse had actually been reduced to selling his hogs to the river-boats, which used the fat for fuel because it was cheaper than wood. In the late 1830s even she had grown disgusted with Missouri. But all that passed. They were selling their produce again. The weather had been better. Money was dear, but they all had their share. They were better off than most. Why, for the first time they even had enough for boughten shoes for everyone in the family that winter.

What would their future have held if they had never known Robert Shortess? She still thought of him with bitterness: the letters and maps he sent them from Oregon. "I never hear of failures here," he'd written. Her brothers-in-law had an adventuresome streak, all right. They were family men but never happy with what they had already. However, Charley had always been prudent. He had a strong, practical nature. He'd always stayed close to what was his through hard work or so she'd thought as she watched Jesse and Lindsay act like men under whom a fire had been set. Emigrant meetings that had been farther and farther away. Lindsay had even advertised in the newspaper to find men of like mind. She remembered when she'd told Charley how foolish she thought his brothers were: the idea of traveling two thousand miles just to live in a country with less than two hundred white folks in it.

She had never really understood it. It had not seemed to matter then, any more than it did now that she did understand—as far as Charley was concerned.

And he had been even worse during the first decade or so of their marriage. It hadn't mattered that he was far from young—a full forty years old. It hadn't mattered that there had been sick spells. Oregon would cure him, he said. In the end, she supposed, it was as simple as the bond of blood; her practical husband, his streak of caution abandoned for kinship's sake. "The Fever" she had heard it called, and it was surely that. A year or so before they themselves had left for Oregon, a man had passed through the settlements with a banner pinned to his wagon that said OREGON OR THE GRAVE. Whether he ever got there they never knew.

It seemed to her that even the good sense of the family women

270

was tainted. Going to Oregon, she told them, was not like going to St. Louis to see the sights. Could they not see the seriousness of their husbands' "talk"? They had both looked at her as if she were peculiar. Maybe Oregon wasn't such a bad idea "for some people," they said. One year later, she looked at Cynthia and Betsy and shared their sorrow. The price for their men's enthusiasm had been dear: two boys lost to the furious torrents of the Columbia. From then on she had forgotten all else save that they were sisters of her heart and women loving their little ones. And there were even more troubles and hardships to follow.

But in Missouri, on that day when they were all making their quilts together, she had felt cut to the very quick. She had never before been excluded. As the eldest and most experienced of the three women, her advice had always been sought. She had felt especially humiliated when she learned that the brothers' plans had been afoot for many more months than she had imagined. It had never been said outright, and she herself had never asked, even years later. Nevertheless, she was certain that Betsy and Cynthia had known she was going to Oregon before she knew herself.

"Oregon, Oregon," even the littlest child whispered. By the winter the murmur had grown to a chorus, and by spring it seemed as if half the settlers in Missouri were considering packing up.

Oh Missouri, sweet Missouri
Where in spring the cycadas
Disperse their yellow parasols
In feather's spin
Missouri swelling deep
Heavy lowland river's place
Farewell!

She had been sixteen times pregnant, losing only one child, who had died in infancy. She had been married just as she turned sixteen and had her first child before her seventeenth birthday. Twenty-five years had passed since she'd delivered her last, little Milton. It pained her heart to think upon him, for like his pappa, he liked his drink.

The house, especially of late, was filled with almost too many

271

grandchildren to name. In the yard below, Albert's boy had been joined by several other young ones.

Thunder in the distance. Her own mamma had told her thunder was made from the potatoes rolling around in the bottom of a gigantic wagon. Whose wagon? God's maybe. Her children and grandchildren liked to hear her say that about the thunder. The little ones in the yard were pointing heavenward and talking about "the potatoes."

As she watched them, it seemed to her truly mysterious and almost miraculous. From two—herself and Charles—there had come so many. It would keep on happening. The children playing in the yard would have children, and then their children would have children, and everyone would be alive in everyone else in a future too distant for her to conceive of.

Watching Albert's little boy at the center of her other grandchildren, she thought about Albert himself and the sort of man he'd grown to be. When he'd been close to his fifteenth birthday, he complained to her one morning about his "having missed the wagon trip and all." She remembered how she had felt as she watched him shoving sourdough biscuits into his mouth. She found it difficult to think him part of her in any way. Yet, impossible as it seemed, the strapping boy at the kitchen table was also the infant she had carried inside her for two thousand miles. Now her womb was withered. Now she was as gray and as "knobby" as the "grannies" she had pointed at with such curiosity when she herself had been a child. But thinking of Albert made her remember how she had almost lost him. Beneath her, the infernal tremble of the wagon, the exhausting heat: On that part of the trip over the Great Sage Plains, the oxteams had moved even more slowly. There had come a day when she felt as if she were breathing in a high wind, only there was no wind. An odd throb—a quickening spread over her belly. She was experienced. She knew it was more than the motion of the unborn child. Something else. Something wrong. By degrees the skin had grown taut and painful. She had never lost a child while carrying it. She had prayed.

The vast expanse of the unending plain was studded with sagebrush and low, evil-smelling tangles of greasewood. Sometimes the stuff grew as high as a big man's waist. The men and boys walked in front of the wagons, trying to clear the way. But this had been a tedious endeavor, especially when they passed over the desiccated and rimrocked regions on the other side of Fort Hall. In that desolate country no emigrant wagon had ever rolled before.

She had been sitting on the wagon seat with Mary, between her and the teamster, Billy Doak. After a while it seemed that the tilting prairies heaved all around her like some immense and foul sea, now gray, now brown-green. Her body rocked, feeling as pliant as a child's cloth baby, except during these moments when sharp pains were slicing up her back.

She had felt better earlier in the journey, robust in fact. Then, she had walked most every day beside the wagon, feeling strong, almost liking it. But that time had passed. Her feet had swollen. "Rest," her body told her. Amidst her collection of "yarbs" and "simples" that she had brought from Missouri there was no remedy for what ailed her. She remembered how helpless she felt.

The three littlest ones were with her in the wagon—John, Lisbon, and Irene had stationed themselves on what was left of their bedding. There they dozed—all curled up together way under the dim canvas, looking like little bears in a cave. She had made the mistake of glancing up at the sun. She saw it turn white. Then it seemed to shimmer and move from side to side in the changeless blue. The next thing she knew, Billy Doak's homely, youthful face was peering down at her. "Mrs. Applegate. Mrs. Applegate!" He had evidently stopped the wagon.

Poor ol' Billy Doak. Even in the midst of her difficulties some part of her still found it possible to be irritated by Billy. More than once during the long journey, she had had to call out to him. In the beginning he had been inclined to push the oxen much too hard and did not always use good sense when trying to control them. Once, when they had been fording the Burnt River, his inexperience had nearly caused them to go under. The oxen had taken their head and the wagon had tipped halfway over. She lost most of their bedding that day, all her candle molds, and a good portion of the cooking gear. Worse, her mother's blue and white demijohn was also at the bottom of the river, along with the few cups that had been so carefully wrapped.

Years passed before she found it in her heart to forgive Billy Doak. Now, as she thought of him, of how tenderly he had lifted

273

her head a little, of the worry and concern in his voice, a softness came. He had tried to be a man. He had done the best that he could.

The children had awakened when the wagon stopped. She heard them whimpering through the opening in the canvas, "Billy, Billy, what's the matter with our ma?" She remembered touching John's and Lisbon's hair as someone helped them down from the wagon. Back then John had been the baby. Later they told her how Lisbon had not wanted to leave her. He'd been a kindhearted, manly little boy. He was going to wait "for his pappa," he said. How could they have known of the damage that was done to him but a few weeks before that would never go away? Only the years would reveal it.

After her confusion lifted somewhat, she recognized the comforting presence of Charles's niece, Harriet (Wingfield-Williams), who had somehow managed to bring some cool water in a cup. "Word has gone back to the cow drivers. Uncle Charley will come soon. Never mind now."

How soothing was Harriet's touch. She had always been grateful to her, and was glad to have given a daughter her name. She'd leaned against Harriet for miles and miles, it seemed. Too, she had felt a little better, doubtless heartened by the thought of Charles's coming. Yet he had not come.

She had been well cared for when they finally stopped for the day. She was very tired, of course. It bothered her that she was not helping Bill Parker with the cooking, and she had told him so when he came by the camping spot. All the greens he had handed over the side to her for the evening meal as he and the other men walked in front lay limp and uncleaned. She and Parker had generally cooked together. It had been their practice to keep the party supplied with wild greens and special edibles she knew about. At Fort Hall some of the half-breed women living there had led her to other plants whose properties she hadn't recognized, for the country was new and strange. Each night she had seen to it that a big stew was simmering and ready that all might partake of. Whenever Dr. Whitman came to their family camp near suppertime, he gladly filled his bowl. "You are doing a great service for our health, Mrs. Applegate," he told her. She had never forgotten the compliment. But that evening, as she waited for Charley, she refused to let anyone impose on Dr. Whitman. Generally, he had traveled with the lighter portion of the emigrant train. Yet he never objected when he was called upon to help their own party. Still, she had no wish to overtax him by causing him to double back. An English doctor—whose name she could no longer remember—had been brought by their camping place. He had felt her forehead and advised her to lie still for some time to come. They had already prepared her a pallet on the ground.

As time passed, she found she was trembling with the queer cold they had come to expect on those prairies, no matter how hot the day. She hadn't the strength to remove her own boots. Nor had she asked for a "extry" coverlet. There were the children to think of and everyone was busy. Traveling all day long, laying the cook fires, doing the cooking, washing up, and the bedding down of all the children and so forth wore people out, especially the women. How well she remembered. And there she had been "parked" upon the ground. She'd drifted off for a while despite the commotion all around her. Who knew how much time had passed before she opened her eyes to see the tall male figure standing at her feet.

"Charles?" she had asked hoarsely. "No, Melinda, it's Jesse. Charles is way out with the animals. Some of the stock has wandered further than it ought. I've come to see to your needs." She said she felt a little better. She wondered whether her brother-in-law had sensed her disappointment. He stooped to pat her gently upon the shoulder. She mustered a smile.

In some ways, she supposed, she had always envied Cynthia. Jesse, especially when he'd been somewhat younger, seemed to feel a certain tenderness toward women. Though he might at times appear brusque to his wife and daughters, he was not inclined to bark and bluster at them or deliberately find fault. Jesse had covered her up, catching the blanket under her feet for warmth. He walked away. She watched the evening ritual of lighting the campfire. He had inserted a cotton rag dusted with gunpowder into the pan of his flintlock. She could not even remember the crack of the gunshot, but seemed to recall the small blue flash of fire afterward. Her sleep was thick and strange.

Before dawn she had awakened with a start. Some creature was calling in the darkness. No one was yet stirring, the fire was gone. The first thing she had done was to straighten herself, smoothing the coarse folds of her skirt. In the night someone had removed her boots; they sat beside her, damp with dew. She remembered struggling to get them on her narrow feet, but was unable to lace them. As she sat there, her belly seemed even higher and pointier than when she'd gone to bed. Some dizziness remained even after she stood on her feet a few moments. She would need to be careful, but she knew that she would be all right. She would not lose the child.

In the privacy of the beginning dawn she removed her rumpled bonnet, her fingers trembling like branches in a wind. Her hair had begun to fall away. It was the first time she had truly taken note of it. Once it had been a fine and mellow brown. Now it had turned to the color of dust, ravaged to the texture of old cornsilk. She remembered how she'd gazed at it standing in the stillness, holding pieces of it in her hands, as if they were bits of fur from some dead animal.

Thunder. She was pulled from her sharper focus of the past back to the storming present.

It had commenced to rain. "Someone's coming, Grand-mammy! In a wagon!" the children chorused.

She responded as they surely knew she would: "Git out of the rain now, all of you! You'll catch a death!" When their grand-mother used a tone like that, they listened, all right. They scurried to the sanctuary of the lower porch.

No thunder now, just the dreary drumming of the rain on the cedar-shaked roof. She saw the spring wagon turn up the road. Coming toward the house. The slow cadence of the horse. The solitary figure upon the seat. Closer and closer it came. She could see what looked to be a man in a broad-brimmed black hat. Who? Jesse? Her eyes had grown weak and weaker.

Jesse was surely come to say farewell to his older brother. Suddenly the weight of the event bore down upon her. He was dying. The last death beneath her roof had been Harriet's. Grieving was an awful thing. She'd thought never to recover. Ellen had died but a few years after that, in her own home. It tore out of a mother's heart to see her daughters leave before she did. Dear Lord, why take the young?! And Ellen with six little children.

A husband was different somehow. Charley was seventy-three years old. He had lived a long life. For almost two years he'd ailed, and, she'd nursed him faithfully like any dutiful wife.

Every now and then he'd rallied. When he'd felt well enough

to leave the place, she knew where he was sure to go. And it was just as well she had known. It deprived the woman in town of some of her "satisfaction."

The winter before, he had surprised them all. Jesse had come, prepared for the worst. Charley had not seen him for quite some time. It had been a true tonic.

How long did they talk, those old grayheads? Lucy had been amazed. They relived Kentucky and the whole of their boyhood. Even after Jesse went, Charley continued to reminisce for several days running; he seemed better and better. A few evenings they'd even spent time talking together. Sitting on the porch: "Melinda!" he'd say to her, "do you remember?" And when his grandchildren came around: "Oh, you young ones should have seen that party of Caws near the river. They had been on a buffalo hunt. . . . Their finery was mighty gaudy too! . . ."

All this was before the woman had called on them the second time, waving her papers and refusing to leave until Charley agreed to sign them. After the woman left it seemed like Charley lost interest in everything again. He'd been writing his recollections down but then stopped. One morning, fearful when he did not answer her knock on his door, she went in. She picked up his papers from the floor and put them in the big chest in her room. She knew there would be no more. Charley's drinking was the worst she'd ever known it. It had taken three of his sons to lift him on the bed. That same morning, the shaking had commenced.

Now her brother-in-law was turning into the yard. His grand-nieces and grandnephews were very quiet as he got down and carefully hitched his horse. There were some standing there all agog who did not recognize his face, only his name. Others, she knew, had no idea whatever that they had an Uncle Lindsay, either. The Klamath country might as well have been on the other side of the earth. It came to her that she had not seen her own sister— her dear beloved Betsy—for more than ten years, nor was she likely to.

The old folks told of the things that gave them pride in themselves. Those who listened, the young and the newcomers mostly, spurred them ever on to more embroidery. In this way perhaps everyone was left happy. Except for her. She had been taught from her earliest years to tell only what was so.

Jesse wore his own troubles like a coat. He seemed bent over with them. Money matters. Betrayed by his important friends, or so she had been given to understand. Perhaps that was why he stayed away. Like her, he was the sort to bear his problems alone. There was another part: Neither he nor Lindsay approved of Charley's dalliance. They cursed the liquor but loved him, albeit from afar.

Suddenly she felt a great wave of pity roll over her. Nor was it for her brother-in-law alone, or for herself. It was for the weakened and swollen body in the room behind her, and for the *man* inside of it whom she had never understood.

In so many ways he had done well by them, her husband. It was a fine, spacious house. Their cupboards had never been empty, and their barns, even in the most difficult of times, had been full. From the time they had settled in Yoncalla, they had lived in peace and harmony with the Indians and their other neighbors. Charley's foolishness would cost them money and had already cost them much in spirit. Even so, she could survive comfortably. The land was hers, the house was large. Her boys would help.

She felt her grief inside her: the tiredness, loneliness. Fifty years beside the man but never inside of him.

She stood perfectly still. She did not see the tall man removing his hat as he made ready to go to the bedside; or the rain-curtained landscape of the Oregon valley where, for so many years, she had made her home:

Oh Missouri I am so far
from thee.
Your sky too broad to hide in hills.
I hear your birds cry now
so softly.
Your red-winged blackbirds
and whippoorwills.

Melinda Applegate   Charles Applegate
1813–1888   1806–1879

TWO-WAY-SEEING

Jesse Applegate Applegate

Several of our subscribers became somewhat alarmed over the non-appearance of this last issue of the Native Son . . . and wrote asking why they did not receive it. Among those enquiring [sic] was one of our agents. . . .

Yoncalla, Oregon
August 8, 1900

Native Son Pub. Co.
  Kloshe Tenas Man:—Klone moon o'coke mika papah wake chaco copa conomox o'coke. . . . Klose mika hyas mamook chaco o'koke papah, copa skookum chickamin kuitan, pee klonas mesika kokshut klose tumtum.

Mika Klose Tillikum
*Sue Burt, Agent

*Granddaughter of Charles Applegate

From an interview with General Elisha L. Applegate,
Pacific Trail Campfires,
Reese B. Kendall, M.D.
Ashland, Oregon, 1891

Now began a struggle to force the Indians upon reservation which lasted for two years, when the harried rightful owner of the soil was notified to gather his families' relics, traps and stock to be in readiness when wagons would be sent to take them to their future homes. These wagons were to be sent to the Umpqua whither the Rogue River and the Coast Indians would gather to be transported to Northern Oregon where they could be watched. . . .

Those aborigines no doubt felt like the Hebrew exiles to Babylon; they did wail their death song for the romantic hill and dale, the limpid streams and beautiful forests which had been their shelter and comfort through unknown ages; and were passing from them forever. Many an Old Oregonian of that day dropped a tear of sympathy.

Those exiles lined the roads and filled the by-ways for weeks before the last dispirited dweller of the forest had reached his new home. Day in and day out was heard the sad refrain in wild minor chords: "Ha-la we-yah" in tones of utter desolation. It was pitiful to see the children hanging to the mother's bedraggled skirts as she labored along, the muddy roads forbidding overloading the teams. They ought to have been treated better. . . . All pity had been lost. . . .

FROM: Robert Metcalfe, Indian Sub-Agent
    Elk Camp

TO: Joel Palmer, Superintendent of Indian Affairs
   Salem
          16 January, 1856

Sir:

I left the Umpqua Reservation * on the 11th with all the Indians that were assembled there on my way North. . . . It was with utmost difficulty I got them started and every morning since I have been on the road I have had to use all my powers of persuasion I

* Coles Valley, Douglas County, Oregon

had at my command and finally threats to get them
started from [each] camp. Today they seated themselves on the road opposite Lindsay Applegate's [near
Yoncalla] and refused to go further but I finally succeeded getting them this far with the exception of
some Calapooyas who were encamped near Applegate's who positively refused to move. And their refusal has been the cause of great dissatisfaction in
[our] camp [here] so much so that I have little hope
of being able to continue on my journey without assistance of a military force.

On the refusal of the Indians to leave Applegate's
today I sent an express to Col. Martin for volunteers
to assist in carrying out your instructions and if it
fails I look for a *general* stampede in camp! The indis-
position on the part of the Indians to leave [this re-
gion] is owing to the interference of some white
settlers in the vicinity.

When I called at Mr. Applegate's for the Indians
I found him and some other men who were sym-
pathizing with the Indians, and who told them that
there were no [as yet official] agents and we [who had
come for them] were a set of inhuman men driving
them from their homes and that they [the Indians]
had rights as well as ourselves!

Now you see what I have to contend with. But I
am determined to take these Indians to the Yamhill
at all hazard unless I am otherwise instructed.

Very Respectfully Yours

R. B. Metcalfe

HERE HE IS APPROACHING

1855

They were an unlikely-looking pair as they set out along the *way-hut*—the pathway that The People had used for thousands of years. The hot summer air was a-whirr with grasshoppers.

The young man was a loper, his gait more youthful than his years, as though he were not yet comfortable with the length of his legs. He was several heads taller than the Indian and he had one bad eye, the blue so scrambled with the white that it appeared to be shot with several tiny stars. He'd done it long years before with his mamma's scissors, poked himself whilst toddling across the puncheon floor in a loghouse that was located in another world altogether: a world called Missouri. This was Oregon. This was Yoncalla. This was yet another place to call home. And he felt that he would like to grow old exactly where he was, as old as the shaman who trod lightly before him, for he, too, felt himself part of the insect-stirring, fragrant, tawny-grassed country surrounding them, content beyond words. But this was not to be.

He was the young moving person who was compelled to say his clan name twice: Jesse Applegate Applegate, a son of "Lin-see." His relatives called him "Jesse A.," or "Jess" to distinguish him from his uncle Jesse, who yet lived in the next valley over. And if the scrawny shaman could have been induced to talk about his feelings for this young man, the shaman might have said that this newcomer was not afraid to listen and had a patient spirit. Whenever he saw the young man coming toward the village, the shaman always blurred the Jesse and the A together, saying in jargon by way of wry salute: "Chako wake siah Yessiay! Here he is approaching, Jesse Ao!"

Jesse Applegate Applegate, author, teacher, amateur ethnographer, 1905. (Courtesy Oregon Historical Society)

Indian Travel

Lolokes psis, which meant "Person-With-Nose-On-Fire," had bowed legs, and hopping was not foreign to him. Jesse A. never saw him run, but he had the feeling the shaman yet had it in him to be fleet. More than that, he was certain that Lolokes psis had the power to leap great distances by ordinary means or otherwise. For a fact, were the Indian's nose not so uncommonly and perpetually red, a name like Quick-Frog-Walker would have suited the shaman better. How old was the Indian? The thong-tied oiled hank of hair hanging down his back was eel-black.

THREE ONE HUNDREDS

There was no telling the actual age of any of the older Indians living in Splashta Alla, the Valley of the Birds. There had been much debate on the subject, especially after the incident with the headman, a fellow who appeared to be around fifty, about the same age as Jesse A.'s uncle Charley. It happened on an afternoon shortly after the headman had purchased his first suit of clothes. Several young cousins had been "humbugging" around the edge of Splashta Alla, not far from Lindsay Applegate's new gristmill. The headman was walking jauntily—in fine fettle, it seemed. His two *klootchmen* (wives) followed him, laden with sacks of flour, their docility so marked, their heads so low, they put to mind a pair of milch cows. As the procession came closer, one of the younger boys took the notion to ask the headman this question: "How many years have you, Mister Halo?" The headman sat down to think his answer through. Finally, he declared that he was "*Mokst tika monuk.* Twice one hundred." The boys were too polite to hoot, but their surprise shown upon their faces. "Ha! Oh!" the headman said to them. "I tell you it is so!" He pointed to an immense old oak nearby, which he stated flatly had been a mere sapling during the time "Mister Halo had been tall as grass." Well, some older boys got wind of it, and a few days later sought out the headman. With his permission, said the boys, they would cut down that oak tree. It would be fine for the rails they needed, and ought to split clean. "Ao-ba," said Mister Halo, "very well." He walked with them to the place, sitting quietly while they wrestled with the oak, which took many shifts on the cross-cut saw, and a full afternoon passed before it fell. Finally, they commenced to count the growth rings, explaining to the headman, who peered over their shoulders, that each ring represented one growing season. Now the headman exhibited no surprise whatever when they passed two hundred and the count went on and on clear to the heartwood, which was a clear amber color, sticky with the juices of life. "Mister Halo!" they exclaimed when they were done, "there are more than three hundred rings on this here oak!" At this revelation the headman said proudly, "You see. It is exactly as

289

I told you before. I am klon tika monuk! Three one hundreds!"

And they never knew if this was Mister Halo's version of a good josh or if he literally believed himself to be as old as that oak tree!

And there were mysteries far deeper than that.

THE-HOUSE-THAT-GRINDS-SEEDS

Ikt yukwa. Ikt yahwa.

One here. One there . . . The path they descended was the same path. Behind them rose the same hills, whose soft summered sides were the color of buckskin. The gray-green outposts of grandfather oaks they'd passed beneath, the heat-muted sky raked with faint white wisps above them, the low sun-bright swales and meadows where camas grew in the valley they both called home, all these were the same. Even so, they saw things differently. Two-way-seeing was going on. Even as they paused together, as if by unspoken agreement; even as they stood there admiring vistas both winsome and wide. *Ikt yukwa. Ikt yahwa.*

Shading his eyes, Jesse A. looked for his father's gristmill and, spying it not too far in the distance, he noted the pleasant redness of the roof, for the cedar shakes he'd helped put on the millhouse had not weathered yet. And when he swung his gaze a little toward the meadow, he saw slow-moving figures and knew them to be the camas harvesters. But something quicker came and he looked up: a hawk. He could see its silhouette against the nearest hill.

The hawk. The shaman had been watching it. He'd seen it dive and miss, its glide renewing now, and the shaman knew many other eyes were watching, too, for the hawk was an important animal person.

The shaman's own people lived in a village which was but one bowshot from the house-that-grinds-seed-into-powder. And as he began his stride again—the young man yet lingering—the shaman considered his friend Lin-see's mill for a moment. From that house-turning-water came the pale stuff the "Bostons'" women called flour.

So *cultus* (bad)-tasting, so strangely named. *Kayek, brat, gravee, pi.*

HALF-A-PEOPLE

Jesse A. liked to watch the deft movements of the digging sticks which brought up bulb after bulb. Too, he enjoyed the gay look of the camas harvesters, their new calico dresses bright as certain birds, their odd singsong voices chirruping in the distance. The Kommema women: mothers and grandmothers. Even tiny girls. Down went their digging sticks, which were smaller versions of their elders'; and they would be trained to watch over their sticks between growing seasons, and eventually their own sticks would be passed down to other girls and they themselves would inherit some larger one. Whose camas stick? Old Deer's? Wind-Blowing's? and before that. . . ? They would know. Some elderly *lamai* (auntie) in the tribe would tell them.

Now appeared two young Kommema women whom Jesse A. had always considered pretty. Sometimes they came around and helped his mother and aunts do the laundering. In return, they received flour and even sugar, when it could be spared.

The one in red looked up, but only fleetingly, for she saw the shaman and did not wish the Evil Eye to be cast upon her. But the shaman looked neither to the left nor to the right, his head held high. He was displeased.

Jesse A. knew that Lolokes psis did not like to see the long dresses of the Moving People upon *klootchmen,* be they young or old. When the shaman first laid eyes upon the headman who had appeared before the tribe in his baggy "Boston" pants and battered hat, Lolokes psis had spit on the ground to show his disgust, or so he told Jesse A. The shaman had then shunned the headman for a day or two—but no longer, Lolokes confessed, for it was not politic to ignore the tribe *tyee,* even if the offense was great. There were other shamans in the vicinity who might whisper things in the headman's ear, in which case Lolokes would lose his influence. And Jesse A. thought about that: Yes, his friend Lolokes was a shrewd old somebody.

Each May since the Applegates had settled in the valley, Jesse A. had admired those selfsame meadows, which were always carpeted with camas blooms so intensely blue that in their unanimity they resembled pools or little lakes. Yet, interspersed in that utter azure were flowers white as bone. These were the flowers of death.

(Drawings courtesy Rosemary Spires)

Camas digger with traditional stick and
tump-lined conical basket.

Camas plant with edible
portion of bulb detached.

Next to the venom of *shugh opoots* (the rattlesnake), white camas
was the worst kind of medicine. Lolokes psis had told him once
that in the wrong hands, white camas was *mamook memaloose*. It
had a killing power.

But now, at the time of harvest, the blossoms had shriveled
and faded, were as brown and translucent as the skin of the
people.

Those girls and women? How did they know? For several seasons now, Jesse A. had spied upon the diggers, but he could not
discern any mark or method through which good camas was distinguished from bad. Why, even the smallest daughters, dug without
supervision; their contributions were simply tossed into their
mothers' baskets to mingle with all the rest.

The baskets themselves—he'd thought—were curious affairs. They were conical, fashioned by the women from willow roots, and each was attached to the bearer by a woven vine-maple tumpline that pressed against the forehead. And a story went along with the basket concerning its special design. Indeed, it sometimes seemed to Jesse A. that everything the native did or made was all bound up with one kind of tradition or superstition or another. Lolokes psis had related that each time a *klootchmen* affixed her basket to her forehead, she was reminded of Snowats. Yes, Snowats (First Woman) had in some way done The People great service *hyas ahnkuttie*, in-the-big-long-ago. Well, sacred design or no— Jesse A. thought to himself—he did not envy the poor Kommema female at the end of a hot day of camas digging.

As the light flickered through the leaves of the last oak grove, Jesse A. saw that he and the shaman had almost reached the fork in the *wayhut*. One path led to his own home—where his family was doubtless readying to sit down to dinner—and the other path led to the simple tribal shelters of Splashta Alla. *Ikt yukwa. Ikt yahwa.*

No—Jesse A. said to himself as he cast a final look at the gaily clad harvesters, whose dresses yet flashed colors between the tree-trunks—he would under no circumstance exchange his lot for that of a native female. For the poor brown women, he knew, endured days that were even longer than his own mother's. And when those persevering *klootchmen* at last arrived at their huts, each basket would surely seem as heavy as a millstone, especially attached as it was by the tumpline to the forehead. Twenty? Thirty pounds maybe. How much would each basket weigh? Skulls would throb. Backs would ache. Not just from hauling camas bulbs, either. In all respects the *klootchmen* served as the tribe's pack animals. But perhaps before serving up the evening meal they'd dose themselves with some queer unsavory remedy to relieve their aches and pains. After which they'd gloat about a job well done. And if they showered Lolokes psis with treats, he would forgive them and overlook their "Boston" clothes.

What exactly would the shaman eat? Jesse A. wondered as he saw him turn off on his path. Camas cakes all patted out? Blackberry pulp? And if times were truly good the feast would be complete with bear grease and the nutlike meat of cut-up grasshoppers. Or so Jesse A. had been told.

But as he hurried down his own path and drew close enough to see that someone had left the millhouse door ajar, Jesse A. sighed and paused. As he closed the door it came to him that when next the camas harvesters returned to Splashta Alla he would accompany them. For he could think of no other way to solve the mystery of the white camas.

Perhaps some old *lamai* knew how to distinguish good from bad and scrutinized each bulb before chucking them into the roasting trench.

How else to explain it? For he had never heard of even one death on account of eating white camas by mistake. . . . Though, God knew, there had been deaths aplenty from other causes. The poor Kommema, whose name meant simply The People. In just four years Jesse A. had seen it happen. He had heard the death song wavering over the village again and again. His own people had brought sickness to the valleys. Now, The People were but half-a-people.

THE YOUNG MAN GROWS OLD

Jesse A. Applegate, Old Soldiers' Home, Roseburg, Oregon, 1906

Now, this may seem queer to you in view of the fact it is evident I don't do much during my "incarceration" here save sit in one chair or another, and maybe walk a little outside on the grounds when some orderly has the time to lead me thence. . . . Nevertheless, I do get tired out, so today I should like to arrange things a little better.

No . . . no . . . I have suffered no ill effects from our long siege of words yesterday—or, more properly, my long siege of words. Truth to tell, last night I tossed and turned some. You got me thinking with your questions. Then it occurred to me I had left out so much on this manuscript Sue Burt and I are trying to "scare up" for the printer. But let us go on. Before we broke off last even', I had given you several bits of tribal "lore," I believe. What? . . . Do I remember the precise nature of the gestures and locutions employed by the old-time native taleteller? No. That art is surely lost or much diluted. Most of the Yoncalla, or Kommema—their name before the whites appeared—are long passed away. . . . By which I mean not only the more venerable members of the clan. I will say more later about the handful who remain. Those of my generation are gone. Be-el (son of Halo, the headman), my boyhood chum, who was somewhat younger than I, died several years ago. The Yoncalla were not blessed with longevity. Be-el lasted far longer than the majority of his clansmen, however.

Be-el? No. The name was not short for Beelzebub, yet a name of some interest. Be-el's name was Paul. Yes. A Christian name. "Paul" was hard for the native to pronounce—"Be-el" was the result. However, Jacob (or Jake) and John tripped more easily upon the native tongue. These were Be-el's brothers.

Did *we* bestow these biblical names? Not the Applegates, nor any other settler, for these names were given long e'er any wagon appeared on the horizon. They were inspired by another—a mysterious figure about whom I will now relate some things that are

297

curious to me, and you also may find them so. . . . But as you are evidently interested in the manner in which the native passed along his stories and traditions, I will first say that the style and content of these narratives never varied from telling to telling, save perhaps for some very minor embellishment. Why, these were bona fide dramatic presentations. In my youth I frequently made it a point to "happen by" the village (a bowshot from Lindsay Applegate's ranch), usually around dusk on certain winter eves, for that was the season the native set aside for storytelling and other indoor activities. I'm afraid I was something of a pest in those days. Whenever possible I induced the older natives to speak of their traditions. Sometimes bits and pieces of legends were gleaned in this manner. But this was merely conversation— not what you might call formal storytelling.

Now, what the old *lamai* told me about the stranger who inspired the naming of Halo's oldest sons falls into the latter category. Nevertheless, it shows some things about how the native thought about the past, so I will attempt to render this as close as memory permits. . . . But to be honest, I remember more of what she said than what I said. I, of course, was listening intently. Why, anything I could learn about him—the mysterious stranger who had come long before we Applegates—was of immense interest to me.

Yes, he had a name. Doubtless bestowed by the tribe. The name was Squiyowhiynoof—"Squee-oh-whee-nōof." Yes indeed, it was quite a "monicker" to haul around, all right.

On the occasion of this particular visit to the village, I arrived about midafternoon. It must have been autumn, too, for the old *lamai* was occupied smashing up acorns. The year was either 1854 or 1855—before most of the Yoncalla were removed to the reservation. I was a young man of not quite twenty. The natives knew me as Jessiay in those days—pronounced by them "Yesiay."

I seem to remember that the old *lamai* was not particularly pleased with the prospect of my company. In any case, this is the sum total of all I was able to extract from her that day.

Hiyu cole . . . many winters . . . *ahnkuttie laly* . . . in-the-little-long-ago . . . a powerful and most remarkable *keelally* . . . medicine man or shaman . . . had appeared in Splashta Alla who lived with The People for a time.

"Where had he come from?" I asked.

She did not know—saying only, "Siah, . . . far," . . . at which point she made an arc with the hand that held the pestle.

Had he come alone?

Yes, she said. Companionless. Some said he had been hurt . . . found by the headman's father or grandfather.

But which one? I must have asked, for I was attempting to fix the event in the time our own people understood.

She replied that such things made no difference—or jargon words to that effect. *All* owned the time, she said, the events, and even the dreams of their *ahnkuttie tillikums*—by which she meant ancestors.

Yet this was too vague for my purposes. I continued to press her until she thrust down her pestle and squinted at me. How well I remember the look. The poor soul was surely almost as blind then as I am now—her eyes were milky yet fierce, especially set in her craggy old face. . . . She wanted to get me out of the way, I'm sure, and "finished me off" by giving a terse version of the following:

One day someone looked up . . . to the west . . . toward the big hill there (Mount Yoncalla). A lonely figure was approaching. He appeared as a bird with a white face whose dark wings moved whenever the wind blew. This was because of his odd raiment— his *iktas*—which The People had never seen before. What he wore was *polaklie*—the color of night—and this [robe] extended clear to the earth—the *illahee* whereon he trod.

I found this revelation fascinating. Surely she was describing a priest or some other man of the cloth. This impression was confirmed somewhat later by Old Halo, and my friend, the tribe's principal shaman, Lolokes psis. As I had never heard of such a mysterious personage before, and I knew Yoncalla to be exceedingly remote in 1849 when Uncle Jesse first arrived, I was anxious for the *lamai* to resume. One of her big-eyed little granddaughters appeared about then, and she went away with her for a moment without so much as a glance in my direction. When she returned and observed me still squatting in her outdoor kitchen, she commenced banging on the mortar bowl again. But I'd grown tired of waiting by then, though my tone was surely exceedingly polite. In some way I asked her what had happened to their adopted shaman, Ol' Squiyowhiynoof.

"Oh that, oh that," she said. But in the end she'd pointed her gnarled finger upward. "*He* is in Saghalie. Yes. Saghalie. . . . Memaloose—dead," as if I had somehow missed her meaning. "His enemies killed him."

"And that," she avowed, as stone rang against stone so hard the acorn paste sputtered forth a little, "is enough." Naught else was added. The interview so closed; I went meekly on my way.

Was he myth or man? you ask. . . . Indeed, ". . . that is the question." Oh, he certainly existed. Not that that diminishes the mystery a whit. For who was "he"? And what on earth was a solitary priest doing wandering around valleys so far inland? For if my calculations are correct, poor Squiyowhiynoof arrived somewhere between 1750 and 1800. I say this because Old Halo sometimes claimed he remembered him from his earliest childhood, but other times Halo implied that the *hyas keelally* (shaman) practiced his new "medicine" in his father's or even his grandfather's era. This coincides with the *lamai*'s version as well.

Thus even if we place the date closer to 1800, it would put Squiyowhiynoof in Yoncalla even before Astoria was established (in 1811) far up the northern coast. Astoria—as you may know—was the first real habitation and fortification in the northwest—excluding doings way up in Canada and Russian Alaska, and Lewis and Clark's Fort Clatsop, of course. It's how we Americans got our foothold way out here. That's another story. . . .

A wandering Spanish friar? That *would* solve it, wouldn't it? . . . Yet I do not think so. You see, the names of the biblical patriarchs Paul, Jacob, and John, which Squiyowhiynoof gave to the Yoncalla, were obviously in English and were passed to the native as such. Of course, I do not know what sound Jacob has in Spanish, and John is Juan—that's close, I suppose. . . . Even so, I am inclined to discard the notion of Squiyowhiynoof's Spanish origin. After all, the California missions were distant. The fellow was alone and on foot. Wounded perhaps. I have of course thought of shipwrecks—the coastline was rough. Yoncalla is but forty miles inland as the crow flies. Yet, think of it! What a risky and dismal trek our sojourner must have had. How many years had he been away from home? But his faith, evidently, remained.

As for proof of our sojourner's existence, I have not yet substantiated it. The evidence I will now present is, admittedly, circumstantial. From the preceding remark, you will now know that for a time I practiced the law, but I liked that even less than I did the rancher's life. Hence, I entered the teaching profession, as I mentioned to you yesterday.

To proceed with my evidence: One day when Be-el and I had risen early so we might spend a long day hunting upon the wooded ridges more or less behind my uncle Charley's place, Be-el led me along an older pathway, one that he himself trod only infrequently. In fact, he said, he had not passed that way for many seasons, and on the last occasion he had been alone and *hyas kwass,*—full of fear. This made me think he might have used the path whilst on his way to his "Quest"—the native boys' initiation into maturity.

No . . . I did not ask him. Those were secret matters. In any case, he doubtless would not have told me . . . nor anyone as far as that goes, unless it were Lolokes.

Well, we had passed some exceedingly old oak trees before we got to the conifers above and beyond. If memory serves, Be-el said something to the effect that these oaks were not far from an upper meadow that the Yoncalla had formerly occupied—before moving to the Splashta Alla village site, I mean. I was interested in the big oak trees we passed because the native always stashed his winter stores in the crotches of them. Sometimes he forgot and a child might find all kinds of Indian stores and relics years later. It was great sport for a growing boy; I know. Often these oaks were far afield. Before my father and uncles arrived the Yoncalla were frequently raided and the oak stashes may have been a way of ensuring that their plunderers did not get away with everything. I wanted to poke around a little in the trees, but Be-el said no. He seemed rather uneasy.

We started to climb a little. Our way was full of huge firs and cedars. Then came a giant cedar. I stopped to admire it. Truly it was as huge as those cedars they call Port Orfords on our southern Oregon coast.

Be-el said he would wait for a moment while I went to look at the *memaloose illahee* (place of the dead).

I was mystified. "What grave?" said I, for the burying ground I was familiar with was elsewhere.

His look was droll. The native—contrary to popular opinion—had quite a sense of humor, and irony, too. I suppose Be-el

301

knew perfectly well I would be surprised, and of course much interested.

I was. For he made it known that Squiyowhiynoof's remains were deposited in the direction he indicated. I was beside myself! I would stand by the mysterious stranger—his resting place, anyway.

Yes, I found it. Why, it even had a headstone and a footstone—not stone or rock, but great slabs of cedar. I missed them at first. They were much overgrown and one had fallen on its side. I would say they were some seven feet from one another. The ground between them was slightly depressed.

I offer up these details because this was not the way the Yoncalla themselves disposed of the remains of their own departed. Their dead were always more or less seated in the earth, the knees drawn up to the chest. Nor did they use markers upon the grave as we know them, although sometimes trinkets and whatnots might dangle over the spot on a post or nearby tree limb.

Now you see what I'm getting at. The lonely grave Be-el led me to was most assuredly that of a white man. Those cedar markers—the wood itself—were much disintegrated, even back in the 1850s.

Did I ever see it again? Never. Yet I seem to see it now—in my imagination, I mean. It was a place that, despite its isolation or perhaps because of it, had an air of serenity. The grave itself was in a very small meadow that had surely had its share of sun in years past, before the trees grew to such a height and cast a certain gloom.

I was a youth, of course, and said to be imaginative or even "sensitive." Some of my brothers and male cousins were of a more rough-and-ready type, I suppose.

Perhaps this explains the feeling I had there in that solitary wood. I felt strangely close to the mysterious man in the grave. I surprised myself by uttering the name. *Squiyowhiynoofff*—it seemed to whisper back to me as those soft-scented cedar boughs trembled a little. It was the wind, of course.

Yet somehow I felt better after I had spoken his name, for it was the only name I knew to call him. I had paid my respects, for surely none but the browsing beasts found their way to that remote graveside.

302

Too, I felt that he must have been a good man. After all, the Yoncalla had seen fit to bury him according to his own customs and had not imposed their own. Surely, at some point when it was clear to him he would never return to the place of his origin, he had let them know how he wished his remains to be disposed of. He who lay there under the Oregon dirt rested upon his back as though sleeping.

Pardon? Oh yes. I did try to find the place again . . . twice. The first attempt was an inspiration born of procrastination: any diversion . . . any excuse to delay my duties at the hated mound! By which I mean the charcoal mound where—annually—my uncle Charley employed us all to help him manufacture the charcoal he used in his blacksmith business for the year forthcoming. We used oak mostly. . . .

Oh, this must have been early in 1856, before my father (Lindsay) had any thought of moving us again. At any rate, I was late for my stint at the charcoal-making spot behind Uncle Charley's early one October morning. I thought to make up for my tardiness by taking a shortcut from our place to his. The mound was close to an oak-covered knoll. In the course of years, we much decimated those old groves.

It was foggy, I recall. The light was eerie and pale and I had only one good 'un—eye, I mean—yet it was a keen eye in those days.

Well, Be-el's pathway seemed like just the thing. I tried to find it—and did—at least a portion of it. It was but a season or so after he'd first taken me to Squiyowhiynoof's graveyard. In short, it occurred to me that since I was in the vicinity I might just as well take a detour to Squiyowhiynoof. I tried and failed. Perhaps had the mists not intervened as they did, I should have found it.

More about old-time charcoal making? It would take too long. The process took us, back then, several days, and each charring was different, emitting its own especial color of smoke. We young firetenders took turns staying up all night long, shoveling wet leaves and ferns so the fire would not flare up and ruin our work, for if someone forgot to be vigilant, there was always the possibility that the mound would explode on us.

It was no fun, I can tell you. Why, we would look black as Nubians after each charring. Our mothers refused to let us in-

303

doors. And of course that kind of work didn't help my eye. I stopped after that year because my bad eye got visited with pus on account of exposing it to all that acrid smoke. It took months for it to heal. Nothing like that had happened since I was a little boy on the trail to Oregon. I didn't regret having to quit charcoal making, I can tell you.

Still, there was one part of the affair I rather liked. Uncle Charley dispensed hard cider each time a fellow finished his stint, and sometimes we'd linger awhile so we would be sure to get our share, passing the jug with him, listening to his stories. He was quite a raconteur, especially if the spirit so moved him—or perhaps I should say *"spirits"* moved him. It's a miracle any of us stumbled to our own dooryards after a night of charcoal making! In fact, as I think of it, sometimes we didn't. We just fell around the campfire and someone would kick us awake when it was time to take our turn again.

In sheep-shearing season, it was more of the same. Hard cider and whatnot, I mean. Now, that *was* a bloody affair. Shearing and imbibing do not mix well.

Still—even Charley's libations weren't enough to take the edge off certain tasks, such as clipping off bull balls or snipping the tails of full-boweled baby lambs. Yet these mundane duties were part and parcel of any Yoncalla rancher's life, along with slaughtering and butchering pig, steer, and deer, not to mention the backbreak of bucking hay and cutting cordwood season after season, year after year.

Thus it came to me I would be better doing something in some more civilized outpost, such as Salem or Albany, say, where I might buy my steaks and chops neatly wrapped in paper and have my firewood delivered to my door.

But I have certainly wandered "whither and thither." Back to our business. My second attempt to find Squiyowhiynoof's grave was about fifteen years ago. I went back to Yoncalla briefly, thinking to tromp around behind Charley's old place again. Be-el was yet alive, but for some reason he couldn't accompany me—perhaps his poor health. Buck came along. . . .

Buck? My cousin—Charley's youngest. He lived there in the house his father built. Still does. His name was George . . . Buck is his nickname. He was called so after one of Charley's favorite oxen. "Buck." It stuck.

No, I didn't find any sign of Squiyowhiynoof's grave. The back hills had been logged. Blackberries had overrun the old trails. I looked for the stump of that huge sentinel cedar but could not find it. In fact, I couldn't find anything in the way of natural landmarks. The countryside was changed greatly. I hardly knew it. Funny what trees do for a place.

Buck, incidentally, was very surprised when I told him the Squiyowhiynoof story. He had never even heard of a grave. Doubtless I was the only white man ever to be privileged to lay eyes upon it. Thus you have only my word for it, but my word is good.

Why did the Yoncalla Indians place Squiyowhiynoof's remains so far away from their own? A perfectly good question. I wondered that myself. Certainly the burying ground they used was very old. I never heard of any other in the vicinity. Their own graveyard occupied a spot sacred to them, I mean. It was close to the strangely marked boulder I spoke of yesterday . . . up on the hill behind rattlesnake country. If we had time I could tell you of an encounter the shaman and I had with a grandfather rattler, but you can read about it in my book, I suppose.

What? The serpent was not feared by them. There's quite a story that goes with that, too, but if you don't mind, I shall continue. It's easy for an old soldier to be tempted off the track.

Soldier? There's much I could say in that line, also, but by Judas Priest, if I understood you, you've only today. "Let us go forth."

Where was I? . . . Oh yes, the grave. I wanted to say something about the medicine man, or shaman, in that connection. Sometimes even a small clan like the Yoncalla had several. Some merely visited. Others dwelt among them—Lolokes for one. It was sometimes a case of too many cooks—they competed for a following, not unlike certain ministers I've known. The denominations were at war, so to speak. It is possible that the shamans of Squiyowhiynoof's era viewed him with some resentment. He "carried the Word"; the "Word" was unfamiliar to them, which surely upset the status quo. Thus they may have felt that he should not be buried next to the rest.

I should say, too, that whatever the case, it is not surprising that Squiyowhiynoof's grave was never visited by the Indians. This was not necessarily a sign of contempt or disrespect. The natives never did too much in the way of graveside commemoration in any case. Now, on the way to the grave they might keen and moan. I heard it many times. Mortality was especially great amongst the Yoncalla children. Any infant had to fight to stay alive. Each winter, the sick were numerous. Not just Indians but settlers, too. Intermittent fever, ague, whooping cough, scrofula . . . scrofula especially attacked the natives. . . . The older people dropped like flies in the '50s. I've heard that it was even worse when the poor Indians were herded toward the reservations. Even after they were relocated, many died before their time. Those Indians who managed to remain in Yoncalla went through it, too; sickness and death. I remember a score or more who were brought by heartsick mothers right to Aunt Melinda's door, yet even she, who had nursed countless persons with astonishing success, could do nothing. It was all the more pathetic, since the Indians put much stock in her herbal remedies. She said it broke her heart to see them coming. It was an awful thing to see the processions going up to the hillside, women clutching the tiny wrapped bodies to their bosoms—preparing to give them up.

Their keening was surely one of the saddest sounds to fall upon the human ear. I've already stated their burial custom. After that, the dearly departed were on their own. Where? Well, in Indian heaven—Saghalie—or so it was hoped, and no further respects were paid.

Oh, for a few days the keening might rise up from the village. Occasionally a bansheelike wail could be heard that set the teeth on edge. But then it was done. No one returned to the grave unless forced to the cemetery because some other had died. That was that. The living went on living.

And all this brings to mind a superstition widely held among the Yoncalla that had to do with the wolf—Quartux, they called him. Strange to say, in those days wolves were sighted most frequently whenever there was an Indian burial. . . . Yes, there were wolves in relatively large numbers in those days. No longer, I understand. I suppose they've been killed off.

No! The Yoncalla *never* hunted the wolf . . . ever! . . . or treated him with anything but respect. Why? Because they believed the wolf to be their benefactor and protector; thus when Quartux commenced to howl, or was seen in a place where the dead person previously had ties or some unfinished business, even the children greeted him, and their elders sang songs of farewell. For it was thought that some persons had difficulty accepting the fact that they were dead—supposedly the wolf offered them assistance by permitting them to inhabit his body until all good-byes had been said.

I will now take a moment to relate a little myth I have heard repeated by countless Indians, which further explains why the wolf was so venerated. I consider it to be the native's version of Genesis.

In the beginning was a mountain and on the mountaintop was a table of stone. On this table was a deposit of matter, jellylike in consistency. . . . Now, it is this part of the myth that I find especially significant because it seems to me the jellylike matter bears a credible resemblance to the substance called protoplasm that Professor Darwin and others claim has given all life its origin!

To continue: Out of this protoplasmic mass grew a living being in the form of—and in fact, was—a woman! First Woman, or Snowats, came forth holding a baby. When she was ready, she came down the mountain carrying that child, whose sacred name was Iswukaw.

At the mountain's base the two were joined by friend Quartux—an accommodating sort of fellow, evidently—for First Woman placed the boy astride the wolf's back and passed a strap of some sort around the child so he should not fall off, pulling it over the wolf's head, just above his eyes, in a kind of primitive harness arrangement! That ends—rather abruptly, to be sure—the story of the beginning of the Kommema or Yoncalla people, and I've never heard a native who could add another word to it.

A practice is said to have emerged out of this legend, incidentally; every native mother carried her baby on her back, though, unlike Quartux, she was not compelled to go about on all fours! The cradleboard and the camas-gathering baskets had vine-maple tumplines that passed over the forehead, reminiscent of Quartux's harness.

I always pitied the native women. In those days they amounted to no more than glorified pack animals. Not only did they carry everything, they were the workers of the clan, save for hunting and other such activities. Before the reservation times, they did the bidding of their lords, who both gamboled and gambled as often as possible. The native woman's contribution to tribal life has been unsung, in my opinion.

No, I knew no female shamans among the Yoncalla, yet the old women were the storytellers. The whole of the Yoncalla theology—for I consider it such—their science of God or gods . . . was a complex affair which demonstrates that the Indians were not only intelligent but a thoughtful people as well, far more so than they or any of their kind were generally given credit for!

The Yoncalla and their northern cousins—the Calapooey—had a veritable pantheon of deities. Why, there was a whole hierarchy of what the Christian would call angels and devils. These were just as elaborate and carefully conceived as the classes of archangels, cherubim, seraphim, and so on. And, like the Christians, the Yoncalla recognized a darker retinue. Yes—the native had the equivalent of Satan and his legions, as well.

If I might be permitted to say so, I'd just as soon "pin my faith" on Worldmaker, Snowats, Quartux, and the rest, for is the Old Testament any less far-fetched? There is nothing resembling protoplasm there! Why, the Hebrew Elohim or Yahweh was said to have made the first man of mud or common clay, and woman from a mere rib! No! To my mind, the quivering jelly atop Snowat's mythical mountain makes more sense than all that business about the Master Potter blowing life into a pile of dirt in order to make a man-vessel.

Speaking of the Old Testament reminds me of something I failed to report earlier concerning the mysterious Squiyowhiynoof . . . an incident Jesse Applegate related to me. . . .

What? Why, I'm referring to my uncle, of course. . . . Yes, indeed. I was named after him . . . "in full," you might say. . . . Where was I? . . .

No . . . no . . . I don't mind an occasional interruption. Naturally, there will come things you don't know as I "soliloquize and parenthesize," as my brother Elisha used to say. Now, if I were 'Lish you might have to resort to jumping up and down, or perhaps strike me with some blunt object to get my attention. My brother was the sort to "hold forth." But as I am not Elisha and still myself—or was when last I checked—I will continue.

I was working up to more evidence . . . building a case for Squiyowhiynoof's influence upon the Yoncalla.

Jesse "the elder" arrived in the Yoncalla country in '49, a year before the rest of us. Naturally, he brought all his books—those that had survived the disasters of the Columbia River at least, when our boats went down. . . . At any rate, as soon as Jesse appeared the Yoncalla descended upon him, full of intense curiosity. At that time, any "civilized" object, a simple spool of thread, a common butter churn, a hammer or anvil, excited the greatest interest on the part of the natives! But my uncle's books—his most prized possessions—met with utter indifference. They'd seen such a thing already, they said, *ahnkuttie laly.* "Talking paper" was old hat to them. Jesse was taken aback. How had the natives seen such a thing as a book, living as they did so far off the beaten track? He thought maybe a trapper of the more bookish sort—for most were not—might have passed by at some time or another. He asked them if the talking paper had been with a *lepiege tillikum* (trap-man).

They replied in the negative, saying that their talking paper had been left to them by Squiyowhiynoof. They said it "disappeared" when they had been raided by other Indians. Before that, however, they evidently had kept it with their tribal relics for many years. One or two of the elders had seen it with their own eyes and described what were surely engravings or prints depicting a *cultus* place under the earth where the incorrigible found themselves, and a place high up—Saghalie—where the obedient might dwell if they followed the teachings espoused by Squiyowhiynoof.

From which we may infer that our sojourner indeed was a "religious," and, most certainly, a Christian.

When we all lived in Yoncalla, my father noted it time and again: The Yoncalla were not light-fingered. They said Squiyowhiynoof instructed them not to help themselves to what was not theirs. Their Great Teacher intoned, "Thou Shalt Not Steal," and they didn't. This, of course, made the Yoncalla excellent neighbors. Elsewhere in Oregon many a native robbed the white man blind . . .but the reverse was also true . . . maybe more so. . . . In a manner of speaking, some white men surely got their "just deserts."

Bad feeling betwixt settlers and natives? Yes, that could be said. After a while the Indian—any Indian—was viewed with distrust. I will point out, however, that such had not always been the case. Settlers arriving before the middle 1840s had no ax to grind

309

with the natives! On the contrary! There was cooperation and sometimes even friendship. Old Caleb, the Calapooey; Quatlee, the Klickitat; King's Girl; and countless of their kin enjoyed our confidence. We felt close to them whilst we lived in the Willamette. Where? On what we called Salt Creek. The three family claims were side by side, not far from the town of Dallas, which, incidentally, was earlier named "Cynthia" in honor of Uncle Jesse's wife. When we were youngsters, white boys and brown kept continual company hunting, fishing, bartering. They were fine folk! From them we learned jargon 'til it became second nature! We grew up speaking it—every one of us.

Why, when old Quatlee—a Klickitat chieftain of some reputation—learned that his friend Jesse Applegate was relocating, he offered to provide an Indian escort all the way to Yoncalla. And, by Jove, he and his braves did exactly that. Dressed in full regalia, too, their horses decorated as fancifully as themselves, proceeding just ahead of the wagons. Ready to fend off any of their red brethren who might take offense, though none did, of course. The Indians living in the Willamette were peaceable people. Not so peaceable were those farther to the south. And even those—the Klamath, Rogue, Takelma, and so forth—became enemies of the white man only after much provocation.

I suppose the bitterness between the two races was inevitable; after all, the history of our continent is rife with such troubles. Yet, in my opinion, the turning point—in Oregon, at least—came on the day that news reached the settlements concerning the Whitman massacre. Queer, is it not, that the good doctor's name itself is so close to white man?!

After the massacre at Waiilatpu in '47, all Indians—Cayuse or not—were cause for alarm. That tragedy so stirred up people that their fears became exaggerated. The Cayuse war resulted.

As it turned out, some of those fears were justified. I myself served briefly in our attempts to rout out the Rogues. For by 1848 there were numerous incidents between emigrants and Indians all along the southern emigrant road. Yes, my father and Uncle Jesse and other brave men cut that route. Fracases grew commonplace after gold was discovered. The Applegate Trail, as many called the southern road, was jammed with those going or returning from the mines. Some of the gold-seekers were of a rougher sort: riff-raff! if

Captain Oliver Cromwell Applegate and two Klamath Indian friends, circa 1920. (Applegate family photograph. Courtesy Douglas County Museum)

I may be forgiven for being blunt. In any case, the coarseness of their character was amply demonstrated by their offenses to native females. To some, the yellow stuff in their poke meant more than common decency. Naturally, all this put the native in a fearsome and vengeful humor. The native cannot be entirely blamed, though many have sought to do so for convenience' sake. After all, the land of southernmost Oregon was exceedingly fecund and beautiful! Many settlers believed that the sooner the Indian was forced to part with it, the better. To that end, many a so-called Christian played his role. In ten years' time the disfranchisement of the native was thought to be complete! It was, save for the bloody war with the Modocs, which was yet to come.

Certain of my kinsmen could surely write a tome on that subject. And lest I be perceived as some old fool ranting, I will make it clear that I know of what I speak.

How could it be otherwise? I was brought up by people who knew all about the Indians and their troubles. My uncle Jesse was called upon from the 1840s onward . . . parleying . . . negotiating . . . and later serving on commissions whose task it was to settle up with the natives. In the sixties or thereabouts, J. W. P. Huntington, a son-in-law of Charley Applegate's, was Superintendent of Indian Affairs for the whole of Oregon! Even closer to home, as far as I was concerned, were the activities of my own father—yes, Lindsay Applegate, at the first Klamath agency. He'd served as subagent there and he had his hands full, or rather I should say tied, by government policies that left both him and the Indians helpless to do what needed doing. What? Well, settlers were squatting on lands set aside for the natives and the government more or less turned its back on the problem. Supplies guaranteed by the treaties failed to arrive. There was graft. . . . Oh, it went on and on. . . . My father finally called it quits. Those were appointed positions, you know. A man had to be of the right political party. Most of the Applegates were "Whiggish." My brother Elisha, by the way, helped found the Republican party in Oregon. Back in Lincoln's era. Naturally, the plight of the natives and my father's troubles were spoken of and agonized over by the family as a whole.

Elisha, Lucien, Ivan, and Oliver . . . four of my brothers worked closely with the Indians, officially and otherwise. Why, Oliver is down there yet! Raising his children right on the reservation. Working with the Klamath people. If anyone wants to know how "Captain O.C." is faring with the Indians, or whether he is considered a friend and benefactor, they have but to ask any native yet living in those parts. O.C.? That stands for Oliver Cromwell—England's Protestant protector—yes. But there is another name given to Oliver: Blywas' lo kay, "Golden-Eagle-Chief." That, in itself, shows something—Oliver is respected. He is one of their own.

Someday a proper history will be written on the subject of how the Oregon Indian was dealt with, at which time many a shady corner will be lit up for all to evaluate! Such is not my task. My task is far more modest, yet there is need of it.

For where in the records appear the stories of the Yoncalla, or of their noble *sachem* Halo, and the House of Fearn? There is plenty to be read about the so-called bad Indian and still more to be said. Why, everyday I receive a dose of such medicine! The old veterans I am quartered with see to that! "Bloodthirsty savages," to hear their chronicle of what passes for history. Some yet fight the odious war with the Modoc, from their wheelchairs!

Which reminds me, I believe I've caught a whiff of something and hear the rattle of a cart way up the corridor. . . . Luncheon is coming, is it not? Yes? I am right then. Blindness has benefits. Some of my faculties are sharpening in this dim world I occupy. No, they cannot help me here. I am resigned to it. Soon I will go home, or rather to my sister's. In the meantime, Sue Burt—my cousin Ellen Applegate's daughter—visits me and acts as my "eyes," for I cannot see enough to write a single word or read either manuscript or galley. She is a faithful girl . . . has a strong interest in history—can speak and even write in jargon, bless her!

And as luncheon always makes me sleepy, I hope I'll be forgiven for the nap that inevitably follows the custard. By four o'clock, I'll be fit again. . . . I shall then resume my "yarns."

JESSE A.'S DREAMS OF THE AFTERNOON

It had been night: the darkest dark. All the darker under the
fringed shadows of the firs. And he was running with the Indian
boys under a thick, ominous fluttering . . . yes . . . that had come
first . . . that smother of wings which filled the senses. Coming
closer and closer until he'd felt the faint but terrible touch of
feathers against his cheek. Or was it the wind of those great wings
beating over their heads? And they were tipped in white or light.
Someone yelling "Run! Run!" *Hyak cooley!* And he had. Stum-
bling then, as a wheel rolling down the hill. Only now it was the
slope behind Uncle Charley's and not Salt Creek at all. Yoncalla.
Rolling. Trees passing. The thing overhead not eagle but owl. Or
both. The shadow following him down . . . lifting only when he'd
reached the old grove where the oaks were closing over him. But
when he looked up, he saw them to be cedars, and now their
rough trunks were somehow illumined. He could feel his back
against the damp-mossed earth. He was folding his arms, yet
something called him up. Carrying him. And he was unafraid,
even as he felt himself flying and rising over the trees, even as he
had looked down . . . seeing the circle of Indians. Naming them
one by one . . . *And the darkness had been his own robe* . . . and all
was sound, mysterious and resonant. The thing he rode was saying
its name over and under him: *Chuchonny-hoof-hoof-hoof.* Who are
you? . . . Who . . . who . . . who. . . ?
    He'd half-awakened then; the ward was atremble with wheeze
and snore—and he'd lost the dream save for the hover of some
great *something* . . . and . . . for a moment there was light beneath
his eyelids, or the memory of light, which by degrees diminished
into shimmering points that he first took to be stars in the firmament. But they were not. They were sparks more gold than silver.
A glittering shower descended. Scented by smoke. And his hands
held something heavy and cool from which arose the heady, fruity
smell of good applejack. And men were laughing in the inky distance, but the tall, portly man before him was thoughtful, as
though considering some question, and he took the jug, lifting it
up until his face seemed to glow, his hatbrim a black halo. It was
Uncle Charley . . . all ruddy, his vest puckering about the belly.
A button missing.

There was no voice, yet his uncle's eyes spoke, telling a story of some kind. Little scenes were revealing themselves, spreading over the embers of the dying fire. At first, he could not see them clearly. The colors and forms shifting and merging. Then, quite distinctly, appeared three men. On horseback. Dismounting. And one Indian. One. Small of stature. Looking up at the horsemen. Eagle feathers and animal tails trailed from his basket hat. And the Indian was bending low, plucking something from the earth. Holding the green thing over his head, shaking it, saying a single word. Once. Twice. Thrice. The word was "Camapheema." The Indian's name. . . .

And now the men in the distance came closer. Shoes echoing in the corridor. A tap, tap, tapping. Talk, not laughter. A familiar voice saying, "Well, gentlemen!" after which he heard his neighbor's bed cranked up, and the crank who lay upon the bed was coughing and asking for water. And it was time. His own eyes opening, seeing nothing. The dream staying with him for some moments so that he knew he was ready—or soon would be . . . Yes. Quite ripe with remembering.

Four O'clock
Awakening

. . . I apologize for the quality of our present refreshment. Water, weak tea, or hot milk! These bland beverages I may summon from the hospital kitchen day or night! But good coffee . . . or something stronger, that a visitor too might partake of? I presume these are deemed too stimulative for a bunch of old veterans! Yet in Europe, I understand, wine is regularly prescribed and thought most salubrious! Such news, however, has not reached the physicians of fair Roseburg. No, it is to be tea, totally—a poor but à propos joke surely! Even so, the diluted Pekoe before you is far better than the stuff my mother and aunts served up when they first arrived in Oregon. That was nothing more than mashed chickpeas strained through old socks! A concoction invented by the French Canadien settlers, or so I've been told.

Did the French Canadiens make wine? Not that I know of. The plant called Oregon grape, alas, is no grape at all. I've never heard that they used the lowly blackberry or elderberry either, as some folks do now, or any other native fruit—of which there are few enough in Oregon. In those early days, no one dared experiment, in any case. The laws were strict from the beginning. The Hudson's Bay Company had regulations concerning spirits and their manufacture in Oregon. A little later the Methodist lobby influenced the provisional government to the same end. If John Barleycorn, Demon Rum, and their relatives had friends in Oregon, they were visited "on the sly"! Of course, once the apple orchards had taken hold, many in the country made cider—for family use. Ofttimes it was allowed to "age." Yet even in the hinterlands, Dame Temperance made headway! "To drink or not to drink?" It has always been an issue with us Webfoots: Yes, I disagree with others in my family. The Applegates have been split on the subject as far back as I can remember. As for but a few examples: My father didn't have much use for liquor yet he "judged not." Uncle Jesse rarely partook of any spirit, including his own cider, which was peculiar, since Jesse made some of the best applejack in the Yoncalla countryside on a press especially built for him! Uncle Charley—a convivial sort of fellow—was another

317

matter altogether, as you may have gathered already. He paid for it in the end, or so Irene and Lucy—his daughters—claim. No woman in the family, as far as I know, had a liking for spirits. Why, some would have sooner spit in a public place than have such beverages in their home. . . .

. . . Oh, how my brother Oliver can harangue on the subject! Doubtless his aversion stems from his work with the Indians, who suffer on account of liquor, God knows. Alcohol and the Indian are a rowdy couple, all right, and the laws enforcing his abstinence are understandable if the poor red man is not to sink to further degradation. But for other men . . . now, how have I got on the unpleasant subject of temperance? On account of the weak tea, I suppose. . . . Ha! I understand myself. I have the vague impression that my nap was moistened by good applejack! But that was no more than a dream . . . spiked by wishful thinking.

Dreams are a queer business, aren't they? I've had them frequently since arriving in Roseburg; perhaps they've been sharpened by abstinence. The other "inmates"—for so I think of us all as we serve out our terms in this monotonous place—have them, too; dreams, I mean. Why, on some nights the wards fairly echo with whoops and inane pronouncements as one fellow or another "thrashes it out" in his sleep. Sometimes an orderly appears to shake the culprit awake. . . . Thus far, however, no one has so plucked me from slumber. If I have nightmares, I am spared the memory of them. Nightmare . . . where did the expression come from in the first place, I mean? *Peshak moosum nanitch!*—The seeing-bad-sleep—that is what the Indians called nightmares: Surely, theirs were more gruesome than those of their white counterparts . . . because their beliefs are populated by evil spirits, demons, and the like. It is a wonder any Indian child ever slept through the night! When I was a youngster, the Calapooeys around Salt Creek scared me silly with their stories about Chuchonnyhoof, the king of the hobgoblins. He was supposedly a big birdlike fellow who swooped down on those who'd gone astray. Chuchonnyhoof . . . Squiyowhiynoof. Well, the "oof" part is certainly the same. I've no idea what either name means. Neither is in jargon.

For my own part, I would rather "see" something "bad" than see nothing at all, for when dreaming I am blessed with sight again. However, I've known men who tremble at the sight of "night's dark horses"! . . . Someone told me recently—Sally Long (Sally Applegate Long, daughter of Jesse)—anyway, it got so Uncle Jesse was afraid to sleep at all. Yes. Her father—my uncle Jesse. He lived with Sally in Yoncalla toward the end of his life. Uncle Jesse died in 1888, if memory serves. At any rate, Sally would hear him prowling about the house half the night until at last exhaustion took him. But no sooner would he shut his eyes, evidently, than a regular "haunt" commenced. He told Sally that various of his dead loved ones appeared, Aunt Cynthia—his wife—at the head of the procession. Sometimes she held Milburn—the little baby that died in Missouri. On other occasions, my little cousin Edward (who drowned in the Columbia) would be hugging her skirts. Each morning, Uncle Jesse would report how Aunt Cynthia always seemed on the verge of telling him something. All night long she stood staring at him, her eyes full of reproach, yet she never spoke. She looked so sad, he said, he could not help but cry. Upon arising, Sally always found him in this state, poor soul. It's surprising to me. Uncle Jesse was never one to demonstrate emotion.

In any event, I am certain that Aunt Cynthia would not have wished to be an instrument of her husband's torture, for no one was kinder than Cynthia Applegate. She stood steadfastly by her husband. It is true, however, that there were many cruel reverses and hardships in later years. After these nightmares over at Sally's, Jesse became increasingly confused. He evidently took to wandering around the countryside. Sometimes, he took a train as far as Linkville (Klamath Falls) or Ashland without telling anybody. Eventually, word would get back to them that he was quartered in some hotel room. Once someone found him half-dazed along the roadway, muttering about one harebrained business venture or another, which he insisted was "bound to bring in money"! . . . When it got too much for Sally and the rest of her bunch, they decided they had no choice but to put him away. He was occasionally violent, too. Where? Uncle Jesse was first at Linkville and then up at Salem . . . in the asylum. After a time he was released, though greatly changed.

I was glad Sally explained the matter to me, for there has been much bitterness about that subject. Others in our family, especially those of us who had long since left Yoncalla, did not understand the circumstances. Even so, I wonder . . . what did such a

319

thing do to a man's spirit . . . to find himself so reduced? . . . Why, Uncle Jesse had blazed trails and served in the first legislature of the land. He had written laws; prominent men respected him. The vice-president of our nation sought his counsel even as men on his homeground made ready to do him in!

Who and for what reason? *Why?!* Because the courts of Oregon and a lawyer said Jesse Applegate owed him money. When all was said and done, Uncle Jesse's only crime was lack of judgment: Jesse signed his bond and placed his trust in one who held high office. This man turned out to be a scoundrel, through and through. . . . Yes, he absconded. Jesse and another man had to come up with the bond. And when the judgment came to "pay up," Jesse Applegate could not, for times were hard and he had suffered business reverses even before the court judged against him.

In the end, Uncle Jesse had neither home nor land to leave his children. They were taken from him. Later, the governor tried to remove the sting somewhat and granted Aunt Cynthia forty acres of her own. She took it way high up on their beloved Mount Yoncalla. I've often thought of that. . . . There they were—Aunt Cynthia and Uncle Jesse—both old people—and they had but to look down the mountain to see the site of their former holdings spreading beneath them. The fine house Jesse had built was no longer his. Instead, he and Aunt Cynthia occupied a modest house of logs. Not long after that, she died. Uncle Jesse was never the same. In my opinion, the combination of these reverses bested him. He began to fail mentally. He had delusions. While at the Salem asylum, I have heard, Uncle Jesse met an old friend. Yes, a fellow patient. Who was it? Why, it was none other than Senator James W. Nesmith, who had not only crossed the plains with Uncle Jesse in '43, but had come to the defense of the Applegate Trail at a time when there was much controversy on that subject. Thus two of Oregon's most illustrious old fathers ended in the same pitiable condition.

Yes, it is sad, is it not? There is no accounting for the twists of Destiny. . . . Nevertheless, it is high time that I return to my principal topic, which is not Jesse Applegate but the Yoncalla tribe from whom the government likewise "tooketh" away. The losses of the Yoncalla and other Indians amounted to more than a plot of ground, as far as that goes. All the wild miles: hillsides, forests, creeks. . . . All that roamed! All that grew! As far as their dark eyes could see. Soon none will be left who can remember the natives' former way of life, nor will there be letters, or keepsakes, or anything whatever to prod the memory. How, I ask, will rite and lore and tribal happening find their way into the record?

Records? There are none . . . save a few treaties and documents drawn up by the Indian agents. I understand that not a single Yoncalla name appears on those treaties. Others, apparently, were permitted to sign away the Yoncalla's land on their behalf, or so it seems.

Of the seventy or so Yoncalla whom I knew in my youth, fewer than a dozen souls remain. These are all members of a single family named Fearn: They are Old Halo's descendants.

When the first settlers arrived, did the Yoncalla jealously guard his *klose illahee*? Did any of Halo's clan let loose a shower of arrows or do anything whatever to discourage the Scotts, Applegates, or any of the countless families who came later? No. . . . The Yoncalla raised not so much as a finger against any white—then or ever! But I will now relate a brief tale that demonstrates how years before any white horsemen or emigrant wagons rolled into Yoncalla, the seeds of apprehension against new people had been sown. Halo told me this years ago—else some other Indian at a later time. No matter, the story was passed around from tribe to tribe. I've even heard it repeated down in the south Klamath country!

It seems that a Calapooian shaman from the Willamette Valley once had a vision. Supposedly he was seated in a grove of alders— near the river called Santiam. At any rate, the shaman shared his vision with his clan. Soon runners and messengers hoofed it down to various of the southern tribes, saying that they were "bringing the Dream." The shaman claimed that a time would come when the *illahee*—the earth—would be all black and its green covering would disappear. This was because some new people were coming to ruin everything. Indeed, when the settlers' plows commenced to overturn the sod, revealing acre upon acre of the dark earth underneath, many an Indian, including Halo, spoke of that old-time prophecy. All had been foretold.

Despite this, Halo did not view the coming of the white man with alarm. On the contrary. You see, even though Uncle Jesse and Father had passed through the Yoncalla country when they

321

scouted the southern route in 1846, and then later on other occasions, they never actually saw an Indian. Yet there was sign everywhere. Clearly, Indians lived in Yoncalla. This was of concern. How could a man consider moving his family to a place where the character of the Indians was unknown? Why, everything depended on whether the native was peaceable or not. Uncle Jesse, you see, already had set his heart on Yoncalla. He knew that he wanted to stake out a claim near the base of the mountain. . . . What? Mount Yoncalla is in reality a very high and handsome hill; it's the principal landmark in that vicinity. As I was saying, as Jesse's mind was more or less made up, and Father was inclining that way, too, it was important to settle any question regarding the disposition of the native. Father and Uncle Jesse, I should say, had been talking it up to Uncle Charley for some time—relocating in Yoncalla, I mean. . . . Oh, Uncle Charley was willing on the face of it, but as he was a practical sort, naturally he had to see the place for himself. He was the oldest. He didn't want to move again unless it was ideally suited to what he had in mind: horses and cattle.

So the three brothers went on a little trip south in '47, but then again it could have been '48. But "it don't matter a whing whang," as a schoolboy I once taught used to say, at least not for present purposes.

How many times have I heard Uncle Charley relate what I'm about to tell you! It stuck in his mind, I guess. He said just the three of them went down there. They'd had a fine jaunt. Everything looked pretty good. But as soon as they rode into the easternmost valley (Scotts Valley) Jesse began acting nervous. He was on the lookout. There were no Indians and d———d little sign. But some. Enough to make Uncle Jesse think he, Dad, and Uncle Charley were deliberately being avoided. There were Indian troubles elsewhere that same season, and Uncle Jesse grew convinced some "bucks" might be hidden and lying in wait to strike. Just about dusk, they'd given up hope of finding any natives and thought to make camp. They'd even discussed the "watch" for the night. Suddenly three or four Indians appeared, as if out of nowhere. Uncle Charley was especially relieved. Their native callers were unarmed. Some jargon passed between both groups: The Indians made it known that they were a sort of welcoming committee and that the three *t'kope tillikums* should follow them to their *hyas tyee*, great headman.

Well, off they went. The headman was in fact rather small in stature. The three Applegates were tall men. They towered over him. Nevertheless, the headman was a dignified fellow. He had on certain ceremonial headgear. Clearly, he had been expecting them. He gave them a speech in fine oratorical style. It was almost as though it were rehearsed. In fact, it was.

It seems the headman had been expecting Uncle Jesse to return for quite some time. He allowed that he had felt it in his *tumtum* (heart) and thumped upon his chest to emphasize the point . . . which is what Uncle Charley always did when relating this story. Yes. Most assuredly. The headman recognized Uncle Jesse from his earlier journeys. A certain spot upon the ridge was pointed out where the Indians had formerly secreted themselves in order to evaluate their white visitors on that day, as well as on other occasions.

Things seemed to be going so well Uncle Charley dipped into his saddlebags so he might dispense the various geegaws they'd brought along—oh, the usual business . . . beads and so forth. The headman was much pleased. All squatted amiably around a fire for a while. When it was time for the three *tillikums* to return to their own camping site, Uncle Jesse decided it was time to "pop the question." How would the *hyas tyee* feel if the three Applegates brought their *klootchmen* and little *tillikums* and *moos moos* to the valleys? Now, this was the part of the episode Uncle Charley was especially taken by. The diminutive *tyee* stood up. He looked thoughtful. Some moments passed as he conferred with certain of his own brethren. Finally, with great solemnity the headman addressed his three white visitors, looking them in the eye, each in his turn. "Once in the long ago time came a t'kope man who had much lametsin [medicine]. He had lived with The People in peace. He was skookum."

After so saying, the headman lifted his hand as if delivering a benediction. Full of trust, the headman gazed at them.

"Klone tillikums. You three men. Six . . . friends. Skookum," the *tyee* said. "Hyas skookum."

Yes. Certainly the headman was referring to Squiyowhiynoof, the "t'kope man" who many years before had lived with the Yon-

323

Skookum. Lindsay, Charles, and Jesse Applegate making their pact with the headman of the Yoncalla tribe, Halo. (Susan Applegate painting. Photograph courtesy Douglas County Museum)

calla. In the mind of the Indian the Applegates would forever be associated with the mysterious black-robed medicine man. Doubtless a smallish clan like the Yoncalla would have been pleased to have white "protectors." In any case—as I have said—their people were regularly raided by other tribes. Nevertheless, I do not underestimate Squiyowhiynoof's lingering influence upon the Yoncalla. His coming in the long ago disposed the Yoncalla to trust. The Applegates were in good stead from the beginning. We were *welcomed.* And this so affected my uncles and my father that they never forgot it. No. They stood by the Yoncalla from then on and vice versa.

What? Why, the headman was none other than Halo, of course. I thought that was understood . . . from his scion grew the large Indian family called Fearn.

Fearn? No, that was not Indian, strictly speaking. Indians did not have surnames, though they were eventually forced to adopt them.

During that first meeting between the Applegates and the Yoncalla, Uncle Jesse asked the *tyee,* "What is your yahhul [name]?"

Now, natives sometimes had several names, some of which were secret. The *tyee* contemplated the name question for a moment, and then, as though inspired, he suddenly plucked up a plant that grew near his feet. Waving it over his head, he was heard to say *"Camapheema!"* several times. The Applegates assumed this was a tribal word meaning "fern." For a while, Old Halo called himself Camapheema, but eventually he took a new name, that of "Mister Halo." He seemed to prefer it. It was given to him by the "Boston," like his new clothes. What? Well, Halo meant "destitute" or "without much" in jargon. Uncle Charley told me the "without much" part came about when Halo lost the youngest of his three wives. Apparently, she made off with his best pony, too.

But Halo never did use the name Fearn himself, even when the Applegates begged him to apply for his own homestead under that name. My father, who then lived in Ashland, made a special trip back to Yoncalla to bring Halo the papers. He wouldn't do it. He said he would not put his "X" on a talking paper that said he was no longer a part of his clan. Not then or ever was Halo heard to utter a single word in English, incidentally. Whether or not he understood it, we never knew. His sons, of course—Jake, Blind John, and Be-el—were different. They knew they had to adapt to the white man's ways in order to survive! Yet Halo, save for his clothes and the "Boston" cabin my father and uncles built for him, stayed Indian through and through. He was a most remarkable individual! Sad to say, most of the traditions of his people passed with him. Save for the queer hieroglyphics on the tribe's hallowed boulder, Halo and his ancestors left no record for future generations. I have a notion that those ciphers are a unique feature of the Yoncalla, by the way. Oh, there are crude pictures dug into the walls of caves in various parts of Oregon and so forth, but they do not resemble—even remotely—the odd markings on what people now call the Halo Rock.

No, I was not privy to what the rock said, or says, rather; nor did Halo's sons seem to know, or perhaps they considered that it was none of the white man's business! As far as white men went, Halo trusted Uncle Charley Applegate more than any other. The two grew old together and shared many confidences in their twilight years, but if Uncle Charley knew what was written upon the rock, he kept it secret!

325

Now all that is left is a "handful of Fearns." As far as I know, Halo's grandsons care more about baseball than they do for the history of their clan. I intend no disrespect in saying so, either. Those off the reserves go out of their way *not* to be Indian. It is safer.

The rest of the Yoncalla? Their numbers were never great and, as I've said, ever dwindling—even before the removal in 1855.

How I remember that sad day—a long winter's march ahead of them—the pathetic lines of natives following the agent's wagon: Lolokes psis, the old *lamai*, the big Indian my mother called Jolly Sides—all . . . all . . . I saw them go until only Halo and his wives remained. Some natives wept openly, others were anxious to depart, at least in the beginning of that exodus. How so? Why, the agent in charge had done his best to color their destination in rosy hues: the Indian reservations called Siletz, Grande Ronde—and the other places—paradise, the agent said.

Of course, it had been no such thing. The native was promised that he would have the best of both worlds: schools, farming implements, and of course "plenty food," and there would be *hyas illahee* for him to wander over and game and fish and festivals, too! Many a Yoncalla believed the agent who came for them. After all, they had always trusted the "t'kope man." The settlers in their vicinity had treated them kindly. Also, some Yoncalla were un-

The sandstone boulder known as Halo Rock with Sumner Brawn standing next to it, circa 1907. (Brawn family photograph. Courtesy Betty Kruse Smith and Douglas County Museum)

326

happy in their own homeland. In each and every valley, fences were going up. Sometimes the hogs rooted in their camas fields, spoiling everything. More settlers were arriving and many were unkind. There was a killing in the neighborhood. An educated Klickitat Indian named Dick Johnson was murdered most brutally so that some greedy whites could have his fine homestead.

Besides, the agent told the Yoncalla that they had to go. It was the new law! he said. Nevertheless, Mister Halo stood his ground and watched his clan depart. Even his sons.

Yes, Indians all over Oregon were rounded up . . . some taken by force! How did Old Halo manage to remain at home? Because he had uncommon courage and *skookum* friends. But I will say more about that in a moment. First, I want to say something of the adventures of Halo's sons: John, Be-el, and Jake.

They told me these things later after they had run away from the reservation. I should say, of all who had been removed, only Be-el and Jake came home. They said that at Grande Ronde a trumpet summoned them to class each day at seven, and even the littlest Indian boy was forced to wear shoes so stiff and ill-fitting that each step was agony. And all were to wear scratchy uniforms that let in the cold. And of course they'd been shorn—like sheep—too. The vermin were terrible in their draughty quarters, where they had not been permitted to stay with their own clansmen, but instead forced to bunk with Indians of other places . . . all crowded together so that disputes broke out . . . and if any native dared to speak in his own tongue, he was flogged within an inch of his life and flogged for other things as well. And food and blankets were scarce, and within a month the game was played out, the agents having firearms while the natives did not. And they were driven so hard in the fields, even the sick ones, that a number died; and one *cultus* white man dallied openly with various Indian women, so that even dignity had been stripped from the natives, for they watched helplessly as their women were corrupted. And that was what had happened at Grande Ronde Reservation, and doubtless the same sorry story was true elsewhere in Oregon.

. . . I beg your pardon. I seem to have got myself all worked up. Too much talking and I become a phlegmy old warhorse! . . . And not a spittoon or basin within reach! No matter . . . my nose rag will do. My sister supplies them. . . . If they aren't the size of

327

Mac Fearn, grandson of Chief Halo, wearing Pendleton blanket and fern headdress, circa 1920. (Applegate family photograph. Courtesy Douglas County Museum)

a small flag, I consider them useless. . . . She has them made up for me. . . . I fear I will need to beg off in a few moments and rest awhile. . . . If further questions arise? . . . Well, they can be mailed to the same sister . . . she will help me answer inquiries. Yes, in a month or less I will be in Ashland again. Of late, I have thought of the truth of this old saying, "There is more time than life."

Now, before my vocalizations are reduced to piteous squeaks, I will finish up, for I promised to tell how Halo managed to stay home. What? . . . Oh yes, I will be glad to send along a book . . . soon Sue Burt will make arrangements with the printer here in Roseburg. I will include some of my poems in the package, and some of my brother Oliver's as well. We are inspired by the same subject: the Indian lore of the Klamath people. Oliver, by the way, has been commended for his literary efforts by none other than the famous Bard of the Sierras. Yes, Joaquin Miller himself. Miller has known various Applegates since back in the 1850's. It is not widely known that Miller is in fact a Webfoot—at least in the beginning. He grew up in Eugene City. Elisha and he both wrote for newspapers, though of the opposite party. Since you seem interested, I should tell you that others in our family take pen in hand from time to time. . . . A few have published or will soon; my sister, in fact, is busy writing of her experiences in the Philippines, Alice Applegate Sargent. Her husband is the general. There have been several "scribblers" in Uncle Charley's and Jesse's clans as well. In my opinion, the most talented of all the Applegates . . . for she had been a budding playwright, poet, novelist, and artist, too . . . is long since dead. No. She was a woman. Beautiful and honey-haired. Long ago, when but sixteen, her bright candle was snuffed out. Has not someone writ that "the good die young!"? Harriet. Or Harriette, as she preferred to spell it. One of Uncle Charley's daughters. How many times Oliver and I said had she lived, she would have outshone the lot of us. She was not only a poet, playwright, and an aspiring novelist, she could draw and paint, too.

But onward . . . for of all the things I have related concerning Halo, it is this last which will best illustrate his staunch character!

The agent, as I already said, came in the winter of 1855. There were, I think, a handful of soldiers in his party, and one or two interpreters. Evidently, the agent did not understand various

Halo wearing "Boston" clothes. This photograph is reproduced from a circa 1890 newspaper engraving. (Courtesy Douglas County Museum)

dialects and his jargon was poor, too. It should be added that a season or so before, the same agent had arranged to parley with the *tyee* of the various clans in the greater vicinity. At this "potlatch"—party—he liberally handed out presents. At the opportune moment, he struck a contract that stated in what manner the native and his land would soon be parted!

Did all understand the terms? No. I know for certain that several Yoncalla believed they were celebrating the Fourth of July. They told me so later!

Nevertheless, after hearing the agent's pretty speech via the interpreter, many permitted their names to be inscribed on the treaty . . . poor souls! None realized that for some, that fateful paper amounted to a death warrant.

No, Halo did not sign. Even then, at that first meeting, his stance was clear. "Wake nika klatawa halvima illahee! I will not go to a strange land!" For some reason, the interpreter did not convey Halo's declaration to the agent, however. A few seasons later, when the agent returned to gather up his charges, he was much dismayed. Where was the Yoncalla's chieftain? He dispatched a search party.

Besides the Yoncalla, there were many other Indians encamped on my father's property; I don't know how many. Perhaps a hundred or upward. These were already on the march and very dispirited. Now came a contentious interlude. Many Indians refused to go on. They said so. My father especially was angry at the agent's attitude. Yes, the fellow was unduly harsh. Why, many of the natives were visibly sick and cold. Others were hungry. Settlers sympathetic to their plight came by to feed them. Uncle Charley and Jesse, my father, and a few others could no longer hold their tongues. As the unhappy native multitude looked on, the sympathetic settlers made certain demands of the agent. They commenced by asking where were his written instructions? They were unsatisfied with the papers the agent showed them. Why, said my father, as far as he was concerned, the Yoncalla and any other Indians could stay right where they were.

Now the agent grew angry. He stated that he found it incredible that white men would side with a bunch of savages who were being removed for their own betterment. Further—poor fellow, he must have been quite red of face—he said that the settlers were interfering with their own government!

"You have no right," he said. Whereupon the settlers banded as one, thwarting the agent's way.

Then Uncle Jesse spoke up—a man named Wilson seconding, the rest cheering: "We are aware of our own rights, yet the Indian has rights as well."

About this time, the soldiers returned, saying they'd found the missing chief. They had been on the point of taking him forcibly, but had decided to come back for the agent. Now, the agent was surely in a high dudgeon. He stormed away after the missing head-man. My father and uncles, however, and some of the rest of us— myself included—decided to lead the agent to Splashta Alla, where we felt our presence would ensure that he did not act rashly.

I will never forget how Halo looked during those troubled mo-ments. He stood still as a rock, his head high, his look dark and sullen. At first, he would say nothing, not even to Lin-see, his *hyas tillikum*. Clearly, his faith in the white man was shaken.

His two wives sat before the doorhole of their dwelling, quivering with fear. And it was no wonder! For as the agent began to bark out his commands, he began swaggering in front of Halo's *klootchmen*. All the while, the agent fingered the Colt revolving pistol in his belt.

He hissed to his interpreter, "Tell the old man he must come with the others to the reservation!"

The message was relayed. What did Halo do? He remained impassive. Finally, he leaned back against the huge black oak be-side his doorway, as though partaking of its ancient strength. These words rang out:

"Pul! Klose memaloose nika, mitlite nika illahee, nika pa-pa memaloose mitlite okoke illahee. Klose pose nika kokwa. Mister Halo wake quash! WAKE NIKA KLATAWA!"

In sober tones, the interpreter relayed the message: "He says, 'Shoot! It is good I die at home. My father died here; his grave is here! 'Tis good I die here and be buried here! Mister Halo is not a coward! I will not go!'"

As the agent drew out his pistol, the *hyas tyee* lifted his hands and tore open his shirt so that his scrawny chest was exposed! "Pul! Pul! Shoot! Shoot!" challenged Halo. The hand that held the revolver was shaking. "Should I?" the agent asked.

To which my father replied, his voice hoarse with indignation,

332

"NO! By God, you won't. . . . Take the rest if you must! But leave Halo and his women here. We will answer for them—"
The agent, doubtless relieved, "led" the rest away.

The Wayhut
Oft' I wonder if they come when twilight shades the vale
Misty phantoms, vapor light that drifts along the trail
Dim the valley slumbers underneath the waning moon
The chilly breath of autumn chants in shifting, vibrant rune
'Mong unmarked graves of ancients whose age long mead of fame
Was written on the sacred rock before the whiteman came
We mark the trail in Halo's name, record the ancient lore
But they who trod the winding path will walk it nevermore.
—Anne Applegate Kruse
Yoncalla, Oregon
1954

MEMORY PICTURES

Irene Applegate

The child Irene had abundant hair. It was not pale—the color of wheat—like her sister Ellen's, nor was it the color of her sister Susan's, a rich coffee-black with a pretty glint to it when the light was just so. Her sister Mary, like Susie, had the dusky, heavy hair of their father, Charles. Lucy, on the other hand, had her mother Melinda's hair and it was not abundant at all, but rather fine and wispy, a soft brownish shade, though Lucy's tended to curl a little when the weather was damp.

Irene's hair was something people always remarked upon because there was so much of it. When she was smaller, it had been on the yellow side, but now it seemed to be growing darker gradually, and it was hard to guess what color it might be when she was full grown. Perhaps it would take on the reddish tint of some of her mother's people. Yet it was not truly red, like her baby brother John's or her oldest brother Jim's. Irene's hair was closer to her brother Lisbon's, which had, as he grew older, turned coppery. Like Lisbon's hair, Irene's had a distinct wave to it, so that even when her mother tried to braid it, or tie it back for neatness' sake, it tended to loosen, tumbling in coils down her back, falling in thick, unruly waves around the child's face.

It was as if Irene's hair refused to be tamed or confined, as if it had to escape.

And it has always been, since she was a little thing, that her mother, when trying to soothe her or comfort her, had simply run her hand over Irene's hair, stroking it, petting it, until the child quieted and relaxed.

But now Irene was embarrassed by her hair, and she would draw her hand over the place where the gander had struck her, trying to hide the spot her mother had cut around, near the crown of her head because the wound had festered and become a hot, hateful carbuncle. There was an English doctor traveling with them on the wagon train who'd finally taken up his knife and lanced the thing. Irene had been terrified. The blood ran red and sticky down her back, matting her hair, and when her mother washed her off, sponging the place, her whole head felt like it was on fire. It hurt so much she hadn't even cried, but the doctor said,

"My, what a *brave* little girl! It's a good thing she has such abundant hair. It will cover the scar in no time at all."

Yes, and it was a good thing, too, that that gander had only struck her head. They had been at Elm Grove, getting ready to turn on the trail to Oregon, when the creature had attacked her. "Lord, Lord!" the woman who owned the bird cried. "Why, my big old gander could of broke off both her little arms!" As it was, the big bird, honking and squawking, had knocked Irene down in the dirt. Her brother Lisbon had finally chased it away, but Irene never forgot the frenzied flapping of the gander's huge gray wings, or the way the bird had dipped his long neck, snakelike somehow, the ugly wedge-shaped head and open bill coming at her, over her, again and again as she lay helpless on the ground.

Later, it turned out she was not as lucky as the doctor had first thought. That carbuncle hadn't healed as it should have, and even after it did, it still seemed like her head ached the whole of the time they were on the way to Oregon. She couldn't even bear to have her mother touch her hair anymore, and though it was growing over the place, covering it up just the way the English doctor said it would, Irene's head still throbbed.

Yet, when she tried to tell her mamma or sister Lucy or aunt Harriet that her head still hurt her sometimes, they acted like they didn't understand what she meant.

And if she went by herself to sit near the warmth of the fire, and held her head in her hands and maybe cried a little bit, the boys would come by and torment her and say, "Ah, Irene! 'Rene's crying again. Does Reney want her mammy?"

And she couldn't even look up, and just held on to her head, trying not to cry out loud. Only her double cousin Ivan—her "twin," the older people called him because he'd been born the same year and almost the same day as she herself—did not taunt her. And Lisbon, who didn't have the streak of pure meanness some of the older boys had, sometimes brought her a cup of water or sat beside her when her head hurt.

Irene was not thick-skinned; she never would be. Where that child got all her peculiar ideas they—the grown-ups—would never know.

And her brothers, sisters, and cousins, seeing that she always took things hard—taking their bait like some serious little fish— tried to tease her out of her humors. She was a dreamy child,

338

sometimes appearing helpless, susceptible (they said), as if she needed and expected more care and consideration than the other little ones. Yet she was a sturdy little thing to look at her, rounded and rosy. But her parents could count on Irene to be first to get the ague, or start the cycle of the family colds and coughs, or complain about some bellyache that had missed everyone else.

Yet for all of that, no one doubted that she was a smart little somebody. She noticed things the other children didn't. A "sensitive," her mother called her; visited by nightmares, imagining things that weren't there, intensely curious about the things that were there.

"Mamma, why does that old lady smoke a pipe? Why did you pick that plant for us to eat and not the other one? Why are we going on the boats now and leaving the wagons behind? They look so sad."

Irene, one of her aunts said once, was a child who looked for trouble, and because she looked for it, she sometimes saw it coming before anyone else did.

When they had camped at The Dalles near the little mission that overlooked the river, Irene awakened in the middle of the night. She could never give herself to sleep as the others did, and in her long life she would always find herself staring into the darkness with strange thoughts and worries hovering over her. And sometimes the things she called "memory pictures" would visit her. And she would see it all again—All. Even the things she wished to forget.

For when she was four years old, a thing happened more terrible than the gander and the throbbing in her head; more terrifying than thunderstorms upon the plain, or the sight of Dr. Whitman singing that mournful church song over the place where they had put the little Hembree boy under the ground on the trail.

She could not stop thinking about it. She shivered with it. Warren and Edward. She had not seen it happen with her own eyes because Aunt Harriet had thrown the quilt over her head in the boat. But she had felt the awful commotion! She could hear the cries of her family.

Now her little body took in the knowledge. And she knew what it meant—all the things the grown-ups were saying to one another. The wind and rain shook the tent and the little girl, lying awake on the ground, trembled and sobbed.

A voice said then, "Now, Reney, don't cry now." And someone else said, "Poor little thing. She's probably hungry." And
Aunt Harriet went for food. She brought some bread spread with
brown sugar that the Hudson's Bay people had sent upriver to feed
the emigrants, and they begged her to partake of it.

"There now, dearie. There." But Irene couldn't make them
understand. She was not hungry. She shook her head and chewed
the bread, all the while crying—tasting the salt in the sugar. She
couldn't make them understand that she was crying about their
boys and the awful thing that had happened to them.

Decades later, some of the old Applegate men who had also
come to Oregon on the family wagons in their childhood considered that Irene's memory was less than perfect. Perhaps they
were right. Irene, after all, had only been four years old when she
made the crossing, and sometimes, it was claimed, her recollections veered toward the fanciful. She got confused, the old men
said, about when things happened on the trail. Her geography had
gotten all mixed up.

But the old men in the family had bolstered their own faltering
memories of childhood by traveling extensively in their adult
lives. Other men, sometimes even their own fathers, had taken
them over the old trails, retracing much of the journey they had
made years before. Her brothers and male cousins had surveyed or
gone soldiering or gold mining, seeing the country Irene had
passed through only once as a small child atop a covered wagon.

She had stayed at home at the Old Place in Yoncalla, her
vistas contracting rather than expanding, a captive of her gender,
her temperament, and her ailments.

Even so, if a little niece or nephew, grandniece or grand-
nephew, truly wanted to hear about traveling all the way to
Oregon on a covered wagon, they asked Aunt 'Rene. When they
listened to Irene Applegate, they didn't hear the cavalcade of
facts, the sort of calendar of the Oregon Trail that the old men in
the family were inclined to tell them about. A child could live
inside Aunt 'Rene's tales. Her "little scenes," as she called them,
her memory pictures, were as perfectly and vividly rendered as the
illustrations in the storybooks their mothers read to them at home.
A child could feel the things Irene described, because Irene still
felt them herself.

Yes. They could almost see the flashing river when Irene

talked about it, and feel their own hands dangling wrist-deep in the cold blue water just as that little girl on the boat had that long ago misty morning, even as they themselves sat mesmerized on the hooked rug, close to their auntie's rocking chair, hearing the creak of the floorboards underneath, watching the old woman's face in the flicker of the gaslight or kerosene lanterns. "Tell us again about the panther. Oh, tell us about the panther and the swans," they begged.

And she would tell the story slowly, building up to the part about the panther, how she had seen all the great white wild swans floating on the river. And because they'd never seen the swans themselves, she would first describe their cry. "Not a honking sound," she'd say. "Not like the big geese that fly over Yoncalla in the autumn. No, it was not a honking sound. It was higher and more musical."

The older children held their breaths, knowing what was coming, for their aunt 'Rene was clearing her throat, getting ready to give the call of the wild whistling swans—"Too whooo . . . too whooo." And each child would feel a chill, for she had come to the part about the panther, which, Irene said, stood some distance away on the riverbank—the huge cat standing under a big fir tree, its head lowered, worrying something at the edge of the water.

"And the thought came to me"—the old sweet voice wavered then—"that the cat was clawing at the body of one of our boys, and I suppose the same thought came to all of us.

"And Uncle Lindsay stood up in the boat closest to us, looking distraught, though his motion was quiet and deliberate. He drew his rifle to his shoulder, taking aim. And everyone was quiet, only the swish, swish of the paddles cutting steadily through the water, closer and closer to that panther."

And she told how they had floated through the swans, which then moved in soundless agitation, sensing something amiss. "And the shot rang out"—Irene would strike the wooden arm of her rocking chair. Once. Quick. So that it startled them. Then she would slowly raise her hands, just as the swans had risen out of the water, so great in number that the air, for a moment, seemed black with white moving swans. "And I was filled with fear and awe," she'd say. "I feel something of it now, just in the telling of it." And the listening children could almost hear the sound; the eerie *too-whooo too-whoooing* of the wild swans as they flew over

341

the river, up and up, until they were no more than a wavering line high in the sky.

"But what about the panther?" the children clamored. And their aunt would draw her hands back into her lap and say quietly, sadly, "No. It was not one of our boys. Only a dead salmon. Uncle Lindsay's shot missed, just landing in the river, splashing water on the big cat's face." And then she'd say, finishing the story, rising from the chair, smoothing her long skirts, "And you know, it was the oddest thing. That big cat looked up at the boat then, just as calm as you please, and then it turned slowly, walking very deliberately around that big tree he'd been standing under, giving us a fine view of his body and great long tail, as if he intended it."

"And the bodies were never found?"

"No, never found. Never. Not Warren, nor Edward, nor Mr. McClellan's, either."

And she would walk to the little door by the fireplace, the door that led to the narrow staircase to her and Aunt Lucy's room. And the children would sigh to see her go. "No, my dearies, no more stories now. Irene is tired."

APPLES

Lucy Applegate

Apple trees are members of the rose family. . . . Even after
they've been picked apples continue to live.
                              —Henry Weil, *The Compleat Apple*

Great-great-aunt Lucy attracted apples the way some people attract yellow jackets or smoke from a campfire. Yet stings and
smarting tears were but temporary vexations. What Lucy's apples
brought to her did not disappear. Apples hovered in her memory.
In more ways than one, they had left their mark.

Not that Lucy had ever been a beauty, her relatives admitted.
Nevertheless, before the accident she had been "tolerable handsome" in a rawboned way. Stately, even. And of course capable.
Any man on their wagon train would have been glad to have her,
for she'd been almost a woman grown—fourteen years old back in
'43—and when the fiddlers played "Money Musk" or "I've Hung
My Heart on a Willow Tree," her feet never seemed to touch the
ground. Yes, those her father called young swains were sniffing
around, all right—only after that apple smote her, Lucy changed.
Her shoulders weren't straight anymore, as though she were perpetually carrying something that weighted her down. And never
again—until she grew stout and middle-aged and got her special
spectacles—did Lucy Applegate seem to approach either person or
thing head on.

The eye: Unless their mothers or big sisters glared at them, or
nudged them, children were inclined to stare at it. Later, they
would whisper among themselves how Aunt Lucy's eye was "jest
like a bully-frog's," for it bulged considerably, and underneath the
curved lens it appeared even larger than it had before. When a
body chatted with Aunt Lucy, it was hard not to be distracted
because the bad eye was always wandering off as though interested
in something else entirely. It had a life of its own.

Yet when a person got used to Aunt Lucy, it was possible to
concentrate on her other eye, which was bright and blue and filled
with all the steadfastness and perfect alertness that everyone always associated with Lucy Applegate.

When that apple got Aunt Lucy, she had been picking just
like everybody else, her sisters said. At that time, they'd all lived

345

Lucy and Irene Applegate seated on side porch of the Old Place, circa 1910. (Gus Peret Collection. Courtesy Douglas County Museum)

up in the Willamette Valley, way north of Yoncalla, never dreaming they'd have to move all over again. They'd been over at a neighbor's orchard since morning, the littlest girls laughing and talking, gathering windfalls mostly. But even after everyone else— including the oldest girls—had called it quits, Lucy kept on working until she had laden her apron many times over and had out-picked the lot of them.

346

Doubtless she was thinking about all the pies, butter, and fruit leather those apples would provide, and how happy their mother would be to have the larder full of something besides dried peas and crocked cabbage, of which there had been a surfeit that season.

Yes, they could see Lucy was tired out, but she saw a particularly fine specimen way up on a branch. "Just this big one," she said, reaching up. Suddenly that apple was on her.

Later, she told them the last thing she ever saw out of that eye splintered like a starburst or a percussion cap exploding at night—brighter than anything.

Then all—she said—grew dark.

Other apples had caused Lucy misery even before her Willamette days; nor had the passage of time lessened her discomfort. She herself was loath to speak of those apples and hated to have the subject brought up by anyone else.

Unlike most of her relatives who had crossed the plains with her as children and who, gathering together in the winter of their lives, shook out their memories one by one, airing them in the company of the others, Lucy preferred forgetting to remembering. No, it did not pleasure her to ruminate about the past. The present was plenty to contend with, she always said. It took all her time.

But other family members—especially if seated around the hearth at the Old Place because a funeral or some other occasion had brought them back to Yoncalla—relished remembering.

It seemed to Lucy that it made no difference to them whether the memory was good or bad. Time, somehow, had distanced them from their younger selves. The past, as they were prone to talk about it, was nothing more than a series of stories in which they themselves were characters, as though they'd become part of a book written by someone else altogether. And in these stories of childhood endlessly recited, certain of the tellers had elevated themselves, becoming homely little heroes and heroines who were both unscathed and invulnerable to all that had gone wrong, all that had hurt them in the long ago.

The fact was, Lucy's temperament was not suited to the slow unfolding of a good story, the others said among themselves. Why, you had to tie that woman down or else follow her from

Lucy in the Gold Fields. ". . . When that apple got Aunt Lucy, she had been picking apples just like everybody else, her sister said . . ." (Susan Applegate painting. Photograph courtesy Douglas County Museum)

chore to chore to have a conversation, especially in her younger days. Telling stories was more in her sister Irene's line.

Lucy's imagination had a fence around it, not unlike the one her brothers had built to enclose her kitchen garden and all her rosebushes years before. And that fence kept the wild creatures who visited each night from doing harm. Only sometimes they got

348

in anyway. And when someone else was bent on remembering what Lucy wanted to forget, it was like a deer jumping over her fence, and there was nothing for it save to survey the damage.

"Remember those apples, Lucy?" She could count on Irene to bring it up. "The ones those sailors threw at you when our little boat passed by that big ol' schooner at Fort Vancouver?"

And despite herself, Lucy would see those apples, bright and ruddy, tumbling down; the dark hull, the shadowy waters splashing. And her little brothers and sisters and cousins all squealing excitedly, and she blushing, beside herself, her knees shaking as she stood up in the mackinaw.

"They were calling to you, Lucy. Shouting. That one fellow blowing kisses from the railing. My, how those sailors carried on. Apple after apple. All we children could think of was how good they'd taste. Why, there had been nothing so fresh and sweet since Missouri. We were counting on you. Lucy will get 'em. We cheered 'til we were hoarse!"

And Lucy, the past breaking over her anew, remembered how apple after apple had drifted away. Red dots caught in the gray Columbia. Nary a one. Forever out of reach. And the children grew silent; the British sailor called down, too, raising his empty hands, "Sorry, Missy!" And the look her father had shot her was full of disgust, and when they'd gone by Uncle Lindsay's mackinaw, the boys averted their eyes. Every child downcast. After that—how could she forget?—she'd felt sorry and sad and mad at herself, because so much that was hard had already befallen them on their way to Oregon. . . . The children . . . She had let them down.

Once, when Irene was having a good spell and ready for company, there'd come a pair of old-men-cousins not seen for many a year—one even more opinionated than he'd been in his youth, the other pleasant.

They'd made a regular camp there before the fireplaces, alternating between both big front rooms as it suited them, and, of course, commenced to talking about the old times from the moment they arrived.

Lucy kept to her work schedule, which was considerable despite the fact she was getting on in years, but in the evenings she felt compelled to be sociable.

For the most part, this meant that she just listened to the

349

others travel o'er mountain, plain, and stream again as she caught up on mending or pushed her heavy sadiron back and forth across the stout, flat-lidded trunk that had come with them in the wagons.

Now and then there'd be a pause while everyone considered what to remember next. And the room was full of hiss for a moment, and steam rose like a mist because she had just sprinkled the linens. This caused one of those old men to remark, "Lucy! Don't you ever rest?"

Irene had answered for her. "No. She never does. Never." Then Irene rocked rhythmically, like a plump pigeon settled on a movable roost, the motion of the rocking chair punctuating her talk. "No . . . Lucy doesn't know the meaning of the word 'rest.' She *never* has."

And they knew this was so, because on an earlier evening Lucy had confided to them that even as a young child she had always been on the verge of exhaustion, adding how she supposed it was simply her lot in life. After all, she had been born the oldest of sixteen children and had always been a little nursemaid to the rest of them.

Their poor mother! Child after child. It seemed for many years that their mamma was either in the sickbed or the birthing bed, Lucy said, and plumb "wore out" all the time. Yet there were all those little people to care for: babies just weaned and little children hardly more than babies. And it got so they'd all call out, "Lucy! Lucy, I need you," because they were down with a head cold or fever, or bent-up with stomach miseries, or just plain scared. Thus, Lucy said, it seemed that she just went from one little bed to another on some nights, and that from the time she was six years old or so until she was twenty, she had never had the luxury of a night's sleep unbroken.

All she had really wanted when she was a child, she sighed, was to sink into some cushy old chair and just sit quiet! But of course she never could. There was too much that needed doing, and too many who needed tending. And it had astonished her that her sisters Ellen, Susie, and Mary still had spunk enough to play and cut up even after their chores were finished. But they were littler, after all, so much was not expected from them.

And so it came to be—the others theorized—that work had simply become a habit with Lucy.

"Now, where's Aunt Lucy keeping herself?" those who arrived unexpectedly would ask as their men took the teams barnward. Over at the henhouse . . . on the kitchen porch, stuffing sausage . . . down at the springhouse, rounding up the little gosling who got away. . . . Then they would either hunt her down or wait her out. Admiring her flowerbeds. Helping themselves to coffee. And of course they'd brought their gaggles of little people, who were fretful because their mammas had taken the notion to drop by the Old Place right around dinnertime.

There they all would be. Everyone awaiting Aunt Lucy so that she might wait on them. Which she did, for there was always plenty to go around and mealtime was no exception. Aunt Lucy saw to it even if it meant she had to stretch out the stew or the cobbler so she didn't get any herself.

Later, when the tableware and old white platters clattered in the dishpans, and the kitchen was abuzz with sisters, sisters-in-law, and the odd lot of female cousins, this one or that one would pour out her heart to her. And no one ever left empty-handed. Onion braids, potatoes, "extry" muskmelons she'd been lucky with that season, tomato preserves, leftover sour biscuits: Up they went into the wagon. And because she knew that one of their husbands had taken to drink again, or some little nephew whose feet weren't all that they should be needed specially made shoes, she'd sometimes slip the wife or mother a little money wrapped in a kerchief, knotted tight so that the gold coins inside wouldn't give themselves away.

People agreed it was a good thing Aunt Lucy had inherited the Old Place when her mamma passed away and she had been left a little money, for had she wanted for anything in her old age, she was just the sort of maiden lady who would have been too proud to let on.

As it was, no one could do anything for her, at least directly. Even a Christmas gift met with reproach, for Aunt Lucy hated to feel as if anyone had put himself out on her account. While she was a generous soul, she considered generosity in others wor-risome—especially if they had families to raise.

Thus people satisfied themselves by sending thank-you notes and pretty cards. Those who'd moved away wrote her long letters by the score, though no one ever expected a correspondence to result. Everyone knew Aunt Lucy hated to write anything down.

Now and then she'd scribble a note at the bottom of one of 'Rene's letters, but her closest kin had almost forgotten what her handwriting looked like, unless they happened upon one of her many lists of things to tend to that she left around the Old Place.

Yet Lucy seemed to appreciate being remembered, and if the sender enclosed or hand-delivered a fancy button of some sort, she would immediately go after the Oriental box where she stored little relics from her girlhood. Out would come the string of buttons she called the "Friendship Loop," the newest addition quickly added to the rest of the collection, her delight so evident she seemed almost childlike for a moment.

Sometimes Aunt Lucy's button collection helped a visiting boy or girl warm up to her. No, her grandnieces said years later, Aunt Lucy wasn't a talker—at least with them—unless lecturing counted. A "talking *to*," in other words. When they had transgressed as children by squabbling over some plaything or by shirking some chore, which like as not was the unhappy duty of hauling the upstairs chamber pots downstairs and thence to that certain hole in the corner of the yard where the obnoxious contents were to be heaved, well, then, Aunt Lucy had plenty to say, all right. "Share and share alike." "Birds in their nest agree." Or "Cleanliness is next to godliness." Those were the familiar homilies that threaded in and out of Aunt Lucy's talk, like neat embroidery stitches on some old sampler.

Yet if she was not too busy or in the right mood, she could be induced to show off her pretties—all those wonderful buttons—and Aunt Lucy would tell just who had sent each one, and when, and whether the particular specimen had been made in Belgium, France, or Germany, or some other place a-way-far-off.

Why, even a half-grown boy didn't mind hearing Aunt Lucy going on about her buttons, it was said. Especially if he were permitted to hold the precious loop. There was something satisfying about fingering the button string. A soft clicking came as each button was turned and carefully examined, its pretty shape or color admired. And the ones set with tiny glass stones, the little girls said, winked up at them like fairy lights.

Some young relatives, who over the years had enjoyed Lucy's Friendship Loop time and again, vowed that when they grew old enough, they would go to the places where some of her buttons

352

came from. They would have all kinds of adventures, but they would not forget to send buttons back to Yoncalla . . . and picture postcards and other things, too. They would not forget Aunt Lucy when they were a-way-far-off.

Only it turned out that just a few of those children went any farther than California or Idaho, yet none ever forgot how Aunt Lucy's face had softened, her bad eye wandering as she told them how she would look forward to all the wonderful things that would someday be coming through the mails. "I'll wait right here," she said. "Right here at home. You can be sure of that."

Lucy was always there. Never went anyplace. Not even to town. It bothered some people. Certain of her older nieces, for instance. "Aunt Lucy," they'd say, "you've martyred yourself to this old place long enough. There's a world out there!" Then they'd try to tantalize her with descriptions of all the wonderful wildflowers that would be blooming up in the high meadows, where they intended to take the light wagon that very afternoon. Or they'd talk about how a little trip was being planned. Yes, they were off to the coast and she ought to go, too. "Fifty years!" they'd exclaim. Here she'd been in Oregon fifty years . . . surely, it was time for her to see the ocean at least once in her life, and the coast would be pure heaven now that the weather had turned. All the dunes and big rocks and the strange caves where sea lions lived.

But it was to no avail. It was always the same: Lucy shaking her head and folding her arms, making excuses: The cow was liable to calf anytime; if she didn't sauce up those early apples they'd picked for her, only the yellow jackets would find them fit for consumption. Besides, who would see to Irene's needs if she were to go away?

And 'Rene could be seen to smile wanly, murmuring, "Oh, go ahead, Lucy. *Someone* will look after me, I suppose. You go enjoy yourself." But Lucy never did.

No, you couldn't budge Aunt Lucy, her nieces complained . . . Lucy in her rock-gray dress.

Yet sometimes they couldn't help noticing her wistful look as they climbed up on the wagon and then arranged their skirts, everyone in high spirits. Except for her. Sometimes they could almost feel something stirring around the edges of her refusal, as though she might finally give in, but whatever was tugging on Lucy was as fleeting and faint as a breeze in August—soon she had that resolute look again. She waved. They pulled away. Stout and indomitable, Lucy has turned her back, is trudging off to her duties.

Now the rattle of wheels, the merry voices, are past hearing—have disappeared in a veil of dust. Where are you, Great-great-aunt Lucy, when the summer air is full of hum and heat, incomparably sweet here at the verge of the kitchen porch where your old Mission rose yet blooms—so deeply planted—profuse and pink, smelling, somehow, of cinnamon?

This comes to me as I open the door: the apple—that ruddy distant cousin of the rose.

Inside this house, coolness reigns. The Seth Thomas clock on the mantel chimes the hour. What hour? I hold your Friendship Loop in my hands now, slowly turning it. All—all who have been here—we are as buttons strung together. Dusk slants its muted light through the windows.

But where are your little kindred, Aunt Lucy? Those family boys and girls who stayed here while their mammas birthed other babes or took their outings coastwise, or nursed some ailing relative for a while on the other side of the valley?

Your little people have not gone off to do their chores, and tonight they will not stir upstairs in their beds, nor will their daddies' wagons and horseless carriages appear in a moment just outside to take them home.

Instead, they sit in their lonely apartments or in convalescent homes that are not homes at all, and some lie in their graves, just as you do, Aunt Lucy.

An image seems to hover beneath the closed lids of my two good eyes. It is you: the Lucy whom those sailors saw, young, flushed to the color of a certain rose, your breasts blooming beneath your bodice. In some forever I see you yet . . . standing in the little boat . . . raising your arms . . .

Apple after apple.

Oh, Aunt Lucy, if I could make all new again, your apron would be filled.

THE SAME

Eva and Evea Applegate

NOVEMBER 20, 1970

Yoncalla, Oregon

The rain has coughed mud, glistened the porch slick. Baby-Blue-Bonnet-Bear shivers outside the kitchen door, mewing. The screen snaps, bangs as Uncle Vince shuffles to the door. "Not too good," he mutters while he shakes his head and juts his flaccid lower lip. "Hasn't got outta bed all day." He says this with practice, without real conviction. "Goddamn cats . . . Eva and her damn cats. Like to get rid of them." There are dishes of condensed milk and leftover scrambled eggs all over the porch. He put them there.

We walk through the kitchen with its afternoon clutter, opened cans of chicken noodle soup, Saltines in torn wax paper, coffee cups, toast crusts. The old-fashioned sink is filled with dishes and scraps of dinner from the night before. "Haven't felt too good myself today," he says, glancing at the sink as we pass. The old dining room, now his sister's and his living quarters, is unbearably warm. Heat rises in waves from the old-fashioned oil stove.

Nothing has changed since my last visit. The aquarium, a gift from the summer, gurgles fitfully, green scum shutting out the last of the goldfish. Vince sees me looking. "Don't know why Rex bought that thing. The devil to clean it." He smiles and pats my shoulder. "How 'bout a little bourbon? Or don't ya do that in a college town?" He doesn't wait for an answer. He is glad for the company and ambles to the kitchen. I am surprised, as usual, by his height. But he is a giant without force or energy. His neck sticks out in front of massive rounded shoulders. He has lost weight. We share the last of the Jim Beam in yellow plastic bathroom glasses. It is three o'clock in the afternoon. I already have a headache. Is it from the interminable rain or from simply being here?

She sleeps in the tiny back room, nearly closet-sized. Perhaps it was a cloakroom once or an entryway to the side porch. The door has been taped against the weather and wind. Nailed shut. Behind the curtain, Eva, my great-aunt, the oldest surviving member of the family, stirs beneath her electric blanket. She

357

knows somehow that I am here despite her deepening sleep of pain-drugs, and waiting. Once she had the run of the house; she would glide with her twin sister down the broad stairway, carrying parasols and books. More than three of my lifetimes ago, for she is nearly ninety. Now she just lies in her cubicle, will rarely stay in the front room for more than a few minutes. Even last summer she would sometimes sit next to the old oil stove, hunching alongside of it like an ancient lizard longing to climb inside the sun. But even in the dry, heat-rising summer she would complain of feeling cold.

"Who is with you, Vince? Shannon?" So, she will come out today. I pull the curtain and help her to sit up. The snowy hair wisps are caught by a jaunty green ribbon. The town nurse who comes each morning to give her the injection has bathed and combed her. I put her slippers on feet so twisted and misshapen by the disease that they resemble claws. She leans against me without real weight. Stooped, gnarled, nearly gnome. The slender body is swollen in all its junctures. For a dozen years she has been trapped inside. I have only known her this way.

She asks for some milk. I put it on the heater. "So cold just from the icebox," she says. She is tired of asking people to do things for her, yet would rather ask me than Vince.

Her younger brother, who is himself in his seventies, escapes to town in his failing Chevrolet. He has a painful heart condition. His biggest fear is that he will die and leave his sister alone. He has promised her she will not go to a "home," and yet grows more weary of his role daily. A lifetime of ailing women: his own wife, then Evea, the other twin sister, and now Eva. A basically gentle man, he has been irascibly obedient to the needs of his kin; the family ethic: circles of dependency and being depended upon.

We are alone then, my great-aunt and I. A calendar room of landscapes and knickknacks. A dirty Persian rug covering yellow linoleum. Two hand-carved cabinets with glass fronts containing gold-edged crystal and tarnished silver teapots, trays, salt cellars. Mickey Spillane paperbacks, magazines spill over the surface of the dining table—an enormous, elegantly worked table built by their father, Buck Applegate. Like the aquarium, my father has brought the books to help "pass the time."

I watch my great-aunt drink her milk from the jelly glass. Watch her hands shake moving it to her lips. Drift . . . I drift.

The old house hovering all around us silent and dark. A dozen rooms or more shut off from light. Old furniture, unopened trunks. Piles of papers, dusty books on dusty shelves. Six generations of the family floating in their photographs across old wooden walls. I feel the smallness of the space we occupy. I imagine the house moving with its many people. I imagine the two of them especially, Evea and Eva.

Evea and Eva, Eva and Evea. The confusing interchangeable names. As if a deliberate attempt had been made from the very beginning to merge them into one being. As if the difference dividing selves were one letter only.

I rummage for the faded clipping Vince has dredged from an old trunk in his room. The outrageous comic-opera headline in florid Gothic Bold:

HOW TWO GIRLS, ALIKE IN FEATURE
VOICE AND MANNER, PLAYED PRANKS
AT OREGON AGRICULTURAL COLLEGE
The Evening Telegram

—January 30, 1904

It swims dead before me—the twins' unprankish handsome faces locked in identical ovals. Around them wreaths, in hurried pen and ink:

> The young women are twins; alike as two peas. If Eva wished to spend an afternoon shopping or taking a beauty sleep at home, Evea would attend recitations for her. And if Evea was doubtful of her ability to pass her examinations, Eva would undertake the task, without the professors being any the wiser.

The attraction of the overwhelming duplication of surfaces. A journey of the eyes. The twins, two exotic, curious creatures. A pair of elegant birds with identical plumage. Long, graceful necks. Heavy-lidded green eyes. Puffs and rolls of dark hair. Two roses. Two brooches. Two lockets. The same. Moving through life, causing heads to turn. Carefully conceived costumes. Ladies of the mirror, balancing one another; inescapable balance of being two, the automatic symmetry. Tilting heads for photographs, manufacturing minute differences. One folding her hands, one not. Veils up or down. One smiling, one sober. Trapped in my hands, in their double ovals gazing up at me. This incredible symbiosis reduced to a boardwalk whim, a "feature" sent up and down the coast.

I hand the clipping to Eva. She cannot see it; searches for her glasses in the small cache of belongings she keeps in the shoebox beside her. Upstairs there are closets alive with dresses. A dozen pair of shoes filling cloth pockets lining the dresser door. Drawers laden with lavender sachets, labeled piles of lace handkerchiefs, gloves with pearl buttons, long silk scarves. She has not been able to climb the stairs for five years now.

She gives up. Laughs at herself, at me, for not knowing better. Tightens the limp red Christmas sweater around her shoulders. "Oh yes," she says, as if she has read the clipping. "Oh yes," the soothing response she has adopted for all occasions. A result of her deafness and her unwillingness to wear the rented hearing aid, also in the shoebox beside her. "Oh yes," a way to participate, to say, "I am here."

I feel vaguely ashamed. She hands me back the clipping. I thought seeing it again might unwind things, make her want to share the past with me. But she is glad to see me because it is the present—a moment. The yellowing paper is more dead to her than it is to me.

And so we move in conversation, our particular ritual of being together. Old-fashioned courtesies. This is the way of our visits; she apologizes for not being able to fix tea. Her expression is of wishing to do simple things for herself once more, like comb her own hair, or move to the bathroom without assistance. It is not complaining, but the admission of her simple day-to-day humiliations. The incomprehensible immobility. The walls thick around her senses and limbs.

And so I ask, "Are you sleeping well?" She looks bewildered. It seems better to write things down, even at the risk of offending her. Large block letters scratch the surface of my notebook. She nods as she reads, then says something which breaks the old rhythms of our being together.

"I am not alone here. There are others."

360

Eva and Evea Applegate, circa 1906. (Applegate family photograph. Courtesy Douglas County Museum)

AT NIGHT?

"At night . . . oh yes, at night sometimes. Floating. Maybe these pills I take for pain. Last night I saw a whirlpool. Coming down a river in a boat. Waters crashing, white stuff all around. Rex was in the boat. Seems like he was little. Called out to him, 'Rex! Rex! but could not save him, no matter how hard I tried. Oh little Rex!' Her eyes are full of tears. She says, 'Vince thinks I am silly and that I keep him up all night. Yes, they are all with me now.'"

WHO IS WITH YOU, AUNT EVA?

"Why all . . . all of the family. Mamma, Pappa, Pauline, Rachel, and Ted. And Evea, oh Evea, my dear, you most of all. They tell me things."

WHAT DO THEY TELL YOU?

"Why, they tell me not to worry, not to worry at all. Not about the house, nor anything. That it will be all right. 'You're not to worry, Eva,' they say always. Makes me feel better." She looks at me searchingly, and says, "I guess you might say that it is a bad sign."

My heart is beating; I feel it thrusting against the walls of my chest. I am inside this old woman, our senses merging. Beneath the marred transparency of skin, beneath the veins, floating blue near the surface. Behind the eyes of watered green, nearly sight-less, minute white islands of cataracts, pupils dilating from the Demerol, the pulse, our pulse, pulls, pushes the skin up and down, slender wrists, blood moving. Family blood. We are connected. I cannot understand it all, but I feel it moving through both of us. Some identical genes, chromosomes. And Evea, her other self, conjoined in ways beyond this sense of mine, even their skin in-terchangeable, transplants of organs, eyes. Seeds in the same garden. From the magic of twos—split cells floating in the blood, beneath the eye of a microscope. Their blood the same, the same. Mine, something the same. Pulse distant. Floating down the river. Her ancestors are mine drowning in the Columbia. Family women

362

calling from the boats: "Men, do not quit the oars! Men! We cannot save the boys!"

It has passed, our joining. I am here with a headache. Aunt Eva is tired. I help her back to bed, get her pill. Tuck her in as I would my children. She closes her eyes. "I'll be back in a few days, Aunt Eva." She cannot hear me.

I wait outside for Vince to come back from town. For my father to pick me up and take me back to the river. The air has that pungent smell. I know where I am without seeing. Restive wood odors coming from the pile of wet wood stacked against the house. The cedar or fir trees? Perhaps the valley mill. The rain mixes things here. It rains forever here.

Journal
Shannon Applegate

In the pickup heading back to the river, a story about the twins: My father had a room at the Army-Navy Club in Washington, D.C., about seven years ago. He was eating lunch one afternoon in the private dining room upstairs (mahogany tables, white linen, crystal glasses. I remember it clearly since Dad and I went there on a rare visit together. A salon space, nearly. Mirrors. Obsequious elderly black waiters, southern style). At any rate, an old man and woman seated at the next table overheard Dad's waiter call him "Colonel Applegate." After the meal, the old gentleman approached him and said, "Pardon me, Colonel. I am interested in your last name. I once had two lovely women serving under me at Walter Reed while I was commandant of the medical corps there. About 1920. Just as the war was ending. They were also Applegates, though I can't recollect their first names just now."

"Why, you must mean my aunts, Evea and Eva," said my father. The old man described them, mentioned that they had been such "look-alikes" and "damned efficient," though their nearly identical names had "played havoc with the duty rosters." He asked after their welfare and Dad told him that Evea had died years before. Well, he thanked my father and wandered off toward the elevator with his wife. A moment or two passed and he returned to my father's table, leaving his wife in the hallway. He stated that he had something special about the "girls" to share with my father, but that he did not want his wife to overhear. Could he come later in the evening to my father's room? My father, curious, agreed that he should come around eight or so.

I can still see the long carpeted hallway leading to my father's room. There were glass cases holding scabbards with silver handles, "U.S." insignias: American Revolution, Civil War, Manila Insurrection, Spanish-American. Military caps and gleaming revolvers. Donated by Major So-and-So, Captain X, 5th Cav. 1903. Elderly men would walk down the hallways at all hours, peering inside those cases. All decked out, old soldiers in their uniforms that never die. And so, the gentleman who visited my father that night, arriving so punctually at eight o'clock, he spent a few moments gazing at the cases and the metal memories within. Then he knocked discreetly at my father's door, holding himself erect, shoulders squared, the way he had all of his military life.

My father offered the old man a drink of Scotch. He evidently had several drinks while warming up to his subject and the reasons for his visit. Finally, after talking about the "club," his war experiences, etc., he said, "Well, Colonel, your two aunties were very handsome women. Women too; not girls, you understand. They were older than some of the other nurses there. Well liked, those two; did their jobs. Naturally, everyone was interested when one of the ladies began seeing old Black Jack Pershing." He went on to describe General Pershing, his dandyism, his flirtations as a younger officer. It seemed that Pershing, having suffered a wound and some paralysis, had retired in the early 1920's, and because of his high rank and prestige was given a whole suite of rooms at the hospital, which he had furnished in his typically luxurious style. He was an older man by then, but continued to command his small staff with as much bravado and mercurial change of mood as ever. Every inch a general in the tradition of the old army. If he was unhappy with the hospital staff's evening meal (which would be wheeled to his room on an elaborate cart), he would send the cart spinning across the room and proceed to instruct some poor aide, obliged to serve out his term with the "old man," to bring French delicacies in for the evening from an expensive Washington restaurant.

"Now, one of those girls was constantly in Black Jack's company. She would arrive early in the evening for the general's physical-therapy treatment and be seen leaving the next morning." On other occasions, the general would be seen walking with one of the twins on the hospital grounds, or one would be seated beside him in his open car when he undertook a rare excursion into the city.

"Have you ever heard your aunties talk about this, Colonel?"

"Why, no, I haven't. Of course, I would probably be the last person they might have told. As far as I know, though, no one in the family ever knew about all this." Knowing my father, he probably added, "Well, I'll be damned." It had certainly been a surprise to him. I expect he was delighted.

"Well, I hope I haven't revealed too many family secrets in any case, Colonel. After all, it was a long time ago. I have always been curious about it. Those girls, well, none of us could tell them

Eva and Evea Applegate, U.S. Army physical therapists during World War I. Shown here at training camp in South Carolina in 1918. (Applegate family photograph. Courtesy Douglas County Museum)

apart, as I have mentioned. After all, the general was an ex-tremely prominent man. One of the most important patients we ever had at Reed, excepting of course various presidents who were at the hospital on and off during my command. When your aunties left the service and went back, the old man was said to be very despondent for several weeks. More short-tempered than ever."

My father's elderly visitor seemed to be in his cups by about ten o'clock. Dad helped him get as far as the elevator. The next day, Dad went back to Mexico and never saw the old gentleman again.

Now, the past ten miles or so, more information from my fa-ther: The twins enlisted in the Army Nursing Corps in 1917 or thereabouts and went through training as therapists at Reed Col-lege in Portland. They wanted to go to France. The army assigned them to two different places for basic training, South Carolina and Minnesota. It was the first time in their lives that they had been separated. Evidently they were miserable and in one way or an-other, after a few months, managed to convince the army that their assignments to different places constituted emotional hard-ship. From then on, their stations were the same. Just as they were about to go to France, the war ended and they were transferred to Walter Reed Hospital in Washington instead. Information and more information. I feel as if my head is about to explode, as if I cannot digest one more bit of data, one more story.

Mind tangles, images: Walter Reed Hospital as the old man talked about it. Nineteen-eighteen. Evea, Eva with starched caps, white uniforms. Black hair in white nets. Down the hospital cor-ridors by two. Passing the machinery of health. Metal con-traptions to set limbs, gleaming leg braces. X-ray equipment with blinking lights and old-fashioned dials.

Glazed eyes of boys in long wards. Too much mustard gas and shrapnel. Trench coughs from the long, wet winter in Lorraine. Evea, Eva, rubbing backs and smiling. Massaging legs that wouldn't walk again. White metal bedsteads, cots, long windows down one side like a greenhouse. Humid Washington. Smells of the sick. Overlooking the gardens and the grounds. The magnolia trees and rows of roses pruned by young men in khaki leggings. Wheelchairs and green lawns. Under arches of honeysuckle. Hid-den benches conclaved circles of bushes. Eva? Evea? Talking softly to Pershing. Black moustache; swaggerstick resting against a high brown boot. The pantleg of a custom-tailored uniform. Evea? Eva? Lowered eyes. Through the boxwood hedge and wall of shrubs. Sweet, heavy scents of flowers and love.

My father says just now, "Well, at least one of them didn't die an old maid. Maybe both of them, huh? You can go ahead and erect that shrine: 'To my dear sainted father [Colonel Rex Applegate], for the best two stories of the family history.' Well, that's right, isn't it? Great-grandfather and the 'other woman,' and now this story."

I don't know what to say to all this. I just asked him how he would like a neon eagle attached to the roof of the old place. Watching him now, driving. There is a sterling silver nameplate on the plastic mahogany dash. COL. REX APPLEGATE, it says, an engraved Ford chevron beside the name—my father, his old army shirt covering a large stomach that thrusts against the steering wheel; his massive hands that navigate the car through the sudden downpour. Below the road, the Umpqua, swollen and muddy.

Time. Too much time. Too late for me to understand everything. Fit the pieces together from the past—from the present even. Aunt Eva is dying back there in the old house. Unrepeatable family blood. Vines covering windows, porch sagging. Windshield wipers swooshing. Leave Oregon in a few days. Leave all this.

In the old house, Vince has taken another pan from the cupboard. More leaks. There are pans all over the house. The rain thickens and spills over the edges of rusted gutters, drips and strikes the metal. He turns on the football game and lights another Philip Morris. Eva calls from her cubicle, "Vince, Vince, have they gone?" Vince does not rise from his chair. "Yep, they have gone, all right." He is absorbed in what the team from Green Bay is doing. "Vince, oh, why don't you answer me? Now they're gone. Gone back to Indiana on the airplane. Oh, and I went to sleep instead of saying good-bye." Her brother walks to the doorway of her tiny room, pulls back the curtain, and looks down at her. Rests against the doorframe and says, "Don't you remember? I told you twice already this morning. They are leaving Sunday." He keeps reminding his sister that she keeps forgetting. His voice has an edge of sarcasm that comes more from his sense of exasperation at the continual interruptions than from anger. Disparagement he knows about; it comes naturally. It is part of the family's internal rhythm. Weaves in and out of all conversations, a substitute for the expression of affection or a defense against pain. But, seeing that his sister is genuinely upset, he adds loudly, "Shannon said she will come out to say good-bye in a few days. There now," he says, patting her brusquely, "that make you feel better?" "Oh, Vince, I still can't hear you. What is it you're saying?" Under his breath, "Oh, forget it . . ." Walks away. Shouts, "Ah, quit your worrying and go back to sleep."

YONCALLA, OREGON, 1893

> I think it always stuck in Mother's craw a little bit about her
> sisters, the twins. I think she felt kind of left out a lot of times.
> —Interview with Kenneth Tulley, only son of Rachel Applegate
> Tulley (older sister of Eva and Evea)

There were special places in the old house. Secret places, even if
everyone did know about them. Outside and inside. Children's
places. And in the late autumn the rains came, flooding the flats
in the valley so that even the chickens were forced to take to the
high ground. Despite the fact that the house was large and spacious with its six bedrooms and double living rooms on the lower
floor, privacy for anyone in the family was a hard thing, a dear
thing. It seemed there were always many houseguests, not to mention five noisy children and three adults.

So they had gone up to the garret. The light from the rain
made everything blue and luminous somehow. The two large windows at either end; the old chimney thrusting through the very
center of the house, dividing the attic exactly in half. They were
to tend the drying stove, for it was the season of nut gathering—
black and English walnuts. The drying racks covered the old floor;
bumpy brown spheres were everywhere. When they walked, some
of them would roll and clatter across the uneven surface of the
floorboards. It made it hard to sneak upstairs because the walnuts
gave them away.

But they had a reason for their special privacy that day, and
could do what they liked as long as they watched the stove. They
sat and explored the pile of old magazines and newspapers that
stretched across the length of the attic. At least forty years' worth
of periodicals, all gloriously illustrated: drawings of cities in Europe, elegant china and glassware, interiors of salons in New York,
heartrending pen-and-ink portrayals of beautiful but troubled
young women who suffered in the stories on adjacent pages.

But mainly they liked the *Godey's Lady's Book*: the fashionable
women in hoop skirts of another era; fringed shawls and cunning
slippers peeping out from silken skirts.

Over their heads were real dress hoops suspended on ropes
from the rafters. Their old aunties, Irene and Lucy, had saved

The George "Buck" Applegate Family in front of the pergola on the east side of the Old Place, circa 1929. From left to right: Rachel Applegate Tulley, Flora, Paul, Eva, Evea, "Buck," and Vincent Applegate. (Gus Peret Collection. Courtesy Douglas County Museum)

literally everything. Everyone in the family saved things, "held on to things." The hoops above were misshapen, hovering birdcages without bottoms. They made queer shadows across the floor and did not, even remotely, resemble the fine damask overskirts with their graceful bell shape shown in the magazines.

They also enjoyed the ads for patent medicines. They would read aloud to one another: "Dr. Kennedy's Supreme Medicinal Remedy . . . Mrs. X of Newport, R.I., reports astonishing results . . . miraculous relief from piles and swollen joints, etc." The bearded Dr. Kennedy, splendid in his sepia cravat, looked kindly and robust. They had discussed sending away for the medicines even though the magazines were very old. The people in their family were sick a great deal, it seemed to them. Mealtime discussions were often concerned with "the cure" for this or that. When their old uncle, Lisbon, was alive, there had been a continuous stream of doctors in and out of the house. They could barely remember that. But then there was Aunt Lucy, who grew ill toward the last, and Aunt Irene, who was still living with them and had a whole shelf filled with tiny bottles: mysterious amber and ruby-red liquids; tiny pouches in her dresser drawer of herbs, "weeds," as she called them, for teas and evil-smelling poultices. Even their pappa took medicine every day for his back pains. The people around them seemed to suffer so. They wondered why their mother had never sent for Dr. Kennedy's Remedy. So much illness made them want to help somehow. In the garret they played at being nurses, but could not decide for certain whether they themselves would be nurses when they were women or whether they would take their mother's calling of schoolteacher. There was, of course, no question that they would both be exactly the same thing.

There were some old quilts in a trunk. Faded patterns of pink and yellow stars. In their mamma's "to be mended" pile, along with outgrown clothing of several generations, there were scraps of fabric. They draped each other in their quilt capes and discussed the costumes they might have their mamma make for them as ladies. She would be old then and have time. Everything made exactly the same, down to the ribbons and the buttons. Wouldn't people look then! Oh, wouldn't they, though!

The time passed gently—the two of them, the two of them. They fed the stove with stubby blocks of fir and watched the little glow grow and then subside. And they were glad that *she* was downstairs with Mamma. Even though she was making sourdough biscuits and they were not. It was a privilege extended to their sister because they had been "snippy" earlier that morning and had made her cry. They had got tired of being bossed, that was all. Rachel could be so high and mighty. Crimped everything. You were supposed to always love "your people," Pappa said, "no matter what." But that couldn't be true. Someone was always arguing with somebody else in the family. Pappa wasn't close to *his* brothers and sisters. Sometimes he even made fun of them.

They felt guilty talking about it and began to whisper. Their voices merged with the swoosh of the wind and the rain outside. "Have you noticed she tries to act like Mamma? She's just a little older than us. Tries to run everybody. Vince and Paulie, too! It's right that we do things the same; we are the same. When we cut our hair yesterday, then *she* cut her hair, too. Wears that blue dress of hers when we wear ours. Do you think Mamma notices?" They grew tired of thinking about it. It was an intrusion, as if their sister were actually with them. "Oh, it's so nice here by ourselves. Oh, look, Ev, look over there!"

Two bassinets of white wicker on stands of white metal with tiny wheels, their insides lined in dusty pink coverlets the color of conch shells. They stood over them, began to rock them back and forth and sing softly to their imaginary selves. Pink babies in white handworked nightdresses. Doll children. From somewhere, deep down inside, small voices rose, floating into the darkening air of the garret. The special sound they had made as very small children. Sounds only they had understood—from some secret source of comprehension, the cadence of sentences without words. They remembered how they had once played near the back of the house where the jasmine grew and climbed all the way to the top of the window. Delicate flowers. The sweet, stirring smell of them. They pulled at the vine with their tiny fingers, exchanging smiles and sounds. Exchanging a handful of dainty yellow stars. The fragrance and pulp of the blossoms giving way in their hands. And they shared this old memory now without speaking of it. Moving their matching cradles back and forth across the old floor in singsong fashion. The walnuts rolled and thumped across the boards like tiny drumbeats.

"*What* are you two doing?! Open this door! You better . . . you

374

better open this door, you two!" Rachel stood at the base of the stairwell, struggling with the latch and feeling her anger move all over her. It settled in two vivid dots on either cheek. It always did. Their sister, you could see it in her face—her large eyes, the same dark hair, but not the same somehow. Her fingers were still sticky from the sourdough, still not able to move the latch. But she managed, finally. And they had been so startled, so deeply engrossed that they had not moved. They were still standing over their bassinets, holding on to the cradles but no longer rocking them. And seeing them so, understanding in a glance what all the "racket" had been about, Rachel felt the old coldness settling over her. Outside. Shivery. Alone. She said from the bottom of her anger, "My, my, look at the two *big* girls now! You were playing baby! I heard you! Making baby sounds! My, my." She said it steadily and carefully, but her fingers grew white, curling around the edge of her apron. "You were supposed to be watching the stove. Just look at it. It's out now." The two younger girls exchanged guilty looks. It was true. There was no glow. "Well, it looks to me that you two just can't be trusted."

1937

It had merely been a question of time. They both knew that. They tried not to talk about it further once the decision was made. They spent the morning transplanting their father's special dahlias. The two women, both nearly sixty, found that the amount of work for the large yard was nearly impossible. Especially now. But restoring their dead father's beautiful bed of dahlias was a matter of sentiment. For a while that morning it seemed like always, the two of them, working and chatting side by side in the sunshine.

For many years, there had just been weekends for such projects. They drove down from Portland regularly, before their mother and father passed away, before they realized that the old home would in the end be their responsibility and not their brother's. Their city friends would sometimes come with them to the country. It was an excursion everyone enjoyed; fires in the fireplace in the winter and autumn, walnut gathering, lazy summer days, the men sometimes hunting in the fir forest in back of the Old Place, the ladies drinking lemonade and sewing under the pergola, the long lattice tunnel laced with sweet pink wild-rose vines. Of course, their friends helped with whatever needed to be done in the yard. All found the changes in their twin hostesses delightful, so unlike their stylish city selves, the two "glorious clotheshorses." At home in Yoncalla, the girls preferred their "working clothes," unlikely combinations of old baggy pants from their brothers' closets, mixes of plaid shirts and flowered scarves. Each had an old floppy garden hat, variously cluttered with vivid wooden cherries or celluloid grapes of eye-stopping purple. That had always been their favorite color. Like the purple shoes with Cuban heels. One pair of Eva's had been purchased in her Oriental period, the tops of each shoe embroidered with exotic water lilies edged with pink and gold thread. Rhinestones bordered the open toes. The anklestraps were of an even deeper shade of purple. Evea's, a bit more sedate but equally dramatic—a throbbing lavender velvet pair of slippers, flat satin bows disguising the straps. Oh, the girls and their purple clothes, purple hose and purple underwear, purple purses of Moroccan leather, which had been custom-dyed. They had stopped dressing exactly alike after returning from Walter Reed in 1920. But they still kept some "themes," as the issues of *Vogue* called it. Eva wore gray often, with variously colored accessories. Evea was fond of black-and-white combinations. For many years, they made good salaries as therapists at the hospital. They could afford to indulge their stylish cravings. But once friends, visiting them in the country unannounced, found them weeding in the garden, each wearing one red shoe and one blue shoe. There had been much good-humored ribbing about this.

But then they were "jolly" girls, quick-witted and lively. It was part of their style; they had always captivated everyone. They were two incredibly handsome women, so identical in appearance as to be confusing even to their close friends. But then after getting to know them, especially professionally, the part of themselves that showed so unmistakably in country life emerged, the commitment to hard work, attention to detail. Clear minds with skills directed toward the care of others. At home they cared for their cow, their dogs, the chickens, a dozen cats. In recent years, they had sought to make repairs on the old home by themselves. They had even undertaken the task of patching the shingles on the roof, Eva climbing the rickety ladder and Evea handing up the nails. They were Oregon girls after all; they knew how to can food and shoot and sew. Of course, it was their sewing that had always been a special skill. When they could not afford to buy what they wanted, they made it. They often laughed at themselves when they removed labels from finery purchased in the Portland dress shops and stitched the old labels inside the new sewing-machine clothing. But they did it anyway, despite their own amusement at their vanity. Their costumes were a primary diversion, a source of conversation and sharing with their women friends, especially after both had passed middle age and the many suitors who had been so ever-present earlier in their lives were married or had died or decided, as they had, that marriage was not what they sought.

Perhaps it was true what their sister Rachel said: "You two girls are too thick for anyone to want to have either of you." Once or twice, they had nearly taken the step. In the end, it was always the same, each of them finding fault with the other's suitor. Rachel and her husband, Ted, had grown exasperated with them.

Both girls lived with their older sister in her Portland home, sharing expenses. Rachel, fond of entertaining and cooking (as her portly figure showed, while her sisters remained slim and glamorous), encouraged her kindhearted husband to bring his friends home for dinner. The evenings were always lively and promising, but after the gentlemen had departed, Eva and Evea would proceed to do imitations of their visitors. More often than not, they were fairly accurate. Even Rachel had to join in the laughter despite her thwarted attempts at matchmaking.

How long ago, long ago. "Tell me the tales that to me were so dear, long long ago, long ago." Their voices floated in the spring air without the resonance they once had when singing a duet, a song they had played on the violins that their daddy, Buck, had carved for them. They had always known that their father, so slow to compliment or touch the people he loved, nonetheless felt a pride in both of them; he viewed their twinship as extraordinary and special, like the things he made with his hands.

Now something had eaten away at the bulbs they transplanted. Too old, too old, rotted by the rain or perhaps eaten by the gray ground squirrels or deer that gathered around the fruit trees at dusk. Evea, wrapped in a shawl, went wordlessly to the bench beneath the Japanese plum tree. Her sister joined her, still holding the trowel in her gloved hand. She said gently, "'Bout time for me to get dressed and go if I want to make it before dark, Eve." Her twin nodded.

Suddenly, it all seemed real—the separation was inevitable. Their working partnership of nearly forty years, the deeper partnership of their spirits and minds through all their sixty years, was coming to a close. They had thought they each had five more years to work before retiring. They had looked forward to coming back to the old home with time and funds sufficient to make it look like it once had. But they were alone now. Just the two of them. And Evea, thinner than ever, frequently ill from the internal gnawings of the cancer that took her strength daily, would stay at the old house alone. Eva hoped that the spring sunshine might have some good effect on her sister. Neither of them could discuss the appalling sense of loneliness that seemed to shadow their divided futures. Evea, standing up and laying a hand on her sister's shoulder, said gaily, "Well, I'm going to take care of all the

The Old Home.
Have you ever been alone?
In your old, old home,
House of a hundred years?
In its silence so quiet, not a voice,
not a sound, not a whisper, not a
name, Only your tears —
The years of yesterday-crowd
your mind, as from room to room
you wander - Once so full of
laughing voices - Now so quiet,
alone, you wonder =
The old Billiard table so dusty
an old leather chair is empty
Books - books - a picture, cold hearth
a letter -
You lift the lid of an old
oaken chest -
Full to the brim of remembrances
boxes of keepsakes, little shoes - a
dress, letters, poems, a rare book -
You smile with delight, at a
forgotten thing, you turn to ask
you are alone —

Your mother's picture - Your
father's chair, a pipe he used to
smoke -
Her knitting, a book of poems,
The old, old clock - Broke -
Oh, the days of yesterday, could
we, but live again -.
It is so lonely, this old home
of a hundred years...
There's dust in the attic
There is dust on the stairs
There is rain on the roof
You can not see for your tears

Evea Applegate - Feb. 13, 1937

anniversary of her father's death
Feb. 13, 1932.

Evea Applegate by rundown Old Place, circa 1937. (Applegate family photograph. Courtesy Douglas County Museum)

380

gardening, Evy. Maybe this year it will all get done, now that there's one of us here all the time." They both knew that she would not be up to the task, nor to many other things that needed doing. There were, of course, a few things she could plan to take care of. Sorting family keepsakes, labeling all the items in the old trunk Lucy and Irene had left to their own mother, Flora. Their father's papers and books. That professor at the university had wanted some of the old things in the house to look over. She would try to assist him in some way. Her sense of continuity and pride in the family was as deep as any Applegate's. She had these thoughts while her sister packed in the room above her. But she dreaded the darkness at night. There was still no electricity in the upper parts of the house. Thank heavens, Vince had put in the bath finally. She was so often ill lately, and would have hated treks to the outhouse in the yard.

Her sister came down the broad steps carrying her suitcase and paper sack full of sewing things. "I'll try to come down on Friday night, Eve. So much is happening now at the hospital. Hard to tell what will come up. Don't forget FDR's talk tonight. I'm going to try to stop in Salem for supper and listen to it."

And as they linked arms and walked to the front drive, the house behind them, Eva thought she had never felt so tired. Turning together to look back at their home, it seemed to her that the Old Place looked rundown and depressing. Even the greening abundance of the oncoming spring and its flowers could not change the effects of rotting boards on the porches, or disguise the raw look of the rain-streaked exterior, so badly in need of paint and repairs. The gigantic wisteria vine with its heavily scented flowers had grown thick and untamed. It blocked all the light from the large upper windows in the front. Evea, sensing her sister's worry and preoccupation, said softly, "You look very nice, Evy. Here, let me tuck your collar in. The facing's come out."

She couldn't help but wonder at their contrast. Eva in her flowered silk shirtwaist, the dyed black hair pulled into a chignon. While she, Evea, had not done her hair that day and had on an old black work dress left from years before. She guessed that she would not dye her own hair any longer, now that she was not working. They shared an embrace laden with the scent of Eva's Persian Lilac cologne that Evea had given her the Christmas before. How alone she was. The big house loomed behind her like a damp and blackening cave.

Eva pulled out of the drive and saw her twin so small in the old doorway. Evea's wave seemed forlorn. She felt a grief that was like death, a tearing in herself. She wondered at the oncoming night, which would find them separate. She wished that the dog had not died.

THE BED

Lisbon Applegate

The floor upstairs still bears its scars—from casters the size of small carriage wheels. The bed which occupied the corner room, the bed built for Lisbon, was an elaborate contraption laden with pulleys and ropes, adjustable wooden slats, ingenious levers, and even a sliding compartment through which he might relieve himself (though at the last he could not even manage that).

I have searched for days in these rooms—in trunks and other secret places of this old house. Yet I have not found Lisbon. I move in a world I do not know, sifting through my sense of the present bit by bit—slipping with my eyes, my hands, my mind into the past. And when I lift the heavy lid of a trunk, time floats, diffuses in particles of dust and light. I unlatch the family faces caught in their hand-sized casings of velvet and tooled leather, yet I have not seen him; there are no mementoes, no loved things. Only this thick smell of things forgotten, stored away. Only a few journals remain—his sister Irene's "scratchings," bound in slim notebooks with paper paisley covers. They lie here in my hands without weight—pieces of skin, pale blue handwriting coursing like fragile veins across the page.

But where is that thing so massively tangible, so heavy it has left potent markings, ruts on the floor? Lisbon's real universe, that bed—its proportions so magnificent that it was a bed with a room, the white slab of mattress extending like an angular peninsula within this hole of whitewashed walls.

He lay quietly most of the time; content it seemed to watch the activity in the side yard. He could turn his head and stare out his tiny window, watching, sometimes for hours, the movements of his brothers in and out of the toolshed, the sparks flying from the small foundry. He listened to the dense bell sound of the hammer striking the homemade anvil. Or he would watch his mother and sisters making soap, stoking their neat little fires, wiping their eyes with the corners of their aprons. Often, he would simply stare at the rough ceiling. Did he listen then to the rhythmic groan of the pump handle as it was worked up and down, up and down? Sometimes it seemed to put him to sleep.

But often, late at night, they would hear him—moving in his bed, rocking it back and forth as a child might to comfort himself.

385

The sound would fill the house. His sisters in the bedroom would watch the ceiling tremble. The others would go back to sleep. Irene would lie there, longing to do something.

One day, in the afternoon, when John O'Rourk, a farmhand, looked up from pumping and saw Lisbon beating his fists on the window, heard him bellowing something indecipherable—on that day there was a shattering of glass and the shrill, mournful sound of a voice that had lost its capacity for humanness. And when O'Rourk and two of Lisbon's brothers thundered up the stairs, the older one, Albert, shouted uselessly, "Stop it! Lisbonnnn, stop it!"

They found Lisbon in a moving shower of glass. He was lunging backward and forward in his bed, as if trying to make it move him out his window, his hands flailing at levers, then dragging the pulleys down—tugging at them like reins. Seeing the men, he stopped. He began to sob, flinging himself against the wide white girth of pillows. They never knew what set him off. They did know that it must not happen again. Miraculously, he had not sustained a single cut, despite glittering shards of glass that rested in his hair like sleet and were removed, piece by piece, by his gentle sister Jane.

On that day, the smallest ties to life and movement were severed. The casters were removed. Oilcloth was placed over the windows. Who could tell then what he watched, perhaps the moving silhouette of fir branches scratching the edge of the window. Or, perhaps, he watched nothing.

But if he did not exert, he did consume. Oh, the endless procession of hand-stitched sheets up and down two flights of stairs, the endless plumping up of goose-feather pillows—all those daily nightly ministrations that spanned thirty years. Oh, that vacant-eyed, full-bladdered boy-man, whose hair alone survived the slipping of the mind's and body's undergirdings. The hair, they said, remained thick, copper-colored, and coiled damply as a child's, even at fifty-three years of age.

Nights then simply blackened and were quiet. Lisbon did not rock his bed. Sleeping arced into wakefulness. They could not be sure except sometimes his eyes were open and sometimes they were not. That he continued to move one hand they did know. A slow heartbeat stroking across the ledge of his bed, the large childish hand, its oil, its body heat, moving across the wood, polishing it to unbearable smoothness. Whether out of love for his prison or as a last surviving link to his senses they did not know. Perhaps it was simply that what goes on living has motion. He existed in a torpor; he was never again heard to make a sound of any kind, as if that last furious frantic driving of his bed had exhausted him forever—finally used him up.

Great-great-aunt Irene—who gave him comfort, spoon-fed, washed, and combed him—boiled the soiled man-sized diapers in a black pot out back, watched the ash-hopper 'til the lye curdled into soap so she could continue to wash out "poor" Lisbon's things. That boy, who was "the brightest, most comely" of the lot, who began to die shortly after his seventh birthday, after the accident, while crossing by wagon to Oregon in 1843.

Memories of the Journey 1843 . . . concerning my brother Lisbon Applegate

. . . We young ones have been warned. Told not to ride in that wagon. Its driver one George Beale by name was a surlie fellow a son of a Missouri slave owner the storie went. We heard many years later that he was hanged along with Andrew Baker (not the Andy Baker on our train). Hanged for the terrible crime of murder. And also that he had taught school someplace above the Willamette settlements but I caint imagine that for he was always snarling at we little folk and would tell such grusome tales about indians and the like that we would have bad dreams. But the boys especially Lisbon and some other boy cousins liked this and would without telling their ma and sometimes without the driver himself a knowing climb atop his wagen. They said George Beale talked to himself when he thought no one was lissening and also that he spent hours digging at pustules on his face. Oh they repeated awfull things to impress we girl cousins I expect. Later George Beale was asked to leave our party. He had done so much that was wrong and mean.

Twas one day as we approached outside of Fort

387

Laramie it happened the crule thing which changed poor Lisbon's life and mine to though I have tried never to regret. None of us were knowing it then. Oh it was hot the prairie brush giving off a peculiar odor we had come to know. It was a slow day the teams having been terrible short on watter for sevral days. I remember I told Mamma as we rocked to and fro on the wagen seat that I felt strange in my stomac. I think I vomited. I asked her "Mamma how far is it now to Oregon?" She wipes my face with her apron and says "I'm afraid its still a long long ways." I asked where my brother was . . . she says Lisbon is riding in Aunt Cynthia's wagen with some other boys. I miss him. We were always together being so close in age. But I guess in the fuss of getting started that morning he had gone off. It seems still so awful to think on—that he was in George Beale's wagen right in front of us and I dident even know it. Oh lord if only I did know. Beale was driving a provision wagen a heavy thing taking a double team of oxen as it was loaded with slabs of salt pork early in the trip and then just flour and the kegs of camp water. Behind the drivers seat there was a built in bin which was lined with coper. A place big enough that two men could have layed down in it. I did not realize that my poor brother had secured himself there or that he had fallen asleep. We were close enough to hear George Beale shouting to his team but could not make out his words. He had pulled his wagen to the side and was moving it towards a little hill off the trail.

Later he told Uncle Jesse he did not believe he could make the grade due to the heavy wagen. Just then the man who had been in front of Beale shouted "there it is the Snake! There it is the Snake River!" Our trail was perilus and narrow. Mamma stood up in our wagen but held on to the buckboard.

"I can see the Fort now!" the man shouted again. I rember Mamma laught I guess it was because we would sleep under a real roof that night and fresh watter was soon to be had. Then I saw it too! The Snake, a sort of brown green color cutting between the gorge below our trail and up a little ways. I thought I could see the fort too the wooden tower away far off and even some smoke waving up from it. Every body was talking with much excitedness it seemed you could hear people in back asking things to us in front. And we were not watching George Beales wagen then nor seeing the bad trouble that was coming. . . ."

Some said later that they had seen the driver beating the oxen up the incline; he was rising too abruptly and the wagon began to slip down the hill. It gained momentum, nearly unbalancing the team of oxen—spitting rocks and dust from the wheels, clattering down to the bottom of the hill. George Beale threw himself out of the wagon, plummeting head first into a patch of sage—all the while cursing and shouting out. A man watching had a good laugh. He got his just deserts, that fellow, and no harm done, as the wagon, lurching to a stop, had remained remarkably upright.

But they did not know about the stowaway, young Lisbon, who was coughed up from the wagon's insides in a flurry of white stuff. The flour had covered him from head to foot and he looked anything but injured as he lay on the ground like some noisy half-done ghost. He was wailing about the spilled flour and worrying that his ma should be angry that he had stowed away and disobeyed her.

After his accident, Lisbon's "fits" began. He, who had been an even-tempered, amiable child, would go into a rage—sometimes fainting and shaking, turning deathly pale. At first the fits were far apart; a month or more might pass in seeming normalcy. Then within the year they became a nearly daily occurrence. His sister Irene "looked after him." When he began to shake, to cry out, she would watch over him, sometimes attempting to embrace him to keep him from doing harm. "Ain't that somethin'," people would say, watching her. "Such a little thing to take *that* on!" At night the girl had nightmares. She would sob, burying her face in her mother's apron. Her thick reddish braids jerking, she would look up and say, "Oh, poor poor Lisbon. I'll take care of him, Ma. He'll get better." Her sense of responsibility for her brother, her oblique sense of guilt, consumed her, and so she stayed at the ranch while her sisters married—she stayed all of her life. She was fifty when he died and, as she said, "past it."

HANDWRITTEN NOTES—FAMILY HISTORY

Today Aunt Eva told me a family story about Lisbon Applegate. When a young man he was still walking and had not at that time been in the wheelchair (now in the attic). "One afternoon someone was to have been watching Lisbon as he strolled

George "Buck" Applegate in the east front room with several of his hand-built devices and the second "memory portrait" of his uncle Jesse Applegate. (Gus Peret Collection. Courtesy Douglas County Museum)

One of "Buck" Applegate's glass-fronted cabinets containing two handcrafted violins made for Eva and Evea Applegate in 1893. (Stephen T. Rose photograph)

in the yard. He wandered off somehow. They say he found two snakes, rattlers some say, though I don't know. He grabbed both of them . . . holding one in each hand, then walked up to this back porch here, right up to the fellow who was to have watched him. Now this is the queer part. He was saying, 'Applegate, Applegate, Applegate' over and over . . . all the while holding those snakes. Pretty soon after he was in the chair all the time—and then in the special bed our daddy had built for him upstairs. I remember seeing him as a small girl."

Great-grandfather, "Buck" he was called by everyone who knew him, designed and constructed Lisbon's bed. It is said he took great pleasure making it; spent hours arranging the networks of rope under the mattress, sanding the fir boards, carving the pegs. But then he always found pleasure making things, inventing things, it would seem, like the sulky plow he had patented in 1881, and those two violins with their delicate inlays of Oregon hardwoods carved for his twin daughters, Evea and Eva. But he was especially proud of the bed, a feat of engineering in his neighborhood. He would take people upstairs to see it with Lisbon still lying in it.

But things drifted from him—Buck was not a businessman and the family land diminished year by year as he sold it. His legacy was his objects; his hybrid apple trees, a few journals scratched hastily in pencil while he was on trips, his hand-built phonograph, four handsome chests and glass-fronted cupboards made from Douglas fir and mountain ash, the violins, and the patent for his plow that he never "followed through" with.

But what does this mean? Is it that I search for the blood then, tracing across Irene's pages and now my own pages? I am a fragment in motion.

I stare out from Lisbon's window, watching the Oregon rain drift and glisten down the big cedar tree. I walk around the edges of the emptied room as if the bed were still here, blocking passage. My passage, Irene's, Lisbon's—even Buck's, the maker. The circle of relations—the bed. The wagon, its movement stopped.

THE OLD PLACE

August 1971

Those first days in the old house were filled with uneasiness as well as exultation. Dog days, Uncle Vince called them, hot and sleepy.

A peculiar silence settled over the ridges, I remember, for the big trucks no longer rumbled back and forth upon the logging roads that rimmed the valley, nor could the incessant burr of chain saws be heard in the distance. The woods were tinder-dry.

But there were other hazards besides fire, and people who knew the country were sure to wear high-topped boots if they had to go up into the hills.

It was the season of rattlesnakes. They were sloughing off their old skins and more apt to strike if caught unawares. Thus my father warned me to stay away from the oak knolls and rocky places. "Just stay put until things cool off," he advised, "close to home."

While Uncle Vince allowed that he had not seen a rattler "right here in the yard" since he'd been "a youngster," he related that just a few weeks before the children and I arrived, the neighbor up the road had had an "upset."

One stifling morning when the summer haze yet crept over everything, foretelling a day even hotter than the one before, Mrs. Warner's dog had barked—which was a good thing, since she was on her way to her vegetable garden. Not twenty feet from her kitchen door, there lay a big fellow, Vince said, and no man being on the place at the time, Mrs. Warner had gone after her little rifle and she'd shot that snake three times before it was done for, after which she'd called him and everyone else.

Snakes. Jessica grew worried about them. The old yard was large and fenced as far as the hayfields. Even so, Jess—with Colin toddling behind her—never ventured farther than the plum tree or lilac bushes, and if Vince or I were out of sight for a moment, little fearful calls rang out and soon they'd trundle back, dragging their toys behind them, "sticking closer," Vince complained, "than yellow jackets to a full apple crate."

Uncle Vince would do what he always did on hot days: "just-a-sit." His "seat" was a handmade wooden chair his father, Buck, had made some fifty years before. If the children weren't pestering him, he would tilt back his chair against the porch wall, his long bony legs extended, and snooze a little, grunting every now and again. Occasionally, if he was in the mood, he would pass on a story of some kind, usually concerning what Jessica called "it-used-to-be's," which she was certain to query me about later. I was grateful for the time Uncle Vince spent with the children. These hours were precious to me. After many days of cleaning and ordering upstairs, I tried to settle down to work.

There was a small room that opened from the large bedroom where the children and I slept. A year before she died, Aunt Eva told me that the little room had once been Lisbon's. I decided to make it my study, partly, I suppose, because I was intrigued by its history.

My father related something even more interesting about that little room. When he'd visited his grandparents as a child, the room had been his overnight quarters. He had stayed at the Old Place frequently, he said, especially in the weeks following his mother's funeral. His grandmother, Flora, slept in the big room

The Old Place, circa 1920. (Gus Peret Collection. Courtesy Douglas County Museum)

next to him, always keeping the door open to make his sleep less fretful. Once, he awakened in the middle of the night and was startled to see a woman in an old-fashioned white dress seated at the foot of his narrow little bed. "She was just looking at me," he said. When he hollered "Grandma," the woman disappeared. The experience had so unnerved him he never again slept in the little room. On hot nights he took his bedroll on the balcony, with only the owls in the big walnut tree disturbing his sleep. On cold nights, he was assigned one of the other five bedrooms.

I was peculiarly drawn to the little room. During that first month in Yoncalla, I settled in, making a place for my desk by shoving several old trunks against the walls. I felt quite comfortable in my hidey-hole, but for some reason I could not work there. In a matter of moments, I would find myself staring out the single tiny window—a window that would not open regardless of how I pulled and pried. I suppose I was simply finding my bearings upstairs, scanning the horizon, the big white house mounting the surrounding fields like an old riverboat.

I could see over and past the orchard, and beyond the fence line, where high grasses shivered in the wind. Black-green ridges rose in the hazy distance. If I looked far enough to the west, the tawny hump of the big hill some people called Old Baldy appeared. Jesse Applegate had named that hill Mount Yoncalla: Yonc—the sound the eagle makes; alla-alla—the nest or home of the eagles.

I thought a great deal about that hill he had called mountain. What had drawn my great-great-grandfather and his brothers to it? How had they felt when they first rode past it, looking for a place to call home? I had a long view from the tiny window. It pulled at me like a tide.

As I sat there, house-high, immersed in those vistas, it seemed to me that I was somehow surrounded by water. Nothing could have been further from the truth. Except for a farmer's pond flashing deep blue under the heat-hazed sky, there was no water nearby. The creeks of that countryside were always bone-dry by July, and our own little valley—called Halo, after an old Indian headman—was notoriously short of water from summer to early autumn. Yet the impression of water surrounding me was always there, perhaps because of the antique glass in the little window over my desk. Its captured bubbles and slight variations in thickness made the landscape appear to blur and move. When I rose from my chair, I walked like a sailor or a diver returning from deep waters. I would settle myself on the airy haven that was the balcony, thinking to read some old book from downstairs or else Irene's "hen's scratchings"—as Uncle Vince called them. But Irene's papers lay leaf-dry on the small white table beside me on most afternoons. I nearly always gave in, closing my eyes—drifting along—floating on the sweetly acrid scent of the boxwood hedges that wafted up to the balcony. I might as well have been in a field of poppies.

I met Irene that first summer. She was very real to me as I read her recollections. One morning, investigating the contents of a stout old trunk—Aunt Lucy's trunk, Vince said—I found a packet of loose papers bound by a slender pink ribbon. The wavering notation was in Aunt Eva's hand: "Irene's notes for the book she was going to write."

I uncovered many unexpected treasures that summer, but Irene's recollections gave me the greatest pleasure. Papers in hand, I ran through both front rooms and the old dining room. I remember I shouted, "Uncle Vince," with as much exuberance as a miner shouting "Eureka!"

When I got to the kitchen, I grew alarmed. The air was thick with smoke and there was a smell of burning grease that even the open door did not dispel. Vince appeared unperturbed, just stood there listening to the radio, holding a spatula in his hand.

"I was frying me some eggs," he said. "They kind of got away from me, I guess."

I watched him douse the iron skillet and scrape the eggs into the sink. His mind was obviously still on his ball game. He would not meet my eyes. I was not about to be put off, regardless of what the team from Phillie was up to. I resolutely turned down the volume on the radio.

"Vince," I said, rattling the papers in front of his nose, "look what I've found."

His look was sour. "Well," he grumbled, "I can't see what you've got until you stop waving it around, now can I? Anyway, my hands are all greased up. Tell me about it but make it quick, will ya?"

"Aunt Irene was going to write a book and it looks like all the notes are in that big trunk in the east room!" Even as I delivered this momentous news, his eyes drifted toward the radio. After a moment, he shrugged and muttered, "Hell, lots of people in this family have been going to write themselves a book. Women mostly. There's stuff like that all over the house."

"Where?" I demanded.

"Well, it seems to me Eva stuck some papers of Irene's in the big desk. Go look there, why don't ya?" Then he sighed, with a more or less tolerant smile. "Now," he said, giving me a little shove, "can I get back to my ball game?"

Irene's handwriting was odd and sometimes nearly indecipherable. She'd written with a pencil that obviously needed sharpening. Her scrawl was so silvery that unless I held it at precisely the right angle it seemed to disappear before my eyes. Transcribing even a single page not infrequently took hours, partly because of the motley array of paper she'd written upon. Sometimes her words slipped in an uneven web over smallish note sheets that had evidently been left by some traveling salesman from "F. S. Meeker & Co., Dealers in Oregon Hops, Salem, Oregon 1898."

Whole sections concerning her girlhood were relegated to the backs of 1918 calendars. These, she'd cut into various sizes, and even though she'd used the blank side, the printer's ink had permeated so that October and its green numbered boxes yet lingered in reverse beneath her descriptions of life on the Oregon Trail. When she had concerned herself with leaving a lefthand margin, her writing inevitably traveled around it so as to use every bit of space, rather like a train running off the track. But most exasperating to me were her unaccountable shifts in direction. Halfway down a page she had elected to write sideways. Sometimes I would discover an account of the same event written all over again, both versions almost verbatim, though the page numbers—faint, elusive, and rarely in the same place twice—would be different.

Later, Vince shed light on the quality of Irene's stationery, though he was somewhat surprised by my question. "Why, back then people used everything and anything."

"But surely if Irene had wanted to, she could have bought decent paper," I responded. "I thought you told me Lucy and Irene were quite well-to-do for their time."

"Yeah. They were quite well fixed. For a pair of old ladies, I mean. But in those days, people held on to things. They held on to everything that was theirs, I mean. My mother was like that, too. Yes. Always putting things away for a rainy day. That's why there's so much old junk in the attic yet today! And Aunt Lucy and Aunt 'Rene, they were a pair of pack rats. Even Mother accused them of it. Those two just couldn't bear to part with anything." He grinned. "Which is why, maybe, they died old maids."

Then he stared for a moment at Jessica and Colin, who were playing on the floor. Then giving me a sly look: "But that wasn't *your* problem, was it?"

One day Jessica sought me out on my balcony roost. "What are you doing, Mommy?" she asked. "Just reading," I told her. "The memories of an old lady who died a long time ago." Jessica was four years old then and loved stories, so I thought I'd share something that Irene had written. I thought it might help her understand why I spent so much time either reading or writing, and why I needed to be alone sometimes to do my work.

"Three greats," I remember telling her. "Your great-great-great-aunt." She held up three fingers.

I explained that Irene had written about something that happened to her when she was a very little girl. "She lived in Missouri then, which is next door to Indiana, where you used to live."

I was placed on the Negro woman's back. My little feet dangling acrosst her big broad breasts in front. She held onto my hands and sang me songs as we trotted along, "The Redbird in the Redbud Tree" . . . while I had been gone with Ruhanna a child had been born and died at our house. I remember that my Mamma [Melinda Applegate] was sick from the birth after that and I would crawl under her bed just to be close to her! I remember *hugging Mamma's shoes* as I could not get to her where she lay on the bed!

How surprised I was to find tears streaming down my face, but then I seemed to cry easily that first summer alone in Oregon.

"What's the matter, Mommy?" Jessica asked, climbing on my lap. How small she was! Fitting herself under my "wing," as she called it. A baby bird.

And I tried to explain what it was that had moved me . . . that poor little girl . . . Irene . . . wanting something she could not have . . . her mother sick . . . Irene—huddling under the bed with only the dust devils for company and only a pair of old shoes to hold on to.

Excerpts from Shannon Applegate's Letters to Friends

August 26, 1971
. . . Have been considering moving into the old house in Yon-calla to stay with my uncle Vince for a few months. He is all alone now. My great-aunt Eva (his sister) died a few months before I arrived in Oregon.

Would love to stay at the old house for a time and work there on my book. Much worry and much joy in this new life of mine. For the time being I am living with my dad on his place on the Umpqua River. Blackberries and cream for breakfast every morning. I love Oregon.

August 30, 1971
. . . Spending as much time as I can with Uncle Vince in Yoncalla. Mentioned the possibility of moving in with him for a time. He seemed delighted. . . . He enjoys talking about the past and I enjoy listening.

August 31, 1971
I have been frantically cleaning the upstairs bedrooms in the old house. About fifty years' worth of dust at least. I aired the quilts on the upper balconies. Coming back from the grocery, looked up and saw them: stars, patchwork, embroidered. Waving and flapping against the railing. Déjà vu. Makes so much sense to be here. I feel at home. Welcome.

September 2, 1971
I must tell you about Susan Applegate. I have found a friend. Like so many things which I have experienced lately, it makes the fact that I am here in Oregon feel more natural, more right. Susan's and my meeting and our emerging friendship brings feelings of utter connectedness.

. . . Her great-grandfather, Albert Applegate, was the brother of Buck (in the piece "The Bed" that I sent you). Her great-great-grandfather, therefore, is also my own—Charles Applegate, who built the old home I'm living in now.

405

When some dear friends visiting from Indiana were here recently we went to the hill in back of the house one night. Milky Way spangling everything. Drank champagne out of paper cups and stared up at the stars reminiscing. Susan had called while we were on the hill and told Uncle Vince that she was coming over. I went back to the house, briefly, to check on the kids, and Vince told me Susan had telephoned again, saying that she had had car trouble and would not be coming after all. After an hour or so had passed I was surprised to hear a car pull up. It was quite late but even so I knew somehow that it was Susan. I literally ran down the hill. . . . "Susan Applegate!" I called. Out of the darkness, a voice, so much like my own, shouted back, "Shannon Applegate!" We embraced on the brow of the hill. I knew at once that we were not strangers at all. Words flowed easily between us. There was no strain. My friends sat and listened to us talking. They said later that they were amazed to observe two such youthful members of the family who were so obviously fascinated by family lore.

Susan and I share another quality that is more easily felt than described: For years each of us has sensed "a part of self" that has wandered, almost as though lost, in the labyrinth of family.

Even so, how different our own histories as individuals. Unlike me, she is no rolling stone. Susan has always lived in Oregon. After she graduated from the university, she came back to Yoncalla. She took a job teaching at a nearby elementary school.

I asked about her growing-up years: Various places in Oregon are named Applegate. The name had a certain "old power" in the southern part of the state during the years when she was growing up. By the time she was in the fifth grade, she said, she had come to resent having the name Applegate. It actually embarrassed her, especially when one schoolteacher or another insisted in singling her out during the part of the year when Oregon history was studied. "Isn't it wunnn-derful," the teacher would say as Susan cringed, "that we have a descendant of such a courageousss pioneeeer family in our midst! Stand up please, Susan . . ."

She had seen nothing "courageous" in the behavior of her Applegate relatives, who liked nothing better than to argue with one another. Why, she wondered, didn't her teacher talk about Susan's own efforts and accomplishments instead of those of her dead relatives? She wanted them to pay attention to the Susan

Applegate family reunion in 1957. (Gus Peret Collection. Courtesy Douglas County Museum)

part and not the Applegate part, she said. Only when she reached the university did her curiosity about the family reemerge.

Life in Yoncalla would be very lonely were it not for one another. Until meeting Susan, I spent most of my time with elderly Yoncalla people. When Susan comes to visit we have wonderful times. We talk and talk about all manner of things. She is an artist. I've shared some of my writing with her—even my poetry. The children adore her. I love it when she lingers in the evenings. The air is heavy and sweet. The old front rooms are cool. Sometimes we sing and dance or listen to music on the portable record player Dad loaned me. How amazing it is to enjoy ourselves in the same front rooms where our ancestors lived.

There were many family fiddlers in the "days-gone-by," as Uncle Vince puts it. He doesn't care much for Janis Joplin, Taj Mahal, or Joni Mitchell, but he claims to like to hear Susan and me singing the "good ol' songs" whenever she brings her guitar with her. This is an important time in my life. I can't say why but I feel it deeply.

By the way, Susan has plump cheeks, "apple cheeks," as you used to call mine. So maybe it's hereditary after all!

September 7, 1971

This past week Uncle Vince died suddenly. He was visiting his son and family in Portland. He had a heart attack. They're bringing him home to bury him in our family cemetery.

It's all very upsetting. I had a great deal of regard for Uncle Vince. We had a few rough spots to work out in terms of living here at the Old Place together; nevertheless, I will miss him. He provided an incredible link to the family's past. I feel a great sense of loss, as if something has been prematurely severed.

All these years of being away from the family. In reality I have had less than three years in which to become close to my elders. In the past six months there have been two deaths. The oldest members of the family are now gone since Uncle Vince's passing. Many things have gone through my mind. I am afraid to remain at the Old Place with only the children for company. I still do not have a car. We are a mile and more from town. The house feels very isolated, though there are one or two neighbors not too far away. Even while Uncle Vince was alive, I experienced a certain lack of ease, especially at night. Except for Susan and occasional visits from Dad I would be "cut off." Our visitors here have tended to be Uncle Vince's old cronies. They will not "call" very much now that he's gone, I think. . . .

September 20, 1971
The evenings since Vince has died have become a ritual of locking doors and pulling shades. I have not intended to be frightened, but I am, I guess. Strange sounds at night when I am alone and the children are asleep. I turn on the classical music station on the radio. Perhaps I am just not used to the physical isolation. The twinkling lights of the little town just across the valley seem incredibly distant. I've never lived in an old house like this. Not sleeping well. Can't tell if the sounds I hear are within or without. Does not change the fact that I hear them, however. Susan comes when she can, but am mainly very alone.

September 30, 1971
Canning some fruit and vegetables, cataloging books and artifacts, cleaning and transcribing old family letters.
. . . The days, even the rainfilled ones, rest easy on me. I love the rain and the house seems like a cozy refuge. But at night the fog smothers the valley. In a locked-in world I walk around carrying an infant whom I cannot seem to comfort as old clocks clang and reverberate in darkened rooms. For the past five nights a multitude of other sounds as well. I will get through this, dammit!! It is eleven o'clock now. This is not like me. Have got to get some sleep! I do know that the sounds do not come from the outside.

October 3, 1971
Susan and I went to Eugene last Saturday night. I was pleased to have finally found someone competent to stay with Jess and Colin. At last!—or so I thought—occasional nights out would be possible. I left the babysitter the phone number of the people who live down the road in the event of some emergency. Suz and I felt like two birds free from our cages! We were having a great time but about ten o'clock I grew uneasy and decided to telephone the sitter. She answered on the first half-ring. "I'm a little scared here, 'Mrs.' Applegate," she said. I used my most reassuring tone and advised her that the house was very old, that large houses had their own sounds at the change of seasons, etc. She had nothing

whatever to be fearful of. "Turn the volume up on the TV," I said, and told her we would be home about twelve-thirty. When we arrived home I was amazed to see our neighbor from "down the road" sitting on the sofa in her red bathrobe and pincurls. Our stalwart babysitter cowered nearby. I felt a little embarrassed. "I just got too scared, 'Mrs.' Applegate," she said pathetically, "all those thumpings and footsteps overhead. They never did let up." I apologized profusely and mumbled something about how it might be squirrels in the attic, even though I knew very well there were none. I gave her an extra dollar to soothe my conscience. Susan said good night and offered to drive both my neighbor and the babysitter to their respective homes.

No sooner had Susan pulled out of the drive when I heard several "thumpings" of my own. Fortunately she decided to return and stay the night with me. I had been standing in the rain for some moments when she arrived. In view of the loudness of the noises the weather seemed a better fate. It was doubtless "very un-Applegate," I told her, but I felt alarmed. Together we checked on the children, who were sleeping soundly. We fixed ourselves some tea and talked in the kitchen for a while discussing such things as mice, wind, temperature changes, the old oil stovepipe, etc. We were not more convinced than the babysitter had been . . . especially after we moved to the sofa in the dining room to sip our tea. Almost immediately we heard the steady tread of footsteps overhead. Just then the old clock bonged three o'clock. I cheerfully reminded Susan that Ingmar Bergman called four A.M. the "hour of the wolf." We began to giggle rather hysterically. We felt like a pair of Girl Scouts who, having heard "The Man with the Golden Arm" or some other ghostly yarn, had permitted adrenaline to lift them to dizzying heights.

As the house grew quiet again we quieted ourselves. The next series of footsteps was even louder. Colin began to cry. We simultaneously rushed to the stairs. We were both shaken and our ascent was desperate. As we arrived on the upper landing Colin stopped crying, but an even more disturbing sound greeted us. We both heard voices, which seemed to come from the far end of the house. We could make out the cadence of what surely were angry sentences exchanged by a man and woman, yet the words were unclear. We agreed that we needed to sleep in the same room as the children. Despite the four or five patchwork quilts we piled over ourselves, and the fact that we shared a double bed, we shivered all night. The voices finally ebbed and the footsteps stopped. About five o'clock or so, just as the sun came up, we fell asleep.

Susan did not stay here last night. You might imagine that I was uneasy. I put off going to bed until the last possible moment. I was getting so freaky I thought of calling both of you but realized it was fairly late back east. Instead, I called my friend in Berkeley. I tried to hold the receiver up so he could hear the noises. It did not work. He suggested that maybe various ancestors were upset by the things I was writing. Perhaps it was Lisbon ("The Bed"). He suggested that I acknowledge my fear by addressing it directly. Once before I had tried to verbalize my fear—but it had been a gesture only, because I was so terrified. But last night I was almost as exhausted as I was frightened. Anything was worth a try. I announced loudly as the footsteps drew closer and closer to the bedroom door, "I am afraid. I am trying to understand you. Some of you I have come to love. I have come to this place with my children to rest and work. I cannot promise you that I will write things about you which are pleasing, but whatever I do will be done with as much honesty and resource as I can muster. Please! Let me rest." Or words to that effect. The event is still too real and close in time for me to look at it. It was possibly the most terrifying moment of my life.

I would like to believe that last night I managed to reach *around* my fear. I realize it is possible to literally emit the scent and vibrations of terror. Surely, this state of mind only amplifies and attracts more that is frightful. In any case, I think it helped to verbalize my feelings. The fact that earlier Susan had shared a similar experience, and that the babysitter, too, had heard the sounds, somewhat renews my confidence in my own sanity. The voices did seem fainter last night after I spoke my piece. Soon afterward the kerosene lantern by the bed dimmed perceptibly, as if muting itself so that I might sleep. I awakened this morning, still sitting upright in bed. It was the deepest sleep I have ever known.

I hate to admit this, my dears, oh, how I wish it were otherwise, but there are definitely sounds overhead at this very moment.

411

October 10, 1971

Susan, after much consideration, has decided to move in here with me. God, I love that woman. In the past week, nights have been much easier and I feel the worst is over. I would not let Susan come here if I thought it was purely a matter of my not being able to handle life alone. Maybe the "folk" in the house understand, finally, that I am not about to be run off the place. Or, perhaps, they were not trying to run me off at all. Am truly delighted at Susan's coming . . . I think it will work out. We are good friends. More than that; I feel some especial family tie: sisters.

October 29, 1971

A letter left for Susan after a night of dreams:

Dear Sister/Cousin/Great-Great-Grand-Daughter of Charles who built this house we suffer through and love. And mostly, Suz, dear you,

The fog floats away. Toys on the porch. Horses in the field. Opal-colored clouds drift overhead. I feel the day and the goodness of it. But this is now. Not last night. Concerning our strange encounter on the stairway and the things you told me about your dreams: I was surprised to find myself writing this; your experience has somehow entered me.

The Dream Chant:
Goosey goosey gander, whither dost thou wander
Upstairs, downstairs, off the edge of the world.

"When I woke up my room was washed silver from the fog," you said. "I've been hearing them again. They were chanting. Two dream voices. I thought I could not open my mouth. I thought my plants were swaying, making new shadows upon the walls. Everything's so white and silver in my room. I am trying not to be afraid. . . . The dreams I have since moving here! I had on an old-fashioned cloak of black taffeta. It made sounds when the wind touched it. A big black bonnet with ribbons. Couldn't see the sun in it. All of me all covered up. Was riding on a stagecoach or some kind of wagon. Boxes piled up around me. Then saw faces of the family standing on the side of the road. Faces that I had

412

seen as a little girl. Faces I had never seen. Then somehow, everyone around a big dining table, like this one that Buck made or
another one with clawlike feet, like my grandpa's in his old place.
And my dad was there. He sat at the head of the table. Candles
flickered. Then it was Dad but not my dad; maybe yours. It was
Charley, too. Just the way he looks in that one tintype in the
album. His old coat on. Everyone was waiting to be served. Smiling expectantly. It was then, it was now. I'm so tired. So shaky.
The past is too thick. I don't want to go back upstairs. I truly can't
do this another night!!"

Susan, I will never forget your face as you said those things. I
wanted to throw myself at your feet and say, "Susan, please don't
think about leaving. Please don't go." But when I finally went to
bed my own dreams came back to me. Only they were not dreams,
but reality stretched taut somehow. There was one bad night in

Family Party in Winter. Susan and Shannon Applegate
talk at table while their great-great-aunt Lucy
Applegate places bread. Other figures in painting
depict family members representing six generations.
A mystic moon hovers over the imagined festivities
on the men's side of the old house. (Susan Applegate
painting. Photograph courtesy Douglas County
Museum)

413

those first days. The shade would not shut. I put a blanket over a window. It was still the heart of August; stifling and hot. But no, I must not leave anything open. Something might get in. It was a room without air. Even the sounds of the children breathing so softly and peacefully did not comfort me. There were footsteps. I sat up in bed. I saw a woman in the oval mirror at the foot of my bed. Black hair streaming down, an old-fashioned nightgown. It was my face. It was not my face. I watched her move her hands, her fingers, as if from a distance. I was literally beside myself. Crazy woman. Scared woman. A child with children. I wondered: Why have I come here? Where will I go? Yet these feelings have passed me. I'm forced to smile despite myself. Two more women in this house alone now: Irene and Lucy. Evea and Eva. Susan and Shannon. Can it be we are not meant to go? And there is this: On a good day there is no place softer or sweeter or homier or more, at certain hours, steeped in light. You have said so yourself.

December 5, 1971
Life here is so varied and extraordinary. Most rough spots of living in the house ironed out except for the heat at night. Use the fireplaces a lot. Entertain, fix dinners, etc., play our music, and sing in the front rooms by the fire. To answer your question: Yes, we have had more "visitors." There seem to be cycles for it . . . times when there are more sounds, manifestations, etc., than other times. When we decided to fix the attic as our "studio"

Let Buck Get His Fiddle
Now my young people think of a plan
To celebrate Christmass the best way you can
Get up your jellies, your pies and good meat
And ask all your kinfolk to come help you eat
And all other young folks that you wish to see
Make them perfectly welcome, jolly and free
And when all are together you'll have a good chance
To make Buck get his fiddle and have a good dance
And go on until morning without any fear
Or as long as you please! Your daddy don't care!

Written by Charles Applegate
circa 1870

Fireplace on the men's side (or east room) as it appeared in 1971.
(Stephen T. Rose photograph)

Fireplace on the women's side (or west room) as it appeared in 1971.
(Stephen T. Rose photograph)

space, for example, each time we discussed rearranging things, the Seth Thomas clock in the front room would bong despite the fact that it hasn't worked for months. One can only make it chime manually. We have decided it is on "psychic" time. After thinking for several weeks that each of us had been singing, humming some tuneless meandering melody every evening around seven o'clock, we discovered that neither of us had been doing it. One evening, friends arrived while we were gone. They stood on the porch, they said, for some moments listening to the "fiddle music," wondering why we didn't answer the door. A few nights ago there was a knock on the east front door. Both Susan and I came to answer it from separate directions. "Well, no one is there, Suz. . . ," I said, half-looking at Susan, who I felt was standing to my right. Noted in my mind that Susan had evidently changed her blouse: a half-perception. Peripheral.

"Why are you talking to me over there? I'm here," said Susan. But she too had the sense of someone standing beside me, looking out the window with us.

It seemed the figure wore a white blouse with long sleeves. Susan was wearing a dark jersey. I was left with a kind of after-image of a young woman's face, with hair pulled back.

In terms of such a distinct visual presence, that is about the most interesting we have experienced to date.

You see, Oregon life in the country is toughening me up. I split firewood. I haul water. I am not much disturbed by our "vis-itors," who are probably not "visitors" at all. We abide here to-gether. When people stay overnight and say in the morning that they heard long skirts trailing down the hall or that someone was talking or humming, and attempt to inquire subtly whether any of us were up about four A.M., we simply smile reassuringly. I hope this does not cause you to think twice about coming to see us next summer. Think of it as an adventure.

417

DEAR UNCLE VINCE

1981
Oregon Coast

Dear Uncle Vince,

Why am I writing to you?—you whom the minister eulogized ten years ago and more; you, lying there alone on an island of dark ribboned flowers; you, whom I loved, however imperfectly, whom I could not bear to look upon as I filed past. I saw only the big hand resting over your heart, the sleeve of your one good suit, a glimpse of your old bald head—the unmistakable peak of an Applegate nose looming over the unseen face.

Uncle Vince, for weeks now I have been pulling and pushing, yet my mind seems closed—the door shut tight or not there at all. A wall. No, the memories of you and me and those days we shared in the old house have not come easily. Even on good days, they seem no more than summer westerlies—like the little gusts I remember that rustle through the orchard every now and then.

The truth is that on most days I have felt as if I were standing on the kitchen porch, calling and calling again, waiting for some wayward child or half-deaf hound who will not come. Yet I feel different this morning: Relieved. Released. Last night I had a dream. The dream:

Darkness had fallen but the sky was a vibrant blue. There was no moon; yet in the distance, the Old Place emanated such a bright white light, it was like the moon, or so I thought to myself as I walked along.

I was following a long, winding brick pathway, which resembled the one you said your father made when you were a boy. After walking for what seemed a long time indeed, I turned to see the landscape from whence I'd come. The ocean was utterly silver. I was not surprised to see it in the least. I knew I'd started there and had climbed over huge rocks to find the path.

I was pleased with myself, feeling calm, not hurrying when I resumed my journey.

But as I came closer and closer to the house, some apprehension began to stir in me. I knew that something or someone was waiting for me up ahead.

421

Mists hovered over the fields on either side of me. I wanted to turn back after a while, for now there was no view at all, but I knew I couldn't. I walked very slowly, concentrating upon the bricks, which were laid unevenly—the moss seeming to eat around their edges even as I watched.

I was still some distance from the glow of the house when I heard the sound. I puzzled over it for some moments. It was resonant but brief, almost bell-like. Suddenly I recognized it. A hoe was striking the earth again and again. I was listening so intently, I lost my sense of self. The pitch was like that of a temple or meditation bell. The sound was all. I was still walking, but it was more like floating, as though caught in some stream or current that was not my own. Yet when I passed beneath the locust trees in the front yard, I heard the black leaves whispering. It was as if they were saying, "Call back your alertness." And I did, feeling incredibly alive again.

The pathway did not lead to the front doors as it does in reality, nor did it pass beneath the lattice of the pergola and on to the kitchen door. Instead, the path bordered an immense flowerbed, and Uncle Vince, I have never seen such dahlias.

All were pearl-white, their long stems wavering slightly with each chime of the hoe. Some had heavy heads, larger than dinner plates, and their fringed petals were almost translucent. Others were daintier and wonderfully iridescent. I left the pathway and found myself amidst the maze of flowers.

Did I hear the sound any longer? I can't remember. Before me I see flowers so tall, they are as a swaying wall of lace. But I seem to be looking down now. I see the blade of the hoe. No. That's not right. What I see first are the shoes, dusty and brown. Now there is the blade. The hoe handle. The hand. The man. I knew who it was, Uncle Vince, from the moment I saw those old shoes. His frayed suspenders clipped to baggy pants, the collarless shirt. How many times have I stared at that face caught in those yellowed photographs? Yes. It was your father. It was Buck. Great-grandfather was tending his night garden. And when I was finally able to return his gaze, his eyes told me that he had known me all my life.

How is such a thing possible? He died—what?—twenty-five years before I was born. I knew that: even as I was dreaming. Yet this morning I still feel it. He knows me, Uncle Vince, or some aspect of me. He knows me and sees me and accepts me, in ways that you never did, and I know him.

He said the most amazing things to me, Uncle Vince. No, not in words. He just kept looking at me, oh so deeply.

But I was afraid of him, those first moments. All manner of things were racing through my mind. After all, I have not always been flattering—in terms of Buck, I mean—and as I stood there, the voices of all those men and women I've interviewed over the years were somehow spliced together, whirring round and round. Buck Applegate: "He may have been brilliant, no doubt about that: inventions and those inlaid violins he made for the twins, and apple trees, too; grafting them and watching over them as if they were babies . . . that acre of wheat Buck grew one time as an experiment, the yield so high and each stock so long it extended clear acrosst the bumper of a Model A, and the people at the agricultural college came down. Yes, it was that good. . . . Why, he could do anything—built hisself a record player and made his own recording, too . . . had the first carbide gas setup in the whole danged valley, so he didn't have to bother with kerosene anymore. . . . Drew pictures, played the fiddle . . . but did Buck Applegate ever bother to turn his clever hands at anything that might make his family a little money? . . . Flora, his wife, she did the work over there. . . . She worried, he whittled and fiddled, holed up in that big front room, and when his poor wife couldn't make ends meet anymore and he realized how hard up they were, what did Buck Applegate do? Why, he sold a little more of the land, got rid of it bit by bit. . . ."

How can a person gloss over such things? And Uncle Vince, you yourself told me that your pappa had failings. How could I not at least allude to all that? And I was standing there, feeling embarrassed and even guilty, arguing with myself, and fearful, yes.

My God, he was looking at me—through me almost—and it came to me suddenly he was reading my thoughts and that nothing whatever had missed him, and I began trembling, fully expecting his anger to fall upon me like a blow.

He put down his hoe. His look was quizzical, then amused in some way, his big white moustache lifting a little as he came toward me. He put his hand upon my shoulder.

How I wish I could remember exactly what passed from his mind to mine.

423

"On the contrary," . . . I remember those words. . . . "I'm very interested in what you and others think of me. How can I know if no one tells me?"

And there was something else, too. This is as close as I'm able to come, because this was more like a feeling, a feeling given expression. In some way he let me know that I was doing exactly what I ought to be doing. Yes. Somehow, in some way what I was doing might *help him.*

Help him? I was quite literally stunned. What did he mean? But we were off then—his old gnarled hand still on my shoulder. He was leading me toward the back porch. And a woman opened the kitchen door. Her hair was incredibly thick and auburn in color. She was very animated: "Why, Shannon," she said aloud, "don't you know me? I'm Irene, of course."

And Uncle Vince, others were there, waiting for me: family women all. But this part is the most remarkable:

The women were not in the west room, making quilts or sewing. No, there they were, sitting around the big table in the east room. They had sheafs of papers in their hands, things I'd written or they had written, old letters and documents. Buck took me there and sat back, enjoying all our talk.

Do you understand? It is your father who has led me to the men's side. Buck: my doorway to you.

"What in the Sam Hill is she going on and on about all this dream business?" I can almost hear you saying. "What's she getting at?"

She. Her. "She's in the kitchen." "She's Rex's girl." "She's trying to write herself a book." "She don't know anything; she's been back east mostly." "Now, what's got into *her?*"

Uncle Vince, I can't remember a single time when you used my given name.

As for the "dream business," I'll have you know that talking about dreaming is an honorable tradition in this family. No, not "just the women," either. I could tell you of a half-dozen dreams that have been passed down in one way or another. The dreamers—all family men: Charley and Jesse, your uncle John and uncle Al and Buck. My own father. Three generations, skipping yours and Grandpa's.

If I'd had my wits back then when you and I lived together, I would have asked you about your dreams. I know you had them. I used to watch you sleeping in your favorite chair. Every so often, you'd mutter something and then you'd tremble a little and jerk your head like some old dog reliving the chase.

Do you know what I'd think when I saw you drifting off, or shoveling hash browns into your mouth, or slouching toward the bathroom in your dingy long johns? "Oh, how the mighty have fallen."

You reminded me of some secondary Faulkner character or one of Hardy's listless Derbyvilles. And who was I, pray? A quite short lady on a very high horse indeed.

In those days, I was straining to fit you into the group portrait I was painting in my mind—"The Three Brothers," I called them. Lindsay, Jesse, and Charles were front and center. Larger than life.

They had led notable lives. *They* had rubbed shoulders with famous men: the doyens of the British and American fur trade, Indian chiefs, missionaries, explorers, and politicians. Why, as a boy, Great-great-great-uncle Lindsay hunted coon with Abraham Lincoln, and Jesse corresponded with governors, senators, and vice-presidents who sought his advice.

Those men were "movers and shakers," trailblazers and lawmakers. Even Great-great-grandfather made his mark, in my mind, however faint. Charley, at least, had the gumption to be well-to-do.

Yet you, Charley's grandson, Buck's beloved baby boy, carried nary a trace of either gumption or genius, as far as I could see. You decided to become a dairy inspector, pleased with yourself because they gave you a county car to drive on your rounds. And before that—someone told me you'd run some little grocery store in a town almost as small as Yoncalla. Oh, you could shoot the breeze amicably enough with the customers, but you had trouble keeping up on your inventory. Those bins of sugar, flour, beans, and macaroni apparently had not inspired you. And who were your friends? Why, their lives had been as prosaic as your own. Retired farmers, ranchers, loggers, and maybe one or two who ventured into the world of commerce: a feed and seed salesman who once had been on the road; a gas-station owner.

I was a snob, Uncle Vince. The countryside, rural folk, it was all new to me. "She" had been back east mostly.

Those elderly cronies of yours who sometimes congregated on

the back porch on summer afternoons. "Dee-vorced?" I'd hear them whisper raspily to you, then they'd look me over when they thought I couldn't see them, as though they were gauging some heifer being auctioned.

How could I feel comfortable? I see that now. Yet I see other things, too. When those old men came to visit, "just-a-sitting" or playing cribbage and talking, why didn't I have the sense to sit quietly and eavesdrop until they got used to having me around? But I always felt the need to interject something or ask something. Right then. No, I couldn't wait. I was a backseat driver trying to steer the conversation toward some subject of more interest to me: Such as what crops had their grandfathers grown in the old days, or when had sheep arrived in the valley? Were they more lucrative than cattle? And they'd stop their own talk then and give me a funny look, those old male relatives of ours with spots on their baggy pants, their belts cinched tight, their shirts drizzled with "snooze" or bacon grease, their knotty, tobacco-stained fingers moving the little matchstick pegs or silently reshuffling the plastic playing cards. You could hear a pin drop. I knew how to stop talk dead in its tracks, all right. Even so, those old men were objects of interest to me—antiques, not unlike the Seth Thomas on the men's side that chimed according to a time all its own, and those rusty, ancient pieces of farm equipment lying along the banks of the old creekbed whose names and uses I did not know.

Yet I felt "right at home" when I visited the wives and sisters of those old men. I could follow a woman around in her kitchen and think nothing of it: shucking corn or coring apples, watching her put up green beans while I washed Mason jars. I didn't expect their undivided attention.

And talk? Yes, talk. The air hummed with it. It positively percolated, mixing with the hiss of the canning kettle or trailing along beside us like smoke as we passed in and out of the kitchen to the vegetable garden and back again:

"Great-aunt Susie was a one . . . people came from miles around to try out her sour biscuits. . . . Jane Applegate painted pictures of wild flowers and sewed up a storm. . . . Irene Applegate? Why, my mother told me that old doctor got out his knives and operated on her cancers right there in an upstairs bedroom. Just imagine. No one would go through that today."

They took to me right away, Uncle Vince, asking me ques-

426

Vincent Applegate, his dog, Carlos, and panoramic view of Old Place.
Mount Yoncalla rises in background, circa 1900. (Gus Peret Collection.
Courtesy Douglas County Museum)

tions: How old were the children? did I get lonely over there? how
did it happen I had a pretty name like Shannon?—so uncommon . . .

And when the talker finally landed on an overstuffed chair,
the talk slowed down somewhat, more or less keeping time with
the clickety-click of the knitting needles or crochet hooks. Anything I wanted to know that they knew, it was gladly told, Uncle
Vince, and when it was time to go, I left feeling I was a part of
something. All these years have passed, yet I have never known
more industrious women. Neither age nor infirmity seemed to
keep them from their appointed rounds. But those old men you
introduced me to never seemed to be around when I called upon
their wives, now that I think about it. And when I saw them in
town or at our place, they were always either sitting or standing.
As though waiting for something. I had that feeling about you
too, Uncle Vince, especially toward the last.

Last week I got out all the old pictures I'd brought from Yoncalla. I was looking for you, I guess. There you were, decked out
for World War I. And in one picture, you had curls to your shoul-

ders and a cunning little suit on. But the best one showed you—oh, you must have been as old as Colin is now—riding on a bull in the front yard. Grandpa was behind you, smiling. And I was smiling too by then, until I found that newspaper clipping at the bottom of the box. The obituary notice.

Uncle Vince, you were born in 1894—though I don't suppose I need to tell you that. Why didn't I ask you about the influenza epidemic; were you at home then or off soldiering? Did you go to Europe? Did Buck ever own a motorcar? Did *you* ever play the violin?

And the story you told me one afternoon—I must not have been listening carefully: the Yoncalla ball team that licked all comers—were all the players named Applegate except for one Indian, or was it the other way around?

Oh, Uncle Vince, I wish I could go to the kitchen now and get the Jim Beam down from the cupboard for you, or fry you an egg or make you a blackberry cobbler. Then, by God, we'd talk; or rather, you'd talk and I'd listen.

But there was one evening close to the end—remember?—when the licorice darkness lapped outside the window, and you and I sat by ourselves inside, sipping our ration of bourbon. And you had shown me how to trim the wicks of those kerosene lamps suspended on the walls of the dining room. "Well, go ahead if you want to," you said, "fire 'em up." We turned off the electric lights and sat there in that still pool of glowing yellow: the room itself and you and I, muted and mellow.

But I was afraid you'd fall asleep on me, and I poked at you a little, trying to stir the talk before it died out altogether.

I think I was asking you about Charley: why he, Jesse, and Lindsay had left their homesteads in the Willamette Valley and headed south to Yoncalla instead.

"Aw, honey," you said, "that's history." You drained your cup and told me how you didn't need to tell me about all that history "stuff" because it was already written up. I should go up to Portland to that historical society, or to the library in Eugene at the college. And you yawned, giving in to the hour and the soft light, and muttering something about how you wished your grandpappy's barrel of whiskey was still out on the back porch.

And this is why I remember. It was at the last. Maybe a week before it happened. You sighed and said, "Well, I guess I don't

Vincent Applegate during World War I. (Applegate family photograph. Courtesy Douglas County Museum)

have to worry what will happen to the Old Place anymore now that you and the kids are here." And there it was again, like a cold current or a chill wind slipping unexpectedly beneath a door. I was so lonely suddenly. The night train whistled as it rumbled past the Yoncalla siding and you shut your eyes, asleep in your rocking chair.

Good-bye, Uncle Vince. It's all said. It's all right.

"She" loves you.

SELECTED, ANNOTATED BIBLIOGRAPHY

Published Works

Applegate, Alex, et al. "Ventures and Adventures of a Party of Webfoot Miners on Their Way to and in the Poly Region of the Northern Mines," *The Call Number* 27 (Fall, 1965) pp. 1–24.

Round-robin diary of various family men and Henry Lane originally sent to Gertrude Applegate in 1862 from Idaho

Applegate, E. L. "Occasional Address," *Transactions of the Oregon Pioneer Association* 16 (1888), pp. 30–34.

A synopsis of autobiographical remarks given at the annual reunion, taken from the *Oregonian*

Applegate, Jesse. "A Day with the Cow Column in 1843," *Overland Monthly* (1868).

This famous essay has been reprinted many times and its original publication date is often cited incorrectly. Appearing in the second issue of one of the era's most prominent literary magazines, the essay was edited by Bret Harte. Though meditative, the essay is free of much of the bitterness and disillusionment that characterizes many of Applegate's later writings.

Applegate, Jesse. "Document: Jesse Applegate to W. H. Rees, Secretary, Oregon Pioneer Association, 25 December 1874," *The Quarterly of the Oregon Historical Society* 20 (1919), pp. 397–399.

Applegate, Jesse A. *Recollections of My Boyhood*. Roseburg, Ore.: Review Publishing Company, 1914.

A well-known, and especially well-written, recollection by Jesse Applegate's nephew. Because of the similarity in names, numerous histories have mistakenly attributed the writings of one man to the other. The perspective of the younger Jesse has been extremely important in the development of *Skookum*'s narratives.

Applegate, Jesse A. *The Yangoler Chief: The Kommema and His Religion* . . . Roseburg, Ore.: Review Publishing Company, 1907.

Since there is little ethnographic information available on the Yangoler (Yoncalla) Indians, this work remains the most important source on that subject. Various poems based upon the lore of the Klamath people also form a portion of the text.

Applegate, Lindsay. "Notes and Reminiscences of Laying Out and Establishing the Old Emigrant Road Into Southern Oregon in the Year 1846," *The Quarterly of the Oregon Historical Society* 1 (1921), pp. 12–15.

Oliver Cromwell Applegate is believed to have assisted his father in writing this article. It originally appeared in the *Ashland Tidings* when O.C. was the editor.

Applegate, Lisbon. "Early History of Chariton Co., Missouri," *The Chariton (Missouri) Courier*, June 30, 1933. Originally published in 1862.

Baker, Abner S. "Experience, Personality, and Memory: Jesse Applegate and John Minto Recall Pioneer Days," *Oregon Historical Quarterly* 81 (1980), pp. 229–259.

Bancroft, Hubert Howe. *History of Oregon*. San Francisco: The History Company, 1888.

The testimony of Jesse Applegate regarding his interactions with Joseph Lane in 1860 is noted in the footnote, page 455.

Beckham, Stephen Dow. *The Indians of Western Oregon: This Land Was Theirs*. Coos Bay, Ore.: Arago Book, 1977.

Beckham, Stephen Dow. *Land of the Umpqua: A History of Douglas County, Oregon*. Roseburg, Ore.: Douglas County Commissioners, 1986.

Beckham, Stephen Dow, Rick Minor, and Kathryn Toepel. *Native American Religious Practices of Southwestern Oregon*. Eugene, Ore.: Heritage Research Association, 1982.

Belknap, George. *Oregon Imprints, 1845–1870*. Eugene: University of Oregon, 1968.

Bowen, William. "The Oregon Frontiersman: A Demographic View," [in] Thomas Vaughan, ed., *The Western Shore* . . . Portland: Oregon Historical Society, n.d.

Bowles, Samuel. *Across the Continent*. New York: Hurd and Houghton, 1865.

Bowles, editor of the *Springfield* (Mass.) *Republican*, and Schuyler Colfax, speaker of the U.S. House of Representatives, were greatly impressed with Jesse Applegate when they visited him in 1864. Along with Edward Bates, Lincoln's attorney general, they praised Jesse Applegate and solicited his opinions on such issues as Reconstruction.

Brown, Wilfred, ed. *This Was a Man: About the Life and Times of Jesse Applegate*. North Hollywood, Calif.: The Camas Press, 1971.

This informally organized anthology about the Applegate family was lovingly hand-set and printed on a letterpress by a descendant of Jesse Applegate. The letters of Rozelle Applegate Putnam are well represented in this volume.

Burnett, Peter H. *Recollections and Opinions of an Old Pioneer*. New York: Da Capo Press, 1969.

This is a reprint of a volume published in New York in 1880. Burnett, California's first governor, was an old friend of the Applegates and a leader in the Great Migration of 1843.

SELECTED, ANNOTATED BIBLIOGRAPHY

Carey, Charles H. *General History of Oregon Through Early Statehood.* Portland, Ore.: Binfords and Mort, 1971.

Carey, Charles H., ed. *The Oregon Constitution and Proceedings and Debates . . .* Salem, Ore., 1926.

Jesse Applegate's desire to prohibit slavery "exclusively" is noted. He was a delegate to the Constitutional Convention in 1857, but withdrew over the same question.

Case, Victoria. *The Quiet Life of Mrs. General Lane.* Garden City, N.Y.: Doubleday and Company, 1952.

Clark, Malcolm, Jr., ed. *Pharisee Among the Philistines: The Diary of Judge Matthew P. Deady, 1871–1892.* Portland: Oregon Historical Society, 1975.

Clark, Malcolm, Jr. *Eden Seekers: The Settlement of Oregon, 1818–1862.* Boston: Houghton Mifflin, 1981.

Clarke, S. A. *The Pioneer Days of Oregon History.* Portland, Ore.: J. K. Gill, 1905.

Davenport, T. W. "Slavery Question in Oregon: 1862 Celebration," *The Quarterly of the Oregon Historical Society* 9 (1908), pp. 364–367.

Davis, H. L. "A Pioneer Captain," *American Mercury Magazine* 86 (1931) pp. 149–159.

A little-known essay by Pulitzer Prize-winning author H. L. Davis. Fascinated by the motives of Jesse Applegate (Davis's mother was related to the Applegates through marriage), he writes of the tragic as well as comic side of many an old-time Oregonian. His observations about land use and conservation are particularly interesting in the light of the present era.

De Voto, Bernard. *The Year of Decision: 1846.* Boston: Little, Brown and Company, 1943.

Dye, Eva Emery. *The Soul of America: an Oregon Iliad.* New York: The Press of the Pioneers, 1934.

Edwards, Glenn Thomas. "The Politics of Railroads, 1869," *The Call Number* 1 (Spring, 1969) pp. 6–24.

Letters between Jesse Applegate and Captain J. C. Ainsworth, one of Oregon's most powerful business leaders and owner of the Oregon Steam Navigation Company

Ellison, Joseph. "Designs for a Pacific Republic, 1843–1862," *The Oregon Historical Quarterly* 31 (1930), pp. 319–342.

Estes, George. *The Stagecoach.* Portland, Ore.: Kiham Stationery and Printing, 1925.

This book, dedicated to Jesse Applegate (to whom the Estes family was related through marriage), is truly unique. About four hundred pages long, peculiarly illustrated, and printed in a limited edition of one thousand, it contains wonderful lore about the Yoncalla Valleys and their people. Much of the work is based upon historical fact. Estes was the son of Elijah Estes, the owner of the

Stri-ped Horse Stage Station near today's Drain, Oregon. Of the foodstuffs, entertainments, social customs, and prejudices of early-day settlers circa 1860, Mr. Estes has much to share.

Evans, Elwood. *History of the Pacific Northwest*. Portland, Oregon: North Pacific History Company, 1889.

In Volume I, Evans writes in detail about the cattle contract between the Applegates and chief trader McKinlay at Fort Walla Walla in 1843. Evans corresponded with Jesse Applegate in regard to this and other historic matters. The basis for the trust and respect Jesse Applegate conferred on the Hudson's Bay Company's chief factor, Dr. John McLoughlin, is explained.

Garth, Thomas R. "Archaeological Excavations at Fort Walla Walla," *The Pacific Northwest Quarterly* 43 (1952), pp. 27–49.

Haines, Francis. *Jacksonville: Biography of a Gold Camp*. Jacksonville, Ore.: Gandee Printing, 1967.

Haines, Francis. *The Applegate Trail: Southern Emigrant Route*. S.l.: Bicentennial Applegate Wagon Trek Committee, 1976.

Hardeman, Nicholas P. *Wilderness Calling: Peter Hardeman Burnett—The Great Migration to Oregon*. Knoxville: University of Tennessee Press, 1977.

Helfrich, Devere. "The Applegate Trail," *Klamath Echoes* 9 (1971).

Helfrich, Devere. "The Applegate Trail, Part II: West of the Cascades, *Klamath Echoes* 14 (1976).

Both special Applegate Trail issues

Helper, Hinton Rowan. *The Impending Crisis of the South: How to Meet It*. New York: Burdick Brothers, 1857.

Elisha Applegate reportedly supplied several "tables" of statistics, which were forwarded to Mr. Helper and incorporated into his final manuscript. The emphasis on the economic crisis, and especially its effect on nonslaveholding whites of middle means, offers insights concerning the politics of the Applegate men and the reasons they emigrated to Oregon.

Hendrickson, James E. *Joe Lane of Oregon: Machine Politics and the Sectional Crisis 1849–1861*. New Haven: Yale University Press, 1967.

This generally excellent work mistakenly places Joseph Lane's alleged pistol accident at Winchester, Oregon, rather than at Mount Yoncalla.

Hill, Dorothy. "The Movement in Oregon for the Establishment of a Pacific Coast Republic," *The Quarterly of the Oregon Historical Society* 17 (1916), pp. 177–199.

Hixon, Adrietta Applegate. *On to Oregon*. Weiser, Idaho: Signal American Printers, 1947.

Inman, Loris. "The Applegate Trail," *Lane County Historian* 1, 2 (1967), pp. 1–16.

Johansen, Dorothy O. *Empire of the Columbia: A History of the Pacific Northwest*. New York: Harper and Row, 1957.

Kaliher, Michael. "The Applegate Trail, 1846–1853," *Journal of the J. Shaw Historical Library* 1 (1986), pp. 7–23.

Kappler, Charles J. *Indian Laws and Treaties*, Vol. I, U. S. Government Printing Office, 1905.

Kendall, Reese. *Pacific Trail Camp-fires*. Chicago: Scroll, 1901.

Two thirds of this volume contains a fascinating interview with Elisha Applegate, which Kendall conducted about 1892. Elisha's adventures as political lecturer in Albany, Oregon, his opinions on Indian affairs, his description of early days on Salt Creek, etc., make this an especially valuable source.

Kruse, Anne Applegate. *The Halo Trail*. Drain, Ore.: The Drain Enterprise, 1954.

Kruse, Anne Applegate. *Yoncalla, Home of Eagles*. Drain, Ore.: The Drain Enterprise, 1950.

Lavender, David. *Westward Vision: The Story of the Oregon Trail*. New York: McGraw-Hill, 1963.

Lewis, Raymond. "The Short, Stormy Life of James D. Fay," *The Table Rock Sentinel: Newsletter of the Southern Oregon Historical Society*, August 1982.

Lomax, Alfred. *Pioneer Woolen Mills in Oregon: History of Wool and the Woolen Textile Industry in Oregon, 1811–1875*. Portland, Ore.: Binfords and Mort, 1941.

McCornack, Elwin. "When the Rebel Flag Flew on the Long Tom," *Lane County Historian* 1 (1961) pp. 14–18.

Minter, Harold. *Umpqua Valley Oregon and Its Pioneers*. Portland, Ore.: Binfords and Mort, 1967.

Minto, John. "From Youth to Age as an American," *The Quarterly of the Oregon Historical Society* 9 (1908), pp. 374–387.

Minto, John. "Reminiscences of Honorable John Minto, Pioneer of 1844," *The Quarterly of the Oregon Historical Society* 2 (1901) pp. 119–167, 209–254.

Morgan, Dale, ed. *Overland in 1846: Diaries and Letters of the California-Oregon Trail*. Georgetown, Calif.: The Talisman Press, 1963.

Volume II is especially noteworthy for its comprehensive and balanced treatment of "Applegate Cut-off" and the attendant controversies.

Nelson, Herbert B. *The Literary Impulse of Pioneer Oregon: Studies in Literature*. Corvallis: Oregon State College Press, 1948.

Platt, Robert Treat. "Oregon and Its Share in the Civil War," *The Quarterly of the Oregon Historical Society* 4 (1903), pp. 89–109.

Ramsey, Jarold, ed. *Coyote Was Going There: Indian Literature of the Oregon Country*. Seattle: University of Washington, 1977.

Rucker, Maude Applegate. *The Oregon Trail and Some of Its Blazers*. New York: Walter Neale, 1930.

Sargent, Alice Applegate. *Following the Flag: Diary of a Soldier's Wife*. Kansas City, Mo.: E. B. Barnett, ca. 1920.

Schafer, Joseph. "Jesse Applegate: Pioneer, Statesman, and Philosopher," *Washington Historical Quarterly* 7 (1907).

Schafer, Joseph. *A History of the Pacific Northwest*. New York: Macmillan, 1926.

Schlesser, Norman. *Bastion of Empire: The Hudson's Bay Company's Fort Umpqua*. Oakland, Ore.: Oakland Printing, 1973.

Stowell, George. "Some Recollections of E. L. Applegate," *The Quarterly of the Oregon Historical Society* 15 (1914), pp. 252–263.

Thomas, Edward Harper. *Chinook: A History and Dictionary of the Northwest Coast Trade Jargon*. Portland, Ore.: Binfords and Mort, 1934.

Thompson, Herbert C. "Memories of Moray Applegate," *Oregon Historical Quarterly* 59 (1958), pp. 15–18.

A member of National Press Club and Overseas Writers, Washington, D.C., contributes a memoir of Moray Applegate, grandson of Lindsay and adventurer in exotic climes.

Unruh, John D., Jr. *The Plains Across: The Overland Emigrants and the Trans-Mississippi West, 1840–1860*. Urbana: University of Illinois, 1979.

U.S. Census. Schedule 1, Population, Douglas County, Oregon, 1860.

Vaughan, Thomas, ed. *Space, Style, and Structure: Building in Northwest America*. Portland: Oregon Historical Society, 1974.

Victor, Frances Fuller. *The River of the West: Life and Adventure in the Rocky Mountains and Oregon . . .* Hanford, Conn.: R. W. Bliss, 1870. (Reprinted 1974, Brooks-Sterling, Oakland, Calif.)

Williams, George. "Political History of Oregon from 1853 to 1865," *The Quarterly of the Oregon Historical Society* 2 (1901), pp. 1–35.

Woodward, Walter C. "The Rise and Early History of Political Parties in Oregon: Part II and VIII," *The Quarterly of the Oregon Historical Society* 12 (1911), pp. 36–163, and 13 (1912), pp. 16–69.

Woodward's lengthy article, published serially, provides a very useful review of a complex subject, especially the Civil War period.

Manuscripts and Interviews

Applegate, Albert. Papers, 1863–1888. Special Collections Department, University of Oregon.

These letters to his family include descriptions of army life as a volunteer on the eastern Oregon "front" during the Civil War period, as well as of a later trip to California and Arizona.

Applegate, Alex. Diaries, 1861–1862. Special Collections Department, University of Oregon.

Volumes I and II contain Yoncalla, Oregon, 1861, diary entries. Vol. III contains "Ventures and Adventures of Webfoot Miners . . . ," cited elsewhere.

Applegate, Charles. Probate Records, Vol. 15, No. 20 (1879). Douglas County Clerk's Office, Roseburg, Oregon.

Applegate, Charles. Reminiscences concerning the overland trip to Oregon in 1843. (Ca. 1876) Douglas County Museum. Roseburg, Oregon.

These reminiscences are accompanied by a sketch for a fairy tale written for one of his granddaughters. Although some historians have suggested that Charles Applegate wrote numerous essays, especially in the 1850s, no other works have been uncovered to date.

Applegate, Eva. Interview with author. Yoncalla, Oregon, November 22, 1969.

Applegate, George "Buck." History of Yoncalla (essay). (Ca. 1920) Douglas County Museum, Roseburg, Oregon.

Applegate, George "Buck." Reflections on the Modoc Wars. (Ca. 1922) Douglas County Museum, Roseburg, Oregon.

Applegate, Irene. Reminiscences concerning the overland trip to Oregon in 1843. (Ca. 1919) Douglas County Museum, Roseburg, Oregon.

Many of these notes and loosely organized essays are written on scraps of paper that include the reverse sides of 1918 calendars. These often-repetitive accounts are interesting as well as endearing because of their childlike perspective and emotional content.

Applegate, Jesse. Notes and communications on Oregon history, 1878. (Bancroft Library, University of California, Berkeley) [Ts. copy] Special Collections Department, University of Oregon.

These notes and communications were a result of interviews and inquiries initiated by Frances Fuller Victor on behalf of Hubert H. Bancroft.

Applegate, Lindsay. Papers, 1863–1891. Special Collections Department, University of Oregon.

This collection contains 287 letters, most relating to his work as subagent at Fort Klamath (1864–1869) and to various aspects of Indian affairs. Includes vouchers, reports, and other administrative documents.

Applegate, Oliver. Papers, 1842–1948. Special Collections Department, University of Oregon.

This collection of almost four thousand letters represents a significant portion of Applegate family correspondence among various branches of the family. Of special interest to the author were the letters between 1842 and 1880, which are filled with family details, local, regional, national, social, personal, and political references. These letters were particularly useful in establishing the chronology for the three narratives that comprise Part I of *Skookum*.

The collection also contains official and unofficial correspondence carried on by Oliver Applegate during the Modoc War and illumines various issues related to the Modoc and Klamath Indians.

Manuscript calendar in University of Oregon Library.

Applegate, O. C., Jr. The Applegates in Klamath County. Douglas County Museum, Roseburg, Oregon.

Accurate and informative, this brief piece notes the work of Lindsay Applegate and his sons in various Oregon Indian agencies.

Applegate, O. C., Jr. Interview with author. Oakland, California, February 9, 1972.

Applegate, Shannon. Destiny's Man Disparaged: Uncle Jesse and His Damnable Road. Paper presented at the Oregon/California Trails Association Convention, August 1986, Carson City, Nevada.

Slated for publication in OCTA's *Overland Journal* sometime in 1988.

Applegate, Susannah G. Jesse Applegate, Oregon's prince of pioneers: biography and history, n.d. [Ts. copy] Douglas County Museum, Roseburg, Oregon.

Exhaustively researched and rewritten several times, this lengthy work is believed to have been authored between 1930 and 1970. It contains countless details concerning the Jesse Applegate family. The author states she intends "to clear the record." Her frequently scathing indictments of Jesse Applegate's critics suggests a perspective that is not always objective. The record she presents is sometimes distorted by the omission of certain important sources. The correspondence between Jesse Applegate and Judge Matthew Deady is meticulously noted, as is the record of suits and countersuits of *Dowell* v. *Applegate*. Ms. Applegate never permitted anyone to read or critique her manuscript. Her monumental effort of over two thousand typewritten pages only became available to the present author in December 1987, via a thoughtful relative. Susannah is the younger sister of another family chronicler, Anne Applegate Kruse.

Burt, Lorene. Interview with author. Eugene, Oregon, August 3, 1972.

Frear, Samuel. Jesse Applegate: An appraisal of an uncommon pioneer. Master's thesis. University of Oregon, 1961.

Kingery, Anna Huntington. Interview with author. Yoncalla, Oregon, November 1, 1971.

Kruse, Anne Applegate. The Applegate story. (Ca. 1955) Special Collections Department, University of Oregon.

Manuscript history of the Applegate family of Yoncalla, written from letters, diaries, and recollections. Transcriptions of Charles Applegate family letters form a substantial portion of this manuscript, and have provided a wealth of corroborative detail to the author that would not otherwise have been available.

In some cases the originals of these letters cannot be located and exist only in transcriptions made by Anne A. Kruse during the 1950s. Original letters are thought to be in the private collection of a descendant of Moray Applegate.

Long, Sallie Applegate. Traditional history of the Applegate family. (Ca. 1902) Oregon Historical Society.

Miller, Clover Belle. Westward movement of Jesse Applegate. (Ca. 1930) [Essay] Douglas County Museum, Roseburg, Oregon.

Contains information concerning Jesse Applegate's library, study, and various furnishings. Ms. Miller interviewed Sally Applegate Long, Jesse's daughter, as well as other elder Applegates.

Miller, Florence. Interview with author. Yoncalla, Oregon, October 2, 1971.

Following this initial interview, Mrs. Miller, close friend and amanuensis of writer Anne Applegate Kruse, offered me extraordinary assistance and encouragement. Her death in 1987 deprived the Applegate-Miller clan of its most beloved historian.

Oregon. Superintendent of Indian Affairs. Records of the Oregon Superintendency of Indian Affairs, 1848–1873. Microcopy 2, RG 75. National Archives, Washington, D.C.

Oregon. Supreme Court. B. F. Dowell, et al. v. D. W. Applegate, et al. File no. 4517 (1892). Oregon State Archives.

The depositions of Mary Mires and H. Thiel contain information concerning Jesse Applegate's house. Records of this protracted and complex series of suits and countersuits are available from various sources, notably the *Federal Reporter*, July, September 1881, and January 1883; *Pacific Reporter*, December 1887; *Oregon Reports*, January 1889; and *Supreme Court Reporter* (No. 209), March 1894.

Pence, Richard. Interview with author. Salem, Oregon, November 15, 1971.

Peret, Hazel Samler. Interview with author. Yoncalla, Oregon, November 1, 1971.

Scott, Levi. From Independence to Independence. [Unpublished diary/reminiscence] Possession of Dean Collins, Sitka, Alaska.

Previously unknown and but recently available to researchers on a largely restricted basis, this reminiscence reveals Levi Scott's relationship to important historical events and persons in southern Oregon.

Titus, Irene Applegate. Interview with author. Eugene, Oregon, November 4, 1971.

Tulley, Kenneth. Interview with author. San Francisco, California, February 9, 1972.

United States. Works Progress Administration. Reminiscences of southern Oregon pioneers. [T.s., 4 vols.] 1938–1939.

The oral-history interviews of Suzanna Irene Burt, Anne Applegate Kruse,

Jennie May Applegate Scott, Virginia Estes Applegate, and John Dial Wilson are useful.

U.S. Bureau of the Census. Census of the United States, 1860. Schedule 1, Population, Douglas County, Oregon.

Voress, Hugh Ellison. The Applegate family in America. [T.s. genealogy] In possession of its author.

A well-organized, chronologically arranged text with indexes to both the Applegates and those related to them through marriage and association. The extensive bibliography includes entries reflecting small histories, essays, etc., which its author has gathered from libraries and persons all over the United States. The index contains 25,000 names. Available through the author.

Waldron, Sue. Family tree of the Applegates of Oregon. 1986. Southern Oregon Historical Society.

This comprehensive family tree was developed in conjunction with an exhibition of Applegate family artworks which toured Ashland, Oregon, in 1986.

Warner, Theresa. Interview with author. Yoncalla, Oregon, October 10, 1971.

Wells, Mary, v. John Applegate. Vol. 39, No. 4, Circuit Court Records of Douglas County, Oregon, 1883.

The nitty-gritty concerning Charles Applegate's alleged mistress who successfully sued his estate. John was the estate's executor and the father of writers Anne Applegate Kruse and Susannah Gertrude Applegate.

Newspapers

Oregon Argus, Oregon City/Salem, 1855–1863.

Oregonian, Portland, Oregon.

Booth, R. A. "The Last of the Calapooias, a White-souled Redman, Passes Away from Earth." May 31, 1918. Written to honor Jake Fearn, son of Halo.

Oregon Sentinel, Jacksonville.

The years 1861 and 1866 frequently name the region's "sympathizers." The oath of the Knights of the Golden Circle is quoted in full (11/9/1861).

Oregon Spectator, Oregon City.

The years 1846–1848 contain much material on the Applegate Trail controversy.

Oregon Statesman, Salem.

The December 10, 1860, issue outlines the "scheme" of the "New Pacific Government."

People's Press, Eugene, Oregon.

This shortlived (1859–1860) Republican newspaper carried regular contributions from Elisha Applegate, one of its editors.

Umpqua Gazette, Scottsburg, Oregon, 1854–1855.

The earliest Douglas County newspaper. Rich with important facts concerning the Umpqua region, especially Scottsburg.

ACKNOWLEDGMENTS

Nearly two decades have passed since I began writing about the Applegate family. Many persons have given generously of their time and advice, and have provided moral, spiritual, and material support. Not all will be mentioned here. Some will find acknowledgment in a succeeding volume now in progress. Others should know that no kindness has gone unappreciated. I have been enriched and sustained by an interdependent web of goodwill and good faith. I could not have completed this work without it.

I am indebted to numerous libraries and museums and to the services of their staff members and volunteers. Changes of residence and employment have altered the lives of many persons who have assisted me. Sadly, three people whose assistance was indispensable in the early years of my research have died: They are George Abdill, the first director of the Douglas County Museum, Roseburg, Oregon; librarian and researcher Lavola Bakken of the same institution, and Martin Schmitt, Curator of Special Collections at the University of Oregon Library.

I wish to thank C. William Burk, former director of the Southern Oregon Historical Society in Jacksonville, Richard Engeman, now with the University of Washington Libraries, and Margaret Haines, manuscript librarian of the Oregon Historical Society, all of whom have been extremely helpful at various times and locations. Marjorie Edens and Carol Harbison of the Southern Oregon Historical Society have been exceptionally tolerant and accessible whenever their help has been needed. Although Ida Clearwater (Southern Oregon Historical Society) and Ella Mae Young (Douglas County Museum) have both retired, they have remained interested in my efforts. Ms. Young, especially, has provided tireless research assistance.

During the years I resided on the Oregon coast, the resourceful and patient librarians at Southwest Oregon College in Coos Bay, Oregon, Dortha McCarthy (director) and Kirk Jones, were of tremendous assistance in locating and procuring necessary research materials. In recent years similar assistance has been forthcoming from David Hutchinson, Marilyn Woodrich, and other members of the reference staff of the Douglas County Library System.

Since 1971 I have come to depend upon the resources of the Douglas County Museum of History and Natural History, an important repository of Applegate photographic and manuscript materials. The director of the museum and his staff have been consistently cooperative. Jena Mitchell, photographic technician, has extended herself on numerous occasions. I am particularly grateful to Kathleen Stavec, the museum's research librarian, who assisted me in the preparation of Skookum's bibliography.

Several scholars and writers, teaching in various of Oregon's institutions of higher learning, have given me much needed encouragement over the years: Among them are Edwin Bingham, Nathan Douthit, Linda Danielson, Peter Jensen, Glenn Love, and Robert Newton. Poet Barbara Drake (Linfield College) and historian Stephen Dow Beckham (Lewis and Clark College) have informally advised me, defended my process and methodology, as well as befriended me when my spirits flagged. Nor must I forget poet-writer Neil Meyers of Purdue University, without whose initial encouragement Skookum might never have been born, and Trudy McMurrin of Salt Lake City.

In 1976 several early Applegate pieces were published in the Northwest Review, a literary quarterly. In 1977, due to the interest of Donald Bodey and Michael Strelow (who was then its editor), these pieces were submitted to the Coordinated Council of Literary Magazines, where they received one of six national awards and attracted the attention of a New York literary agent. Strelow, as well as other past and present editors and staff of the Northwest Review, deserve credit for their dedication to the Pacific Northwest's literary arts and artists.

Ron Finne, Madronna Holden, David Johnson, Esther Stutzman, and John Thomas are but a few of the artists, writers, and thinkers who have inspired me. It is my good fortune to count them as friends.

I should like to pay special tribute to David Carr, Bette Li Porter, and Kathy Moritz, as well as my dear husband, Daniel Robertson, for assisting in the preparation of Skookum's text and illustrations. Rosemary Spires's maps and other, artistic contributions are deeply appreciated.

Many friends whose names do not appear here have helped me keep my sense of humor and have frequently come to my rescue. I cannot refrain from mentioning Margaret Broshear by name.

I will assume that Susan Applegate's presence in *Skookum*'s narratives and her wonderful paintings offer adequate testimony to the important part she has played in my personal as well as creative life. I have written about her parents, Fred and Jane Applegate, elsewhere, but here I wish to acknowledge their special and continuous caring, which, over the years, contributed so much to my and my children's sense of belonging.

Finally, I wish to acknowledge my father, Rex Applegate, for his commitment to the preservation of our family's history. It has not always been easy to maintain the old house built by his great-grandfather, Charles Applegate. It is a blessing to the living generations of Applegates that the artifacts and historical surroundings of the family as a whole have found such a willing and faithful steward.

There are persons far from Oregon who have believed in this book and in me. Literary agent Ellen Levine deserves special acknowledgment for without her this book might never have reached across the miles. James Landis and more recently, Jane Meara, have been extraordinarily patient and understanding editors. To these three warm-hearted New Yorkers, I say thank you and hyas skookum.

Index

Abernethy, Governor, 93–94, 97
abolitionists, 144
ahnkuttie laly, 214
alcohol, 67, 266–267, 277, 278,
  304, 317–318
Ambrose family, 127, 196–197
Applegate, Albert, 242, 272, 386,
  405
Applegate, Alena, 246
Applegate, Alexander, 221, 223,
  231, 236, 242, 254–255
Applegate, Charles, 21
  as blacksmith, 61
  Civil War and, 205–207
  death of, 276–278
  drinking habits of, 67, 266–267,
    277, 278, 304, 317–318
  Elisha and, 28–29, 146
  as father, 28–29, 91, 191–192,
    236–237, 242, 255
  health of, 212
  home of, 115–128, 165, 266,
    371, 405
  hospitality of, 118–119,
    125–127
  on Idaho mines, 236–237
  Indians and, 322–325, 331
  on Lindsay, 133–134, 136–137
  Missouri departure of, 21, 268–
    269, 270
  photograph of, *140*
  political involvement of, 155,
    160–161, 164
  on river journey, 34, 44
  at Salt Creek, 59, 62–63,
    67–71, 85–86, 87

as sheep farmer, 127–128, 148,
  213, 215–216, 229, 304
southern expedition by, 103
Thornton controversy and, 80,
  81, 83
wealth of, 178, 425
Yoncalla move of, 109, 322
Applegate, Cynthia Miller:
  death of, 320
  hospitality of, 185, 188, 247,
    248
  household moves and, 102–103
  marriage of, 94–96, 98–99,
    275, 319
  as mother, 71, 92, 95, 257, 259
  photograph of, *177*
  on river journey, 35, 43
  at Salt Creek, 63, 64, 65, 68,
    87, 89
  superstitions of, 43
  Thornton controversy and,
    80–81
  town named for, 310
Applegate, Edward Bates, 36, 51,
  52, 153, 339, 342
Applegate, Elisha Lindsay, 249
  childhood of, 27–29
  family visit by, 139–164
  health of, 145–146
  on Indian exile, 281–282
  on Jesse, 163
  as journalist, 141, 329
  naming of, 27
  political involvement of,
    141–144, 153, 312
  on river journey, 33–34, 50, 51

447